the PARIS REVIEW

Interviews, III

the PARIS REVIEW
Interviews, III

WITH AN INTRODUCTION BY
MARGARET ATWOOD

PICADOR • NEW YORK

THE PARIS REVIEW INTERVIEWS, III. Copyright © 2008 by The Paris Review. All rights reserved. Printed in the United States of America. For information, address Picador, 175 Fifth Avenue, New York, N.Y. 10010.

See also pp. 445–46 for individual copyright information.

www.picadorusa.com

Picador® is a U.S. registered trademark and is used by St. Martin's Press under license from Pan Books Limited.

For information on Picador Reading Group Guides, please contact Picador.
E-mail: readinggroupguides@picadorusa.com

The Library of Congress has catalogued the first volume as follows:

The Paris review interviews, I / with an introduction by Margaret Atwood.—3rd ed.
    p. cm.
  ISBN-13: 978-0-312-36175-4 (v. 1)
  ISBN-10: 0-312-36175-0 (v. 1)
  1. Authors, American—20th century—Interviews.   2. Authors, English—
20th century—Interviews.   3. American literature—20th century—History
and criticism.   4. English literature—20th century—History and criticism.
5. Authorship.   I. Atwood, Margaret, 1939–   II. Paris review.
  PS225.P26   2006
  823'.9109—dc22

                                                                    2006051097

ISBN-13: 978-0-312-36315-4 (v. 3)
ISBN-10: 0-312-36315-X (v. 3)

First Edition: November 2008

10 9 8 7 6 5 4 3 2 1

Contents

Introduction

by Margaret Atwood

In 1953, when George Plimpton became the first editor of *The Paris Review*, I was thirteen. The Second World War had been over for a mere eight years; the Korean War was just ending; the hydrogen bomb loomed over us; and Joseph McCarthy and the redbaiters were in full spate. Cars had extraterrestrial fins; Elvis Presley was about to gyrate to immortality; television was a clunky box with a flickering screen, thought to hypnotize those who became addicted to it. Radio and the movies still ruled, as did Marilyn Monroe. It was an era of extreme popular culture.

Paradoxically, it was also a time when serious writing held a larger chunk of the stage, and when—thanks to the paperback—such writing was widely available to the general reading public: you could buy Faulkner and Steinbeck and J. D. Salinger and even classics like *Wuthering Heights* in the corner drugstore, often with lurid covers featuring girls who looked like Jane Russell bursting out of their ill-buttoned blouses. *Life* magazine regularly featured writers such as Robert Frost, Ernest Hemingway, Isak Dinesen, and beatniks such as Jack Kerouac, though only after they had already become celebrities. For North America at that time was a place where only the making of war or money was considered a truly serious pursuit: writers were tolerated as sideshow artists, but they were respected only if they'd made it financially. Eudora Welty summed up this attitude in one of her stories: "If you're so smart, why ain't you rich?"

From the first, *The Paris Review* saw itself as a home for good writers—those good writers who hadn't yet become famous enough for *Life* or rich enough to be respected by society at large. Instead, the *Review* decided, they were to be respected—or not—on the basis of their achievements as writers. Why *The Paris Review*, rather than "The New York Review" or "The Chicago Review"? Paris was still cheap, still intellectually alive, and thus still the place you felt you should go to write if you were young and romantic and broke, and dedicated to your art.

When Plimpton took on the *Review*'s editorship he was twenty-six, a high-energy American oddball fond of practical jokes. Under his madcap sway, wild parties and improbable locations for its editorial offices were an integral part of the *Review*'s early image. Perhaps he originally conceived of *The Paris Review* as one more whimsical caper in a world in which everything seemed extreme and skewed and changing so fast you couldn't get a fix on it, where the consecration of your time and the effort to produce such a thing as a literary review ranked at least as high as swallowing a hundred goldfish.

By the time the fifties were over and I had grown up and was writing myself, *The Paris Review* was no longer a caper. It had become an institution, and its collection of interviews with writers was already the gold standard for such things. In a sense, *The Paris Review* had invented its own form, for although writers had been the subjects of interviews for many years, these had been newspaper interviews of the what-do-you-eat-for-breakfast kind, or the lion-hunting genre so deplored by many characters in the fiction of Henry James, or the kind in which writers pontificated on the issues of their day. But the *Paris Review* interviews were different.

Over time, the *Review* developed a huge ambition, not unlike that of a butterfly collector: all writers of note were to be drawn into their net, or at least as many as possible. To read the entire collection is to be given an unequalled overview of the complex, multidimensional writing world during the last half century. Also, the *Paris Review* interviews did not treat writers as celebrities or freaks or quasi-experts on subjects other than their own, but as sober professionals engaged in the writing life. Nor are these interviews abstract distillations of theory: they're presented as real conversations between imperfect individuals, during which both participants might eat or drink, get testy, misunderstand each other, stonewall, gossip, pull the legs off their fellow writers, rage against fate. Insofar as words on a page can re-create the flavor of a personality, these interviews do it.

There are many tips and helpful hints, which, if the interviews were cookbooks, would involve such craft-lore things as parsley drying and how to tell if an egg is addled. We all appreciate such tips: maybe they'll help us, maybe they won't, but it's nice to know there are some. (Here are mine: read your manuscript with a ruler; you catch the typos better that way. Make a birth chart for your characters; then you'll always know how old they are.)

Finally, as many have said, these interviews are a great encouragement to other writers, especially at moments of wavering faith. *Why am I doing such an eccentric thing as writing? Is it just undigested neurosis? Why spend all day in a room, in the company of a bunch of people who don't really exist? What good does it do the world? Isn't it unhealthy? Why waste the paper?* Every writer has such thoughts from time to time, and to know that others have had them too is reassuring: *I am not the only one who has viewed the page with loathing.* Not only that, but there's no obvious positive correlation between good writing and commercial success—good does not equal profitable—but on the other hand, there isn't a negative one— profitable does not equal bad. It's reassuring to know that anyone who's kept at it over time has written a few clunkers. And sometimes—not always, but sometimes—the writer knows quite well which ones those are. But look: the clunkers are survivable, we find in these accounts of writing lives, because after some defeating piece that, despite endless rewriting, never quite came right, there will be a clear masterwork. And that too is encouraging.

But above all, writers—alone so much of the time—realize through these interviews that they are not alone. Others have also doubted and blocked and messed up; others have been poor and neglected; others have been dragged into literary bun-fights and been trashed in the press; others have kept going and overcome obstacles and perse-vered. Young writers read the *Paris Review* interviews the way a pre-vious generation read *The Pilgrim's Progress*: this, then, is the way, bestrewn with dangers and temptations, and over there are the mon-sters.

And there are rewards and pleasures too, the moments of glee, the consciousness of a job well done: for the writing life has its joys as well as its sorrows. If not, why would anyone do it?

the PARIS REVIEW

Interviews, III

Ralph Ellison

The Art of Fiction

When *Invisible Man*, Ralph Ellison's first novel, received the National Book Award for 1953, the author in his acceptance speech noted with dismay and gratification the conferring of the award to what he called an "attempt at a major novel." His gratification was understandable, so, too, his dismay when one considers the amount of objectivity Mr. Ellison can display toward his own work. He felt the state of U.S. fiction to be so unhappy that it was an "attempt" rather than an achievement that received the important award.

Many of us will disagree with Mr. Ellison's evaluation of his own work. Its crackling, brilliant, sometimes wild, but always controlled prose warrants this; so does the care and logic with which its form is revealed, and not least its theme: that of a young Negro who emerges from the South and—in the tradition of James's Hyacinth Robinson and Stendhal's Julien Sorel—moves into the adventure of life at large.

In the summer of 1954, Mr. Ellison came abroad to travel and lecture. His visit ended in Paris where for a very few weeks he mingled with the American expatriate group to whom his work was known and of much interest. The day before he left he talked to us in the Café de la Mairie du VIe about art and the novel.

Ralph Ellison takes both art and the novel seriously. And the Café de la Mairie has a tradition of seriousness behind it, for here was written Djuna Barnes's spectacular novel, *Nightwood*. There is a tradition, too, of speech and eloquence, for Miss Barnes's hero, Dr. O'Connor, often drew a crowd of listeners to his mighty rhetoric. So here gravity

. (Later he goes into catalyptic state in coffee pot where proprietor
thinks hes drunk and props him up outside where he can see and hear
muggers rob white-man lookingfor prostitutes; then he is rolled by these
two and lies helpless; then by cripple , then by child. Around corner

I walked back to Harlem at top speed, never slackening my pace until 590

black faces began to dominate the streets. God, what had come over me?
What had happened to people couldn't they see me? didn't they know that
I was nothing like what they ? First the eviction and now this.
One group as confused as the other! Had I become invisible? And then
had a terrifying thought: Perhaps I was everything, nothing ,depending
                    upon
upon who was looking me at the moment! Hadn't I acted the role of
priest as quickly as I had played ? This was
frightening, because I hadn't wanted to do either--or at least
I had gone along, and who knew?I would do
next? Perhaps someone whisper a bank
robber--a Dillenger or RobinHood-- to find myself masked
and gun demanding all the banknotes a teller. And what
if someone took the notion that I was a moron?I might find myself arrested
for indecent exposure. This would have to stop now,today, I thought as I
passed shootinggallery. I knew who I was, perhaps, but not what I was.
And what I appeared to be to others was liable to get me into serious
trouble. doubt thepolice were looking for me this
very minute But I wasn't sure; perhaps by now
had come to look like anybody and everyone and not even could
look at a man an determine the quality of his voice. And yet I remembered,
stepping around a car that had stopped too far into the intersection ,
that certain types Negro did
many of our alto and contralto singers tended to be short dark girls....
Anyway, they couldn't look at me at tell what I'd say in a speech, anymore
than the cover of Leroy's diary what he had to say inside. Besides, I know what I would say myself. Lord, how simple life had
seemed on the campus where everyone had had his name and his role
Well, I was tired, perhaps that was the explaination. Perhaps I was

is in the air, and rhetoric, too. While Mr. Ellison speaks, he rarely pauses, and although the strain of organizing his thought is sometimes evident, his phraseology and the quiet, steady flow and development of ideas are overwhelming. To listen to him is rather like sitting in the back of a huge hall and feeling the lecturer's faraway eyes staring directly into your own. The highly emphatic, almost professorial intonations startle with their distance, self-confidence, and warm undertones of humor.

—*Alfred Chester & Vilma Howard, 1955*

RALPH ELLISON

Let me say right now that my book is not an autobiographical work.

INTERVIEWER

You weren't thrown out of school like the boy in your novel?

ELLISON

No. Though, like him, I went from one job to another.

INTERVIEWER

Why did you give up music and begin writing?

ELLISON

I didn't give up music, but I became interested in writing through incessant reading. In 1935 I discovered Eliot's *The Waste Land*, which moved and intrigued me but defied my powers of analysis—such as they were—and I wondered why I had never read anything of equal intensity and sensibility by an American Negro writer. Later on, in New York, I read a poem by Richard Wright, who, as luck would have it, came to town the next week. He was editing a magazine called *New Challenge* and asked me to try a book review of Waters E. Turpin's *These Low Grounds*. On the basis of this review, Wright suggested that I try a short story, which I did. I tried to use my knowledge of riding freight trains. He liked the story well enough to accept it, and it got as far as the galley proofs when it was bumped from the issue because there was too much material. Just after that the magazine failed.

INTERVIEWER

But you went on writing—

ELLISON

With difficulty, because this was the recession of 1937. I went to Dayton, Ohio, where my brother and I hunted and sold game to earn a living. At night I practiced writing and studied Joyce, Dostoyevsky, Stein, and Hemingway. Especially Hemingway; I read him to learn his sentence structure and how to organize a story. I guess many young writers were doing this, but I also used his description of hunting when I went into the fields the next day. I had been hunting since I was eleven, but no one had broken down the process of wing-shooting for me, and it was from reading Hemingway that I learned to lead a bird. When he describes something in print, believe him; believe him even when he describes the process of art in terms of baseball or boxing; he's been there.

INTERVIEWER

Were you affected by the social realism of the period?

ELLISON

I was seeking to learn and social realism was a highly regarded theory, though I didn't think too much of the so-called proletarian fiction even when I was most impressed by Marxism. I was intrigued by Malraux, who at that time was being claimed by the communists. I noticed, however, that whenever the heroes of *Man's Fate* regarded their condition during moments of heightened self-consciousness, their thinking was something other than Marxist. Actually they were more profoundly intellectual than their real-life counterparts. Of course, Malraux was more of a humanist than most of the Marxist writers of that period—and also much more of an artist. He was the artist-revolutionary rather than a politician when he wrote *Man's Fate*, and the book lives not because of a political position embraced at the time but because of its larger concern with the tragic struggle of humanity. Most of the social realists of the period were concerned less with tragedy than with injustice. I wasn't, and am not, *primarily* concerned with injustice, but with art.

INTERVIEWER

Then you consider your novel a purely literary work as opposed to one in the tradition of social protest.

ELLISON

Now, mind, I recognize no dichotomy between art and protest. Dostoyevsky's *Notes from Underground* is, among other things, a protest against the limitations of nineteenth-century rationalism; *Don Quixote*, *Man's Fate*, *Oedipus Rex*, *The Trial*—all these embody protest, even against the limitation of human life itself. If social protest is antithetical to art, what then shall we make of Goya, Dickens, and Twain? One hears a lot of complaints about the so-called protest novel, especially when written by Negroes, but it seems to me that the critics could more accurately complain about the lack of craftsmanship and the provincialism which is typical of such works.

INTERVIEWER

But isn't it going to be difficult for the Negro writer to escape provincialism when his literature is concerned with a minority?

ELLISON

All novels are about certain minorities: The individual is a minority. The universal in the novel—and isn't that what we're all clamoring for these days?—is reached only through the depiction of the specific man in a specific circumstance.

INTERVIEWER

But still, how is the Negro writer, in terms of what is expected of him by critics and readers, going to escape his particular need for social protest and reach the "universal" you speak of?

ELLISON

If the Negro, or any other writer, is going to do what is expected of him, he's lost the battle before he takes the field. I suspect that all the agony that goes into writing is borne precisely because the writer longs for acceptance—but it must be acceptance on his own terms. Perhaps, though, this thing cuts both ways: The Negro novelist draws his blackness too tightly around him when he sits down to write— that's what the antiprotest critics believe—but perhaps the white reader draws his whiteness around himself when he sits down to read. He doesn't want to identify himself with Negro characters in terms of our immediate racial and social situation, though on the deeper human level identification can become compelling when the situation is revealed artistically. The white reader doesn't want to get too close, not even in an imaginary re-creation of society. Negro writers have felt this, and it has led to much of our failure.

Too many books by Negro writers are addressed to a white audience. By doing this the authors run the risk of limiting themselves to the audience's presumptions of what a Negro is or should be; the tendency is to become involved in polemics, to plead the Negro's humanity. You know, many white people question that humanity, but I don't think that Negroes can afford to indulge in such a false issue. For us, the question should be, what are the specific *forms* of that humanity, and what in our background is worth preserving or abandoning. The clue to this can be found in folklore, which offers the first drawings of any group's character. It preserves mainly those situations which have repeated themselves again and again in the history of any given group. It describes those rites, manners, customs, and so forth, which insure the good life, or destroy it; and it describes those boundaries of feeling, thought, and action which that particular group has found to be the limitation of the human condition. It projects this wisdom in symbols which express the group's will to survive; it embodies those values by which the group lives and dies. These drawings may be crude, but they are nonetheless profound in that they represent the group's attempt to humanize the world. It's no accident that great literature, the product of individual artists, is erected upon this humble base.

The hero of Dostoyevsky's *Notes from Underground* and the hero of Gogol's "The Overcoat" appear in their rudimentary forms far back in Russian folklore. French literature has never ceased exploring the nature of the Frenchman. Or take Picasso—

How does Picasso fit into all this?

Why, he's the greatest wrestler with forms and techniques of them all. Just the same, he's never abandoned the old symbolic forms of Spanish art: the guitar, the bull, daggers, women, shawls, veils, mirrors. Such symbols serve a dual function: they allow the artist to speak of complex experiences and to annihilate time with simple lines and curves; and they allow the viewer an orientation, both emotional and associative, which goes so deep that a total culture may resound in a simple rhythm, an image. It has been said that Escudero could recapitulate the history and spirit of the Spanish dance with a simple arabesque of his fingers.

But these are examples from homogeneous cultures. How representative of the American nation would you say Negro folklore is?

The history of the American Negro is a most intimate part of American history. Through the very process of slavery came the building of the United States. Negro folklore, evolving within a larger culture which regarded it as inferior, was an especially courageous expression. It announced the Negro's willingness to trust his own experience, his own sensibilities as to the definition of reality, rather than allow his masters to define these crucial matters for him. His experience is that of America and the West, and is as rich a body of experience as one would find anywhere. We can view it narrowly as something exotic, folksy, or "low-down," or we may identify ourselves with it and recognize it as an important segment of the larger

American experience—not lying at the bottom of it, but intertwined, diffused in its very texture. I can't take this lightly or be impressed by those who cannot see its importance; it is important to *me*. One ironic witness to the beauty and the universality of this art is the fact that the descendants of the very men who enslaved us can now sing the spirituals and find in the singing an exaltation of their own humanity. Just take a look at some of the slave songs, blues, folk ballads; their possibilities for the writer are infinitely suggestive. Some of them have named human situations so well that a whole corps of writers could not exhaust their universality. For instance, here's an old slave verse:

> Ole Aunt Dinah, she's just like me
> She work so hard she want to be free
> But ole Aunt Dinah's gittin' kinda ole
> She's afraid to go to Canada on account of the cold.

> Ole Uncle Jack, now he's a mighty "good nigger"
> You tell him that you want to be free for a fac'
> Next thing you know they done stripped the skin off your back.

> Now ole Uncle Ned, he want to be free
> He found his way north by the moss on the tree
> He cross that river floating in a tub
> The patateroller give him a mighty close rub.

It's crude, but in it you have three universal attitudes toward the problem of freedom. You can refine it and sketch in the psychological subtleties and historical and philosophical allusions, action and whatnot, but I don't think its basic definition can be exhausted. Perhaps some genius could do as much with it as Mann has done with the Joseph story.

INTERVIEWER

Can you give us an example of the use of folklore in your own novel?

ELLISON

Well, there are certain themes, symbols, and images which are based on folk material. For example, there is the old saying among Negroes: If you're black, stay back; if you're brown, stick around; if you're white, you're right. And there is the joke Negroes tell on themselves about their being so black they can't be seen in the dark. In my book this sort of thing was merged with the meanings which blackness and light have long had in Western mythology: evil and goodness, ignorance and knowledge, and so on. In my novel the narrator's development is one through blackness to light; that is, from ignorance to enlightenment, invisibility to visibility. He leaves the South and goes North; this, as you will notice in reading Negro folk tales, is always the road to freedom—the movement upward. You have the same thing again when he leaves his underground cave for the open.

It took me a long time to learn how to adapt such examples of myth into my work—also ritual. The use of ritual is equally a vital part of the creative process. I learned a few things from Eliot, Joyce, and Hemingway, but not how to adapt them. When I started writing, I knew that in both *The Waste Land* and *Ulysses*, ancient myth and ritual were used to give form and significance to the material; but it took me a few years to realize that the myths and rites which we find functioning in our everyday lives could be used in the same way. In my first attempt at a novel, which I was unable to complete, I began by trying to manipulate the simple structural unities of *beginning*, *middle*, and *end*, but when I attempted to deal with the psychological strata—the images, symbols, and emotional configurations—of the experience at hand, I discovered that the unities were simply cool points of stability on which one could suspend the narrative line, and that beneath the surface of apparently rational human relationships there seethed a chaos before which I was helpless. People rationalize what they shun or are incapable of dealing with; these superstitions and their rationalizations become ritual as they govern behavior. The rituals become social forms, and it is one of the functions of the artist to recognize them and raise them to the level of art.

I don't know whether I'm getting this over or not. Let's put it this way: Take the "Battle Royal" passage in my novel, where the boys are blindfolded and forced to fight each other for the amusement of the white observers. This is a vital part of behavior pattern in the South, which both Negroes and whites thoughtlessly accept. It is a ritual in preservation of caste lines, a keeping of taboo to appease the gods and ward off bad luck. It is also the initiation ritual to which all greenhorns are subjected. This passage states what Negroes will see I did not have to invent; the patterns were already there in society so that all I had to do was present them in a broader context of meaning. In any society there are many rituals of situation which, for the most part, go unquestioned. They can be simple or elaborate, but they are the connective tissue between the work of art and the audience.

INTERVIEWER

Do you think a reader unacquainted with this folklore can properly understand your work?

ELLISON

Yes, I think so. It's like jazz; there's no inherent problem which prohibits understanding but the assumptions brought to it. We don't all dig Shakespeare uniformly, or even "Little Red Riding Hood." The understanding of art depends finally upon one's willingness to extend one's humanity and one's knowledge of human life. I noticed, incidentally, that the Germans, having no special caste assumptions concerning American Negroes, dealt with my work simply as a novel. I think the Americans will come to view it that way in twenty years— if it's around that long.

INTERVIEWER

Don't you think it will be?

ELLISON

I doubt it. It's not an important novel. I failed of eloquence and many of the immediate issues are rapidly fading away. If it does last, it will be simply because there are things going on in its depth that are of more permanent interest than on its surface. I hope so, anyway.

INTERVIEWER

Have the critics given you any constructive help in your writing, or changed in any way your aims in fiction?

ELLISON

No, except that I have a better idea of how the critics react, of what they see and fail to see, of how their sense of life differs with mine and mine with theirs. In some instances they were nice for the wrong reasons. In the United States—and I don't want this to sound like an apology for my own failures—some reviewers did not see what was before them because of this nonsense about protest.

INTERVIEWER

Did the critics change your view of yourself as a writer?

ELLISON

I can't say that they did. I've been seeing by my own candle too long for that. The critics did give me a sharper sense of a larger audience, yes; and some convinced me that they were willing to judge me in terms of my writing rather than in terms of my racial identity. But there is one widely syndicated critical bankrupt who made liberal noises during the thirties and has been frightened ever since. He attacked my book as a "literary race riot." By and large, the critics and readers gave me an affirmed sense of my identity as a writer. You might know this within yourself, but to have it affirmed by others is of utmost importance. Writing is, after all, a form of communication.

INTERVIEWER

When did you begin *Invisible Man*?

ELLISON

In the summer of 1945. I had returned from the sea, ill, with advice to get some rest. Part of my illness was due, no doubt, to the fact that I had not been able to write a novel for which I'd received a Rosenwald Fellowship the previous winter. So on a farm in Vermont, where I was reading *The Hero* by Lord Raglan and speculating on the nature of Negro leadership in the United States, I wrote the first paragraph of *Invisible Man*, and was soon involved in the struggle of creating the novel.

INTERVIEWER

How long did it take you to write it?

ELLISON

Five years with one year out for a short novel which was unsatisfactory, ill-conceived, and never submitted for publication.

INTERVIEWER

Did you have everything thought out before you began to write *Invisible Man*?

ELLISON

The symbols and their connections were known to me. I began it with a chart of the three-part division. It was a conceptual frame with most of the ideas and some incidents indicated. The three parts represent the narrator's movement from, using Kenneth Burke's terms, purpose to passion to perception. These three major sections are built up of smaller units of three which mark the course of the action and which depend for their development upon what I hoped was a consistent and developing motivation. However, you'll note that the maximum insight on the hero's part isn't reached until the final section. After all, it's a novel about innocence and human error, a struggle through illusion to reality. Each section begins with a sheet of paper; each piece of paper is exchanged for another and contains a definition of his identity, or the social role he is to play as defined for him by others. But all say essentially the same thing: "Keep this nigger boy running." Before he could have some voice in his own destiny, he had to discard these old identities and illusions; his enlightenment couldn't come until then. Once he recognizes the hole of darkness into which these papers put him, he has to burn them. That's the plan and the intention; whether I achieved this is something else.

INTERVIEWER

Would you say that the search for identity is primarily an American theme?

ELLISON

It is *the* American theme. The nature of our society is such that we are prevented from knowing who we are. It is still a young society, and this is an integral part of its development.

INTERVIEWER

A common criticism of first novels is that the central incident is either omitted or weak. *Invisible Man* seems to suffer here; shouldn't we have been present at the scenes which are the dividing lines in the book—namely, when the Brotherhood organization moves the narrator downtown, then back uptown?

ELLISON

I think you missed the point. The major flaw in the hero's character is his unquestioning willingness to do what is required of him by others as a way to success, and this was the specific form of his "innocence." He goes where he is told to go; he does what he is told to do; he does not even choose his Brotherhood name. It is chosen for him and he accepts it. He has accepted party discipline and thus cannot be present at the scene since it is not the will of the Brotherhood leaders. What is important is not the scene but his failure to question their decision. There is also the fact that no single person can be everywhere at once, nor can a single consciousness be aware of all the nuances of a large social action. What happens uptown while he is downtown is part of his darkness, both symbolic and actual. No, I don't feel that any vital scenes have been left out.

INTERVIEWER

Why did you find it necessary to shift styles throughout the book; particularly in the prologue and epilogue?

ELLISON

The prologue was written afterwards, really—in terms of a shift in the hero's point of view. I wanted to throw the reader off balance—make him accept certain nonnaturalistic effects. It was really a memoir written underground, and I wanted a foreshadowing through which I hoped the reader would view the actions which took place in the main body of the book. For another thing, the styles of life presented are different. In the South, where he was trying to fit into a traditional pattern and where his sense of certainty had not yet been challenged, I felt a more naturalistic treatment was adequate. The college trustee's speech to the students is really an echo of a certain kind of Southern rhetoric and I enjoyed trying to re-create it. As the hero passes from the South to the North, from the relatively stable to the swiftly changing, his sense of certainty is lost and the style becomes expressionistic. Later on during his fall from grace in the Brotherhood it becomes somewhat surrealistic. The styles try to express both his state of consciousness and the state of society. The epilogue was necessary to complete the action begun when he set out to write his memoirs.

INTERVIEWER

After four hundred pages you still felt the epilogue was necessary?

ELLISON

Yes. Look at it this way. The book is a series of reversals. It is the portrait of the artist as a rabble-rouser, thus the various mediums of expression. In the epilogue the hero discovers what he had not discovered throughout the book: you have to make your own decisions; you have to think for yourself. The hero comes up from underground because the act of writing and thinking necessitated it. He could not stay down there.

INTERVIEWER

You say that the book is a series of reversals. It seemed to us that this was a weakness, that it was built on a series of provocative situations which were canceled by the calling up of conventional emotions.

I don't quite see what you mean.

Well, for one thing, you begin with a provocative situation of the American Negro's status in society. The responsibility for this is that of the white American citizen; that's where the guilt lies. Then you cancel it by introducing the Communist Party, or the Brotherhood, so that the reader tends to say to himself, Ah, they're the guilty ones. They're the ones who mistreat him, not us.

I think that's a case of misreading. And I didn't identify the Brotherhood as the C.P., but since you do, I'll remind you that they too are white. The hero's invisibility is not a matter of being seen, but a refusal to run the risk of his own humanity, which involves guilt. This is not an attack upon white society! It is what the hero refuses to do in each section which leads to further action. He must assert and achieve his own humanity; he cannot run with the pack and do this—this is the reason for all the reversals. The epilogue is the most final reversal of all; therefore it is a necessary statement.

And the love affairs—or almost love affairs—

I'm glad you put it that way. The point is that when thrown into a situation which he thinks he wants, the hero is sometimes thrown at a loss; he doesn't know how to act. After he had made this speech about the Place of the Woman in Our Society, for example, and was approached by one of the women in the audience, he thought she wanted to talk about the Brotherhood and found that she wanted to talk about brother-and-*sister*hood. Look, didn't you find the book at all *funny*? I felt that such a man as this character would have been incapable of a love affair; it would have been inconsistent with his personality.

INTERVIEWER

Do you have any difficulty controlling your characters? E. M. Forster says that he sometimes finds a character running away with him.

ELLISON

No, because I find that a sense of the ritual understructure of the fiction helps to guide the creation of characters. Action is the thing. We are what we do and do not do. The problem for me is to get from A to B to C. My anxiety about transitions greatly prolonged the writing of my book. The naturalists stick to case histories and sociology and are willing to compete with the camera and the tape recorder. I despise concreteness in writing, but when reality is deranged in fiction, one must worry about the seams.

INTERVIEWER

Do you have difficulty turning real characters into fiction?

ELLISON

Real characters are just a limitation. It's like turning your own life into fiction: you have to be hindered by chronology and fact. A number of the characters just jumped out, like Rinehart and Ras.

INTERVIEWER

Isn't Ras based on Marcus Garvey?

ELLISON

No. In 1950 my wife and I were staying at a vacation spot where we met some white liberals who thought the best way to be friendly was to tell us what it was like to be Negro. I got mad at hearing this from people who otherwise seemed very intelligent. I had already sketched Ras, but the passion of his statement came out after I went upstairs that night feeling that we needed to have this thing out once and for all and get it done with; then we could go on living like people and individuals. No conscious reference to Garvey is intended.

What about Rinehart? Is he related to Rinehart in the blues tradition, or Django Reinhardt, the jazz musician?

There is a peculiar set of circumstances connected with my choice of that name. My old Oklahoma friend, Jimmy Rushing, the blues singer, used to sing one song with a refrain that went:

> Rinehart, Rinehart,
> it's so lonesome up here
> on Beacon Hill,

which haunted me, and as I was thinking of a character who was a master of disguise, of coincidence, this name with its suggestion of inner and outer came to my mind. Later I learned that it was a call used by Harvard students when they prepared to riot, a call to chaos. Which is very interesting, because it is not long after Rinehart appears in my novel that the riot breaks out in Harlem. Rinehart is my name for the personification of chaos. He is also intended to represent America and change. He has lived so long with chaos that he knows how to manipulate it. It is the old theme of *The Confidence Man*. He is a figure in a country with no solid past or stable class lines; therefore he is able to move about easily from one to the other. . . .

You know, I'm still thinking of your question about the use of Negro experience as material for fiction. One function of serious literature is to deal with the moral core of a given society. Well, in the United States the Negro and his status have always stood for that moral concern. He symbolizes among other things the human and social possibility of equality. This is the moral question raised in our two great nineteenth-century novels, *Moby-Dick* and *Huckleberry Finn*. The very center of Twain's book revolves finally around the boy's relations with Nigger Jim and the question of what Huck should do about getting Jim free after the two scoundrels had sold him. There is a magic here worth conjuring, and that reaches to the very nerve of the American consciousness—so why should I abandon it? Our so-called race problem has now lined up with the world problems of colonialism and the struggle of the West to gain the allegiance of the remaining non-white people who have thus far remained outside the communist sphere; thus its possibilities for art have increased rather than lessened. Looking at the novelist as manipulator and depicter of moral problems, I ask myself how much of the achievement of democratic ideals in the United States has been affected by the steady pressure of Negroes and those whites who were sensitive to the implications of our condition, and I know that without that pressure the position of our country before the world would be much more serious than it is even now. Here is part of the social dynamics of a great society. Perhaps the discomfort about protest in books by Negro authors comes because, since the nineteenth century, American literature has avoided profound moral searching. It was too painful and besides there were specific problems of language and form to which the writers could address themselves. They did wonderful things, but perhaps they left the real problems untouched. There are exceptions, of course, like Faulkner who has been working the great moral theme all along, taking it up where Mark Twain put it down.

I feel that with my decision to devote myself to the novel I took on one of the responsibilities inherited by those who practice the craft in the United States: that of describing for all that fragment of the huge diverse American experience which I know best, and which offers me the possibility of contributing not only to the growth of the literature but to the shaping of the culture as I should like it to be. The American novel is in this sense a conquest of the frontier; as it describes our experience, it creates it.

Georges Simenon

The Art of Fiction

M r. Simenon's study in his rambling white house on the edge of Lakeville, Connecticut, after lunch on a January day of bright sun. The room reflects its owner: cheerful, efficient, hospitable, controlled. On its walls are books of law and medicine, two fields in which he has made himself an expert; the telephone directories from many parts of the world to which he turns in naming his characters; the map of a town where he has just set his forty-ninth Maigret novel; and the calendar on which he has Xed out in heavy crayon the days spent writing the Maigret—one day to a chapter—and the three days spent revising it, a labor which he has generously interrupted for this interview.

In the adjoining office, having seen that everything is arranged comfortably for her husband and the interviewer, Mme. Simenon returns her attention to the business affairs of a writer whose novels appear six a year and whose contracts for books, adaptations, and translations are in more than twenty languages.

With great courtesy and in a rich voice which gives to his statements nuances of meaning much beyond the ordinary range, Mr. Simenon continues a discussion begun in the dining room.

—*Carvel Collins, 1955*

GEORGES SIMENON

Just one piece of general advice from a writer has been very useful to me. It was from Colette. I was writing short stories for *Le Matin*, and

Above, the eleven-by-sixteen-inch calendar sheet on which Simenon marked off in black each day of his writing *The Brothers Rico*, one chapter a day, and in red the three days spent revising it. Below, the two sides of a seven-by-ten brown manila envelope on which Simenon began consciously shaping the characters of *The Brothers Rico* two days before he began the novel on July 14, 1952.

Colette was literary editor at that time. I remember I gave her two short stories and she returned them and I tried again and tried again. Finally she said, Look, it is too literary, always too literary. So I followed her advice. It's what I do when I write, the main job when I rewrite.

INTERVIEWER

What do you mean by "too literary"? What do you cut out, certain kinds of words?

SIMENON

Adjectives, adverbs, and every word which is there just to make an effect. Every sentence which is there just for the sentence. You know, you have a beautiful sentence—cut it. Every time I find such a thing in one of my novels it is to be cut.

INTERVIEWER

Is that the nature of most of your revision?

SIMENON

Almost all of it.

INTERVIEWER

It's not revising the plot pattern?

SIMENON

Oh, I never touch anything of that kind. Sometimes I've changed the names while writing: a woman will be Helen in the first chapter and Charlotte in the second, you know; so in revising I straighten this out. And then, cut, cut, cut.

INTERVIEWER

Is there anything else you can say to beginning writers?

SIMENON

Writing is considered a profession, and I don't think it is a profession. I think that everyone who does not *need* to be a writer, who thinks he can do something else, ought to do something else. Writing is not a profession but a vocation of unhappiness. I don't think an artist can ever be happy.

INTERVIEWER

Why?

SIMENON

Because, first, I think that if a man has the urge to be an artist, it is because he needs to find himself. Every writer tries to find himself through his characters, through all his writing.

INTERVIEWER

He is writing for himself?

SIMENON

Yes. Certainly.

INTERVIEWER

Are you conscious there will be readers of the novel?

SIMENON

I know that there are many men who have more or less the same problems I have, with more or less intensity, and who will be happy to read the book to find the answer—if the answer can possibly be found.

INTERVIEWER

Even when the author can't find the answer do the readers profit because the author is meaningfully fumbling for it?

SIMENON

That's it. Certainly. I don't remember whether I have ever spoken to you about the feeling I have had for several years. Because society today is without a very strong religion, without a firm hierarchy of social classes, and people are afraid of the big organization in which they are just a little part, for them reading certain novels is a little like looking through the keyhole to learn what the neighbor is doing and thinking— does he have the same inferiority complex, the same vices, the same temptations? This is what they are looking for in the work of art. I think many more people today are insecure and are in search of themselves.

There are now so few literary works of the kind Anatole France wrote, for example, you know—very quiet and elegant and reassuring. On the contrary, what people today want are the most complex books, trying to go into every corner of human nature. Do you understand what I mean?

INTERVIEWER

I think so. You mean this is not just because today we think we know more about psychology but because more readers need this kind of fiction?

SIMENON

Yes. An ordinary man fifty years ago—there are many problems today which he did not know. Fifty years ago he had the answers. He doesn't have them anymore.

INTERVIEWER

A year or so ago you and I heard a critic ask that the novel today return to the kind of novel written in the nineteenth century.

SIMENON

It is impossible, completely impossible, I think. Because we live in a time when writers do not always have barriers around them, they can try to present characters by the most complete, the most full expression. You may show love in a very nice story, the first ten months of two lovers, as in the literature of a long time ago. Then you have a second kind of story: they begin to be bored; that was the literature of the end of the last century. And then, if you are free to go further, the man is fifty and tries to have another life, the woman gets jealous, and you have children mixed in it; that is the third story. We are the third story now. We don't stop when they marry, we don't stop when they begin to be bored, we go to the end.

INTERVIEWER

In this connection, I often hear people ask about the violence in modern fiction. I'm all for it, but I'd like to ask why you write of it.

SIMENON

We are accustomed to see people driven to their limit.

INTERVIEWER

And violence is associated with this?

SIMENON

More or less. We no longer think of a man from the point of view of some philosophers; for a long time man was always observed from the point of view that there was a God and that man was the king of creation. We don't think anymore that man is the king of creation. We see man almost face-to-face. Some readers still would like to read very reassuring novels, novels which give them a comforting view of humanity. It can't be done.

INTERVIEWER

Then if the readers interest you, it is because they want a novel to probe their troubles? Your role is to look into yourself and—

SIMENON

That's it. But it's not only a question of the artist's looking into himself but also of his looking into others with the experience he has of himself. He writes with sympathy because he feels that the other man is like him.

INTERVIEWER

If there were no readers would you still write?

SIMENON

Certainly. When I began to write I didn't have the idea my books would sell. More exactly, when I began to write I did commercial pieces—stories for magazines and things of that kind—to earn my living, but I didn't call it writing. But for myself, every evening, I did some writing without any idea that it would ever be published.

INTERVIEWER

You probably have had as much experience as anybody in the world in doing what you have just called commercial writing. What is the difference between it and noncommercial?

SIMENON

I call "commercial" every work, not only in literature but in music and painting and sculpture—any art—which is done for such-and-such a public or for a certain kind of publication or for a particular collection. Of course, in commercial writing there are different grades. You may have things which are very cheap and some very good. The books of the month, for example, are commercial writing; but some of them are almost perfectly done, almost works of art. Not completely, but almost. And the same with certain magazine pieces; some of them are wonderful. But very seldom can they be works of art, because a work of art can't be done for the purpose of pleasing a certain group of readers.

INTERVIEWER

How does this change the work? As the author you know whether or not you tailored a novel for a market, but, looking at your work from the outside only, what difference would the reader see?

SIMENON

The big difference would be in the concessions. In writing for any commercial purpose you have always to make concessions.

INTERVIEWER

To the idea that life is orderly and sweet, for example?

SIMENON

And the view of morals. Maybe that is the most important. You can't write anything commercial without accepting some code. There is always a code—like the code in Hollywood, and in television and radio. For example, there is now a very good program on television, it is probably the best for plays. The first two acts are always first class. You have the impression of something completely new and strong, and then at the end the concession comes. Not always a happy end, but something comes to arrange everything from the point of view of a morality or philosophy—you know. All the characters, who were beautifully done, change completely in the last ten minutes.

INTERVIEWER

In your noncommercial novels you feel no need to make concessions of any sort?

SIMENON

I never do that, never, never, never. Otherwise I wouldn't write. It's too painful to do it if it's not to go to the end.

INTERVIEWER

You have shown me the manila envelopes you use in starting novels. Before you actually begin writing, how much have you been working consciously on the plan of that particular novel?

SIMENON

As you suggest, we have to distinguish here between consciously and unconsciously. Unconsciously I probably always have two or three, not novels, not ideas about novels, but themes in my mind. I never even think that they might serve for a novel; more exactly, they are the things about which I worry. Two days before I start writing a novel I consciously take up one of those ideas. But even before I consciously take it up I first find some atmosphere. Today there is a little sunshine here. I might remember such-and-such a spring, maybe in some small Italian town, or some place in the French provinces or in Arizona, I don't know, and then, little by little, a small world will come into my mind, with a few characters. Those characters will be taken partly from people I have known and partly from pure imagination—you know, it's a complex of both.

And then the idea I had before will come and stick around them. They will have the same problem I have in my mind myself. And the problem—with those people—will give me the novel.

INTERVIEWER

This is a couple of days before?

SIMENON

Yes, a couple of days. Because as soon as I have the beginning I can't bear it very long; so the next day I take my envelope, take my telephone book for names, and take my town map—you know, to see exactly where things happen. And two days later I begin writing. And the beginning will be always the same; it is almost a geometrical problem: I have such a man, such a woman, in such surroundings. What can happen to them to oblige them to go to their limit? That's the question. It will be sometimes a very simple incident, anything which will change their lives. Then I write my novel chapter by chapter.

INTERVIEWER

What has gone on the planning envelope? Not an outline of the action?

SIMENON

No, no. I know nothing about the events when I begin the novel. On the envelope I put only the names of the characters, their ages, their families. I know nothing whatever about the events that will occur later. Otherwise it would not be interesting to me.

INTERVIEWER

When do the incidents begin to form?

SIMENON

On the eve of the first day I know what will happen in the first chapter. Then, day after day, chapter after chapter, I find what comes later. After I have started a novel I write a chapter each day, without ever missing a day. Because it is a strain, I have to keep pace with the novel. If, for example, I am ill for forty-eight hours, I have to throw away the previous chapters. And I never return to that novel.

INTERVIEWER

When you did commercial fiction, was your method at all similar?

SIMENON

No. Not at all. When I did a commercial novel I didn't think about that novel except in the hours of writing it. But when I am doing a novel now I don't see anybody, I don't speak to anybody, I don't take a phone call—I live just like a monk. All the day I am one of my characters. I feel what he feels.

INTERVIEWER

You are the same character all the way through the writing of that novel?

SIMENON

Always, because most of my novels show what happens around one character. The other characters are always seen by him. So it is in this character's skin I have to be. And it's almost unbearable after five or six days. That is one of the reasons my novels are so short; after eleven days I can't—it's impossible. I have to—it's physical. I am too tired.

INTERVIEWER

I should think so. Especially if you drive the main character to his limit.

SIMENON

Yes, yes.

INTERVIEWER

And you are playing this role with him, you are—

SIMENON

Yes. And it's awful. That is why, before I start a novel—this may sound foolish here, but it is the truth—generally a few days before the start of a novel I look to see that I don't have any appointments for eleven days. Then I call the doctor. He takes my blood pressure, he checks everything. And he says, OK.

INTERVIEWER

Cleared for action.

SIMENON

Exactly. Because I have to be sure that I am good for the eleven days.

INTERVIEWER

Does he come again at the end of the eleven days?

SIMENON

Usually.

INTERVIEWER

His idea or yours?

SIMENON

It's his idea.

INTERVIEWER

What does he find?

SIMENON

The blood pressure is usually down.

INTERVIEWER

What does he think of this? Is it all right?

SIMENON

He thinks it is all right but unhealthy to do it too often.

INTERVIEWER

Does he ration you?

SIMENON

Yes. Sometimes he will say, Look, after this novel take two months off. For example, yesterday he said, OK, but how many novels do you want to do before you go away for the summer? I said, Two. OK, he said.

INTERVIEWER

Fine. I'd like to ask now whether you see any pattern in the development of your views as they have worked out in your novels.

SIMENON

I am not the one who discovered it, but some critics in France did. All my life, my literary life, if I may say so, I have taken several problems for my novels, and about every ten years I have taken up the same problems from another point of view. I have the impression that I will never, probably, find the answer. I know of certain problems I have taken more than five times.

INTERVIEWER

And do you know that you will take those up again?

SIMENON

Yes, I will. And then there are a few problems—if I may call them problems—that I know I will never take again, because I have the impression that I went to the end of them. I don't care about them anymore.

INTERVIEWER

What are some of the problems you have dealt with often and expect to deal with in the future?

SIMENON

One of them, for example, which will probably haunt me more than any other is the problem of communication. I mean communication between two people. The fact that we are I don't know how many millions of people, yet communication, complete communication, is completely impossible between two of those people, is to me one of the biggest tragic themes in the world. When I was a young boy I was afraid of it. I would almost scream because of it. It gave me such a sensation of solitude, of loneliness. That is a theme I have taken I don't know how many times. But I know it will come again. Certainly it will come again.

INTERVIEWER

And another?

SIMENON

Another seems to be the theme of escape. Between two days changing your life completely: without caring at all what has happened before, just go. You know what I mean?

INTERVIEWER

Starting over?

SIMENON

Not even starting over. Going to nothing.

INTERVIEWER

I see. Is either of these themes or another not far in the offing as a subject, do you suppose? Or is it harmful to ask this?

SIMENON

One is not very far away, probably. It is something on the theme of father and child, of two generations, man coming and man going. That's not completely it, but I don't see it neatly enough just yet to speak about it.

INTERVIEWER

This theme could be associated with the theme of lack of communication?

SIMENON

That's it; it is another branch of the same problem.

INTERVIEWER

What themes do you feel rather certain you will not deal with again?

SIMENON

One, I think, is the theme of the disintegration of a unit, and the unit was generally a family.

INTERVIEWER

Have you treated this theme often?

SIMENON

Two or three times, maybe more.

INTERVIEWER

In the novel *Pedigree*?

SIMENON

In *Pedigree* you have it, yes. If I had to choose one of my books to live and not the others, I would never choose *Pedigree*.

INTERVIEWER

What one might you choose?

SIMENON

The next one.

INTERVIEWER

And the next one after that?

SIMENON

That's it. It's always the next one. You see, even technically I have the feeling now that I am very far away from the goal.

INTERVIEWER

Apart from the next ones, would you be willing to nominate a published novel to survive?

SIMENON

Not one. Because when a novel is finished I have always the impression that I have not succeeded. I am not discouraged, but I see—I want to try again.

But one thing—I consider my novels about all on the same level, yet there are steps. After a group of five or six novels I have a kind of—I don't like the word *progress*—but there seems to be a progress. There is a jump in quality, I think. So every five or six novels there is one I prefer to the others.

INTERVIEWER

Of the novels now available, which one would you say was one of these?

SIMENON

The Brothers Rico. The story might be the same if instead of a gangster you had the cashier of one of our banks or a teacher we might know.

INTERVIEWER

A man's position is threatened and he will do anything to keep it?

SIMENON

That's it. A man who always wants to be on top with the small group where he lives. And who will sacrifice anything to stay there. And he may be a very good man, but he made such an effort to be where he is that he will never accept not being there anymore.

INTERVIEWER

I like the simple way that novel does so much.

SIMENON

I tried to do it very simply, simply. And there is not a single "literary" sentence there, you know? It's written as if by a child.

INTERVIEWER

You spoke earlier about thinking of atmosphere when you first think of a novel.

SIMENON

What I mean by atmosphere might be translated by "the poetic line." You understand what I mean?

INTERVIEWER

Is "mood" close enough?

SIMENON

Yes. And with the mood goes the season, goes the detail—at first it is almost like a musical theme.

INTERVIEWER

And so far in no way geographically located?

SIMENON

Not at all. That's the atmosphere for me, because I try—and I don't think I have done it, for otherwise the critics would have discovered it—I try to do with prose, with the novel, what generally is done with poetry. I mean I try to go beyond the real, and the explainable ideas, and to explore the man—not doing it by the sound of the words as the poetical novels of the beginning of the century tried to do. I can't explain technically but—I try to put in my novels some things which you can't explain, to give some message which does not exist practically. You understand what I mean? I read a few days ago that T. S. Eliot, whom I admire very much, wrote that poetry is necessary in plays having one kind of story and not in plays having another, that it depends on the subject you treat. I don't think so. I think you may have the same secret message to give with any kind of subject. If your vision of the world is of a certain kind you will put poetry in everything, necessarily.

But I am probably the only one who thinks there is something of this kind in my books.

INTERVIEWER

One time you spoke about your wish to write the "pure" novel. Is this what you were speaking of a while ago—about cutting out the "literary" words and sentences—or does it also include the poetry you have just spoken of?

SIMENON

The pure novel will do only what the novel can do. I mean that it doesn't have to do any teaching or any work of journalism. In a pure novel you wouldn't take sixty pages to describe the South or Arizona or some country in Europe. Just the drama, with only what is absolutely part of this drama. What I think about novels today is almost a translation of the rules of tragedy into the novel. I think the novel is the tragedy for our day.

INTERVIEWER

Is length important? Is it part of your definition of the pure novel?

SIMENON

Yes. That sounds like a practical question, but I think it is important, for the same reason you can't see a tragedy in more than one sitting. I think that the pure novel is too tense for the reader to stop in the middle and take it up the next day.

INTERVIEWER

Because television and movies and magazines are under the codes you have spoken of, I take it you feel the writer of the pure novel is almost obligated to write freely.

SIMENON

Yes. And there is a second reason why he should be. I think that now, for reasons probably political, propagandists are trying to create a type of man. I think the novelist has to show man as he is and not the man of propaganda. And I do not mean only political propaganda; I mean the man they teach in the third grade of school, a man who has nothing to do with man as he really is.

INTERVIEWER

What is your experience with conversion of your books for movies and radio?

SIMENON

These are very important for the writer today. For they are probably the way the writer may still be independent. You asked me before whether I ever change anything in one of my novels commercially. I said, No. But I would have to do it without the radio, television, and movies.

INTERVIEWER

You once told me Gide made a helpful practical suggestion about one of your novels. Did he influence your work in any more general way?

SIMENON

I don't think so. But with Gide it was funny. In 1935 my publisher said he wanted to give a cocktail party so we could meet, for Gide had said he had read my novels and would like to meet me. So I went, and Gide asked me questions for more than two hours. After that I saw him many times, and he wrote me almost every month and sometimes oftener until he died—always to ask questions. When I went to visit him I always saw my books with so many notes in the margins that they were almost more Gide than Simenon. I never asked him about them; I was very shy about it. So now I will never know.

INTERVIEWER

Did he ask you any special kinds of questions?

SIMENON

Everything, but especially about the mechanism of my—may I use the word? it seems pretentious—creation. And I think I know why he was interested. I think Gide all his life had the dream of being the creator instead of the moralist, the philosopher. I was exactly his opposite, and I think that is why he was interested.

I had the same experience two years later with Count Keyserling. He wrote me exactly the same way Gide did. He asked me to visit him at Darmstadt. I went there and he asked me questions for three days and three nights. He came to see me in Paris and asked me more questions and gave me a commentary on each of my books. For the same reason.

Keyserling called me an *imbécile de génie*.

INTERVIEWER

I remember you once told me that in your commercial novels you would sometimes insert a noncommercial passage or chapter.

SIMENON

Yes, to train myself.

INTERVIEWER

How did that part differ from the rest of the novel?

SIMENON

Instead of writing just the story, in this chapter I tried to give a third dimension, not necessarily to the whole chapter, perhaps to a room, to a chair, to some object. It would be easier to explain it in the terms of painting.

INTERVIEWER

How?

SIMENON

To give the weight. A commercial painter paints flat; you can put your finger through. But a painter—for example, an apple by Cézanne has weight. And it has juice, everything, with just three strokes. I tried to give to my words just the weight that a stroke of Cézanne's gave to an apple. That is why most of the time I use concrete words. I try to avoid abstract words, or poetical words, you know, like *crepuscule*, for example. It is very nice, but it gives nothing. Do you understand? To avoid every stroke which does not give something to this third dimension.

On this point, I think that what the critics call my atmosphere is nothing but the impressionism of the painter adapted to literature. My childhood was spent at the time of the Impressionists and I was always in the museums and exhibitions. That gave me a kind of sense of it. I was haunted by it.

INTERVIEWER

Have you ever dictated fiction, commercial or any other?

SIMENON

No. I am an artisan; I need to work with my hands. I would like to carve my novel in a piece of wood. My characters—I would like to have them heavier, more three-dimensional. And I would like to make a man so that everybody, looking at him, would find his own problems in this man. That's why I spoke about poetry, because this goal looks more like a poet's goal than the goal of a novelist. My characters have a profession, have characteristics; you know their age, their family situation, and everything. But I try to make each one of those characters heavy, like a statue, and to be the brother of everybody in the world. And what makes me happy is the letters I get. They never speak about my beautiful style; they are the letters a man would write to his doctor or his psychoanalyst. They say, You are one who understands me. So many times I find myself in your novels. Then there are pages of their confidences; and they are not crazy people. There are crazy people, too, of course; but many are on the contrary people who— even important people. I am surprised.

INTERVIEWER

Early in your life did any particular book or author especially impress you?

SIMENON

Probably the one who impressed me most was Gogol. And certainly Dostoyevsky, but less than Gogol.

INTERVIEWER

Why do you think Gogol interested you?

SIMENON

Maybe because he makes characters who are just like everyday people but at the same time have what I called a few minutes ago the third dimension I am looking for. All of them have this poetic aura. But not the Oscar Wilde kind—a poetry which comes naturally, which is there, the kind Conrad has. Each character has the weight of sculpture, it is so heavy, so dense.

INTERVIEWER

Dostoyevsky said of himself and some of his fellow writers that they came out from Gogol's "Overcoat," and now you feel you do too.

SIMENON

Yes. Gogol. And Dostoyevsky.

INTERVIEWER

When you and I were discussing a particular trial while it was going on a year or two ago, you said you often followed such newspaper accounts with interest. Do you ever in following them say to yourself, This is something I might some day work into a novel?

SIMENON

Yes.

INTERVIEWER

Do you consciously file it away?

SIMENON

No. I just forget I said it might be useful some day, and three or four or ten years later it comes. I don't keep a file.

INTERVIEWER

Speaking of trials, what would you say is the fundamental difference, if there is any, between your detective fiction—such as the Maigret which you finished a few days ago—and your more serious novels?

SIMENON

Exactly the same difference that exists between the painting of a painter and the sketch he will make for his pleasure or for his friends or to study something.

INTERVIEWER

In the Maigrets you look at the character only from the point of view of the detective?

SIMENON

Yes. Maigret can't go inside a character. He will see, explain, and understand; but he does not give the character the weight the character should have in another of my novels.

INTERVIEWER

So in the eleven days spent writing a Maigret novel your blood pressure does not change much?

SIMENON

No. Very little.

INTERVIEWER

You are not driving the detective to the limit of his endurance.

SIMENON

That's it. So I only have the natural fatigue of being so many hours at the typewriter. But otherwise, no.

INTERVIEWER

One more question, if I may. Has published general criticism ever in any way made you consciously change the way you write? From what you say I should imagine not.

SIMENON

Never. I have a very, very strong will about my writing, and I will go my way. For instance, all the critics for twenty years have said the same thing: It is time for Simenon to give us a big novel, a novel with twenty or thirty characters. They do not understand. I will never write a big novel. My big novel is the mosaic of all my small novels. You understand?

Issue 9, 1955

Isak Dinesen

The Art of Fiction

It was, in a sense, typecasting, when a few years ago a film was planned that would have shown us Garbo playing the role of Isak Dinesen in a screen version of *Out of Africa* . . . for the writer is, like the actress, a Mysterious Creature of the North. Isak Dinesen is really the Danish Baroness Karen Christentze Blixen-Finecke and is the daughter of Wilhelm Dinesen, author of a classic nineteenth-century work, *Boganis' Jagtbreve* (*Letters from the Hunt*). Baroness Blixen has published under different names in various countries: usually Isak Dinesen, but also Tania Blixen and Karen Blixen. Old friends call her Tanne, Tanya, and Tania. Then there is a delightful novel she preferred not to acknowledge for a while, though any reader with half an eye could guess the baroness hiding behind the second pseudonym, Pierre Andrezel. Literary circles have buzzed with legends about her: She is really a man; he is really a woman; "Isak Dinesen" is really a brother-and-sister collaboration; "Isak Dinesen" came to America in the 1870s; she is really a Parisienne; he lives at Elsinore; she stays mostly in London; she is a nun; he is very hospitable and receives young writers; she is difficult to see and lives a recluse; she writes in French; no, in English; no, in Danish; she is really—and so the buzzing never stopped.

In 1934 the house of Haas & Smith (later absorbed by Random House) brought out a book called *Seven Gothic Tales* which Mr. Haas had accepted on first reading. It became a bestseller. A favorite among writers and painters, the book was discussed from first appearance as of some permanence.

The roads round Pisa.

Herman von Spiegelhausen, a
young poet of note birth was
travelling in Italy in the spring
of 1822. He was in a way
driving going from place to place
in search of peace of mind and
happiness, which he did not
find.

One fine May eve he stopped
at a little inn on the road to
Pisa. — The air was clear as
glass and filled with sweet scent
and a golden, clamour light,
a lot of swallows were owing
about in it. While they made
his supper ready Herman
walked down the road along which
a big row of high poplars grew,

A manuscript page from a draft of "The Roads Round Pisa"
by Isak Dinesen.

Outside the canon of modern literature, like an oriole outside a cage of moulting linnets, "Isak Dinesen" offers to her readers the unending satisfaction of the tale told: "And then what happened? . . . Well, then . . ." Her storyteller's, or ballad maker's, instinct, coupled with an individual style of well-ornamented clarity, led Hemingway, accepting the Nobel Prize, to protest it should have gone to Dinesen.

—*Eugene Walter, 1956*

SCENE ONE

Rome, early summer, 1956. The first dialogue takes place in a sidewalk restaurant in the Piazza Navona, that long space, once flooded, where mock naval battles raged. The twilight is darkening the sky to an iris color; against it the obelisk that stands amidst Bernini's figures seems pale and weightless. At a café table sit Baroness Blixen, her secretary and traveling companion, Clara Svendsen, and the interviewer. The baroness is like a personage from one of her own tales. Slim, straight, chic, she is dressed in black, with long black gloves and a black Parisian hat that comes forward to shadow her remarkable eyes that are lighter in color at the top than at the bottom. Her face is slender and distinguished; around her mouth and eyes play the faint ghosts of smiles, changing constantly. Her voice is pleasing, being soft but with enough force and timbre for one to hear at once that this is a lady with opinions of both grave profundity and of most enchanting frivolity. Her companion, Miss Svendsen, is a fresh-faced young person with a charming smile.

ISAK DINESEN

Interview? Oh, dear . . . well, yes, I suppose so . . . but not a list of questions or a third degree, I hope . . . I was interviewed a short time ago . . . terrible . . .

CLARA SVENDSEN

Yes, there was a man who came for a documentary film . . . it was like a catechism lesson . . .

DINESEN

Couldn't we just talk together as we've been doing, and you could write down what you like?

INTERVIEWER

Yes, then you could scratch out some things and scribble in others.

DINESEN

Yes. I ought not to undertake too much. I've been ill for over a year and in a nursing home. I really thought I should die. I planned to die, that is, I made preparations. I expected to.

SVENDSEN

The doctor in Copenhagen told me: "Tania Blixen is very clever, but the cleverest thing she's ever done is to survive these two operations."

DINESEN

I even planned a last radio talk . . . I have made a number of radio talks on all kinds of subjects, in Denmark . . . they seem to enjoy me as a radio speaker there . . . I planned a talk on how easy it was to die . . . not a morbid message, I don't mean that, but a message of, well, cheer . . . that it was a great and lovely experience to die. But I was too ill, you know, to get it done. Now, after being so long in the nursing home and so ill, I don't feel I do really belong to this life. I am hovering like a seagull. I feel that the world is happy and splendid and goes on but that I'm not part of it. I've come to Rome to try and get into the world again. Oh, look at the sky now!

INTERVIEWER

Do you know Rome well? How long since you've been here?

DINESEN

A few years ago, when I had an audience with the pope. I first came in 1912 as a young girl, staying with my cousin and best friend, who was married to our Danish ambassador to Rome. We rode in the Borghese Gardens then, every day. There were carriages with all the great beauties of the day in them, and one stopped and chatted. It was delightful. Now look at these motors and motor-bicycles and noise and rushing about. It's what the young today want, though: Speed is the greatest thing for them. But when I think of riding my horse—I always had a horse when I was a girl—I feel that something very precious is lost to them today. Children of my day lived differently. We had little in the way of toys, even in great houses. Modern mechanical play-things, which furnish their own motion, had hardly come into exis-tence. We had simpler toys and had to animate them. My love of marionettes springs from this, I think. I've tried my hand at writing marionette plays. One might, of course, buy a hobbyhorse, but we loved better a knotted stick personally chosen in the woods, which our imagination could turn into Bucephalus or Pegasus. Unlike children of today, who are content from birth to be observers . . . we were cre-ators. Young people today are not acquainted with the elements or in touch with them. Everything is mechanical and urban: Children are raised up without knowing live fire, living water, the earth. Young peo-ple want to break with the past, they hate the past, they don't want to even hear of it, and one can partly understand it. The near past to them is nothing but a long history of wars, which to them is without interest. It may be the end of something, of a kind of civilization.

INTERVIEWER

But loathe leads to love: They may be led in a circle back to a tradi-tion. I should be frightened of indifference more.

DINESEN

Perhaps. And I myself, you know, I should like to love what they love. Now, I love jazz. I think it's the only new thing in music in my lifetime. I don't prefer it to the old music, but I enjoy it very much.

INTERVIEWER

Much of your work seems to belong to the last century. For in-stance, *The Angelic Avengers*.

DINESEN

Oh, that's my illegitimate child! During the German occupation of Denmark I thought I should go mad with boredom and dullness. I wanted so to be amused, to amuse myself, and besides I was short of money, so I went to my publisher in Copenhagen and said, Look here, will you give me an advance on a novel and send me a stenographer to dictate it to? They said they would, and she appeared, and I started dictating. I had no idea at all of what the story would be about when I began. I added a little every day, improvising. It was very baffling to the poor stenographer.

SVENDSEN

Yes, she was used to business letters, and when she'd type the story from her shorthand notes, she'd put numbers sometimes like "the 2 terrified girls" or "his 1 love."

DINESEN

I'd start one day by saying, Then Mr. So-and-so entered the room, and the stenographer would cry out, Oh dear, but he can't! He died yesterday in chapter seventeen. No, I prefer to keep *The Angelic Avengers* my secret.

INTERVIEWER

I loved it, and I remember it had excellent notices. Did many people guess that you had written it?

DINESEN

A few.

INTERVIEWER

And what about *Winter's Tales*? That came out in the midst of the war—how did you get the book to America?

DINESEN

I went to Stockholm—not in itself an easy thing to accomplish—and, what was even more difficult, took the manuscript with me. I went to the American embassy and asked them if they didn't have planes going to the United States every day, and if they couldn't take the manuscript, but they said they only carried strictly political or diplomatic papers, so I went to the British embassy and asked them, and they asked could I supply references in England, and I could (I had many friends in the cabinet, among them Anthony Eden), so they cabled to check this, then said yes they could, which started the manuscript on its way to America.

INTERVIEWER

I'm ashamed of the American embassy. They surely could have taken it.

DINESEN

Oh, don't be too hard on them. I owe a lot to my American public. Anyway, with the manuscript I sent a letter to my American publishers just telling them that everything was in their hands, and that I couldn't communicate with them at all, and I never knew anything of how *Winter's Tales* was received until after the war ended, when suddenly I received dozens of charming letters from American soldiers and sailors all over the world: The book had been put into Armed Forces Editions—little paper books to fit a soldier's pocket. I was very touched. They sent me two copies of it; I gave one to the king of Denmark and he was pleased to see that, after all, some voice had spoken from his silent country during that dark time.

INTERVIEWER

And you were saying about your American public?

DINESEN

Yes, I shall never forget that they took me in at once. When I came back from Africa in 1931, after living there since 1914, I had lost all the money I had when I married because the coffee plantation didn't pay, you know; I asked my brother to finance me for two years while I prepared *Seven Gothic Tales*, and I told him that at the end of two years I'd be on my own. When the manuscript was ready, I went to England, and one day at luncheon there was the publisher Huntington, and I said, Please, I have a manuscript and I wish you'd look at it. He said, What is it? and when I replied, A book of short stories, he threw up his hands and cried, No! and I begged, Won't you even look at it? and he said, A book of short stories by an unknown writer? No hope! Then I sent it to America, and it was taken right away by Robert Haas, who published it, and the general public took it and liked it, and they have always been faithful. No, thank you, no more coffee. I'll have a cigarette.

INTERVIEWER

Publishers everywhere are boneheaded. It's the traditional lament of the author.

DINESEN

The amusing thing is that after the book was published in America, Huntington wrote to Robert Haas praising it and begging for the address of the author, saying he must have the book for England. He had met me as Baroness Blixen, while Mr. Haas and I had never seen one another. Huntington never connected me with Isak Dinesen. Later he did publish the book in England.

INTERVIEWER

That's delightful; it's like something from one of the tales.

DINESEN

How lovely to sit here in the open, but we must be going, I think. Shall we continue our discussion on Sunday? I should like to see the Etruscan things at the Villa Giulia. We might chat a little then. Oh, look at the moon!

INTERVIEWER

Splendid. I'll find a taxi.

SCENE TWO

Rainy, warm Sunday noon. The Etruscan Collection in the Villa Giulia is not too crowded because of the weather. The Baroness Blixen is now attired in a suit of reddish brown wool and a conical ochre-colored straw hat that again shadows her extraordinary eyes. As she strolls through the newly arranged Etruscan figures, pottery, and jewelry, she seems as remote as they from the ordinary gallery-goers who are pattering through. She walks slowly, very erect, stopping to gaze lingeringly at those details that please her.

DINESEN

How could they get that blue, do you suppose? Powdered lazuli? Look at that pig! In the north we give a great mythological importance to the pig. He's a kind of minion of the sun. I suppose because his sweet fat helps to keep us warm in the darkest and coldest time. Very intelligent animal . . . I love all animals. I have a huge dog in Denmark, an Alsatian; he's enormous. I take him walking. If I survive him, I think I shall get a very small dog—a pug. Though I wonder if it's possible to get a pug now. They used to be very fashionable. Look at the lions on that sarcophagus. How could the Etruscans have known the lion? In Africa it was the animal that I loved the most.

INTERVIEWER

You must have known Africa at its best. What made you decide to go?

DINESEN

When I was a young girl, it was very far from my thoughts to go to Africa, nor did I dream then that an African farm should be the place in which I should be perfectly happy. That goes to prove that God has a greater and finer power of imagination than we have. But at the time when I was engaged to be married to my cousin Bror Blixen, an uncle of ours went out to Africa big-game hunting and came back all filled with praise of the country. Theodore Roosevelt had been hunting there then, too; East Africa was in the news. So Bror and I made up our minds to try our luck there, and our relations on both sides financed us in buying the farm, which was in the highlands of Kenya, not far from Nairobi. The first day I arrived there, I loved the country and felt at home, even among unfamiliar flowers, trees, and animals, and changing clouds over the Ngong hills, unlike any clouds I had ever known. East Africa then was really a paradise, what the Red Indians called "happy hunting grounds." I was very keen on shooting in my young days, but my great interest all through my many years in Africa was the African natives of all tribes, in particular the Somali and the Masai. They were beautiful, noble, fearless, and wise people. Life was not easy running a coffee plantation. Ten thousand acres of farmland, and locusts and drought . . . and too late we realized that the table land where we were located was really too high for raising coffee successfully. Life out there was, I believe, rather like eighteenth-century England: one might often be hard up for cash, but life was still rich in many ways, with the lovely landscape, dozens of horses and dogs, and a multitude of servants.

INTERVIEWER

I suppose that you began to write seriously there?

DINESEN

No, I really began writing before I went to Africa, but I never once wanted to be a writer. I published a few short stories in literary reviews in Denmark when I was twenty years old, and the reviews encouraged me, but I didn't go on—I don't know, I think I had an intuitive fear of being trapped. Also, when I was quite young, for a while I studied painting at the Danish Royal Academy of Fine Arts; then I went to Paris in 1910 to study with Simon and Menard, but [*she chuckles*] . . . but I did little work. The impact of Paris was too great; I felt it was more important to go about and see pictures, to see Paris, in fact. I painted a little in Africa, portraits of the natives mostly, but every time I'd get to work, someone would come up and say an ox has died or something, and I'd have to go out in the fields. Later, when I knew in my heart I should have to sell the farm and go back to Denmark, I did begin to write. To put my mind to other things I began to write tales. Two of the

Gothic Tales were written there. But earlier, I learned how to tell tales. For, you see, I had the perfect audience. White people can no longer listen to a tale recited. They fidget or become drowsy. But the natives have an ear still. I told stories constantly to them, all kinds. And all kinds of nonsense. I'd say, "Once there was a man who had an elephant with two heads . . ." and at once they were eager to hear more. Oh? Yes, but Memsahib, how did he find it, and how did he manage to feed it? or whatever. They loved such invention. I delighted my people there by speaking in rhyme for them; they have no rhyme, you know, had never discovered it. I'd say things like "Wakamba na kula mamba" ("The Wakamba tribe eats snakes"), which in prose would have infuriated them, but which amused them mightily in rhyme. Afterwards they'd say, Please, Memsahib, talk like rain, so then I knew they had liked it, for rain was very precious to us there. Oh, here's Miss Svendsen. She's Catholic, so she went off today to hear a special cardinal. Now we'll go buy some postcards. Hope there is one of the lions.

SVENDSEN

Good morning.

DINESEN

Clara, you must see the delightful lions; then we'll get some postcards and go for lunch.

Postcards are found, a taxi is summoned, umbrellas opened, the party runs for taxi, drives off through the rainy Borghese Gardens.

SCENE THREE

The Casino Valadier is a fashionable restaurant in the Gardens, just above the Piazza del Popolo, and commands a fine view of Rome. After a brief glimpse of the rain-grayed city from the flooded terrace, the party goes into a brocaded room, with considerably shaded girandoles, brightly colored carpets, and pictures.

DINESEN

I'll sit here so I can see everything.

INTERVIEWER

Pleasant place, isn't it?

DINESEN

Yes, very pleasant, and I recognize it. I was here in 1912. Every now and again here in Rome I recognize very vividly a place I've visited then. [*Pause.*] Oh, I shall go mad!

INTERVIEWER

What is it?

DINESEN

Look how crooked that picture is! [*Indicates blackened portrait across room.*]

INTERVIEWER

I'll straighten it. [*Goes to it.*]

DINESEN

No, more to the right.

INTERVIEWER

Like this?

DINESEN

That's better.

*Two solemn gentlemen at table beneath portrait
indicate bewilderment.*

SVENDSEN

It's like that at home. So much traffic passes, and I have always to straighten the pictures.

DINESEN

I live on the North Sea, halfway between Copenhagen and Elsinore.

INTERVIEWER

Perhaps halfway between Shiraz and Atlantis?

DINESEN

Halfway between that island in *The Tempest* and wherever I am. I'll have a cigarette now. Do you mind if we just stay here for a while? I hate to change once I'm installed in a décor I like. People are always telling me to hurry up or come on and do this or do that. Once when I was sailing around the Cape of Good Hope and there were albatrosses, people kept saying, Why do you stay on deck? Come on in. They said, It's time for lunch, and I said, Damn lunch. I said, I can eat lunch any day, but I shan't see albatrosses again. Such wingspread!

INTERVIEWER

Tell me about your father.

DINESEN

He was in the French army, as was my grandfather. After the Franco-Prussian War, he went to America and lived with the Plains Indians in the great middle part of your country. He built himself a little hut and named it after a place in Denmark where he had been very happy as a young man—Frydenlund ("Happy Grove"). He hunted animals for their skins and became a fur trader. He sold his skins mostly to the Indians, then used his profits to buy them gifts. A little community grew up around him, and now Frydenlund is, I believe, the name of a locality in the state of Wisconsin. When he returned to Denmark, he wrote his books. So you see, it was natural for me, his daughter, to go off to Africa and live with the natives and, after returning home, to write about it. He also, incidentally, wrote a volume of his war experiences called *Paris Under the Commune*.

And how is it that you write in English?

It was quite natural to do so. I was partly schooled in England after being taught always by governesses at home. Because of that, I lack knowledge of plain facts which are common coinage for others. But those governesses were ambitious: They did teach languages, and one of them put me to translating *The Lady of the Lake* into Danish. Then, in Africa, I had been seeing only English people, really. I had spoken English or Swahili for twenty years. And I read the English poets and English novelists. I prefer the older writers, but I remember when I first read Huxley's *Chrome Yellow*, it was like biting into an unknown and refreshing fruit.

Most of your tales are laid in the last century, aren't they? You never write about modern times.

I do, if you consider that the time of our grandparents, that just-out-of-reach time, is so much a part of *us*. We absorb so much without being aware. Also, I write about characters who together *are* the tale. I begin, you see, with a flavor of the tale. Then I find the characters, and they take over. They make the design, I simply permit them their liberty. Now, in modern life and in modern fiction there is a kind of atmosphere and above all an interior movement—inside the characters—which is something else again. I feel that in life and in art people have drawn a little apart in this century. Solitude is now the universal theme. But I write about characters within a design, how they act upon one another. Relation with others is important to me, you see, friendship is precious to me, and I have been blessed with heroic friendships. But time in my tales is flexible. I may begin in the eighteenth century and come right up to World War I. Those times have been sorted out, they are clearly visible. Besides, so many novels that we think are contemporary in subject with their date of publication—think of Dickens or Faulkner or Tolstoy or Turgenev—are really set in an earlier period, a generation or so back. The present is always unsettled, no one has had time to contemplate it in tranquillity. I was a painter before I was a writer . . . and a painter never wants the subject right under his nose; he wants to stand back and study a landscape with half-closed eyes.

INTERVIEWER

Have you written poetry?

DINESEN

I did as a young girl.

INTERVIEWER

What is your favorite fruit?

DINESEN

Strawberries.

INTERVIEWER

Do you like monkeys?

DINESEN

Yes, I love them in art—in pictures, in stories, in porcelain—but in life they somehow look so sad. They make me nervous. I like lions and gazelles. . . . Do you think I look like a monkey? [*Here, the baroness refers to an earlier conversation where someone had suggested that if the tale "The Monkey" were ever filmed, she should play the character of the Chanoiness who turns into a monkey.*]

INTERVIEWER

Of course. But you must understand that there are many kinds of monkeys. [*The interviewer has copied out a passage from Ivan Sanderson's* The Monkey Kingdom *for the baroness's delectation and now reads it.*] "The definition of 'monkey' has not, however, been satisfactorily resolved. This apparently simple question, moreover, requires careful examination before we may proceed in our story, for, although we are not solely or even primarily interested in mere monkeys, we cannot, without its resolution, attempt the greater galaxy of life-forms to which they belong."

DINESEN

But no tale can proceed without examining apparently simple questions. And no tail, either.

SCENE FOUR

Now we are on the parapets of the central tower of the Castle of Sermonetta, perched on a hill amidst a clustering town, about an hour and a half south of Rome. We have crossed a moated drawbridge, climbed a rickety ladder-stair. We have seen remains of fourteenth-century frescoes, and in the tower stronghold seen scrawled phrases and drawings on the wall, fresh as new, from when Napoleonic soldiers were incarcerated here. Now the party comes out, shading their eyes. Below, the Pontine plain stretches green and gold to the sea, bathed in bright afternoon sunlight. We can see tiny figures miles below working amidst the bean fields and the peach orchards.

INTERVIEWER

I think it is curious that practically no critic nor reviewer in either America or England has pointed out the great comic element in your works. I hope we might speak a little of the comic spirit in your tales.

DINESEN

Oh, I'm glad you mentioned that! People are always asking me what is the significance of this or that in the tales—What does this symbolize? What does that stand for? And I always have a difficult time making them believe that I intend everything as it's stated. It would be terrible if the explanation of the work were outside the work itself. And I do often intend a comic sense, I love a joke, I love the humorous. The name *Isak* means "laughter." I often think that what we most need now is a great humorist.

INTERVIEWER

What humorists in the English language please you?

DINESEN

Well, Mark Twain, for example. But then all the writers I admire usually have a vein of comic spirit. Writers of tales always do, at least.

INTERVIEWER

Who are writers of tales that appeal to you, or with whom you feel a kinship?

DINESEN

E. T. A. Hoffman, Hans Andersen, Barbey d'Aurevilly, La Motte Fouqué, Chamisso, Turgenev, Hemingway, Maupassant, Stendhal, Chekhov, Conrad, Voltaire . . .

SVENDSEN

Don't forget Melville! She calls me Babu after the character in *Benito Cereno*, when she doesn't refer to me as Sancho Panza.

INTERVIEWER

Heavens, you've read them all!

DINESEN

I am really three thousand years old and have dined with Socrates.

INTERVIEWER

Pardon?

DINESEN

Because I was never told what I must read or what I mustn't read, I did read everything that fell into my hands. I discovered Shakespeare very early in life, and now I feel that life would be nothing without him. One of my new stories is about a company of actors playing *The Tempest*, incidentally. I love the novelists no one reads anymore: Walter Scott, for instance. Oh, and I like Melville very much, and the *Odyssey*, the Norse sagas—Have you read the Norse sagas? I love Racine, too.

INTERVIEWER

I remember your observation on the Norse mythology in one of the *Winter's Tales*.* It's very interesting to me, incidentally, how you have chosen the tale for your form.

DINESEN

It came naturally to me. My literary friends at home tell me that the heart of my work is not in the idea but in the line of the tale. Something you can tell, like one can tell *Ali Baba and the Forty Thieves* but one could not tell *Anna Karenina*.

INTERVIEWER

But there are some who find your tales "artificial" . . .

DINESEN

Artificial? Of course they are artificial. They were meant to be, for such is the essence of the tale-telling art. And I felt I acknowledged that . . . or rather, pointed it out . . . by calling my first tales "Gothic." When I used the word *Gothic*, I didn't mean the real Gothic, but the imitation of the Gothic, the Romantic age of Byron, the age of Horace Walpole, who built Strawberry Hill, the age of the Gothic Revival . . . you know Walpole's *Castle of Otranto*, of course?

---

* "And I have wondered, while I read," says the young nobleman in "Sorrow-Acre," "that we have not till now understood how much our Nordic mythology in moral greatness surpasses that of Greece and Rome. If it had not been for the physical beauty of the ancient gods, which has come down to us in marble, no modern mind could hold them worthy of worship. They were mean, capricious, and treacherous. The gods of our Danish forefathers are as much more divine than they as the Druid is nobler than the Augur."

INTERVIEWER

Yes, indeed. In a tale, the plot is all-important, isn't it?

DINESEN

Yes, it is. I start with a tingle, a kind of feeling of the story I will write. Then come the characters, and they take over, they make the story. But all this ends by being a plot. For other writers, that seems an unnatural thing. But a proper tale has a shape and an outline. In a painting the frame is important. Where does the picture end? What details should one include? Or omit! Where does the line go that cuts off the picture? People always ask me, they say, In "The Deluge at Norderney," were those characters drowned or saved at the end? (You remember they are trapped in a loft during a flood and spend the night recounting their stories while awaiting rescue.) Well, what can I reply? How can I tell them? That's outside the story. I really don't know!

INTERVIEWER

Do you rewrite your tales very much?

DINESEN

Oh, I do, I do. It's hellish. Over and over again. Then when I think I'm finished, and Clara copies them out to send to the publishers, I look over them, and have a fit, and rewrite again.

SVENDSEN

In one tale there was a lesser character called Mariana the Rat who ran an inn called The Lousing-Comb. The publishers mentioned her in the text for the book jacket, but by the time they had the final proofs, she had been removed from the tale. It must have caused mystification.

INTERVIEWER

Many people are mystified by the tale "The Monkey."

DINESEN

Yes, I grow weary from the questions people ask me about that particular tale. But that is a fantastic story; it should be interpreted that way. The principle is this: Let the monkey resolve the mess when the plot has got too complicated for the human characters. But people say, "What does it mean?" *That's* what it means. . . . [*She pauses, with a little laugh.*] It would be a bad thing if I could explain the tale better than what I have already said in the tale. As I never tire of pointing out, the story should be *all*.

INTERVIEWER

Everyone would be interested to know just how one of your tales takes shape. Especially those with tales within the tale. Take "The Deluge at Norderney," for instance . . . it seems so inevitable and ordered, but if one studies it, the design is amazing. . . . How did—

DINESEN

Read it, read it, and you'll see how it's written!

EPILOGUE

For epilogue here, let's append a passage from the Baroness Blixen's "Albondocani," a long series of connected tales still unfinished at the time of the author's death in 1962. This excerpt is from "The Blank Page," published in *Last Tales* (1957). An old woman who earns her living by storytelling is speaking:

"With my grandmother," she said, "I went through a hard school. 'Be loyal to the story,' the old hag would say to me, 'be eternally and unswervingly loyal to the story.' 'Why must I be that, Grandmother?' I asked her. 'Am I to furnish you with reasons, baggage?' she cried. 'And you mean to be a story-teller! Why, you are to become a storyteller, and I shall give you the reasons! Hear then: Where the storyteller is loyal, eternally and unswervingly loyal to the story, there, in the end, silence will speak. Where the story has been betrayed, silence is but emptiness. But we, the faithful, when we have spoken our last word, will hear the voice of silence. Whether a small snotty lass understands it or not.'

"Who then," she continues, "tells a finer tale than any of us? Silence does. And where does one read a deeper tale than upon the most perfectly printed page of the most precious book? Upon the blank page. When a royal and gallant pen, in the moment of its highest inspiration, has written down its tale with the rarest ink of all—where, then, may one read a still deeper, sweeter, merrier, and more cruel tale than that? Upon the blank page."

Issue 14, 1956

Evelyn Waugh

The Art of Fiction

The interview which follows is the result of two meetings on successive days at the Hyde Park Hotel, London, during April 1962.

I had written to Mr. Waugh earlier asking permission to interview him, and in this letter I had promised that I should not bring a tape recorder with me. I imagined, from what he had written in the early part of *The Ordeal of Gilbert Pinfold*, that he was particularly averse to them.

We met in the hall of the hotel at three in the afternoon. Mr. Waugh was dressed in a dark blue suit with a heavy overcoat and a black homburg hat. Apart from a neatly tied, small, brown-paper parcel, he was unencumbered. After we had shaken hands and he had explained that the interview would take place in his own room, the first thing he said was, "Where is your machine?"

I explained that I hadn't brought one.

"Have you sold it?" he continued as we got into the lift. I was somewhat nonplussed. In fact, I had at one time owned a tape recorder, and I had indeed sold it three years earlier, before going to live abroad. None of this seemed very relevant. As we ascended slowly, Mr. Waugh continued his cross-questioning about the machine. How much had I bought it for? How much had I sold it for? Whom did I sell it to?

"Do you have shorthand, then?" he asked as we left the lift.

I explained that I did not.

A manuscript page from *Basil Seal Rides Again* by Evelyn Waugh.

"Then it was very foolhardy of you to sell your machine, wasn't it?"

He showed me into a comfortable, soberly furnished room, with a fine view over the trees across Hyde Park. As he moved about the room he repeated twice under his breath, "The horrors of London life! The horrors of London life!"

"I hope you won't mind if I go to bed," he said, going into the bathroom. From there he gave me a number of comments and directions:

"Go and look out of the window. This is the only hotel with a civilized view left in London. . . . Do you see a brown-paper parcel? Open it, please."

I did so.

"What do you find?"

"A box of cigars."

"Do you smoke?"

"Yes. I am smoking a cigarette now."

"I think cigarettes are rather squalid in the bedroom. Wouldn't you rather smoke a cigar?"

He reentered, wearing a pair of white pajamas and metal-rimmed spectacles. He took a cigar, lit it, and got into bed.

I sat down in an armchair at the foot of the bed, juggling notebook, pen, and enormous cigar between hands and knees.

"I shan't be able to hear you there. Bring up that chair." He indicated one by the window, so I rearranged my paraphernalia as we talked of mutual friends. Quite soon he said, "When is the inquisition to begin?"

I had prepared a number of lengthy questions—the reader will no doubt detect the shadows of them in what follows—but I soon discovered that they did not, as I had hoped, elicit long or ruminative replies. Perhaps what was most striking about Mr. Waugh's conversation was his command of language: his spoken sentences were as graceful, precise, and rounded as his written sentences. He never faltered, nor once gave the impression of searching for a word. The answers he gave to my questions came without hesitation or qualification, and any attempt I made to induce him to expand a reply generally resulted in a rephrasing of what he had said before.

I am well aware that the result on the following pages is unlike the majority of *Paris Review* interviews; first it is very much shorter, and secondly, it is not "an interview in depth." Personally, I believe that Mr. Waugh did not lend himself, either as a writer or as a man, to the form of delicate psychological probing and self-analysis which are characteristic of many of the other interviews. He would consider impertinent an attempt publicly to relate his life and his art, as was demonstrated conclusively when he appeared on an English television program, *Face to Face*, some time ago and parried all such probing with brief, flat, and, wherever possible, monosyllabic replies.

However, I should like to do something to dismiss the mythical image of Evelyn Waugh as an ogre of arrogance and reaction. Although he carefully avoided taking part in the marketplace of literary life, of conferences, prize giving, and reputation building, he was, nonetheless, both well informed and decided in his opinions about his contemporaries and juniors. Throughout the three hours I spent with him he was consistently helpful, attentive, and courteous, allowing himself only minor flights of ironic exasperation if he considered my questions irrelevant or ill-phrased.

—*Julian Jebb*, 1963

INTERVIEWER

Were there attempts at other novels before *Decline and Fall*?

EVELYN WAUGH

I wrote my first piece of fiction at seven: *The Curse of the Horse Race*. It was vivid and full of action. Then, let's see, there was *The World to Come*, written in the meter of *Hiawatha*. When I was at school I wrote a five-thousand-word novel about modern school life. It was intolerably bad.

INTERVIEWER

Did you write a novel at Oxford?

WAUGH

No. I did sketches and that sort of thing for the *Cherwell* and for a paper Harold Acton edited—*Broom*, it was called. The *Isis* was the official
undergraduate magazine: it was boring and hearty, written for beer
drinkers and rugger players. The *Cherwell* was a little more frivolous.

INTERVIEWER

Did you write your life of Rossetti at that time?

WAUGH

No. I came down from Oxford without a degree, wanting to be a
painter. My father settled my debts and I tried to become a painter. I
failed as I had neither the talent nor the application—I didn't have the
moral qualities.

INTERVIEWER

Then what?

WAUGH

I became a prep-school master. It was very jolly and I enjoyed it
very much. I taught at two private schools for a period of nearly two
years and during this I started an Oxford novel which was of no interest. After I had been expelled from the second school for drunken-
ness, I returned penniless to my father. I went to see my friend
Anthony Powell, who was working with Duckworth, the publishers,
at the time, and said, I'm starving. (This wasn't true: my father fed
me.) The director of the firm agreed to pay me fifty pounds for a brief
life of Rossetti. I was delighted, as fifty pounds was quite a lot then. I
dashed off and dashed it off. The result was hurried and bad. I
haven't let them reprint it again. Then I wrote *Decline and Fall*. It was
in a sense based on my experiences as a schoolmaster, yet I had a
much nicer time than the hero.

INTERVIEWER

Did *Vile Bodies* follow on immediately?

WAUGH

I went through a form of marriage and traveled about Europe for some months with this consort. I wrote accounts of these travels which were bundled together into books and paid for the journeys, but left nothing over. I was in the middle of *Vile Bodies* when she left me. It was a bad book, I think, not so carefully constructed as the first. Separate scenes tended to go on for too long—the conversation in the train between those two women, the film shows of the dotty father.

INTERVIEWER

I think most of your readers would group these two novels closely together. I don't think that most of us would recognize that the second was the more weakly constructed.

WAUGH [*briskly*]

It was. It was secondhand, too. I cribbed much of the scene at the customs from Firbank. I popularized a fashionable language, like the beatnik writers today, and the book caught on.

INTERVIEWER

Have you found that the inspiration or starting point of each of your novels has been different? Do you sometimes start with a character, sometimes with an event or circumstance? Did you, for example, think of the ramifications of an aristocratic divorce as the center of *A Handful of Dust*, or was it the character of Tony and his ultimate fate which you started from?

WAUGH

I wrote a story called *The Man Who Liked Dickens*, which is identical to the final part of the book. About two years after I had written it, I became interested in the circumstances which might have produced this character; in his delirium there were hints of what he might have been like in his former life, so I followed them up.

INTERVIEWER

Did you return again and again to the story in the intervening two years?

WAUGH

I wasn't haunted by it, if that's what you mean. Just curious. You can find the original story in a collection got together by Alfred Hitchcock.

INTERVIEWER

Did you write these early novels with ease or—

WAUGH

Six weeks' work.

INTERVIEWER

Including revisions?

WAUGH

Yes.

INTERVIEWER

Do you write with the same speed and ease today?

WAUGH

I've got slower as I grow older. *Men at Arms* took a year. One's memory gets so much worse. I used to be able to hold the whole of a book in my head. Now if I take a walk whilst I am writing, I have to hurry back and make a correction, before I forget it.

INTERVIEWER

Do you mean you worked a bit every day over a year, or that you worked in concentrated periods?

WAUGH

Concentrated periods. Two thousand words is a good day's work.

INTERVIEWER

E. M. Forster has spoken of "flat characters" and "round characters"; if you recognize this distinction, would you agree that you created no "round" characters until *A Handful of Dust*?

WAUGH

All fictional characters are flat. A writer can give an illusion of depth by giving an apparently stereoscopic view of a character— seeing him from two vantage points; all a writer can do is give more or less information about a character, not information of a different order.

INTERVIEWER

Then do you make no radical distinction between characters as differently conceived as Mr. Prendergast and Sebastian Flyte?

WAUGH

Yes, I do. There are the protagonists and there are characters who are furniture. One gives only one aspect of the furniture. Sebastian Flyte was a protagonist.

INTERVIEWER

Would you say, then, that Charles Ryder was the character about whom you gave the most information?

WAUGH

No, Guy Crouchback. [*A little restlessly*] But look, I think that your questions are dealing too much with the creation of character and not enough with the technique of writing. I regard writing not as investigation of character, but as an exercise in the use of language, and with this I am obsessed. I have no technical psychological interest. It is drama, speech, and events that interest me.

INTERVIEWER

Does this mean that you continually refine and experiment?

WAUGH

Experiment? God forbid! Look at the results of experiment in the case of a writer like Joyce. He started off writing very well, then you can watch him going mad with vanity. He ends up a lunatic.

INTERVIEWER

I gather from what you said earlier that you don't find the act of writing difficult.

WAUGH

I don't find it easy. You see, there are always words going round in my head: some people think in pictures, some in ideas. I think entirely in words. By the time I come to stick my pen in my inkpot these words have reached a stage of order which is fairly presentable.

INTERVIEWER

Perhaps that explains why Gilbert Pinfold was haunted by voices—by disembodied words.

WAUGH

Yes, that's true—the word made manifest.

INTERVIEWER

Can you say something about the direct influences on your style? Were any of the nineteenth-century writers an influence on you? Samuel Butler, for example?

WAUGH

They were the basis of my education, and, as such, of course I was affected by reading them. P. G. Wodehouse affected my style directly. Then there was a little book by E. M. Forster called *Pharos and Pharillon*—sketches of the history of Alexandria. I think that Hemingway made real discoveries about the use of language in his first novel, *The Sun Also Rises*. I admired the way he made drunk people talk.

INTERVIEWER

What about Ronald Firbank?

WAUGH

I enjoyed him very much when I was young. I can't read him now.

INTERVIEWER

Why?

WAUGH

I think there would be something wrong with an elderly man who could enjoy Firbank.

INTERVIEWER

Whom do you read for pleasure?

WAUGH

Anthony Powell. Ronald Knox, both for pleasure and moral edification. Erle Stanley Gardner.

INTERVIEWER

And Raymond Chandler!

WAUGH

No. I'm bored by all those slugs of whiskey. I don't care for all the violence either.

INTERVIEWER

But isn't there a lot of violence in Gardner?

WAUGH

Not of the extraneous lubricious sort you find in other American crime writers.

INTERVIEWER

What do you think of other American writers, of Scott Fitzgerald or William Faulkner, for example?

WAUGH

I enjoyed the first part of *Tender Is the Night*. I find Faulkner intolerably bad.

INTERVIEWER

It is evident that you reverence the authority of established institutions—the Catholic Church and the army. Would you agree that on one level both *Brideshead Revisited* and the army trilogy were celebrations of this reverence?

WAUGH

No, certainly not. I reverence the Catholic Church because it is true, not because it is established or an institution. *Men at Arms* was a kind of uncelebration, a history of Guy Crouchback's disillusion with the army. Guy has old-fashioned ideas of honor and illusions of chivalry; we see these being used up and destroyed by his encounters with the realities of army life.

INTERVIEWER

Would you say that there was any direct moral to the army trilogy?

WAUGH

Yes, I imply that there is a moral purpose, a chance of salvation, in every human life. Do you know the old Protestant hymn which goes: "Once to every man and nation/Comes the moment to decide"? Guy is offered this chance by making himself responsible for the upbringing of Trimmer's child, to see that he is not brought up by his dissolute mother. He is essentially an unselfish character.

INTERVIEWER

Can you say something about the conception of the trilogy? Did you carry out a plan which you had made at the start?

WAUGH

It changed a lot in the writing. Originally I had intended the second volume, *Officers and Gentlemen*, to be two volumes. Then I decided to lump them together and finish it off. There's a very bad transitional passage on board the troop ship. The third volume really arose from the fact that Ludovic needed explaining. As it turned out, each volume had a common form because there was an irrelevant ludicrous figure in each to make the running.

INTERVIEWER

Even if, as you say, the whole conception of the trilogy was not clearly worked out before you started to write, were there not some things which you saw from the beginning?

WAUGH

Yes, both the sword in the Italian church and the sword of Stalingrad were, as you put it, there from the beginning.

INTERVIEWER

Can you say something about the germination of *Brideshead Revisited*?

WAUGH

It is very much a child of its time. Had it not been written when it was, at a very bad time in the war when there was nothing to eat, it would have been a different book. The fact that it is rich in evocative description—in gluttonous writing—is a direct result of the privations and austerity of the times.

INTERVIEWER

Have you found any professional criticism of your work illuminating or helpful? Edmund Wilson, for example?

WAUGH

Is he an American?

INTERVIEWER

Yes.

WAUGH

I don't think what they have to say is of much interest, do you? I think the general state of reviewing in England is contemptible—both slovenly and ostentatious. I used to have a rule when I reviewed books as a young man never to give an unfavorable notice to a book I hadn't read. I find even this simple rule is flagrantly broken now. Naturally I abhor the Cambridge movement of criticism, with its horror of elegance and its members mutually encouraging uncouth writing. Otherwise, I am pleased if my friends like my books.

INTERVIEWER

Do you think it just to describe you as a reactionary?

WAUGH

An artist must be a reactionary. He has to stand out against the tenor of the age and not go flopping along; he must offer some little opposition. Even the great Victorian artists were all anti-Victorian, despite the pressures to conform.

INTERVIEWER

But what about Dickens? Although he preached social reform he also sought a public image.

WAUGH

Oh, that's quite different. He liked adulation and he liked showing off. But he was still deeply antagonistic to Victorianism.

INTERVIEWER

Is there any particular historical period, other than this one, in which you would like to have lived?

WAUGH

The seventeenth century. I think it was the time of the greatest drama and romance. I think I might have been happy in the thirteenth century, too.

INTERVIEWER

Despite the great variety of the characters you have created in your novels, it is very noticeable that you have never given a sympathetic or even a full-scale portrait of a working-class character. Is there any reason for this?

WAUGH

I don't know them, and I'm not interested in them. No writer before the middle of the nineteenth century wrote about the working classes other than as grotesques or as pastoral decorations. Then when they were given the vote certain writers started to suck up to them.

INTERVIEWER

What about Pistol . . . or much later, *Moll Flanders* and—

WAUGH

Ah, the criminal classes. That's rather different. They have always had a certain fascination.

INTERVIEWER

May I ask you what you are writing at the moment?

WAUGH

An autobiography.

INTERVIEWER

Will it be conventional in form?

WAUGH

Extremely.

INTERVIEWER

Are there any books which you would like to have written and have found impossible?

WAUGH

I have done all I could. I have done my best.

Issue 30, 1963

William Carlos Williams

The Art of Poetry

Rutherford, New Jersey: Number nine stands on a terrace at the foot of Ridge Road, just where it angles into Park Avenue and the stores along the main street. For fifty years the sign beside the walk read WILLIAM C. WILLIAMS, M. D. Now it carries the name of his son, with an arrow pointing to the side entrance and the new office wing. In his last years, Dr. Williams's health suffered from a series of strokes that made it difficult for him to speak and impaired his physical vigor, so that there would often be a delay before he appeared, pushing out the aluminum storm door and retreating a step or two, extending welcome with a kind of hesitant warmth. On the occasion of the interview, he moved more deliberately than ever, but his greeting was still at pains to be personal. A leisurely progress brought us upstairs past a huge, two-story painting of the Williamsburg Bridge filling the stairwell, to the study, a room at the back of the house, overlooking the yard. An electric typewriter, which Dr. Williams could no longer use, was at the desk, and, though he could scarcely read, a copy of *The Desert Music and Other Poems*, opened to "The Descent," was propped up in the open drawer. In a corner of the room, over a metal filing cabinet, was an oil painting hung against a wallpaper of geometric simplicity. We sat a little away from the desk, toward the window, with the microphone lying on a stack of small magazines between us.

At the time of these talks, in April 1962, William Carlos Williams was in his seventy-ninth year, author of forty published volumes from

As Weehawken ### to Hamilton
to Provence we'll say, he hated it
of which he knew nothing and cared less
and used it inhis scheems - so
founding the counding which was to
increase to be the wonder of the world
in its day

which was to exceed his london on which he patterened it

(A key figure in the development)

                    If any one is important more important
        - point of a dagger-
than the edge of a knife or a poem is: or an irrelevance #
in the life of a people: see Da Da or the murders of a
Staline

        or a Li Po

                        or an obscre Montezuma

or a forgotten Socrates or Aristotle before the destruction
of the library of Alexandria (as note derisively by Berad Shaw)
by fire in which the poes of Sappho were lost

        and brings us (Alex was born out of wedlock)

        illegitimately perversion ##### righed though that alone
does not a make a poet or a statesman

- Wahington was a six foot four man with a wakk voice and a slow
mind which made it inconvenient for him to move fast - and so he
stayed. He had a will bred in the slow woods so that when he
moved the world moved out of has way.

A fragment from the continuation of *Paterson* by William Carlos Williams.

Poems, 1909, a collection so rare that Mrs. Williams has had trouble holding on to a copy, down through various collected editions and the successive books of *Paterson* to *The Desert Music* and *Journey to Love*. Both of these last volumes were written in an unusual recovery of creative power after Dr. Williams's first serious illness in 1952. Now, with customary impatience, he was fretting to see his latest collection, *Pictures from Brueghel*, scheduled for publication in June. The doorbell never rang but he expected some word from New Directions, though it was still early in spring.

Because it was so hard for Dr. Williams to talk, there was no question of discoursing on topics suggested in advance, and the conversation went on informally, for an hour or two at a time, over several days. The effort it took the poet to find and pronounce words can hardly be indicated here. Many of the sentences ended in no more than a wave of the hand when Mrs. Williams was not present to finish them. But whatever the topic, the poet's mind kept coming back to the technical matters that interested him in his later years. One of these was his concern with "idiom," the movements of speech that he felt to be especially American, as opposed to English. A rival interest was the "variable foot," a metrical device that was to resolve the conflict between form and freedom in verse. The question whether one had not to assume a fixed element in the foot as the basis for meter drew only a typical Williams negative, slightly profane, and no effort was made to pursue this much further. As a result, the notion of some mysterious "measure" runs through the interview like an unlaid ghost, promising enough pattern for shapeliness, enough flexibility for all the subtleties of idiom. No wonder a copy of "The Descent" was in evidence as we began; for however much one may argue over the theory of this verse, it is hard to resist the performance.

On March 4, 1963, William Carlos Williams died in his sleep, at home, of a cerebral hemorrhage that was not unexpected. Two months later, *Pictures from Brueghel* was awarded the Pulitzer Prize for poetry, and Mrs. Williams accepted, in his name, the Gold Medal for Poetry from the National Institute of Arts and Letters. Though he did not see this interview in print, he approved it in its final stages.

Mrs. Williams reports him as having been much entertained by her part in the second half of it.

—*Stanley Koehler, 1964*

WILLIAM CARLOS WILLIAMS

Well, what's to be done?

INTERVIEWER

I would like to ask you about this new measure that I see here—

WILLIAMS

If I could only talk.

INTERVIEWER

Perhaps we might begin with Rutherford, whether you thought it was a good environment for you.

WILLIAMS

A very bad environment for poets. We didn't take anything seriously—in Ruth—in Rutherford. We didn't take poetry very seriously. As far as recording my voice in Rutherford—I read before the ladies, mostly.

INTERVIEWER

You mean the Women's Club? How did they like it?

WILLIAMS

Very much: they applauded. I was quite a hero. [*Picking up a volume*] I remember "By the Road to the Contagious Hospital" was one of the ones I read. The hospital was up in Clifton. I was always intent on saying what I had to say in the accents that were native to me. But I didn't know what I was doing. I knew that the measure was intended to record—something. But I didn't know what the measure was. I stumbled all over the place in these earlier poems. For instance, in this one here ["Queen-Ann's Lace"]. I would divide those lines differently now. It's just like the later line, only not opened up in the same way.

INTERVIEWER

You were saying that Rutherford was a bad environment for poets.

WILLIAMS

Yes. But except for my casual conversations about the town, I didn't think anything of it at all. I had a great amount of patience with artisans.

INTERVIEWER

Did you mean it when you said medicine was an interference which you resented?

WILLIAMS

I didn't resent it at all. I just wanted to go straight ahead.

INTERVIEWER

And medicine was not on the way?

WILLIAMS

I don't know whether it would be. I used to give readings at the high school and Fairleigh Dickinson. I was sympathetic with these audiences. I was talking about the same people that I had to do with as patients, and trying to interest them. I was not pretending: I was speaking to them as if they were interested in the same sort of thing.

INTERVIEWER

But were they? Perhaps they felt the double nature of your role, as both poet and doctor, was something of a barrier.

WILLIAMS

No, no. The language itself was what intrigued me. I thought that we were on common territory there.

INTERVIEWER

Did you write the short stories on a different "level" than the poems—as a kind of interlude to them?

WILLIAMS

No, as an alternative. They were written in the form of a conversation which I was partaking in. We were in it together.

INTERVIEWER

Then the composition of them was just as casual and spontaneous as you have suggested. You would come home in the evening and write twelve pages or so without revising?

WILLIAMS

I think so. I was coming *home*. I was placing myself in continuation of a common conversation.

INTERVIEWER

You have insisted that there cannot be a seeking for words in literature. Were you speaking of prose as well as poetry?

WILLIAMS

I think so. Not to choose between words.

INTERVIEWER

Certainly the word does matter though.

WILLIAMS

It does matter, very definitely. Strange that I could say that.

INTERVIEWER

But when you had come home, and were continuing the experience of reality—

WILLIAMS

Reality. Reality. My vocabulary was chosen out of the intensity of my concern. When I was talking in front of a group, I wasn't interested in impressing them with my power of speech, but only with the seriousness of my intentions toward them. I had to make them come alive.

INTERVIEWER

You have said you felt trapped in Rutherford, that you couldn't get out, never had any contact with anyone here. Do you still feel that Rutherford hasn't provided enough of the contact you managed to find during the twenties, in New York, with the Others group? Was that a genuine contribution to your development?

WILLIAMS

That was not a literary thing exactly. But it was about writing—intensely so. We were speaking straight ahead about what concerned us, and if I could have overheard what I was saying then, that would have given me a hint of how to phrase myself, to say what I had to say. Not after the establishment, but speaking straight ahead. I would gladly have traded what I have tried to say for what came off my tongue, naturally.

INTERVIEWER

Which was not the same?

WILLIAMS

Not free enough. What came off in this writing, finally—*this* writing [*pointing to* "The Descent"]—that was pretty much what I wanted to say, in the way I wanted to say it, then. I was searching in this congeries. I wanted to say something in a certain tone of my voice which would be exactly how I wanted to say it, to measure it in a certain way.

INTERVIEWER

Was this in line with what the others in the group were trying to do?

WILLIAMS

I don't think they knew what they were trying to do; but in effect it was. I couldn't speak like the academy. It had to be modified by the conversation about me. As Marianne Moore used to say, a language dogs and cats could understand. So I think she agrees with me fundamentally. Not the speech of English country people, which would have something artificial about it; not that, but language modified by *our* environment; the American environment.

INTERVIEWER

Your own background is pretty much a mixture of English and Spanish, isn't it? Do you think the Spanish has had any influence on your work?

WILLIAMS

There might have been a permanent impression on my mind. It was certainly different from the French. French is too formal; the Spanish language isn't. They were broad men, as in *El Cid*, very much broader than the French. My relation to language was a curious thing. My father was English, but Spanish was spoken in my home. I didn't speak it, but I was read to in Spanish. My mother's relatives used to come up and stay two or three months.

INTERVIEWER

You have said you equated Spanish with the "romantic." Is that a designation you would shrink from?

WILLIAMS

No, not shrink from.

INTERVIEWER

What I was getting at is that you have kept the name "Carlos."

WILLIAMS

I had no choice but to keep the "Carlos."

INTERVIEWER

I understand Solomon Hoheb, your mother's father, was Dutch.

WILLIAMS

Maybe. The Spanish came from the Sephardic Jews. Though the English was strong indeed, through my grandfather.

INTERVIEWER

You've been more conscious of the Spanish, then, than of the other.

WILLIAMS

Yes! I've insisted on breaking with my brother's memory of the Williamses as English. All one needs to do is look at my nose. Flossie says, I love your nose. And the hell with my nose, after all. The thing that concerns me is the theory of what I was determined to do with measure, what you encounter on the page. It must be transcribed to the page from the lips of the poet, as it was with such a master as Sappho. "The Descent" was very important to me in that way.

INTERVIEWER

You mean that is where it finally happened?

WILLIAMS

Yes, there it happened; and before that it didn't. I remember writing this (*trying to read*):

The descent beckons
as the ascent beckoned.
Memory is a kind . . .

INTERVIEWER

. . . of accomplishment.

WILLIAMS

A sort of renewal
even
an initiation, since the spaces it opens are new places.

You see how I run that line? I was very much excited when I wrote this. I had to do something. I was sitting there with the typewriter in front of me. I was attempting to imitate myself (I think I can't even see it at all) but it didn't come alive to me.

INTERVIEWER

It seems to me you were reading it just now.

WILLIAMS

More or less. But something went wrong with me. I can't make it out any more. I can't type.

INTERVIEWER

Would a tape recorder or a dictaphone be uncongenial?

WILLIAMS

No, anything that would serve me I'd gladly adopt.

INTERVIEWER

The appearance of this poem on the page suggests you were conscious of it as a thing—something for the eye.

WILLIAMS

Yes, very good. I was conscious of making it even. I wanted it to read regularly.

INTERVIEWER

Not just to please the eye?

WILLIAMS

The total effect is very important.

INTERVIEWER

But the care in placing the words—did you ever feel you would be as happy painting?

WILLIAMS

I'd like to have been a painter, and it would have given me at least as great a satisfaction as being a poet.

INTERVIEWER

But you say you are a "word man."

WILLIAMS

Yes, that took place early in my development. I was inducted early into my father's habit of reading—that made me a poet, not a painter. My mother was a painter. Her brother Carlos won the Grand Prix— the Gros Lot it was called—then he financed her to go to Paris, to study painting. Then the money ran out.

INTERVIEWER

And she met your father through Carlos, whom he knew in—

WILLIAMS

Puerto Plata. My father was a businessman, interested in South America. But he always loved books. He used to read poetry to me. Shakespeare. He had a group who used to come to our house, a Shakespeare club. They did dramatic readings. So I was always interested in Shakespeare, and Grandmother was interested in the stage—my father's mother. Emily Dickinson, her name was. Isn't that amazing?

INTERVIEWER

Quite a coincidence: I notice a picture of her namesake over the desk.

WILLIAMS

Emily was my patron saint. She was also an American, seeking to divide the line in some respectable way. We were all of us Americans.

INTERVIEWER

Then you did read a good bit of her at some stage, with your father?

WILLIAMS

My father didn't know anything about Emily Dickinson. He was sold on Shakespeare. [*Doorbell rings. WCW makes his way downstairs to answer it.*]

INTERVIEWER [*As he returns*]

You say you were hoping it might be the new volume?

WILLIAMS

Yes. I am keenly disappointed. But that's always the way it is with me—my life's blood dripping away. Laughlin has been a wonderful friend, but it's always so goddamn *slow*! I have still the illusion that I will be able to talk when I make these connections. It's possible, because I am an emotional creature, and if I could only talk, to you for instance. Here is a person well-intentioned toward me, meaning yourself, and I can't talk to him. It makes me furious.

INTERVIEWER

It's good of you to put up with this business at all. We were talking about painting and the theater and poetry. Was that a natural progression for you?

WILLIAMS

More or less; stemming from frustration. I was wondering—I was seeking to be articulate.

INTERVIEWER

At one point you wanted to be an actor.

WILLIAMS

I had no skill as an actor. But through Dad's reading, the plays of Shakespeare made an impression on me. He didn't *want* them to necessarily, just to read them—as words, that came off as speech.

INTERVIEWER

How did this interest in words make you interested in poetry as opposed, say, to writing novels?

WILLIAMS

That didn't have any connection.

INTERVIEWER

The words weren't sufficiently important in prose?

WILLIAMS

No. I never thought I was a very good prose writer anyway. But when I speak of Emily Dickinson—she was an independent spirit. She did her best to get away from too strict an interpretation. And she didn't want to be confined to rhyme or reason. (Even in Shakespeare, the speech of the players: it was annoying to him to have to rhyme, for God's sake.) And she followed the American idiom. She didn't know it, but she followed it nonetheless. I was a better poet.

INTERVIEWER

You are speaking about language now, not form.

WILLIAMS

Yes; her native speech. She was a wild girl. She chafed against restraint. But she speaks the spoken language, the idiom, which would be deformed by Oxford English.

INTERVIEWER

This new measure of yours, in the later poems, is meant then to accommodate the American speech rhythms.

WILLIAMS

Yes. It's a strange phenomenon, my writing. I think what I have been searching for—

INTERVIEWER

You were suggesting that Emily Dickinson had something to do with it; and her objection to rhyme. But that you were a better poet.

WILLIAMS

Oh, yes [*laughing*]. She was a real good guy. I thought I was a better poet because the American idiom was so close to me, and she didn't get what the poets were doing at that time—writing according to a new method, not the English method, which wouldn't have made much sense to an American. Whitman was on the right track, but when he switched to the English intonation, and followed the English method of recording the feet, he didn't realize it was a different method, which was not satisfactory to an American. Everything started with Shakespeare.

INTERVIEWER

Because it was meant to be spoken?

WILLIAMS

Yes. But when the Shakespearean line was recorded, it was meant to be a formal thing, divided in the English method according to what was written on the page. The Americans shouldn't tolerate that. An Englishman—an English rhetorician, an actor—will speak like Shakespeare, but it's only rhetorical. He can't be true to his own speech. He has to change it in order to conform.

INTERVIEWER

You think it is easier for the English to conform, in poetry, to their kind of speech pattern than it is for an American? You don't think for example that Frost is as true to the American idiom as you are trying to be?

WILLIAMS

No, I don't think so. Eliot, on the other hand, was trying to find a way to record the speech and he didn't find it. He wanted to be regular, to be true to the American idiom, but he didn't find a way to do it. One has to bow down finally, either to the English or to the American.

INTERVIEWER

Eliot went to England; you stayed here.

WILLIAMS

To my sorrow.

INTERVIEWER

To your sorrow? What do you mean by that?

WILLIAMS [*yielding, perhaps*]

It is always better to stick to something.

INTERVIEWER

It's rare to find someone who has. Eliot says he would not be the same if he had stayed. You have said there was a great virtue in the kind of isolation you experienced here.

WILLIAMS

A key question.

INTERVIEWER

And you have been called our most valuable homespun sensitivity.

WILLIAMS

"Homespun sensitivity." Very good.

INTERVIEWER

But you still feel it was a bad environment.

WILLIAMS

It was native, but I doubt that it was very satisfactory to me personally. Though it did provide the accent, which satisfied me.

INTERVIEWER

Do you think you could have picked a better one? Do you think you would have been happier in Boston, or Hartford, or New York, or Paris?

WILLIAMS

I might have picked a better one, if I had wanted to—which I did. But if I lived there—if its language was familiar to me, if that was the kind of conversation which I heard, which I grew up with—I could tolerate the vulgarity because it forced me to speak in a particular manner. Not the English intonation.

INTERVIEWER

Do you still feel that the English influence on Eliot set us back twenty years?

WILLIAMS

Very definitely. He was a conformist. He wanted to go back to the iambic pentameter; and he did go back to it, very well; but he didn't acknowledge it.

INTERVIEWER

You say that you could never be a calm speaker, so that this unit you use, which isn't either a foot or a line necessarily, and which works by speech impulses, this is meant to reflect also your own nervous habit of speech—in which things come more or less in a rush.

WILLIAMS

Common sense would force me to work out some such method.

INTERVIEWER

You do pause, though, in the midst of these lines.

WILLIAMS

Very definitely.

INTERVIEWER

Then what is the integrity of the line?

WILLIAMS

If I was consistent in myself it would be very much more effective than it is now. I would have followed much closer to the indicated divisions of the line than I did. It's too haphazard.

INTERVIEWER

The poetry? You admit that in prose, but—

WILLIAMS

In poetry also. I think I was too haphazard.

INTERVIEWER

In the later poems—like "The Orchestra" here—you think there is still some work to do?

WILLIAMS

It's not successful. It would be classical if it had the proper division of lines. "Reluctant mood," "stretches and yawns." What the devil is that? It isn't firmly enough stated. It's all very complicated—but I can't go on.

INTERVIEWER

You mean you can't find a theory to explain what you do naturally.

WILLIAMS

Yes. It's all in the ear. I wanted to be regular. To continue that—

INTERVIEWER

[*picking up a copy of* Paterson V, *from which some clippings fall to the floor*]
These opening lines—they make an image on the page.

WILLIAMS

Yes, I was imitating the flight of the bird.

INTERVIEWER

Then it's directed—

WILLIAMS

To the eyes. Read it.

INTERVIEWER

"In old age the mind casts off . . ."

WILLIAMS

In old age
the mind
casts off
rebelliously
an eagle
from its crag

INTERVIEWER

Did you ever think of using any other city as subject for a poem?

WILLIAMS

I didn't dare any mention of it in *Paterson*, but I thought strongly of Manhattan when I was looking about for a city to celebrate. I thought it was not particularized enough for me, not American in the sense I wanted. It was near enough, God knows, and I was familiar enough with it for all my purposes—but so was Leipzig, where I lived

for a year when I was young, or Paris. Or even Vienna or even Fras-
cati. But Manhattan escaped me.

INTERVIEWER

Someone remarks in one of these clippings that there is no reason
the poem should ever end. Part four completes the cycle, five renews
it. Then what?

WILLIAMS [*Laughing*]

Go on repeating it. At the end—the last part, the dance—

INTERVIEWER

"We can know nothing and can know nothing but the dance . . ."

WILLIAMS

The dance, to dance to a measure
contrapuntally,
satyrically, the tragic foot.

That has to be interpreted; but how are you going to interpret it?

INTERVIEWER

I don't presume to interpret it; but perhaps the satyrs represent the
element of freedom, of energy within the form.

WILLIAMS

Yes. The satyrs are understood as action, a dance. I always think
of the Indians there.

INTERVIEWER

Is anything implied, in "contrapuntally," about the nature of the foot?

WILLIAMS

It means *musically*—it's a musical image. The Indians had a beat in
their own music, which they beat with their feet. It isn't an image ex-

actly, a poetic image. Or perhaps it is. The beat goes according to the image. It should all be so simple; but with my damaged brain—

INTERVIEWER

We probably shouldn't be trying to reduce a poetic statement to prose, when we have *The Desert Music* here: "Only the poem . . ."

WILLIAMS

"The counted poem, to an exact measure."

INTERVIEWER

You think it should be more exact then, than you have yet made it.

WILLIAMS

Yes, it should be more exact, in Milton's sense. Milton counted the syllables.

INTERVIEWER

"And I could not help thinking of the wonders of the brain that hears that music."

WILLIAMS

Yes.

INTERVIEWER

"And of our skill *sometimes* to record it." Do you still feel that such modesty is in order?

WILLIAMS

Modesty is in order, God knows—facing the universe of sound.

INTERVIEWER

At least you are not talking about painting now.

WILLIAMS

No. I'm more or less committed to poetry.

Talking with Mrs. Williams—the Flossie of White Mule—*is like going on with a conversation with Dr. Williams: the same honesty, the same warmth, mixed perhaps with briskness and reserve. The living room of their house reflects the interests they have had in common—the paintings, the flowers, the poetry. For fifty years the daily mail brought letters, books, journals, to accumulate in corners and cupboards and on tables around the edges of the room: books from authors and publishers, books with dedications to WCW, or titles borrowed from his poems; and the whole lot of those almost anonymous little magazines that he encouraged with contributions: poems, articles, the inevitable "visit with WCW." On the first day of these particular interviews, a new hi-fi set still in its crate stood in the middle of the room, a gift from the second son, Paul. Now, while waiting for Dr. Williams to come in, Mrs. Williams put on a record, and we listened to the poet's voice for a while, recorded in this same room with occasional sounds of local traffic coming through. It was an aging voice, unmodulated and didactic, but curiously effective in reading the late poems. Mrs. Williams talked about the town of Rutherford, and the poet's brother Edgar, an architect with plans for improving life along the Passaic. She talked of the house when they first moved into it, and of her early impressions of Bill Williams as a young man, at a stage of their life when he was generally off in New York at the clinics, or at various literary gatherings.*

INTERVIEWER

Did you have to be converted to poetry, in those early days?

MRS. WILLIAMS

No, I was sympathetic. Of course, Bill never paid much attention to me. He used to come to see my sister, who was quite a bit older. She played the piano, and Bill played the violin—not very well. And Edgar sang. Bill didn't read his poetry to me then. He read some to my sister, but she didn't think much of it. Bill's early verse was pretty bad.

INTERVIEWER

I understand Dr. Williams wrote a sonnet a day for a year, when he was at Pennsylvania. Edgar says he called it brainwash, or something worse.

MRS. WILLIAMS

Meeting Ezra Pound seemed to make a difference. It was not really a literary relationship at first. They were too wholly different, but I think that was the turning point. From that time Bill began seriously to want to write poetry. But he realized he couldn't make a living at it.

INTERVIEWER

How did he happen to become a doctor?

MRS. WILLIAMS

His father wanted him to be a dentist. Bill was willing to try. But he hated it. Bill was just too nervous to stand in one spot. But he loved being a doctor, making house calls, and talking to people.

INTERVIEWER

He didn't care to be a surgeon?

MRS. WILLIAMS

He didn't have the long fingers he thought a surgeon should have. That's why he was never a good violinist. But he and Edgar both had ability with their hands. Edgar was a master at drawing, and Bill used to paint. And of course he loves to garden. Two years ago he turned over that whole garden for me when he could scarcely use his right arm. Things would really grow for him.

INTERVIEWER

Was there much literary life in Rutherford?

MRS. WILLIAMS

Not until much later. We had no literary contacts in Rutherford at all: except for Miss Owen, who taught the sixth grade. She knew what Bill was trying to do.

INTERVIEWER

I had the feeling Dr. Williams felt there was no real response to his poetry, even when he read to local groups.

MRS. WILLIAMS

They took what they could get, and ignored the rest—it just wasn't for them. I think to this day very few people in Rutherford know anything about Bill's writing.

INTERVIEWER

Is that a comment on the town or the writing?

MRS. WILLIAMS

I think both. It's a lower-middle-class type of mind, and Bill has never attracted a general audience. My mother used to try to get me to influence him.

INTERVIEWER

To write more conventionally?

MRS. WILLIAMS

Yes. Some of it I didn't like myself, but I never interfered. And I was never blamed for not liking it. [*Telephone rings*] I'll get it, Bill. [*Answering*] Is it an emergency? No, there are no office hours on Friday. [*Returning from phone*] A patient for young Bill. He left the answering service off. That's what happens.

INTERVIEWER

I suppose you are used to that by now.

MRS. WILLIAMS [*groaning*]
Yes, by now, I'm afraid I am.

INTERVIEWER
Is Dr. Williams not writing now?

MRS. WILLIAMS
No, not for over a year; he can't. He just can't find the words.

INTERVIEWER
Was he writing very much when you were first engaged?

MRS. WILLIAMS
No; once in a while he would send me a poem. But he was busy building up his practice. After we were married he wrote more. I saw to it that he had time, and I made it pleasant for people who came here—because I liked them myself. They were much more interesting than most of the local people. Everyone you can think of used to be in and out. We were the only ones who had a permanent address in all that time. For fifty years, this was headquarters for them all. There was Marsden Hartley—that was his only pastel, over the divan there. He was broke and wanted to go to Germany, so he had an auction at Stieglitz's gallery. An American Place. Bill bought another one at the same time, an unfinished oil up in the study. Maxwell Bodenheim came and stayed a couple of weeks once. He almost drove us crazy. (He was supposed to have a broken arm but Bill was never convinced of it.) He was quite dirty and disagreeable. He couldn't eat carrots, though we had to have them, for the children's sake. And he stuttered terribly. One day we received a telegram from him saying: send two hundred dollars at once am going to marry a very beautiful girl. Maxwell. He was later found murdered in his apartment in New York, with his wife, if she was his wife; probably not the one in the telegram. Then there was Wallace Gould, whom you may not know, a friend of Hartley's from Maine. His mother was an American Indian. And Marianne Moore used to come out with her mother.

Bill's writing developed tremendously in that period. There was a group up at Grantwood, near Fort Lee. Malcolm Cowley was in it; and Marcel Duchamp, Man Ray, Alfred Kreymborg. Robert Brown had the one solid house; the others all lived around in their little shacks. Later on they used to meet in New York, at Lola Ridge's place. She had a big, barnlike studio. I suppose today you would call her a communist, though I never heard any talk of that kind. She was older than most of the young writers. Then there was John Reed, who wrote *Ten Days That Shook the World*; and Louise Bryant—they were all in that group. And there we were. There were arguments; they were all very serious about their writing. They used to get up and read—they would always read. It used to be deadly sometimes. But then I wasn't *too* interested in the group, and after all I had two small children. And then in the thirties, there were the Friends of William Carlos Williams—Ford Madox Ford's group. Toward the end we had a big party for them out here. But that was rather ridiculous. Bill says it was poor old Ford's last gasp for—you know, a group around him. He was dying on his feet. And he did die a couple of years later.

INTERVIEWER

How did you get along with Ezra Pound?

MRS. WILLIAMS

Pound was never around. Pound came over in . . . I think, 1938 to get an honorary degree at Hamilton. And he spent two days with us when he was released from Saint Elizabeth's in 1958, before he sailed for Italy. I wouldn't know what to say of this last impression. He was self-centered, as always. You couldn't talk to him; it was impossible. The only one he ever talked to nicely was Win Scott. It just happened that Win came out to see us, and they got along beautifully. Ezra always tried to tell Bill off, but they got along as friends over the years. Bill wasn't afraid of him; their letters used to be rather acrimonious, back and forth.

INTERVIEWER [*to WCW looking in*]

Apparently those letters don't represent your final attitude?

WILLIAMS

No; the only thing that I remember was the attitude of Flossie's father—

MRS. WILLIAMS

But that has nothing to do with Ezra's last visit here, dear.

WILLIAMS

Just a passing comment. [*withdraws*]

MRS. WILLIAMS

Bill and Ezra wrote quite a number of letters to each other when the war started; they were on such opposite sides. Ezra was definitely pro-Fascist, much as he may deny it, and Bill was just the opposite. Not pro-Semitic but not anti-Semitic either, by any means.

INTERVIEWER

After the war, wasn't there some local concern about Dr. Williams's so-called communism?

MRS. WILLIAMS

That was in 1952, when Bill was going down to take the chair of poetry. Senator McCarthy was in the news then, and they were frightened to death in Washington. There was a woman who was lobbying for a reform in poetry, who had no use for free verse. She had a little periodical, I've forgotten the name of it, and she wrote a letter saying what an outrage it was that a man like that—

INTERVIEWER

Of course, this was all in the aftermath of the Bollingen award to Pound.

MRS. WILLIAMS

Bill had nothing to do with that. But if he had been a member of the Fellows then, he would certainly have voted for him.

INTERVIEWER

Was Dr. Williams ever asked to testify against Pound?

MRS. WILLIAMS

They questioned him two or three times. They wanted him to listen to some records and swear it was Pound. Bill couldn't do that, but he said he would tell them frankly what he knew. And that was all. Every time we went down to Washington, Bill went to see him.

INTERVIEWER

Going back to the First World War: perhaps this isn't something you want to go into, but there were some local reactions then, weren't there?

MRS. WILLIAMS

Against Germans. Yes; that would involve Bill because he was married to me. Bill's mother made my life one hell because I was partly German. Though she wasn't living with us then.

INTERVIEWER

So with one thing and another—Greenwich Village, communism, and the Germans—

MRS. WILLIAMS

Bill was always in a controversy. But I think he stood his ground very well through it all.

WILLIAMS [*coming in, and with his hands on
Mrs. Williams' shoulders*]

Maybe you've had enough.

MRS. WILLIAMS

Oh, Bill, it's all right. Don't worry about me. Go out and take a walk.

INTERVIEWER [*to WCW*]

Do you have any recollection of writing a play for the PTA. years ago? It was on some local issue, like putting in a school nurse, on which you took a liberal view.

WILLIAMS

I can't think. I was certainly interested in plays. But the only person I ever worked with was Kitty Hoagland.

MRS. WILLIAMS

That was *Many Loves*, much later. Kitty didn't come until the thirties. But Bill wrote four or five small plays during those early years. One about the Dutch around this area; and a very nice little play called *The Apple Tree* that was going to be done at the Provincetown, but Alfred Kreymborg lost it. And a Puritan play, *Betty Putnam*, that was acted over at the Tennis Club. Do you remember the old tennis courts over on Montross Avenue? There was a very active young group connected with it.

INTERVIEWER

But the town itself didn't quite get all this, I suppose. [*To WCW*] Your brother Edgar says it's a narrow town, and what you have done is in spite of it.

WILLIAMS

Yes. There were some aristocrats back there who would have nothing to do with budding genius.

INTERVIEWER

Not to mention political matters. Edgar says that in the political club which your father started, you were always the liberal.

WILLIAMS

Yes, to my sorrow.

INTERVIEWER

To your sorrow?

MRS. WILLIAMS

He doesn't mean it! I don't see why—

WILLIAMS

Do I mean it? For God's sake, my friends have all been pretty disillusioned friends.

INTERVIEWER

Marianne Moore, who knows you pretty well, says you were always a bit "reckless."

WILLIAMS

I guess she's right. I was a Unitarian. And Unitarians are liberals.

MRS. WILLIAMS

I think Bill has always been willing to be reckless. There was the social credit business for instance, that Bill got involved in in the thirties. They wanted to give a kind of dividend to the people to increase purchasing power. There were large meetings in New York and down at the University of Virginia. But that was about the end of it. In fact many of those involved withdrew from it when they saw how things were going, with the war coming on and all. Some of them were so nervous about that whole episode they wouldn't even speak to Bill. That's the difference. I don't say Bill was naïve; perhaps it was honesty. Bill isn't a radical or a communist or anything else. He's an honest man. And if he gets into it with both feet, it's just too bad. That's the way it's been.

INTERVIEWER [*to WCW*]

Right?

WILLIAMS

[*Agrees, laughing.*]

INTERVIEWER

If we could talk a few more minutes about personal matters—how did you enjoy Saint Thomas? I understand you have just come back from there.

WILLIAMS

I could stay there forever, with reservations, of course. Saint Thomas is the place where my father grew up. I remember a photograph of the blizzard area—oh, for God's sake, I mean the hurricane—in eighty-eight.

MRS. WILLIAMS

Bill, dear, I'm sorry, but it must have been in the seventies. It was when your father was a boy.

WILLIAMS [*with a sigh*]

Yes, yes, yes. [*Laughs*] I remember a story of the hurricane. Thoroughly documented. How first the water went out of the harbor and left it dry, the ships lying on their beams' ends, and then another shudder and an earthquake worse than they ever had in the area. And I have a distinct memory of some photographs of my father, taken at perhaps twenty-one years of age. I was very much interested in making contact with his memory.

MRS. WILLIAMS

It was a good trip, but Bill gets restless. And it's too difficult at our age.

WILLIAMS

I think we'll not go again.

INTERVIEWER

To get back for a minute to the troubles of 1952—do you think you were working too hard at that time?

WILLIAMS

I was interested in the process of composition—in the theory of it. And I *was* working pretty hard at it. But I couldn't make much of it.

MRS. WILLIAMS

Bill had a contract with Random House for three books. There was no hurry; but that's the only way Bill can work. And he doesn't want to look things over, which is his worst fault. *The Build-Up* was written then. I'm afraid Bill garbled that one. It was just impatience. And he didn't want me to read the things either. I wish I had, there were so many errors in the *Autobiography*. That was inexcusable. Then, one night in the winter of forty-eight, Bill felt a pain in his chest, shoveling out the car. He kept going until February. I used to drive around with him on house calls. But it was too much.

WILLIAMS

I had a heart attack. Perhaps it was a good thing. I thought I was God almighty, I guess, in general. But I got over that one.

MRS. WILLIAMS

There wasn't any kind of cerebral trouble until 1950 or so. Bill had given up medicine and we were going down to take the chair of poetry in Washington. But in 1952, when we were up visiting the Abbotts, in New York, Bill had a serious stroke.

WILLIAMS

I tried to play it down. I was conscious, and rational; and I could joke about it. But I was in a strange house, and I needed to get home. I couldn't write—

MRS. WILLIAMS

Then suddenly you could hardly understand him.

WILLIAMS

That was the end. I was through with life.

MRS. WILLIAMS

No, it wasn't the end. You had a lot of life left. You had a whole play running through your mind while you were lying there, *The Cure*. You thought it out and dictated the notes to me. You wrote it when we got home.

INTERVIEWER

That was something of a change in approach.

WILLIAMS

Yes, the novels I just did as I went along, at first though I tried to think them out as well as I could.

MRS. WILLIAMS

Of course *White Mule* was about a baby, Bill's favorite subject. But most of the later poems were written after the stroke. Bill used to say things like spelling didn't matter, and he would never correct at all. I think he did much better work after the stroke slowed him down.

WILLIAMS [*perhaps grudgingly*]

The evidence is there.

INTERVIEWER

It was when you were at the Abbotts' that someone read Theocritus to you.

WILLIAMS

Yes, Mrs. Gratwick; I asked her to. Theocritus was always strong in my mind. But I wasn't capable of hearing it in the Greek. I'm in an unfortunate position, because I don't have the original language. For example, I started to take Latin at Horace Mann, but the teacher was withdrawn, to my infinite regret. That was the end of that—all my life, that was the end. And I always regretted, too, that I didn't know Greek. I don't know, as far as the Theocritus was concerned, whether it came first, or the stroke.

MRS. WILLIAMS

You had talked of doing an adaptation.

INTERVIEWER

Why Theocritus?

WILLIAMS

The pastoral nature of it gave me a chance to spread myself. It was Greek, and it appealed to me; and it was a wonderful chance to record my feeling of respect for the Greek classics.

INTERVIEWER

There was a change in the verse in the fifties. Was this the first time you tried the new measure?

WILLIAMS

"The Descent" was the first. I regard that as an experiment in the variable foot.

INTERVIEWER

You said earlier that you were almost unconscious when you wrote it.

WILLIAMS

Yes, I was. I was very much excited. I wasn't conscious of doing anything unusual but I realized that something had occurred to me, which was a very satisfying conclusion to my poetic process. Something happened to my line that completed it, completed the rhythm, or at least it was satisfying to me. It was still an irregular composition—but not too much so—but I couldn't complete it. I had written that poem to retain the things which *would* have been the completion of the poem. But as for picking the thing up and going on with it, I had to acknowledge I was licked. I didn't dare fool with the poem so that it would have been more rigid; I wouldn't have wanted that.

INTERVIEWER

You felt there was nothing more you could do with it?

WILLIAMS

Nothing more. I felt all that I could do with it had been done, but it was not complete. I returned to it; but the irregularity of that poem could not be repeated by me. It was too . . . I've forgotten.

INTERVIEWER

You feel it wasn't a perfect poem?

WILLIAMS

It was too regular. There were variations of mood which would have led me to make a different poem out of it.

INTERVIEWER

And you don't think anything after "The Descent" goes beyond it?

WILLIAMS

No. I always wanted to do something more with it, but I didn't know how.

MRS. WILLIAMS

There was one written quite a long time before: that was the start of it. Then there was the "Daphne and Virginia"—Virginia, of course, was Paul's wife, and Daphne is Bill's. That poem always makes me sad. "The Orchestra" was written in 1954 or 1955, I think. Bill wrote quite a lot after he had the stroke.

It's really amazing what he has done; and he gave readings, too, in Saint Louis, Chicago, Savannah—

WILLIAMS

I couldn't break through.

MRS. WILLIAMS

Harvard, Brandeis, Brown. We took two trips to the coast after that—to UCLA, the University of California, Washington—

WILLIAMS

I've been going downhill rapidly.

INTERVIEWER

And the *Pictures from Brueghel*?

WILLIAMS

Yes, those are late, very late. But they are too regular.

INTERVIEWER

Did you ever grow any fonder of the academic world after your trips around the campuses?

MRS. WILLIAMS

They liked *him*, at least. And the girls' colleges all loved him.

WILLIAMS

The high point was the appearance at Wellesley. It was a very successful impromptu appearance, a reading. I always remember the satisfaction I got pleasing the ladies—the kids.

INTERVIEWER

Beginning with the Women's Club in Rutherford.

WILLIAMS

Always. I was always for the ladies.

MRS. WILLIAMS

Bill has always been fond of women, and terribly disappointed not to have had a sister. And he never had a daughter. But women liked him; they sensed that he was sympathetic, and they could talk to him.

WILLIAMS

Very sympathetic.

INTERVIEWER

Just one or two more questions. Do you think your medical training—your discipline in science—has had any effect on your poetry?

WILLIAMS

The scientist is very important to the poet, because his language is important to him.

INTERVIEWER

To the scientist?

WILLIAMS

Well, and the poet. I don't pretend to go too far. But I have been taught to be accurate in my speech.

INTERVIEWER

But not scholastic. Someone has said you would not make so much of the great American language if you had been judicious about things.

WILLIAMS

It's a point well taken. The writing of English is a great pastime. The only catch to that is when a man adds the specification *English*. That is purely accidental and means nothing. Any language could be inserted in its place. But the restrictions that are accepted in the classics of a language enclose it in a corset of mail, which becomes its chief distinction.

MRS. WILLIAMS

Bill has always experimented. He was never satisfied to keep doing the same thing. And he has been severely criticized. But I think some of the younger poets are benefiting from it. Like Charles Tomlinson, and Robert Creeley—they've learned a lot from Bill. David Ignatow—any number of them. Allen Ginsberg was a good friend for many years.

WILLIAMS

I am a little concerned about the form. The art of the poem nowadays is something unstable, but at least the construction of the poem should make sense; you should know where you stand. Many questions haven't been answered as yet. Our poets may be wrong, but what can any of us do with his talent but try to develop his vision, so that through frequent failures we may learn better what we have missed in the past.

INTERVIEWER

What do you think you yourself have left of special value to the new poets?

WILLIAMS

The variable foot—the division of the line according to a new method that would be satisfactory to an American. It's all right if you are not intent on being national. But an American is forced to try to give the intonation. Either it *is* important or it is not important. It must have occurred to an American that the question of the line *was* important. The American idiom has much to offer us that the English language has never heard of. As for my own elliptic way of approach, it may be baffling, but it is not unfriendly, and not, I think, entirely empty.

MRS. WILLIAMS

All the young people come out to see Bill. Charles Olson has been here a lot. Denise Levertov was out last week. Then there is Robert Wallace, Muriel Rukeyser, Charles Bell, Tram Combs. Charles Tomlinson stopped in on his way back to England.

WILLIAMS

Yes. He is writing in my vein. He's even conscious of copying me. I don't think he is too popular with his contemporaries. But it does look suspiciously like the beginning of something in England. I defer to you. But—do you have an example of his poems there?

INTERVIEWER

He seems to be carrying on the new measure. Do you have any comment?

WILLIAMS

The lines are not as I would have done, not loose enough. Not enough freedom. He didn't ignore the rules enough to make it really satisfactory.

INTERVIEWER

But you think he shows your influence in England, finally. That must be a satisfaction.

WILLIAMS

It is.

MRS. WILLIAMS

I think Bill will shortly be published in England.

INTERVIEWER

You would think they might have appreciated the American idiom.

WILLIAMS

Not *my* American idiom.

MRS. WILLIAMS [*looking about among the books*]

These are some translations of Bill's poems in Italian—the early poems, *Paterson*, *The Desert Music*.

WILLIAMS

Yes, I was very pleased by those.

MRS. WILLIAMS

Here are some selected poems in German: *Gedichte*, 1962.

WILLIAMS

I'm alive—

MRS. WILLIAMS

There is a selection coming out now in Czechoslovakia. And here is an anthology of "American lyrics" in Norwegian—

WILLIAMS

I'm still alive!

Issue 32, 1964

Harold Pinter

The Art of Theater

Harold Pinter had recently moved into a five-story 1820 Nash house facing Regent's Park in London. The view from the floor-through top floor where he has installed his office overlooks a duck pond and a long stretch of wooded parkland; his desk faces this view, and in late October 1966, when the interview took place, the changing leaves and the hazy London sun constantly distracted him as he thought over questions or began to give answers. He speaks in a deep, theater-trained voice that comes rather surprisingly from him, and indeed is the most remarkable thing about him physically. When speaking he almost always tends to excessive qualification of any statement, as if coming to a final definition of things were obviously impossible. One gets the impression—as one does with many of the characters in his plays—of a man so deeply involved with what he's thinking that roughing it into speech is a painful necessity.

He was not working at any writing projects when the interview took place, and questions about his involuntary idleness (many questions came back to it without meaning to) were particularly uncomfortable for him. His own work is alternatively a source of mystery, amusement, joy, and anger to him; in looking it over he often discovered possibilities and ambiguities that he had not noticed or had forgotten. One felt that if only he would rip out his telephone and hang black curtains across the wide windows he would be much happier, though he insists that the "great boredom one has with oneself" is unrelated to his environment or his obligations.

When he wrote his first plays, in 1957, he was homeless, constantly on tour as an actor with a repertory stage company, playing all sorts of parts in obscure seaside resorts and provincial cities. His wife, the actress Vivien Merchant, toured with him, but when she became pregnant in 1958 it was necessary for them to find a home, and they took a basement room in London's shabby Notting Hill Gate section, in a building where Mr. Pinter worked as a caretaker to pay his rent. When their son was born they borrowed enough money to move to a less shabby district in Chiswick, but both had to return to full-time acting when Mr. Pinter's first full-length play, *The Birthday Party*, was a full-scale flop in 1958. The production of *The Caretaker* in 1960 produced enough money for a move to the middle-class district of Kew, and then, thinking he could live on his writings, Mr. Pinter moved his family to a bowfronted Regency house in the south-coast seaside town of Worthing. But the two-hour drive to London became imperative too often, and so they moved once again, to a rented flat in Kensington, until Mr. Pinter's lucrative film scripts made it possible for them to buy the Regent's Park house. Though it is not yet completely renovated, the size and comfort of it are impressive, as is Mr. Pinter's office, with a separate room nearby for his secretary and a small bar equally nearby for the beer and Scotch that he drinks steadily during the day, whether working or not. Bookshelves line half the area, and a velvet chaise longue faces the small rear garden. On the walls are a series of Feliks Topolski sketches of London theater scenes; a poster of the Montevideo production of *El Cuidador*; a small financial balance sheet indicating that his first West End production, *The Birthday Party*, earned two hundred sixty pounds in its disastrous week's run; a Picasso drawing; and his citation from when he was named to the Order of the British Empire last spring. "The year after the Beatles," he emphasizes.

—Lawrence M. Bensky, 1966

INTERVIEWER

When did you start writing plays, and why?

HAROLD PINTER

My first play was *The Room*, written when I was twenty-seven. A friend of mine called Henry Woolf was a student in the drama department at Bristol University at the time when it was the only drama department in the country. He had the opportunity to direct a play, and as he was my oldest friend he knew I'd been writing, and he knew I had an idea for a play, though I hadn't written any of it. I was acting in rep at the time, and he told me he had to have the play the next week to meet his schedule. I said this was ridiculous; he might get it in six months. And then I wrote it in four days.

INTERVIEWER

Has writing always been so easy for you?

PINTER

Well, I had been writing for years, hundreds of poems and short pieces of prose. About a dozen had been published in little magazines. I wrote a novel as well; it's not good enough to be published, really, and never has been. After I wrote *The Room*, which I didn't see performed for a few weeks, I started to work immediately on *The Birthday Party*.

INTERVIEWER

What led you to do that so quickly?

PINTER

It was the process of writing a play that had started me going. Then I went to see *The Room*, which was a remarkable experience. Since I'd never written a play before, I'd of course never seen one of mine performed, never had an audience sitting there. The only people who'd ever seen what I'd written had been a few friends and my wife. So to sit in the audience—well, I wanted to piss very badly throughout the whole thing, and at the end I dashed out behind the bicycle shed.

INTERVIEWER

What other effect did contact with an audience have on you?

PINTER

I was very encouraged by the response of that university audience, though no matter what the response had been I would have written *The Birthday Party*, I know that. Watching first nights, though I've seen quite a few by now, is never any better. It's a nerveracking experience. It's not a question of whether the play goes well or badly. It's not the audience reaction, it's *my* reaction. I'm rather hostile toward audiences—I don't much care for large bodies of people collected together. Everyone knows that audiences vary enormously; it's a mistake to care too much about them. The thing one should be concerned with is whether the performance has expressed what one set out to express in writing the play. It sometimes does.

INTERVIEWER

Do you think that without the impetus provided by your friend at Bristol you would have gotten down to writing plays?

PINTER

Yes, I think I was going to write *The Room*. I just wrote it a bit quicker under the circumstances; he just triggered something off. *The Birthday Party* had also been in my mind for a long time. It was sparked off from a very distinct situation in digs when I was on tour. In fact, the other day a friend of mine gave me a letter I wrote to him in nineteen-fifty-something, Christ knows when it was. This is what it says: "I have filthy insane digs, a great bulging scrag of a woman with breasts rolling at her belly, an obscene household, cats, dogs, filth, tea strainers, mess, oh bullocks, talk, chat rubbish shit scratch dung poison, infantility, deficient order in the upper fretwork, fucking roll on." Now the thing about this is *that* was *The Birthday Party*—I was in those digs, and this woman was Meg in the play, and there was a fellow staying there in Eastbourne, on the coast. The whole thing remained with me, and three years later I wrote the play.

INTERVIEWER

Why wasn't there a character representing you in the play?

PINTER

I had—I have—nothing to say about myself, directly. I wouldn't know where to begin. Particularly since I often look at myself in the mirror and say, Who the hell's that?

INTERVIEWER

And you don't think being represented as a character on stage would help you find out?

PINTER

No.

INTERVIEWER

Have your plays usually been drawn from situations you've been in? *The Caretaker*, for example.

PINTER

I'd met a few, quite a few, tramps—you know, just in the normal course of events, and I think there was one particular one . . . I didn't know him very well, he did most of the talking when I saw him. I bumped into him a few times, and about a year or so afterward he sparked this thing off.

INTERVIEWER

Had it occurred to you to act in *The Room*?

PINTER

No, no—the acting was a separate activity altogether. Though I wrote *The Room*, *The Birthday Party*, and *The Dumb Waiter* in 1957, I was acting all the time in a repertory company, doing all kinds of jobs, traveling to Bournemouth and Torquay and Birmingham. I finished *The Birthday Party* while I was touring in some kind of farce, I don't remember the name.

INTERVIEWER

As an actor, do you find yourself with a compelling sense of how roles in your plays should be performed?

PINTER

Quite often I have a compelling sense of how a role should be played. And I'm proved—equally as often—quite wrong.

INTERVIEWER

Do you see yourself in each role as you write? And does your acting help you as a playwright?

PINTER

I read them all aloud to myself while writing. But I don't see myself in each role—I couldn't play most of them. My acting doesn't impede my playwriting because of these limitations. For example, I'd like to write a play—I've frequently thought of this—entirely about women.

INTERVIEWER

Your wife, Vivien Merchant, frequently appears in your plays. Do you write parts for her?

PINTER

No. I've never written any part for any actor, and the same applies to my wife. I just think she's a very good actress and a very interesting actress to work with, and I want her in my plays.

INTERVIEWER

Acting was your profession when you first started to write plays?

PINTER

Oh, yes, it was all I ever did. I didn't go to university. I left school at sixteen—I was fed up and restless. The only thing that interested me at school was English language and literature, but I didn't have Latin and so couldn't go on to university. So I went to a few drama schools, not studying seriously; I was mostly in love at the time and tied up with that.

INTERVIEWER

Were the drama schools of any use to you as a playwright?

PINTER

None whatsoever. It was just living.

INTERVIEWER

Did you go to a lot of plays in your youth?

PINTER

No, very few. The only person I really liked to see was Donald Wolfit, in a Shakespeare company at the time. I admired him tremendously; his Lear is still the best I've ever seen. And then I was reading, for years, a great deal of modern literature, mostly novels.

INTERVIEWER

No playwrights—Brecht, Pirandello . . . ?

PINTER

Oh, certainly not, not for years. I read Hemingway, Dostoyevsky, Joyce, and Henry Miller at a very early age, and Kafka. I'd read Beckett's novels, too, but I'd never heard of Ionesco until after I'd written the first few plays.

INTERVIEWER

Do you think these writers had any influence on your writing?

PINTER

I've been influenced *personally* by everyone I've ever read—and I read all the time—but none of these writers particularly influenced my writing. Beckett and Kafka stayed with me the most—I think Beckett is the best prose writer living. My world is still bound up by other writers—that's one of the best things in it.

INTERVIEWER

Has music influenced your writing, do you think?

PINTER

I don't know how music can influence writing; but it has been very important for me, both jazz and classical music. I feel a sense of music continually in writing, which is a different matter from having been influenced by it. Boulez and Webern are now composers I listen to a great deal.

INTERVIEWER

Do you get impatient with the limitations of writing for the theater?

PINTER

No. It's quite different; the theater's much the most difficult kind of writing for me, the most naked kind, you're so entirely restricted. I've done some film work, but for some reason or other I haven't found it very easy to satisfy myself on an original idea for a film. *Tea Party*, which I did for television, is actually a film, cinematic, I wrote it like that. Television and films are simpler than the theater—if you get tired of a scene you just drop it and go on to another one. (I'm exaggerating, of course.) What *is* so different about the stage is that you're just *there*, stuck—there are your characters stuck on the stage, you've got to live with them and deal with them. I'm not a very inventive writer in the sense of using the technical devices other playwrights do—look at Brecht! I can't use the stage the way he does, I just haven't got that kind of imagination, so I find myself stuck with these characters who are either sitting or standing, and they've either got to walk out of a door, or come in through a door, and that's about all they can do.

INTERVIEWER

And talk.

PINTER

Or keep silent.

INTERVIEWER

After *The Room*, what effect did the production of your next plays have on your writing?

PINTER

The Birthday Party was put on at the Lyric, Hammersmith in London. It went on a little tour of Oxford and Cambridge first, and was very successful. When it came to London it was completely massacred by the critics—absolutely slaughtered. I've never really known why, nor am I particularly interested. It ran a week. I've framed the statement of the box-office takings: two hundred sixty pounds, including a first night of one hundred forty pounds and the Thursday matinee of two pounds, nine shillings—there were six people there. I was completely new to writing for the professional theater, and it was rather a shock when it happened. But I went on writing—the BBC were very helpful. I wrote *A Slight Ache* on commission from them. In 1960 *The Dumb Waiter* was produced, and then *The Caretaker*. The only really bad experience I've had was *The Birthday Party*; I was so green and gauche—not that I'm rosy and confident now, but comparatively . . . Anyway, for things like stage design I didn't know how to cope, and I didn't know how to talk to the director.

INTERVIEWER

What was the effect of this adversity on you? How was it different from unfavorable criticism of your acting, which surely you'd had before?

PINTER

It was a great shock, and I was very depressed for about forty-eight hours. It was my wife, actually, who said just that to me: You've had bad notices before, et cetera. There's no question but that her common sense and practical help got me over that depression, and I've never felt anything like that again.

INTERVIEWER

You've directed several of your plays. Will you continue to do so?

PINTER

No. I've come to think it's a mistake. I work much as I write, just moving from one thing to another to see what's going to happen next. One tries to get the thing . . . *true*. But I rarely get it. I think I'm more useful as the author closely involved with a play: as a director I think I tend to inhibit the actors, because however objective I am about the text and try not to insist that *this is what's meant*, I think there is an obligation on the actors too heavy to bear.

INTERVIEWER

Since you are an actor, do actors in your plays ever approach you and ask you to change lines or aspects of their roles?

PINTER

Sometimes, quite rarely, lines are changed when we're working together. I don't at all believe in the anarchic theater of so-called creative actors—the actors can do that in someone else's plays. Which wouldn't, however, at all affect their ability to play in mine.

INTERVIEWER

Which of your plays did you first direct?

PINTER

I codirected *The Collection* with Peter Hall. And then I directed *The Lover* and *The Dwarfs* on the same bill at the Arts. *The Lover* didn't stand much of a chance because it was my decision, regretted by everyone—except me—to do *The Dwarfs*, which is apparently the most intractable, impossible piece of work. Apparently ninety-nine people out of a hundred feel it's a waste of time, and the audience hated it.

INTERVIEWER

It seems the densest of your plays in the sense that there's quite a bit of talk and very little action. Did this represent an experiment for you?

PINTER

No. The fact is that *The Dwarfs* came from my unpublished novel, which was written a long time ago. I took a great deal from it, particularly the kind of state of mind that the characters were in.

INTERVIEWER

So this circumstance of composition is not likely to be repeated?

PINTER

No. I should add that even though it is, as you say, more dense, it had great value, great interest for me. From my point of view, the general delirium and states of mind and reactions and relationships in the play—although terribly sparse—are clear to me. I know all the things that aren't said, and the way the characters actually look at each other, and what they mean by looking at each other. It's a play about betrayal and distrust. It does seem very confusing and obviously it can't be successful. But it was good for me to do.

INTERVIEWER

Is there more than one way to direct your plays successfully?

PINTER

Oh, yes, but always around the same central truth of the play—if that's distorted, then it's bad. The main difference in interpretation comes from the actors. The director can certainly be responsible for a disaster, too—the first performance of *The Caretaker* in Germany was heavy and posturized. There's no blueprint for any play, and several have been done entirely successfully without me helping in the production at all.

INTERVIEWER

When you are working on one, what is the key to a good writer-director relationship?

PINTER

What is absolutely essential is avoiding all defensiveness between author and director. It's a matter of mutual trust and openness. If that isn't there, it's just a waste of time.

INTERVIEWER

Peter Hall, who has directed many of your plays, says that they rely on precise verbal form and rhythm, and when you write "pause" it means something other than "silence," and three dots are different from a full stop. Is his sensitivity to this kind of writing responsible for your working well together?

PINTER

Yes, it is, very much so. I do pay great attention to those points you just mentioned. Hall once held a dot and pause rehearsal for the actors in *The Homecoming*. Although it sounds bloody pretentious, it was apparently very valuable.

INTERVIEWER

Do you outline plays before you start to write them?

PINTER

Not at all. I don't know what kind of characters my plays will have until they . . . well, until they *are*. Until they indicate to me what they are. I don't conceptualize in any way. Once I've got the clues I follow them—that's my job, really, to follow the clues.

INTERVIEWER

What do you mean by clues? Can you remember how one of your plays developed in your mind—or was it a line-by-line progression?

PINTER

Of course I can't remember exactly how a given play developed in my mind. I think what happens is that I write in a very high state of excitement and frustration. I follow what I see on the paper in front of me—one sentence after another. That doesn't mean I don't have a

dim, possible overall idea—the image that starts off doesn't just en-
gender what happens immediately, it engenders the possibility of an
overall happening, which carries me through. I've got an idea of what
might happen—sometimes I'm absolutely right, but on many occasions I've been proved wrong by what does actually happen. Sometimes I'm going along and I find myself writing "C. comes in" when I
didn't know that he was going to come in; he *had* to come in at that
point, that's all.

INTERVIEWER

In *The Homecoming*, Sam, a character who hasn't been very active
for a while, suddenly cries out and collapses several minutes from the
end of the play. Is this an example of what you mean? It seems abrupt.

PINTER

It suddenly seemed to me right. It just came. I knew he'd have to
say something at one time in this section and this is what happened,
that's what he said.

INTERVIEWER

Might characters therefore develop beyond your control of them,
changing your idea—even if it's a vague idea—of what the play's
about?

PINTER

I'm ultimately holding the ropes, so they never get too far away.

INTERVIEWER

Do you sense when you should bring down the curtain, or do you
work the text consciously toward a moment you've already determined?

PINTER

It's pure instinct. The curtain comes down when the rhythm
seems right—when the action calls for a finish. I'm very fond of curtain lines, of doing them properly.

INTERVIEWER

Do you feel your plays are therefore structurally successful? That you're able to communicate this instinct for rhythm to the play?

PINTER

No, not really, and that's my main concern, to get the structure right. I always write three drafts, but you have to leave it eventually. There comes a point when you say, That's it, I can't do anything more. The only play that gets remotely near to a structural entity which satisfies me is *The Homecoming*. *The Birthday Party* and *The Caretaker* have too much writing. I want to iron it down, eliminate things. Too many words irritate me sometimes, but I can't help them, they just seem to come out—out of the fellow's mouth. I don't really examine my works too much, but I'm aware that quite often in what I write, some fellow at some point says an awful lot.

INTERVIEWER

Most people would agree that the strength in your plays lies in just this verbal aspect, the patterns and force of character you can get from it. Do you get these words from people you've heard talking—do you eavesdrop?

PINTER

I spend *no* time listening in that sense. Occasionally I hear something, as we all do, walking about. But the words come as I'm writing the characters, not before.

INTERVIEWER

Why do you think the conversations in your plays are so effective?

PINTER

I don't know. I think possibly it's because people fall back on anything they can lay their hands on verbally to keep away from the danger of knowing, and of being known.

INTERVIEWER

What areas in writing plays give you the most trouble?

PINTER

They're all so inextricably interrelated I couldn't possibly judge.

INTERVIEWER

Several years ago, *Encounter* had an extensive series of quotations from people in the arts about the advisability of Britain's joining the Common Market. Your statement was the shortest anyone made: "I have no interest in the matter and do not care what happens." Does this sum up your feeling about politics, or current affairs?

PINTER

Not really. Though that's exactly what I feel about the Common Market—I just don't care a damn about the Common Market. But it isn't quite true to say that I'm in any way indifferent to current affairs. I'm in the normal state of being very confused—uncertain, irritated, and indignant in turns, sometimes indifferent. Generally, I try to get on with what I can do and leave it at that. I don't think I've got any kind of social function that's of any value, and politically there's no question of my getting involved because the issues are by no means simple—to be a politician you have to be able to present a simple picture even if you don't see things that way.

INTERVIEWER

Has it ever occurred to you to express political opinions through your characters?

PINTER

No. Ultimately, politics do bore me, though I recognize they are responsible for a good deal of suffering. I distrust ideological statements of any kind.

INTERVIEWER

But do you think that the picture of personal threat that is sometimes presented on your stage is troubling in a larger sense, a political sense, or doesn't this have any relevance?

PINTER

I don't feel myself threatened by *any* political body or activity at all. I like living in England. I don't care about political structures—they don't alarm me, but they cause a great deal of suffering to millions of people.

I'll tell you what I really think about politicians. The other night I watched some politicians on television talking about Vietnam. I wanted very much to burst through the screen with a flamethrower and burn their eyes out and their balls off and then inquire from them how they would assess this action from a political point of view.

INTERVIEWER

Would you ever use this anger in a politically oriented play?

PINTER

I have occasionally out of irritation thought about writing a play with a satirical point. I once did, actually, a play that no one knows about. A full-length play written after *The Caretaker*. Wrote the whole damn thing in three drafts. It was called *The Hothouse* and was about an institution in which patients were kept: all that was presented was the hierarchy, the people who ran the institution; one never knew what happened to the patients or what they were there for or who they were. It was heavily satirical, and it was quite useless. I never began to like any of the characters; they really didn't live at all. So I discarded the play at once. The characters were so purely cardboard. I was intentionally—for the only time, I think—trying to make a point, an explicit point, that these were nasty people and I disapproved of them. And therefore they didn't begin to live. Whereas in other plays of mine every single character, even a bastard like Goldberg in *The Birthday Party*, I care for.

INTERVIEWER

You often speak of your characters as living beings. Do they become so after you've written a play? While you're writing it?

PINTER

Both.

INTERVIEWER

As real as people you know?

PINTER

No, but different. I had a terrible dream, after I'd written *The Caretaker*, about the two brothers. My house burned down in the dream,
and I tried to find out who was responsible. I was led through all sorts
of alleys and cafés and eventually I arrived at an inner room somewhere and there were the two brothers from the play. And I said, So
you burned down my house. They said, Don't be too worried about
it, and I said, I've got everything in there, everything, you don't realize what you've done, and they said, It's all right, we'll compensate
you for it, we'll look after you all right—the younger brother was
talking—and thereupon I wrote them out a check for fifty quid. . . . I
gave *them* a check for fifty quid!

INTERVIEWER

Do you have a particular interest in psychology?

PINTER

No.

INTERVIEWER

None at all? Did you have some purpose in mind in writing the
speech where the older brother describes his troubles in a mental hospital at the end of act two in *The Caretaker*?

PINTER

Well, I had a purpose in the sense that Aston suddenly opened his mouth. My purpose was to let him go on talking until he was finished and then . . . bring the curtain down. I had no ax to grind there. And the one thing that people have missed is that it isn't necessary to conclude that everything Aston says about his experiences in the mental hospital is true.

INTERVIEWER

There's a sense of terror and a threat of violence in most of your plays. Do you see the world as an essentially violent place?

PINTER

The world *is* a pretty violent place, it's as simple as that, so any violence in the plays comes out quite naturally. It seems to me an essential and inevitable factor.

I think what you're talking about began in *The Dumb Waiter*, which from my point of view is a relatively simple piece of work. The violence is really only an expression of the question of dominance and subservience, which is possibly a repeated theme in my plays. I wrote a short story a long time ago called "The Examination," and my ideas of violence carried on from there. That short story dealt very explicitly with two people in one room having a battle of an unspecified nature, in which the question was one of who was dominant at what point and how they were going to be dominant and what tools they would use to achieve dominance and how they would try to undermine the other person's dominance. A threat is constantly there: it's got to do with this question of being in the uppermost position, or attempting to be. That's something of what attracted me to do the screenplay of *The Servant*, which was someone else's story, you know. I wouldn't call this violence so much as a battle for positions; it's a very common, everyday thing.

INTERVIEWER

Do these ideas of everyday battles, or of violence, come from any experiences you've had yourself?

PINTER

Everyone encounters violence in some way or other. It so happens I did encounter it in quite an extreme form after the war, in the East End, when the fascists were coming back to life in England. I got into quite a few fights down there. If you looked remotely like a Jew you might be in trouble. Also, I went to a Jewish club, by an old railway arch, and there were quite a lot of people often waiting with broken milk bottles in a particular alley we used to walk through. There were one or two ways of getting out of it—one was a purely physical way, of course, but you couldn't do anything about the milk bottles—*we* didn't have any milk bottles. The best way was to talk to them, you know, sort of, Are you all right? Yes, I'm all right. Well, that's all right then, isn't it? And all the time keep walking toward the lights of the main road.

Another thing: we were often taken for communists. If you went by, or happened to be passing, a fascist street meeting and looked in any way antagonistic—this was in Ridley Road market, near Dalston Junction—they'd interpret your very being, especially if you had books under your arms, as evidence of your being a communist. There was a good deal of violence there, in those days.

INTERVIEWER

Did this lead you toward some kind of pacifism?

PINTER

I was fifteen when the war ended. There was never any question of my going when I was called up for military service three years later: I couldn't see any point in it at all. I refused to go. So I was taken in a police car to the medical examination. Then I had two tribunals and two trials. I could have gone to prison—I took my toothbrush to the trials—but it so happened that the magistrate was slightly sympathetic, so I was fined instead, thirty pounds in all. Perhaps I'll be called up again in the next war, but I won't go.

INTERVIEWER

Robert Brustein has said of modern drama, "The rebel dramatist becomes an evangelist proselytizing for his faith." Do you see yourself in that role?

PINTER

I don't know what he's talking about. I don't know for what faith I could possibly be proselytizing.

INTERVIEWER

The theater is a very competitive business. Are you, as a writer, conscious of competing against other playwrights?

PINTER

Good writing excites me, and makes life worth living. I'm never conscious of any competition going on here.

INTERVIEWER

Do you read things written about you?

PINTER

Yes. Most of the time I don't know what they're talking about; I don't really read them all the way through. Or I read it and it goes—if you asked me what had been said, I would have very little idea. But there are exceptions, mainly nonprofessional critics.

INTERVIEWER

How much are you aware of an audience when you write?

PINTER

Not very much. But I'm aware that this is a public medium. I don't want to *bore* the audience, I want to keep them glued to what happens. So I try to write as *exactly* as possible. I would try to do that anyway, audience or no audience.

INTERVIEWER

There is a story—mentioned by Brustein in *The Theater of Revolt*—that Ionesco once left a performance of Genet's *The Blacks* because he felt he was being attacked, and the actors were enjoying it. Would you ever hope for a similar reaction in your audience? Would you react this way yourself?

PINTER

I've had that reaction—it's happened to me recently here in London, when I went to see *US*, the Royal Shakespeare Company's anti-Vietnam War production. There was a kind of attack—I don't like being subjected to propaganda, and I detest soapboxes. I want to present things clearly in my own plays, and sometimes this does make an audience very uncomfortable, but there's no question about causing offense for its own sake.

INTERVIEWER

Do you therefore feel the play failed to achieve its purpose—inspiring opposition to the war?

PINTER

Certainly. The chasm between the reality of the war in Vietnam and the image of what *US* presented on the stage was so enormous as to be quite preposterous. If it was meant to lecture or shock the audience I think it was most presumptuous. It's impossible to make a major theatrical statement about such a matter when television and the press have made everything so clear.

INTERVIEWER

Do you consciously make crisis situations humorous? Often an audience at your plays finds its laughter turning against itself as it realizes what the situation in the play actually is.

PINTER

Yes, that's very true, yes. I'm rarely consciously writing humor, but sometimes I find myself laughing at some particular point that has

suddenly struck me as being funny. I agree that more often than not
the speech only *seems* to be funny—the man in question is actually
fighting a battle for his life.

INTERVIEWER

There are sexual undertones in many of these crisis situations,
aren't there? How do you see the use of sex in the theater today?

PINTER

I do object to one thing to do with sex: this scheme afoot on the
part of many "liberal-minded" persons to open up obscene language
to general commerce. It should be the dark secret language of the un-
derworld. There are very few words—you shouldn't kill them by
overuse. I have used such words once or twice in my plays, but I
couldn't get them through the Lord Chamberlain. They're great,
wonderful words, but must be used very sparingly. The pure publicity of freedom of language fatigues me, because it's a demonstration
rather than something said.

INTERVIEWER

Do you think you've inspired any imitations? Have you ever seen
anything in a film or theater that struck you as, well, Pinteresque?

PINTER

That word! These damn words and that word *Pinteresque*
particularly—I don't know what they're bloody well talking about! I
think it's a great burden for me to carry, and for other writers to carry.
Oh, very occasionally I've thought listening to something, Hello, that
rings a bell. But it goes no further than that. I really do think that writers write on . . . just write, and I find it difficult to believe I'm any
kind of influence on other writers. I've seen very little evidence of it,
anyway; other people seem to see more evidence of it than I do.

INTERVIEWER

The critics?

PINTER

It's a great mistake to pay any attention to *them*. I think, you see, that this is an age of such overblown publicity and overemphatic pinning down. I'm a very good example of a writer who can write, but I'm not as good as all that. I'm just a writer; and I think that I've been overblown tremendously because there's a dearth of really fine writing, and people tend to make too much of a meal. All you can do is try to write as well as you can.

INTERVIEWER

Do you think your plays will be performed fifty years from now? Is universality a quality you consciously strive for?

PINTER

I have no idea whether my plays will be performed in fifty years, and it's of no moment to me. I'm pleased when what I write makes sense in South America or Yugoslavia—it's gratifying. But I certainly don't strive for universality—I've got enough to strive for just writing a bloody play!

INTERVIEWER

Do you think the success you've known has changed your writing?

PINTER

No, but it did become more difficult. I think I've gone beyond something now. When I wrote the first three plays in 1957 I wrote them from the point of view of *writing* them; the whole world of putting on plays was quite remote—I knew they could never be done in the reps I was acting in, and the West End and London were somewhere on the other side of the moon. So I wrote these plays completely unself-conscious. There's no question that over the years it's become more difficult to preserve the kind of freedom that's essential to writing, but when I do write, it's there. For a while it became more difficult to avoid the searchlights and all that. And it took me five years to write a stage play, *The Homecoming*, after *The Caretaker*. I did a lot of things in the meantime, but writing a stage play, which is what I really wanted to do, I couldn't. Then I wrote *The Homecoming*, for good or bad, and I felt much better. But *now* I'm back in the same boat—I want to write a play, it buzzes all the time in me, and I can't put pen to paper. Something people don't realize is the great boredom one has with oneself, and just to see those words come down again on paper, I think: Oh Christ, everything I do seems to be predictable, unsatisfactory, and hopeless. It keeps me awake. Distractions don't matter to me—if I had something to write I would write it. Don't ask me why I want to keep on with plays at all!

INTERVIEWER

Do you think you'd ever use freer techniques as a way of starting writing again?

PINTER

I can enjoy them in other people's plays—I thought the *Marat/Sade* was a damn good evening, and other very different plays like *The Caucasian Chalk Circle* I've also enjoyed. But I'd never use such stage techniques myself.

INTERVIEWER

Does this make you feel behind the times in any way?

PINTER

I *am* a very traditional playwright—for instance I insist on having a curtain in all my plays. I write curtain lines for that reason! And even when directors like Peter Hall or Claude Regy in Paris want to do away with them, I insist they stay. For me everything has to do with shape, structure, and overall unity. All this jamboree in happenings and eight-hour movies is great fun for the people concerned, I'm sure.

INTERVIEWER

Shouldn't they be having fun?

PINTER

If they're all having fun I'm delighted, but count me out completely, I wouldn't stay more than five minutes. The trouble is I find it all so *noisy*, and I like quiet things. There seems to be such a jazz and jaggedness in so much modern art, and a great deal of it is inferior to its models: Joyce contains so much of Burroughs, for example, in his experimental techniques, though Burroughs is a fine writer on his own. This doesn't mean I don't regard myself as a contemporary writer: I mean, I'm *here*.

Issue 39, 1966

John Cheever

The Art of Fiction

The first meeting with John Cheever took place in the spring of 1969, just after his novel *Bullet Park* was published. Normally, Cheever leaves the country when a new book is released, but this time he had not, and as a result many interviewers on the East Coast were making their way to Ossining, New York, where the master storyteller offered them the pleasures of a day in the country—but very little conversation about his book or the art of writing.

Cheever has a reputation for being a difficult interviewee. He does not pay attention to reviews, never rereads his books or stories once published, and is often vague about their details. He dislikes talking about his work (especially into "one of those machines") because he prefers not to look where he has been, but where he's going.

For the interview Cheever was wearing a faded blue shirt and khakis. Everything about him was casual and easy, as though we were already old friends. The Cheevers live in a house built in 1799, so a tour of buildings and grounds was obligatory. Soon we were settled in a sunny second-floor study where we discussed his dislike of window curtains, a highway construction near Ossining that he was trying to stop, traveling in Italy, a story he was drafting about a man who lost his car keys at a nude theater performance, Hollywood, gardeners and cooks, cocktail parties, Greenwich Village in the thirties, television reception, and a number of other writers named John (especially John Updike, who is a friend).

Although Cheever talked freely about himself, he changed the subject when the conversation turned to his work. *Aren't you bored*

Sovereign *Government* *one stop* *of the world* *Search* *all that* *Every where*

The main entrance to Falconer--the only entrance for
convicts,their visitors and the staff--was crowned by an
esuctheon representing Liberty,Justice and,between the two,
the power of legislation. Liberty wore a mob-cap and carried a
pike. Legislation was the federal eagle,armed with hunting arrows.
Justice was conventional;blinded,vaguely erotic in her clinging
robes and armed with a headsman's sword. The bas-relief was
bronze but black these days--as black as unpolished anthracite or
onyex. How many hundreds had passed under this--this last
souvenir they would see of man's struggle for cohreence. Hundreds,
one guessed,thousands,millions was close. Above the escutchen was
a declension of the place-names:Falconer Jail 1871,Falconer
Reformatory,Falconer Federal Penitionary,Falconer State Prison,
Falconer Correctional Facility and the last,which had never
caught on:Daybreak House. Now cons were inmates,the assholes
were officers and the warden was a superindendent. Fame is
chancey,God knows but Falconer--with it's limited accomodations
for two thousand miscreants was as famous as Old Bailey. Gone
was the water-torture,the striped suits,the lack-stepkthe balls
and chains and there was a soft-ball field where the gallows had
stood but at the time of which I'm writing leg-irons were still
used in Auburn. You could tell the men from Auburn by the noise
they made.

A manuscript page from *Falconer* by John Cheever.

with all this talk? Would you like a drink? Perhaps lunch is ready, I'll
just go downstairs and check. A walk in the woods, and maybe a swim
afterwards? Or would you rather drive to town and see my office? Do
you play backgammon? Do you watch much television?

During the course of several visits we did in fact mostly eat, drink,
walk, swim, play backgammon, or watch television. Cheever did not
invite me to cut any wood with his chain saw, an activity to which he
is rumored to be addicted. On the day of the last taping, we spent an
afternoon watching the New York Mets win the World Series from the
Baltimore Orioles, at the end of which the fans at Shea Stadium tore
up plots of turf for souvenirs. "Isn't that amazing," he said repeat-
edly, referring both to the Mets and their fans.

Afterward we walked in the woods, and as we circled back to the
house, Cheever said, "Go ahead and pack your gear, I'll be along in a
minute to drive you to the station" . . . upon which he stepped out of
his clothes and jumped with a loud splash into a pond, doubtless
cleansing himself with his skinny-dip from one more interview.

—*Annette Grant, 1976*

INTERVIEWER

I was reading the confessions of a novelist on writing novels: "If
you want to be true to reality, start lying about it." What do you think?

JOHN CHEEVER

Rubbish. For one thing the words "truth" and "reality" have no
meaning at all unless they are fixed in a comprehensible frame of reference. There are no stubborn truths. As for lying, it seems to me that
falsehood is a critical element in fiction. Part of the thrill of being told
a story is the chance of being hoodwinked or taken. Nabokov is a
master at this. The telling of lies is a sort of sleight of hand that dis-
plays our deepest feelings about life.

INTERVIEWER

Can you give an example of a preposterous lie that tells a great deal
about life?

CHEEVER

Indeed. The vows of holy matrimony.

INTERVIEWER

What about verisimilitude and reality?

CHEEVER

Verisimilitude is, by my lights, a technique one exploits in order to assure the reader of the truthfulness of what he's being told. If he truly believes he is standing on a rug, you can pull it out from under him. Of course, verisimilitude is also a lie. What I've always wanted of verisimilitude is probability, which is very much the way I live. This table seems real, the fruit basket belonged to my grandmother, but a madwoman could come in the door any moment.

INTERVIEWER

How do you feel about parting with books when you finish them?

CHEEVER

I usually have a sense of clinical fatigue after finishing a book. When my first novel, *The Wapshot Chronicle*, was finished, I was very happy about it. We left for Europe and remained there, so I didn't see the reviews and wouldn't know of Maxwell Geismar's disapproval for nearly ten years. *The Wapshot Scandal* was very different. I never much liked the book, and when it was done I was in a bad way. I wanted to burn the book. I'd wake up in the night and I would hear Hemingway's voice— I've never actually heard Hemingway's voice, but it was conspicuously his—saying, This is the small agony. The great agony comes later. I'd get up and sit on the edge of the bathtub and chain-smoke until three or four in the morning. I once swore to the dark powers outside the window that I would never, *never* again try to be better than Irving Wallace. It wasn't so bad after *Bullet Park*, where I'd done precisely what I wanted: a cast of three characters, a simple and resonant prose style, and a scene where a man saves his beloved son from death by fire. The manuscript was received enthusiastically everywhere, but when Benjamin

DeMott dumped on it in the *Times*, everybody picked up their marbles and ran home. I ruined my left leg in a skiing accident and ended up so broke that I took out working papers for my youngest son. It was simply a question of journalistic bad luck and an overestimation of my powers. However, when you finish a book, whatever its reception, there is some dislodgment of the imagination. I wouldn't say derangement. But finishing a novel, assuming it's something you want to do and that you take very seriously, is invariably something of a psychological shock.

INTERVIEWER

How long does it take the psychological shock to wear off? Is there any treatment?

CHEEVER

I don't quite know what you mean by treatment. To diminish shock I throw high dice, get sauced, go to Egypt, scythe a field, screw. Dive into a cold pool.

INTERVIEWER

Do characters take on identities of their own? Do they ever become so unmanageable that you have to drop them from the work?

CHEEVER

The legend that characters run away from their authors—taking up drugs, having sex operations, and becoming president—implies that the writer is a fool with no knowledge or mastery of his craft. This is absurd. Of course, any estimable exercise of the imagination draws upon such a complex richness of memory that it truly enjoys the expansiveness—the surprising turns, the response to light and darkness—of any living thing. But the idea of authors running around helplessly behind their cretinous inventions is contemptible.

INTERVIEWER

Must the novelist remain the critic as well?

CHEEVER

I don't have any critical vocabulary and very little critical acumen, and this is, I think, one of the reasons I'm always evasive with interviewers. My critical grasp of literature is largely at a practical level. I use what I love, and this can be anything. Cavalcanti, Dante, Frost, anybody. My library is terribly disordered and disorganized; I tear out what I want. I don't think that a writer has any responsibility to view literature as a continuous process. I believe that very little of literature is immortal. I've known books in my lifetime to serve beautifully, and then to lose their usefulness, perhaps briefly.

INTERVIEWER

How do you "use" these books . . . and what is it that makes them lose their "usefulness"?

CHEEVER

My sense of "using" a book is the excitement of finding myself at the receiving end of our most intimate and acute means of communication. These infatuations are sometimes passing.

INTERVIEWER

Assuming a lack of critical vocabulary, how, then, without a long formal education, do you explain your considerable learning?

CHEEVER

I am not erudite. I do not regret this lack of discipline, but I do admire erudition in my colleagues. Of course, I am not uninformed. That can be accounted for by the fact that I was raised in the tag end of cultural New England. Everybody in the family was painting and writing and singing and especially reading, which was a fairly common and accepted means of communication in New England at the turn of the decade. My mother claimed to have read *Middlemarch* thirteen times; I daresay she didn't. It would take a lifetime.

INTERVIEWER

Isn't there someone in *The Wapshot Chronicle* who has done it?

CHEEVER

Yes, Honora . . . or I don't remember who it is . . . claims to have read it thirteen times. My mother used to leave *Middlemarch* out in the garden and it got rained on. Most of it is in the novel; it's true.

INTERVIEWER

One almost has a feeling of eavesdropping on your family in that book.

CHEEVER

The *Chronicle* was not published—and this was a consideration—until after my mother's death. An aunt who does not appear in the book said, I would never speak to him again if I didn't know him to be a split personality.

INTERVIEWER

Do friends or family often think they appear in your books?

CHEEVER

Only—and I think everyone feels this way—in a discreditable sense. If you put anyone in with a hearing aid, then they assume that you have described them . . . although the character may be from another country and in an altogether different role. If you put people in as infirm or clumsy or in some way imperfect, then they readily associate. But if you put them in as beauties, they never associate. People are always ready to accuse rather than to celebrate themselves, especially people who read fiction. I don't know what the association is. I've had instances when a woman will cross a large social floor and say, Why did you write that story about me? And I try to figure out what story I've written. Well, ten stories back apparently I mentioned someone with red eyes; she noticed that she had bloodshot eyes that day and so she assumed that I'd nailed her.

INTERVIEWER

They feel indignant, that you have no right to their lives?

CHEEVER

It would be nicer if they thought of the creative aspect of writing. I don't like to see people who feel that they've been maligned when this was not anyone's intention. Of course, some young writers try to be libelous. And some old writers, too. Libel is, of course, a vast source of energy. But these are not the pure energies of fiction, but simply the libelousness of a child. The sort of thing one gets in freshman themes. Libel is not one of my energies.

INTERVIEWER

Do you think narcissism is a necessary quality of fiction?

CHEEVER

That's an interesting question. By narcissism we mean, of course, clinical self-love, an embittered girl, the wrath of Nemesis, and the rest of eternity as a leggy plant. Who wants that? We do love ourselves from time to time; no more, I think, than most men.

INTERVIEWER

What about megalomania?

CHEEVER

I think writers are inclined to be intensely egocentric. Good writers are often excellent at a hundred other things, but writing promises a greater latitude for the ego. My dear friend Yevtushenko has, I claim, an ego that can crack crystal at a distance of twenty feet; but I know a crooked investment banker who can do better.

INTERVIEWER

Do you think that your inner screen of imagination, the way you project characters, is in any way influenced by film?

CHEEVER

Writers of my generation and those who were raised with films have become sophisticated about these vastly different mediums and know what is best for the camera and best for the writer. One learns to skip the crowd scene, the portentous door, the banal irony of zooming into the beauty's crow's-feet. The difference in these crafts is, I think, clearly understood, and as a result no good film comes from an adaptation of a good novel. I would love to write an original screenplay if I found a sympathetic director. Years ago René Clair was going to film some of my stories, but as soon as the front office heard about this, they took away all the money.

INTERVIEWER

What do you think of working in Hollywood?

CHEEVER

Southern California always smells very much like a summer night . . . which to me means the end of sailing, the end of games, but it isn't that at all. It simply doesn't correspond to my experience. I'm very much concerned with trees . . . with the nativity of trees, and when you find yourself in a place where all the trees are transplanted and have no history, I find it disconcerting.

I went to Hollywood to make money. It's very simple. The people are friendly and the food is good, but I've never been happy there, perhaps because I only went there to pick up a check. I do have the deepest respect for a dozen or so directors whose affairs are centered there and who, in spite of the overwhelming problems of financing films, continue to turn out brilliant and original films. But my principal feeling about Hollywood is suicide. If I could get out of bed and into the shower, I was all right. Since I never paid the bills, I'd reach for the phone and order the most elaborate breakfast I could think of, and then I'd try to make it to the shower before I hanged myself. This is no reflection on Hollywood, but it's just that I seemed to have a suicide complex there. I don't like the freeways, for one thing. Also, the

pools are too hot . . . eighty-five degrees, and when I was last there, in
late January, in the stores they were selling yarmulkes for dogs—my
God! I went to a dinner and across the room a woman lost her balance
and fell down. Her husband shouted over to her, When I told you to
bring your crutches, you wouldn't listen to me. That line couldn't be
better!

INTERVIEWER

What about another community—the academic? It provides so
much of the critical work . . . with such an excessive necessity to categorize and label.

CHEEVER

The vast academic world exists like everything else, on what it can
produce that will secure an income. So we have papers on fiction, but
they come out of what is largely an industry. In no way does it help
those who write fiction or those who love to read fiction. The whole
business is a subsidiary undertaking, like extracting useful chemicals
from smoke. Did I tell you about the review of *Bullet Park* in *Ram-
parts*? It said I missed greatness by having left St. Boltophs. Had I
stayed, as Faulkner did in Oxford, I would have probably been as
great as Faulkner. But I made the mistake of leaving this place, which,
of course, never existed at all. It was so odd to be told to go back to a
place that was a complete fiction.

INTERVIEWER

I suppose they meant Quincy.

CHEEVER

Yes, which it wasn't. But I was very sad when I read it. I understood what they were trying to say. It's like being told to go back to a
tree that one spent fourteen years living in.

INTERVIEWER

Who are the people that you imagine or hope read your books?

CHEEVER

All sorts of pleasant and intelligent people read the books and write thoughtful letters about them. I don't know who they are, but they are marvelous and seem to live quite independently of the prejudices of advertising, journalism, and the cranky academic world. Think of the books that have enjoyed independent lives. *Let Us Now Praise Famous Men. Under the Volcano. Henderson the Rain King.* A splendid book like *Humboldt's Gift* was received with confusion and dismay, but hundreds of thousands of people went out and bought hardcover copies. The room where I work has a window looking into a wood, and I like to think that these earnest, lovable, and mysterious readers are in there.

INTERVIEWER

Do you think contemporary writing is becoming more specialized, more autobiographical?

CHEEVER

It may be. Autobiography and letters may be more interesting than fiction, but still, I'll stick with the novel. The novel is an acute means of communication from which all kinds of people get responses that you don't get from letters or journals.

INTERVIEWER

Did you start writing as a child?

CHEEVER

I used to tell stories. I went to a permissive school called Thayerland. I loved to tell stories, and if everybody did their arithmetic—it was a very small school, probably not more than eighteen or nineteen students—then the teacher would promise that I would tell a story. I told serials. This was very shrewd of me, because I knew that if I didn't finish the story by the end of the period, which was an hour, then everyone would ask to hear the end during the next period.

INTERVIEWER

How old were you?

CHEEVER

Well, I'm inclined to lie about my age, but I suppose it was when I was eight or nine.

INTERVIEWER

You could think of a story to spin out for an hour at that age?

CHEEVER

Oh, yes. I could then. And I still do.

INTERVIEWER

What comes first, the plot?

CHEEVER

I don't work with plots. I work with intuition, apprehension, dreams, concepts. Characters and events come simultaneously to me. Plot implies narrative and a lot of crap. It is a calculated attempt to hold the reader's interest at the sacrifice of moral conviction. Of course, one doesn't want to be boring . . . one needs an element of suspense. But a good narrative is a rudimentary structure, rather like a kidney.

INTERVIEWER

Have you always been a writer, or have you had other jobs?

CHEEVER

I drove a newspaper truck once. I liked it very much, especially during the World Series, when the Quincy paper would carry the box scores and full accounts. No one had radios, or television— which is not to say that the town was lit with candles, but they used to wait for the news; it made me feel good to be the one delivering the good news. Also, I spent four years in the army. I was seventeen when I sold my first story, "Expelled," to *The New Republic*. *The New Yorker* started taking my stuff when I was twenty-two. I was supported by *The New Yorker* for years and years. It has been a very pleasant association. I sent in twelve or fourteen stories a year. At the start I lived in a squalid slum room on Hudson Street with a broken windowpane. I had a job at MGM with Paul Goodman, doing synopses. Jim Farrell, too. We had to boil down just about every book published into either a three-, five-, or twelve-page précis for which you got something like five dollars. You did your own typing. And, oh, carbons.

INTERVIEWER

What was it like writing stories for *The New Yorker* in those days? Who was the fiction editor?

CHEEVER

Wolcott Gibbs was the fiction editor very briefly, and then Gus Lobrano. I knew him very well; he was a fishing companion. And, of course, Harold Ross, who was difficult but I loved him. He asked preposterous queries on a manuscript—everyone's written about that—something like thirty-six queries on a story. The author always thought it outrageous, a violation of taste, but Ross really didn't care. He liked to show his hand, to shake the writer up. Occasionally he was brilliant. In "The Enormous Radio" he made two changes. A diamond is found on the bathroom floor after a party. The man says, "Sell it, we can use a few dollars." Ross had changed "dollars" to "bucks," which was absolutely perfect. Brilliant. Then I had "the radio came softly" and Ross penciled in another "softly." "The radio came softly, softly." He was absolutely right. But then there were twenty-nine other suggestions like, "This story has gone on for twenty-four hours and no one has eaten anything. There's no mention of a meal." A typical example of this sort of thing was Shirley Jackson's "The Lottery," about the stoning ritual. He hated the story; he started turning vicious. He said there was no town in Vermont where there were rocks of that sort. He nagged and nagged and nagged. It was not surprising. Ross used to scare the hell out of me. I would go in for lunch. I never knew Ross was coming, until he'd bring in an eggcup. I'd sit with my back pressed against my chair. I was really afraid. He was a scratcher and a nose picker, and the sort of man who could get his underwear up so there was a strip of it showing between his trousers and his shirt. He used to hop at me, sort of jump about in his chair. It was a creative, destructive relationship from which I learned a great deal, and I miss him.

INTERVIEWER

You met a lot of writers during that time, didn't you?

CHEEVER

It was all terribly important to me, since I had been brought up in a small town. I was in doubt that I could make something of myself as a writer until I met two people who were very important to me: one was Gaston Lachaise and the other was E. E. Cummings. Cummings I loved, and I love his memory. He did a wonderful imitation of a wood-burning locomotive going from Tiflis to Minsk. He could hear a pin falling in soft dirt at the distance of three miles. Do you remember the story of Cummings's death? It was September, hot, and Cummings was cutting kindling in the back of his house in New Hampshire. He was sixty-six or sixty-seven or something like that. Marion, his wife, leaned out the window and asked, Cummings, isn't it frightfully hot to be chopping wood? He said, I'm going to stop now, but I'm going to sharpen the ax before I put it up, dear. Those were the last words he spoke. At his funeral Marianne Moore gave the eulogy. Marion Cummings had enormous eyes. You could make a place in a book with them. She smoked cigarettes as though they were heavy, and she wore a dark dress with a cigarette hole in it.

INTERVIEWER

And Lachaise?

CHEEVER

I'm not sure what to say about him. I thought him an outstanding artist and I found him a contented man. He used to go to the Metropolitan—where he was not represented—and embrace the statues he loved.

INTERVIEWER

Did Cummings have any advice for you as a writer?

CHEEVER

Cummings was never paternal. But the cant of his head, his wind-in-the-chimney voice, his courtesy to boobs, and the vastness of his love for Marion were all advisory.

INTERVIEWER

Have you ever written poetry?

CHEEVER

No. It seems to me that the discipline is very different . . . another language, another continent from that of fiction. In some cases short stories are more highly disciplined than a lot of the poetry that we have. Yet the disciplines are as different as shooting a twelve-gauge shotgun and swimming.

INTERVIEWER

Have magazines asked you to write journalism for them?

CHEEVER

I was asked to do an interview with Sophia Loren by the *Saturday Evening Post*. I did. I got to kiss her. I've had other offers but nothing as good.

INTERVIEWER

Do you think there's a trend for novelists to write journalism, as Norman Mailer does?

CHEEVER

I don't like your question. Fiction must compete with first-rate reporting. If you cannot write a story that is equal to a factual account of battle in the streets or demonstrations, then you can't write a story. You might as well give up. In many cases, fiction hasn't competed successfully. These days the field of fiction is littered with tales about the sensibilities of a child coming of age on a chicken farm, or a whore who strips her profession of its glamour. The *Times* has never been so full of rubbish in its recent book ads. Still, the use of the word "death" or "invalidism" about fiction diminishes as it does with anything else.

INTERVIEWER

Do you feel drawn to experiment in fiction, to move toward bizarre things?

CHEEVER

Fiction *is* experimentation; when it ceases to be that, it ceases to be fiction. One never puts down a sentence without the feeling that it has never been put down before in such a way, and that perhaps even the substance of the sentence has never been felt. Every sentence is an innovation.

INTERVIEWER

Do you feel that you belong to any particular tradition in American letters?

CHEEVER

No. As a matter of fact, I can't think of any American writers who could be classified as part of a tradition. You certainly can't put Updike, Mailer, Ellison, or Styron in a tradition. The individuality of the writer has never been as intense as it is in the United States.

INTERVIEWER

Well, would you think of yourself as a realistic writer?

CHEEVER

We have to agree on what we mean before we can talk about such definitions. Documentary novels, such as those of Dreiser, Zola, Dos Passos—even though I don't like them—can, I think, be classified as realistic. Jim Farrell was another documentary novelist; in a way, Scott Fitzgerald was, though to think of him that way diminishes what he could do best . . . which was to try to give a sense of what a very particular world was like.

Do you think Fitzgerald was conscious of documenting?

I've written something on Fitzgerald, and I've read all the biographies and critical works, and wept freely at the end of each one—cried like a baby—it is such a sad story. All the estimates of him bring in his descriptions of the '29 crash, the excessive prosperity, the clothes, the music, and by doing so, his work is described as being heavily dated . . . sort of period pieces. This all greatly diminishes Fitzgerald at his best. One always knows reading Fitzgerald what time it is, precisely where you are, the kind of country. No writer has ever been so true in placing the scene. But I feel that this isn't pseudohistory, but his sense of being alive. All great men are scrupulously true to their times.

Do you think your works will be similarly dated?

Oh, I don't anticipate that my work will be read. That isn't the sort of thing that concerns me. I might be forgotten tomorrow; it wouldn't disconcert me in the least.

But a great number of your stories defy dating; they could take place anytime and almost anyplace.

That, of course, has been my intention. The ones that you can pinpoint in an era are apt to be the worst. The bomb-shelter story ("The Brigadier and the Golf Widow") is about a level of basic anxiety, and the bomb shelter, which places the story at a very particular time, is just a metaphor . . . that's what I intended anyhow.

INTERVIEWER

It was a sad story.

CHEEVER

Everyone keeps saying that about my stories, Oh, they're so sad. My agent, Candida Donadio, called me about a new story and said, Oh, what a beautiful story, it's so sad. I said, All right, so I'm a sad man. The sad thing about "The Brigadier and the Golf Widow" is the woman standing looking at the bomb shelter in the end of the story and then being sent away by a maid. Did you know that *The New Yorker* tried to take that out? They thought the story was much more effective without my ending. When I went in to look at page proofs, I thought there was a page missing. I asked where the end of the story was. Some girl said, Mr. Shawn thinks it's better this way. I went into a very deep slow burn, took the train home, drank a lot of gin, and got one of the editors on the telephone. I was by then loud, abusive, and obscene. He was entertaining Elizabeth Bowen and Eudora Welty. He kept asking if he couldn't take this call in another place. Anyhow, I returned to New York in the morning. They had reset the whole magazine—poems, newsbreaks, cartoons—and replaced the scene.

INTERVIEWER

It's the classic story about what *The New Yorker* is rumored to do: remove the last paragraph and you've got a typical *New Yorker* ending. What is your definition of a good editor?

CHEEVER

My definition of a good editor is a man I think charming, who sends me large checks, praises my work, my physical beauty, and my sexual prowess, and who has a stranglehold on the publisher and the bank.

INTERVIEWER

What about the beginning of stories? Yours start off very quickly. It's striking.

CHEEVER

Well, if you're trying as a storyteller to establish some rapport with your reader, you don't open by telling him that you have a headache and indigestion and that you picked up a gravelly rash at Jones Beach. One of the reasons is that advertising in magazines is much more common today than it was twenty to thirty years ago. In publishing in a magazine you are competing against girdle advertisements, travel advertisements, nakedness, cartoons, even poetry. The competition almost makes it hopeless. There's a stock beginning that I've always had in mind. Someone is coming back from a year in Italy on a Fulbright scholarship. His trunk is opened in customs, and instead of his clothing and souvenirs, they find the mutilated body of an Italian seaman, everything there but the head. Another opening sentence I often think of is, "The first day I robbed Tiffany's it was raining." Of course, you can open a short story that way, but that's not how one should function with fiction. One is tempted because there has been a genuine loss of serenity, not only in the reading public, but in all our lives. Patience, perhaps, or even the ability to concentrate. At one point when television first came in no one was publishing an article that couldn't be read during a commercial. But fiction is durable enough to survive all of this. I don't like the short story that starts out "I'm about to shoot myself" or "I'm about to shoot you." Or the Pirandello thing of "I'm going to shoot you or you are going to shoot me, or we are going to shoot someone, maybe each other." Or the erotic thing, either: "He started to undo his pants, but the zipper stuck . . . he got the can of three-in-one oil . . ." and on and on we go.

INTERVIEWER

Certainly your stories have a fast pace, they move along.

CHEEVER

The first principle of aesthetics is either interest or suspense. You can't expect to communicate with anyone if you're a bore.

INTERVIEWER

William Golding wrote that there are two kinds of novelists: One lets meaning develop with the characters or situations, and the other has an idea and looks for a myth to embody it. He's an example of the second kind. He thinks of Dickens as belonging to the first. Do you think you fit into either category?

CHEEVER

I don't know what Golding is talking about. Cocteau said that writing is a force of memory that is not understood. I agree with this. Raymond Chandler described it as a direct line to the subconscious. The books that you really love give the sense, when you first open them, of having been there. It is a creation, almost like a chamber in the memory. Places that one has never been to, things that one has never seen or heard, but their fitness is so sound that you've been there somehow.

INTERVIEWER

But certainly you use a lot of resonances from myths . . . for example, references to the Bible and Greek mythology.

CHEEVER

It's explained by the fact that I was brought up in southern Massachusetts, where it was thought that mythology was a subject that we should all grasp. It was very much a part of my education. The easiest way to parse the world is through mythology. There have been thousands of papers written along those lines—Leander is Poseidon and somebody is Ceres, and so forth. It seems to be a superficial parsing. But it makes a passable paper.

INTERVIEWER

Still, you want the resonance.

CHEEVER

The resonance, of course.

INTERVIEWER

How do you work? Do you put ideas down immediately, or do you walk around with them for a while, letting them incubate?

CHEEVER

I do both. What I love is when totally disparate facts come together. For example, I was sitting in a café reading a letter from home with the news that a neighboring housewife had taken the lead in a nude show. As I read I could hear an Englishwoman scolding her children: "If you don't do thus and so before Mummy counts to three" was her line. A leaf fell through the air, reminding me of winter and of the fact that my wife had left me and was in Rome. There was my story. I had an equivalently great time with the close of "Goodbye, My Brother" and "The Country Husband." Hemingway and Nabokov liked these. I had everything in there: a cat wearing a hat, some naked women coming out of the sea, a dog with a shoe in his mouth, and a king in golden mail riding an elephant over some mountains.

INTERVIEWER

Or ping-pong in the rain?

CHEEVER

I don't remember what story that was.

INTERVIEWER

Sometimes you played ping-pong in the rain.

CHEEVER

I probably did.

INTERVIEWER

Do you save up such things?

CHEEVER

It isn't a question of saving up. It's a question of some sort of gal-
vanic energy. It's also, of course, a question of making sense of one's
experiences.

INTERVIEWER

Do you think that fiction should give lessons?

CHEEVER

No. Fiction is meant to illuminate, to explode, to refresh. I don't
think there's any consecutive moral philosophy in fiction beyond ex-
cellence. Acuteness of feeling and velocity have always seemed to me
terribly important. People look for morals in fiction because there has
always been a confusion between fiction and philosophy.

INTERVIEWER

How do you know when a story is right? Does it hit you right the
first time, or are you critical as you go along?

CHEEVER

I think there is a certain heft in fiction. For example, my latest
story isn't right. I have to do the ending over again. It's a question, I
guess, of trying to get it to correspond to a vision. There is a shape,
a proportion, and one knows when something that happens is
wrong.

INTERVIEWER

By instinct?

CHEEVER

I suppose that anyone who has written for as long as I have . . . It's
probably what you'd call instinct. When a line falls wrong, it simply
isn't right.

INTERVIEWER

You told me once you were interested in thinking up names for characters.

CHEEVER

That seems to me very important. I've written a story about men with a lot of names, all abstract, names with the fewest possible allusions: Pell, Weed, Hammer, and Nailles, of course, which was thought to be arch, but it wasn't meant to be at all. . . .

INTERVIEWER

Hammer's house appears in "The Swimmer."

CHEEVER

That's true, it's quite a good story. It was a terribly difficult story to write.

INTERVIEWER

Why?

CHEEVER

Because I couldn't ever show my hand. Night was falling, the year was dying. It wasn't a question of technical problems, but one of imponderables. When he finds it's dark and cold, it has to have happened. And, by God, it did happen. I felt dark and cold for some time after I finished that story. As a matter of fact, it's one of the last stories I wrote for a long time, because then I started on *Bullet Park*. Sometimes the easiest-seeming stories to a reader are the hardest kind to write.

INTERVIEWER

How long does it take you to write such a story?

CHEEVER

Three days, three weeks, three months. I seldom read my own work. It seems to be a particularly offensive form of narcissism. It's like playing back tapes of your own conversation. It's like looking over your shoulder to see where you've run. That's why I've often used the image of the swimmer, the runner, the jumper. The point is to finish and go on to the next thing. I also feel, not as strongly as I used to, that if I looked over my shoulder I would die. I think frequently of Satchel Paige and his warning that you might see something gaining on you.

INTERVIEWER

Are there stories that you feel particularly good about when you are finished?

CHEEVER

Yes, there were about fifteen of them that were absolutely BANG! I loved them, I loved everybody—the buildings, the houses, wherever I was. It was a great sensation. Most of these were stories written in the space of three days and which run to about thirty-five pages. I love them, but I can't read them; in many cases, I wouldn't love them any longer if I did.

INTERVIEWER

Recently you have talked bluntly about having a writer's block, which had never happened to you before. How do you feel about it now?

CHEEVER

Any memory of pain is deeply buried, and there is nothing more painful for a writer than an inability to work.

INTERVIEWER

Four years is a rather long haul on a novel, isn't it?

CHEEVER

It's about what it usually takes. There's a certain monotony in this way of life, which I can very easily change.

INTERVIEWER

Why?

CHEEVER

Because it doesn't seem to me the proper function of writing. If possible, it is to enlarge people. To give them their risk, if possible to give them their divinity, not to cut them down.

INTERVIEWER

Do you feel that you had diminished them too far in *Bullet Park*?

CHEEVER

No, I didn't feel that. But I believe that it was understood in those terms. I believe that Hammer and Nailles were thought to be social casualties, which isn't what I intended at all. And I thought I made my intentions quite clear. But if you don't communicate, it's not anybody else's fault. Neither Hammer nor Nailles were meant to be either psychiatric or social metaphors; they were meant to be two men with their own risks. I think the book was misunderstood on those terms. But then I don't read reviews, so I don't really know what goes on.

INTERVIEWER

How do you know when the literary work is finished to your satisfaction?

CHEEVER

I have never completed anything in my life to my absolute and lasting satisfaction.

INTERVIEWER

Do you feel that you're putting a lot of yourself on the line when you are writing?

CHEEVER

Oh yes, oh yes! When I speak as a writer I speak with my own voice—quite as unique as my fingerprints—and I take the maximum risk at seeming profound or foolish.

INTERVIEWER

Does one get the feeling while sitting at the typewriter that one is godlike, or creating the whole show at once?

CHEEVER

No, I've never felt godlike. No, the sense is of one's total usefulness. We all have a power of control, it's part of our lives: we have it in love, in work that we love doing. It's a sense of ecstasy, as simple as that. The sense is that "this is my usefulness, and I can do it all the way through." It always leaves you feeling great. In short, you've made sense of your life.

INTERVIEWER

Do you feel that way during or after the event? Isn't work, well, work?

CHEEVER

I've had very little drudgery in my life. When I write a story that I really like, it's . . . why, wonderful. That is what I can do, and I love it while I'm doing it. I can feel that it's good. I'll say to Mary and the children, All right, I'm off, leave me alone. I'll be through in three days.

Issue 67, 1976

Joyce Carol Oates

The Art of Fiction

J oyce Carol Oates is the rarest of commodities, an author modest about her work, though there is such a quantity of it that she has three publishers—one for fiction, one for poetry, and a "small press" for more experimental work, limited editions, and books her other publishers simply cannot schedule. And despite the added demands of teaching, she continues to devote much energy to *The Ontario Review*, a literary quarterly that her husband edits and for which she serves as a contributing editor.

Ms. Oates is striking-looking and slender, with dark hair and large, inquiring eyes. She is highly attractive but not photogenic; no photo has ever done justice to her appearance, which conveys grace and high intelligence. If her manner is taken for aloofness—as it sometimes has been—it is, in fact, a shyness that the publication of thirty-three books, the production of three plays, and the winning of the National Book Award has not displaced.

This interview began at her Windsor home in the summer of 1976 before she and her husband moved to Princeton. When interviewed, her speaking voice was, as always, soft and reflective. One receives the impression that she never speaks in anything but perfectly formed sentences. Ms. Oates answered all questions openly while curled with her Persian cats upon a sofa. (She is a confirmed cat lover and recently took in two more kittens at the Princeton house.)

Talk continued during a stroll by the banks of the Detroit River where she confessed to having sat for hours, watching the horizon

xx other customers in <u>Rinaldi's</u> to overhear. Voice shrill,
laughter shrill. Must guard against excitement. ...A true
gift, such women possess; "artistic arrangement of life" a
phrase I think I read somewhere. Can't remember. She wants
to understand me but will not invade me like the others.
Sunshine: her hair. (Though it is brown, not very unusual.
But always clean.) Sunshine: dispelling of demons. Intimacy
always a danger. Intimacy/hell/intimacy/hell. Could possibly
make love to her thinking of XXXXXXXXXX or (say) the boy with
the kinky reddish hair on the bicycle...but sickening to think
of. What if. What if an attack of laughter. Hysterical gig-
gling. And. Afterward. Such shame, disgust. She would not
laugh of course but might be wounded for life: cannot exaggerate
the dangers of intimacy, on my side or hers. The Secret between
us. My secret, not hers. Our friendship--nearly a year now--
on my footing, never hers. Can't deny what others have known
before me, the pleasure of secrecy, taking of risks.

--With XXXXXXXXX etc. last night, unable to wake this morning
till after ten; already at work; sick headache, dryness of
mouth, throat. But no fever. Temperature normal. XXXXXXXXXXXX
so bitter, speaks of having been blackmailed by some idiot,
but (in my opinion) it all happened years ago, not connected
with his position here in town. Teaches juniors, seniors.
Advises Drama Club. Tenure. I'm envious of him & impatient
with his continual bitterness. Rehashing of past. What's the
point of it? Of course, he is over forty (how much over forty
is his secret) and I am a decade younger, x maybe fifteen years
younger. Will never turn into that. Hag's face, lines around
mouth, eyes. Grotesque moustache: trying to be 25 years old
& misses by a x mile.... Yet my pen-and-ink portrait of him
is endearing. Delighted, that it should please even him. &
did not mind the CA$H. Of course I am talented & of course
misused at the agency but refuse to be bitter like the others.
XXXXXXXXXX lavish, flattery and money. I deserve both but
don't expect everyone to recognize me...in no hurry...can't
demand fame overnight. Would I want fame anyway???? Maybe not.
With XXXXXXXXXXX's hundred dollars bought her that $35 book of
Toulouse-Lautrec's work, dear Henri, perhaps should not have
risked x it with her but genuinely thought she would like it.
Did not think, as usual. She seemed grateful enough, thanking
me, surprised, said she'd received only a few cards from home
& a predictable present from her mother, certainly did not
expect anything ffom me--"But aren't you saving for a trip to
Europe"--remembers so much about me, amazing--so sweet--unlike
XXXXXXXXXX who calls me by the names of strangers and is
vile. His image with me till early afternoon, tried to vomit
in the first-floor lavatory where no one from the office might stomach
drop in, dry heaving gasps, not so easy to do on an empty ~~stomach~~
Mind over matter??????   Not with "Farrell van Buren"!

--A complete day xxxx wasted. Idiotic trendy "collage" for
MacKenzie's Diary, if you please. Cherubs, grinning teenagers,
trophies. An "avant-garde" look to it. Haha. Looking forward
to lay-out for the Hilton & Trader Vic's, at least some precedent
to work from <u>and resist</u>.   ...Could send out my Invisible Soldiers
to hack up a few of these bastards, smart-assed paunchy hags
bossing me around. Someday things will be different. (Of course

A manuscript page from a short story by Joyce Carol Oates.

and the boats, and dreaming her characters into existence. She sets these dreams physically onto paper on a writing table in her study, which faces the river.

Additional questions were asked in New York during the 1976 Christmas season, when Ms. Oates and her husband attended a seminar on her work, which was part of that year's Modern Language Association convention. Many of the questions in this interview were answered via correspondence. She felt that only by writing out her replies could she say precisely what she wished to, without possibility of misunderstanding or misquotation.

—*Robert Phillips, 1978*

INTERVIEWER

We may as well get this one over with first: you're frequently charged with producing too much.

JOYCE CAROL OATES

Productivity is a relative matter. And it's really insignificant: What is ultimately important is a writer's strongest books. It may be the case that we all must write many books in order to achieve a few lasting ones—just as a young writer or poet might have to write hundreds of poems before writing his first significant one. Each book as it is written, however, is a completely absorbing experience, and feels always as if it were *the* work I was born to write. Afterward, of course, as the years pass, it's possible to become more detached, more critical.

I really don't know what to say. I note and can to some extent sympathize with the objurgatory tone of certain critics, who feel that I write too much because, quite wrongly, they believe they ought to have read most of my books before attempting to criticize a recently published one. (At least I *think* that's why they react a bit irritably.) Yet each book is a world unto itself and must stand alone, and it should not matter whether a book is a writer's first, or tenth, or fiftieth.

INTERVIEWER

About your critics—do you read them, usually? Have you ever learned anything from a book review or an essay on your work?

OATES

Sometimes I read reviews, and without exception I will read critical essays that are sent to me. The critical essays are interesting on their own terms. Of course, it's a pleasure simply to discover that someone has read and responded to one's work; being understood, and being praised, is beyond expectation most of the time. . . . The average review is a quickly written piece not meant to be definitive. So it would be misguided for a writer to read such reviews attentively. All writers without exception find themselves clapperclawed from time to time; I think the experience (provided one survives it) is wonderfully liberating: After the first death there is no other. . . . A writer who has published as many books as I have has developed, of necessity, a hide like a rhino's, while inside there dwells a frail, hopeful butterfly of a spirit.

INTERVIEWER

Returning to the matter of your "productivity": have you ever dictated into a machine?

OATES

No, oddly enough I've written my last several novels in longhand first. I had an enormous, rather frightening stack of pages and notes for *The Assassins*, probably eight hundred pages—or was it closer to a thousand? It alarms me to remember. *Childwold* needed to be written in longhand, of course. And now everything finds its initial expression in longhand and the typewriter has become a rather alien thing—a thing of formality and impersonality. My first novels were all written on a typewriter: first draft straight through, then revisions, then final draft. But I can't do that any longer.

The thought of dictating into a machine doesn't appeal to me at all. Henry James's later works would have been better had he resisted that curious sort of self-indulgence, dictating to a secretary. The roaming garrulousness of ordinary speech is usually corrected when it's transcribed into written prose.

INTERVIEWER

Do you ever worry—considering the vast body of your work—if you haven't written a particular scene before, or had characters say the same lines?

OATES

Evidently, there are writers (John Cheever, Mavis Gallant come immediately to mind) who never reread their work, and there are others who reread constantly. I suspect I am somewhere in the middle. If I thought I *had* written a scene before, or written the same lines before, I would simply look it up.

INTERVIEWER

What kind of work schedule do you follow?

OATES

I haven't any formal schedule, but I love to write in the morning, before breakfast. Sometimes the writing goes so smoothly that I don't take a break for many hours—and consequently have breakfast at two or three in the afternoon on good days. On school days, days that I teach, I usually write for an hour or forty-five minutes in the morning, before my first class. But I don't have any formal schedule, and at the moment I am feeling rather melancholy, or derailed, or simply lost, because I completed a novel some weeks ago and haven't begun another . . . except in scattered, stray notes.

INTERVIEWER

Do you find emotional stability is necessary in order to write? Or can you get to work whatever your state of mind? Is your mood reflected in what you write? How do you describe that perfect state in which you can write from early morning into the afternoon?

OATES

One must be pitiless about this matter of "mood." In a sense, the writing will *create* the mood. If art is, as I believe it to be, a genuinely transcendental function—a means by which we rise out of limited, parochial states of mind—then it should not matter very much what states of mind or emotion we are in. Generally I've found this to be true: I have forced myself to begin writing when I've been utterly exhausted, when I've felt my soul as thin as a playing card, when nothing has seemed worth enduring for another five minutes . . . and somehow the activity of writing changes everything. Or appears to do so. Joyce said of the underlying structure of *Ulysses*—the Odyssean parallel and parody—that he really didn't care whether it was plausible so long as it served as a bridge to get his "soldiers" across. Once they were across, what does it matter if the bridge collapses? One might say the same thing about the use of one's self as a means for the writing to get written. Once the soldiers are across the stream . . .

INTERVIEWER

What does happen when you finish a novel? Is the next project one that has been waiting in line? Or is the choice more spontaneous?

OATES

When I complete a novel I set it aside, and begin work on short stories, and eventually another long work. When I complete *that* novel I return to the earlier novel and rewrite much of it. In the meantime the second novel lies in a desk drawer. Sometimes I work on two novels simultaneously, though one usually forces the other into the background. The rhythm of writing, revising, writing, revising, et cetera, seems to suit me. I am inclined to think that as I grow older I will come to be infatuated with the art of revision, and there may come a time when I will dread giving up a novel at all. My next novel, *Unholy Loves*, was written around the time of *Childwold*, for instance, and revised after the completion of that novel, and again revised this past spring and summer. My reputation for writing quickly and effortlessly notwithstanding, I am strongly in favor of intelligent, even fastidious revision, which is, or certainly should be, an art in itself.

Do you keep a diary?

I began keeping a formal journal several years ago. It resembles a sort of ongoing letter to myself, mainly about literary matters. What interests me in the process of my own experience is the wide range of my feelings. For instance, after I finish a novel I tend to think of the experience of having written it as being largely pleasant and challenging. But in fact (for I keep careful records) the experience is various: I do suffer temporary bouts of frustration and inertia and depression. There are pages in recent novels that I've rewritten as many as seventeen times, and a story, "The Widows," which I revised both before and after publication in *The Hudson Review*, and then revised slightly again before I included it in my next collection of stories—a fastidiousness that could go on into infinity.

Afterward, however, I simply forget. My feelings crystallize (or are mythologized) into something much less complex. All of us who keep journals do so for different reasons, I suppose, but we must have in common a fascination with the surprising patterns that emerge over the years—a sort of arabesque in which certain elements appear and reappear, like the designs in a well-wrought novel. The voice of my journal is very much like the one I find myself using in these replies to you: the voice in which I think or meditate when I'm not writing fiction.

Besides writing and teaching, what daily special activities are important to you? Travel, jogging, music? I hear you're an excellent pianist?

We travel a great deal, usually by car. We've driven slowly across the continent several times, and we've explored the South and New England and of course New York State with loving thoroughness. As a pianist I've defined myself as an "enthusiastic amateur," which is about the most merciful thing that can be said. I like to draw, I like to listen to music, and I spend an inordinate amount of time doing nothing. I don't even think it can be called daydreaming.

I also enjoy that much-maligned occupation of housewifery, but hardly dare say so, things being what they are today. I like to cook, to tend plants, to garden (minimally), to do simple domestic things, to stroll around shopping malls and observe the qualities of people, overhearing snatches of conversations, noting people's appearances, their clothes, and so forth. Walking and driving a car are part of my life as a writer, really. I can't imagine myself apart from these activities.

INTERVIEWER

Despite critical and financial success, you continue to teach. Why?

OATES

I teach a full load at the University of Windsor, which means three courses. One is creative writing, one is the graduate seminar (in the Modern Period), the third is an oversize (one hundred and fifteen students) undergraduate course that is lively and stimulating but really too swollen to be satisfying to me. There is, generally, a closeness between students and faculty at Windsor that is very rewarding, however. Anyone who teaches knows that you don't *really* experience a text until you've taught it, in loving detail, with an intelligent and responsive class. At the present time I'm going through Joyce's work with nine graduate students and each seminar meeting is very exciting (and draining) and I can't think, frankly, of anything else I would rather do.

INTERVIEWER

It is a sometimes publicized fact that your professor husband does not read most of your work. Is there any practical reason for this?

OATES

Ray has such a busy life of his own, preparing classes, editing *The Ontario Review* and so forth, that he really hasn't time to read my work. I do, occasionally, show him reviews, and he makes brief comments on them. I would have liked, I think, to have established an easygoing relationship with some other writers, but somehow that never came about. Two or three of us at Windsor do read one another's poems, but criticism as such is minimal. I've never been able to respond very fully to criticism, frankly, because I've usually been absorbed in another work by the time the criticism is available to me. Also, critics sometimes appear to be addressing themselves to works other than those I remember writing.

INTERVIEWER

Do you feel in any way an expatriate or an exile, living in Canada?

OATES

We are certainly exiles of a sort. But we would be, I think, exiles if we lived in Detroit as well. Fortunately, Windsor is really an international, cosmopolitan community, and our Canadian colleagues are not intensely and narrowly nationalistic.

But I wonder—doesn't everyone feel rather exiled? When I return home to Millerport, New York, and visit nearby Lockport, the extraordinary changes that have taken place make me feel like a stranger; the mere passage of time makes us all exiles. The situation is a comic one, perhaps, since it affirms the power of the evolving community over the individual, but I think we tend to feel it as tragic. Windsor is a relatively stable community, and my husband and I have come to feel, oddly, more at home here than we probably would anywhere else.

INTERVIEWER

Have you ever consciously changed your lifestyle to help your work as a writer?

OATES

Not really. My nature is orderly and observant and scrupulous, and deeply introverted, so life wherever I attempt it turns out to be claustral. Live like a bourgeois, Flaubert suggested, but I was living like that long before I came across Flaubert's remark.

INTERVIEWER

You wrote *Do with Me What You Will* during your year living in London. While there you met many writers such as Doris Lessing, Margaret Drabble, Colin Wilson, Iris Murdoch—writers you respect, as your reviews of their work indicate. Would you make any observations on the role of the writer in society in England versus that which you experience here?

OATES

The English novelist is almost without exception an observer of society. (I suppose I mean "society" in its most immediate, limited sense.) Apart from writers like Lawrence (who doesn't seem altogether *English*, in fact) there hasn't been an intense interest in subjectivity, in the psychology of living, breathing human beings. Of course, there have been marvelous novels. And there *is* Doris Lessing, who writes books that can no longer be categorized: fictional parable, autobiography, allegory . . . ? And John Fowles. And Iris Murdoch.

But there is a feel to the American novel that is radically different. We are willing to risk being called "formless" by people whose ideas of form are rigidly limited, and we are wilder, more exploratory, more ambitious, perhaps less easily shamed, less easily discouraged. The intellectual life, as such, we tend to keep out of our novels, fearing the sort of highly readable but ultimately disappointing cerebral quality of Huxley's work . . . or, on a somewhat lower level, C. P. Snow's.

INTERVIEWER

The English edition of *Wonderland* has a different ending from the American. Why? Do you often rewrite published work?

OATES

I was forced to rewrite the ending of that particular novel because it struck me that the first ending was not the correct one. I have not rewritten any other published work (except, of course, for short stories, which sometimes get rewritten before inclusion in a book) and don't intend to if I can possibly help it.

INTERVIEWER

You've written novels on highly specialized fields, such as brain surgery. How do you research such backgrounds?

OATES

A great deal of reading, mainly. Some years ago I developed a few odd symptoms that necessitated my seeing a doctor, and since there was for a time talk of my being sent to a neurologist, I nervously and superstitiously began reading the relevant journals. What I came upon so chilled me that I must have gotten well as a result. . . .

INTERVIEWER

In addition to the novel about medicine, you've written one each on law, politics, religion, spectator sports: Are you consciously filling out a "program" of novels about American life?

OATES

Not really consciously. The great concern with medicine really grew out of an experience of some duration that brought me into contact with certain thoughts of mortality: of hospitals, illnesses, doctors, the world of death and dying and our human defenses against such phenomena. (A member of my family to whom I was very close died rather slowly of cancer.) I attempted to deal with my own very inchoate feelings about these matters by dramatizing what I saw to be contemporary responses to mortality. My effort to wed myself with a fictional character and our synthesis in turn with a larger, almost allegorical condition resulted in a novel that was difficult to write and also, I suspect, difficult to read.

A concern with law seemed to spring naturally out of the thinking many of us were doing in the sixties: What is the relationship between law and civilization, what hope has civilization without law, and yet what hope has civilization *with* law as it has developed in our tradition? More personal matters blended with the larger issues of crime and guilt, so that I felt I was able to transcend a purely private and purely local drama that might have had emotional significance for me, but very little beyond that; quite by accident I found myself writing about a woman conditioned to be unnaturally "passive" in a world of hearty masculine combat—an issue that became topical even as the novel *Do with Me What You Will* was published, and is topical still, to some extent.

The "political" novel, *The Assassins*, grew out of two experiences I had some years ago, at high-level conferences involving politicians, academic specialists, lawyers, and a scattering—no, hardly that—of literary people. (I won't be more specific at the moment.) A certain vertiginous fascination with work which I noted in my own nature I was able to objectify (and, I think, exaggerate) in terms of the various characters' fanaticism involving their own "work"—most obviously in Andrew Petrie's obsession with "transforming the consciousness of America." *The Assassins* is about megalomania and its inevitable consequences, and it seemed necessary that the assassins be involved in politics, given the peculiar conditions of our era.

The new "religious" novel, *Son of the Morning*, is rather painfully autobiographical, in part—but only in part. The religion it explores is not institutional but rather subjective, intensely personal, so as a novel it is perhaps not like the earlier three I have mentioned, or the racing novel, *With Shuddering Fall*. Rather, *Son of the Morning* is a novel that begins with wide ambitions and ends very, very humbly.

INTERVIEWER

Somewhere in print you called *The Assassins* the favorite of your novels. It received very mixed reviews. I've often thought that book was misread. For instance, I think the "martyr" in that novel arranged for his own assassination, true? And that his wife was never really attacked outside the country house; she never left it. Her maiming was all confined within her head.

OATES

What a fine surprise! You read the scene exactly as it was meant to be read. Even well-intentioned reviewers missed the point; so far as I know, only two or three people read Yvonne's scene as I had intended it to be read. Yet the hallucinatory nature of the "dismemberment" scene is explicit. And Andrew Petrie did, of course, arrange for his own assassination, as the novel makes clear in its concluding pages.

The novel has been misread, of course, partly because it's rather long and I think reviewers, who are usually pressed for time, simply treated it in a perfunctory way. I'm not certain that it is my favorite novel. But it is, or was, my most ambitious. It involved a great deal of effort, the collating of passages (and memories) that differ from or contradict one another. One becomes attached to such perverse, maddening ugly ducklings, but I can't really blame reviewers for being impatient with the novel. As my novels grow in complexity they please me more and please the "literary world" hardly at all—a sad situation, but not a paralyzing one.

INTERVIEWER

It's not merely a matter of complexity. One feels that your fiction has become more and more urgent, more subjective and less concerned with the outward details of this world—especially in *Childwold*. Was that novel a deliberate attempt to write a "poetic novel"? Or is it a long poem?

OATES

I don't see that *Childwold* is not concerned with the outward details of the world. In fact, it's made up almost entirely of visual details—of the natural world, of the farm the Bartletts own, and of the small city they gravitate to. But you are right, certainly, in suggesting that it is a poetic novel. I had wanted to create a prose poem in the form of a novel, or a novel in the form of a prose poem: The exciting thing for me was to deal with the tension that arose between the image-centered structure of poetry and the narrative-centered and linear structure of the interplay of persons that constitutes a novel. In other words, poetry focuses upon the image, the particular thing, or emotion, or feeling, while prose fiction focuses upon motion through time and space. The one impulse is toward stasis, the other toward movement. Between the two impulses there arose a certain tension that made the writing of the novel quite challenging. I suppose it is an experimental work, but I shy away from thinking of my work in those terms: It seems to me there is a certain self-consciousness about anyone who sets himself up as an "experimental" writer. All writing is experimental.

But experimentation for its own sake doesn't much interest me; it seems to belong to the early sixties, when Dadaism was being rediscovered. In a sense we are all post-*Wake* writers and it's Joyce, and only Joyce, who casts a long terrifying shadow. . . . The problem is that virtuoso writing appeals to the intellect and tends to leave one's emotions untouched. When I read aloud to my students the last few pages of *Finnegans Wake*, and come to that glorious, and heartbreaking, final section ("But you're changing, acoolsha, you're changing from me, I can feel"), I think I'm able to communicate the almost overwhelmingly beautiful emotion behind it, and the experience certainly leaves *me* shaken, but it would be foolish to think that the average reader, even the average intelligent reader, would be willing to labor at the *Wake*, through those hundreds of dense pages, in order to attain an emotional and spiritual sense of the work's wholeness, as well as its genius. Joyce's *Ulysses* appeals to me more: That graceful synthesis of the "naturalistic" and the "symbolic" suits my temperament. . . . I try to write books that can be read in one way by a literal-minded reader, and in quite another way by a reader alert to symbolic abbreviation and parodistic elements. And yet, it's the same book—or nearly. A trompe l'oeil, a work of "as if."

INTERVIEWER

Very little has been made of the humor in your work, the parody. Some of your books, like *Expensive People*, *The Hungry Ghosts*, and parts of *Wonderland*, seem almost Pinteresque in their absurd humor. Is Pinter an influence? Do you consider yourself a comedic writer?

OATES

There's been humor of a sort in my writing from the first; but it's understated, or deadpan. Pinter has never struck me as very funny. Doesn't he really write tragedy?

I liked Ionesco at one time. And Kafka. And Dickens (from whom Kafka learned certain effects, though he uses them, of course, for different ends). I respond to English satire, as I mentioned earlier. Absurdist or dark or black or whatever: What isn't tragic belongs to the comic spirit. The novel is nourished by both and swallows both up greedily.

INTERVIEWER

What have you learned from Kafka?

OATES

To make a jest of the horror. To take myself less seriously.

INTERVIEWER

John Updike has been accused of a lack of violence in his work. You're often accused of portraying too much. What is the function of violence in your work?

OATES

Given the number of pages I have written, and the "violent" incidents dispersed throughout them, I rather doubt that I am a violent writer in any meaningful sense of the word. Certainly, the violence is minimal in a novel like *them*, which purported to be a naturalistic work set in Detroit in the sixties; real life is much more chaotic.

INTERVIEWER

Which of your books gave you the greatest trouble to write? And which gave the greatest pleasure or pride?

OATES

Both *Wonderland* and *The Assassins* were difficult to write. *Expensive People* was the least difficult. I am personally very fond of *Childwold*, since it represents, in a kind of diffracted way, a complete world made of memory and imagination, a blending together of different times. It always surprises me that other people find that novel admirable because, to me, it seems very private . . . the sort of thing a writer can do only once.

Aside from that, *Do with Me What You Will* gives me a fair amount of pleasure, and, of course, I am closest to the novel I finished most recently, *Son of the Morning*. (In general, I think we are always fondest of the books we've just completed, aren't we? For obvious reasons.) But then I think of Jules and Maureen and Loretta of *them* and I wonder if perhaps that isn't my favorite novel, after all.

INTERVIEWER

For whom do you write—yourself, your friends, your "public"? Do you imagine an ideal reader for your work?

OATES

Well, there are certain stories, like those in *The Hungry Ghosts*, which I have written for an academic community and, in some cases, for specific people. But in general the writing writes itself—I mean a character determines his or her "voice" and I must follow along. Had I my own way the first section of *The Assassins* would be much abbreviated. But it was impossible to shut Hugh Petrie up once he got going and, long and painful and unwieldy as his section is, it's nevertheless been shortened. The problem with creating such highly conscious and intuitive characters is that they tend to perceive the contours of the literary landscape in which they dwell and, like Kasch of *Childwold*, try to guide or even to take over the direction of the narrative. Hugh did not want to die, and so his section went on and on, and it isn't an exaggeration to say that I felt real dismay in dealing with him.

Son of the Morning is a first-person narration by a man who is addressing himself throughout to God. Hence the whole novel is a prayer. Hence the ideal reader is, then, God. Everyone else, myself included, is secondary.

INTERVIEWER

Do you consider yourself religious? Do you feel there is a firm religious basis to your work?

OATES

I wish I knew how to answer this. Having completed a novel that is saturated with what Jung calls the God-experience, I find that I know less than ever about myself and my own beliefs. I have beliefs, of course, like everyone—but I don't always believe in them. Faith comes and goes. God diffracts into a bewildering plenitude of elements—the environment, love, friends and family, career, profession, "fate," biochemical harmony or disharmony, whether the sky is slate-gray or a bright mesmerizing blue. These elements then coalesce again into something seemingly unified. But it's a human predilection, isn't it?—our tendency to see, and to wish to see, what we've projected outward upon the universe from our own souls? I hope to continue to write about religious experience, but at the moment I feel quite drained, quite depleted. And as baffled as ever.

INTERVIEWER

You mention Jung. Is Freud also an influence? Laing?

OATES

Freud I have always found rather limited and biased; Jung and Laing I've read only in recent years. As an undergraduate at Syracuse University I discovered Nietzsche, and it may be the Nietzschean influence (which is certainly far more provocative than Freud's) that characterizes some of my work. I don't really know, consciously. For me, stories usually begin—or began, since I write so few of them now—out of some magical association between characters and their settings. There are some stories (I won't say which ones) that evolved almost entirely out of their settings, usually rural.

INTERVIEWER

Your earliest stories and novels seem influenced by Faulkner and by Flannery O'Connor. Are these influences you acknowledge? Are there others?

OATES

I've been reading for so many years, and my influences must be so vast—it would be very difficult to answer. An influence I rarely mention is Thoreau, whom I read at a very impressionable age (my early teens), and Henry James, O'Connor and Faulkner certainly, Katherine Anne Porter, and Dostoyevsky. An odd mixture.

INTERVIEWER

The title *Wonderland*, and frequent other allusions in your work, point toward a knowledge of, if not an affinity for, Lewis Carroll. What is the connection, and is it an important one?

OATES

Lewis Carroll's *Alice in Wonderland* and *Through the Looking Glass* were my very first books. Carroll's wonderful blend of illogic and humor and horror and justice has always appealed to me, and I had a marvelous time teaching the books last year in my undergraduate course.

INTERVIEWER

Was there anything you were particularly afraid of as a child?

OATES

Like most children, I was probably afraid of a variety of things. The unknown? The possibility of those queer fortuitous metamorphoses that seem to overtake certain of Carroll's characters? Physical pain? Getting lost? . . . My proclivity for the irreverent and the nonsensical was either inspired by Carroll or confirmed by him. I was always, and continue to be, an essentially mischievous child. This is one of my best-kept secrets.

INTERVIEWER

You began writing at a very early age. Was it encouraged by your family? Was yours a family of artistic ambitions?

OATES

In later years my parents have become "artistic," but when they were younger, and their children were younger, they had no time for anything much except work. I was always encouraged by my parents, my grandmother, and my teachers to be creative. I can't remember when I first began to tell stories—by drawing, it was then—but I must have been very young. It was an instinct I followed quite naturally.

INTERVIEWER

Much of your work is set in the 1930s, a period during which you were merely an infant at best. Why is that decade so important to your work or vision?

OATES

Since I was born in 1938, the decade is of great significance to me. This was the world of my parents, who were young adults at the time, the world I was born into. The thirties seem in an odd way still "living" to me, partly in terms of my parents' and grandparents' memories, and partly in terms of its treatment in books and films. But the twenties are too remote—lost to me entirely! I simply haven't had the imaginative power to get that far back.

I identify very closely with my parents in ways I can't satisfactorily explain. The lives they lived before I was born seem somehow accessible to me. Not directly, of course, but imaginatively. A memory belonging to my mother or father seems almost to "belong" to me. In studying old photographs I am struck sometimes by a sense of my being contemporary with my parents—as if I'd known them when they were, let's say, only teenagers. Is this odd? I wonder. I rather suspect others share in their family's experiences and memories without knowing quite how.

INTERVIEWER

When we were undergraduates together at Syracuse, you already were something of a legend. It was rumored you'd finish a novel, turn it over, and immediately begin writing another on the back side. When both sides were covered, you'd throw it all out, and reach for clean paper. Was it at Syracuse you first became aware you were going to be a writer?

OATES

I began writing in high school, consciously training myself by writing novel after novel and always throwing them out when I completed them. I remember a three-hundred-page book of interrelated stories that must have been modeled on Hemingway's *In Our Time* (I hadn't yet read *Dubliners*), though the subject matter was much more romantic than Hemingway's. I remember a bloated, trifurcated novel that had as its vague model *The Sound and the Fury*. . . . Fortunately, these experiments were thrown away and I haven't remembered them until this moment.

Syracuse was a very exciting place academically and intellectually for me. I doubt that I missed more than half a dozen classes in my four years there, and none of them in English.

INTERVIEWER

I remember you were in a sorority. It is incredible to contemplate you as a sorority girl.

OATES

My experience in a sorority wasn't disastrous, but merely despairing. However, I did make some close friends in the sorority, so the experience wasn't a total loss. I would never do it again, certainly. In fact, it's one of the three or four things in my entire life I would never do again.

INTERVIEWER

Why was life in a Syracuse sorority so despairing? Have you written about it?

OATES

The racial and religious bigotry; the asininity of secret ceremonies; the moronic emphasis upon activities totally unrelated to—in fact antithetical to—intellectual exploration; the bullying of the presumably weak by the presumably strong; the deliberate pursuit of an attractive "image" for the group as a whole, no matter how cynical the individuals might have been; the aping of the worst American traits— boosterism, God-fearingism, smug ignorance, a craven worship of conformity; the sheer *mess* of the place once one got beyond the downstairs . . . I tried to escape in my junior year, but a connection between sororities and the dean of women and the university-housing office made escape all but impossible, and it seemed that, in my freshman naïveté, I had actually signed some sort of contract that had "legal" status . . . all of which quite cowed me. I remember a powdered and perfumed alum explaining the sorority's exclusion of Jews and blacks: You see, we have conferences at the Lake Placid Club, and wouldn't it be a shame if *all* our members couldn't attend . . . Why, it would be embarrassing for them, wouldn't it?

I was valedictorian of my class, the class of 1960. I fantasized beginning my address by saying, "I managed to do well academically at Syracuse despite the concerted efforts of my sorority to prevent me . . ."

I haven't written about it, and never will. It's simply too stupid and trivial a subject. To even *care* about such adolescent nonsense one would have to have the sensitivity of a John O'Hara, who seems to have taken it all seriously.

INTERVIEWER

I recall you won the poetry contest at Syracuse in your senior year. But your books of poetry appeared relatively later than your fiction. Were you always writing poetry?

OATES

No, I really began to write poetry later. The poetry still comes with difficulty, I must admit. Tiny lyric asides, droll wry enigmatic statements: They aren't easy, are they? I'm assembling a book which I think will be my last—of poems, I mean. No one wants to read a novelist's poetry. It's enough—too much, in fact—to deal with the novels. Strangely enough, my fellow poets have been magnanimous indeed in accepting me as a poet. I would not have been surprised had they ignored me, but, in fact, they've been wonderfully supportive and encouraging. Which contradicts the general notion that poets are highly competitive and jealous of one another's accomplishments . . .

INTERVIEWER

You say no one wants to read a novelist's poetry. What about Robert Penn Warren? John Updike? Erica Jong? I suppose Allen Tate and James Dickey are poets who happened to write novels. . . .

OATES

I suppose I was thinking only of hypothetical reactions to my own poetry. Robert Penn Warren aside, however, there *is* a tendency on the part of critics to want very much to categorize writers. Hence one is either a writer of prose or of poetry. If Lawrence hadn't written those novels he would have been far more readily acclaimed as one of the greatest poets in the language. As it is, however, his poetry has been neglected. (At least until recently.)

INTERVIEWER

By the North Gate, your first book, is a collection of short stories, and you continue to publish them. Is the short story your greatest love? Do you hold with the old adage that it is more difficult to write a good story than a novel?

OATES

Brief subjects require brief treatments. There is *nothing* so difficult as a novel, as anyone knows who has attempted one; a short story is bliss to write set beside a novel of even ordinary proportions.

But in recent years I haven't been writing much short fiction. I don't quite know why. All my energies seem to be drawn into longer works. It's probably the case that my period of greatest productivity is behind me, and I'm becoming more interested in focusing upon a single work, usually a novel, and trying to "perfect" it section by section and page by page.

INTERVIEWER

Nevertheless, you've published more short stories, perhaps, than any other serious writer in America today. I remember that when you chose the twenty-one stories to compose *The Wheel of Love*, you picked from some ninety that had been in magazines the two years since your previous collection. What will become of the seventy or so stories you didn't include in that collection? Were some added to later collections? Will you ever get back and pick up uncollected work?

OATES

If I'm serious about a story, I preserve it in book form; otherwise I intend it to be forgotten. This is true of course for poems and reviews and essays as well. I went back and selected a number of stories that for thematic reasons were not included in *The Wheel of Love*, and put them into a collection called *The Seduction and Other Stories*. Each of the story collections is organized around a central theme and is meant to be read as a whole—the arrangement of the stories being a rigorous one, not at all haphazard.

INTERVIEWER

You don't drink. Have you tried any consciousness-expanding drugs?

OATES

No. Even tea (because of caffeine) is too strong for me. I must have been born with a rather sensitive constitution.

INTERVIEWER

Earlier you mentioned Hugh Petrie in *The Assassins*. He is but one of many deranged characters in your books. Have you known any genuine madmen?

OATES

Unfortunately, I have been acquainted with a small number of persons who might be considered mentally disturbed. And others, strangers, are sometimes drawn my way; I don't know why.

Last week when I went to the university, I wasn't allowed to teach my large lecture class because, during the night, one of my graduate students had received a telephone call from a very angry, distraught man who announced that he intended to kill me. So I had to spend several hours sequestered away with the head of our department and the head of security at the university and two special investigators from the Windsor city police. The situation was more embarrassing than disturbing. It's the first time anyone has so explicitly and publicly threatened my life—there have been sly, indirect threats made in the past, which I've known enough not to take seriously.

(The man who called my student is a stranger to us all, not even a resident of Windsor. I have no idea why he's so angry with me. But does a disturbed person really need a reason . . . ?)

INTERVIEWER

How about the less threatening, but nonetheless hurtful, reactions of friends and relatives—any reactions to conscious or unconscious portraits in your work?

OATES

My parents (and I, as a child) appear very briefly in *Wonderland*, glimpsed by the harassed young hero on his way to, or from, Buffalo. Otherwise there are no portraits of family or relatives in my writing. My mother and father both respond (rather touchingly at times) to the setting of my stories and novels, which they recognize. But since there is nothing of a personal nature in the writing, I have not experienced any difficulties along those lines.

INTERVIEWER

Aside from the singular incident at the university, what are the disadvantages of being famous?

OATES

I'm not aware of being famous, especially here in Windsor, where the two major bookstores, Coles, don't even stock my books. The number of people who are "aware" of me, let alone who read my writing, is very small. Consequently I enjoy a certain degree of invisibility and anonymity at the university, which I might not have at an American university—which is one of the reasons I am so much at home here.

INTERVIEWER

Are you aware of any personal limitations?

OATES

Shyness has prevented me from doing many things; also the amount of work and responsibility here at Windsor.

INTERVIEWER

Do you feel you have any conspicuous or secret flaw as a writer?

OATES

My most conspicuous flaw is . . . well, it's so conspicuous that anyone could discern it. And my secret flaw is happily secret.

INTERVIEWER

What are the advantages of being a woman writer?

OATES

Advantages! Too many to enumerate, probably. Since, being a woman, I can't be taken altogether *seriously* by the sort of male critics who rank writers one, two, three in the public press, I am free, I suppose, to do as I like. I haven't much sense of, or interest in, competition; I can't even grasp what Hemingway and the epigonic Mailer mean by battling it out with the other talent in the ring. A work of art has never, to my knowledge, displaced another work of art. The living are no more in competition with the dead than they are with the living. . . . Being a woman allows me a certain invisibility. Like Ellison's *Invisible Man*. (My long journal, which must be several hundred pages by now, has the title *Invisible Woman*. Because a woman, being so mechanically judged by her appearance, has the advantage of hiding within it—of being absolutely whatever she knows herself to be, in contrast with what others imagine her to be. I feel no connection at all with my physical appearance and have often wondered whether this was a freedom any man—writer or not— might enjoy.)

INTERVIEWER

Do you find it difficult to write from the point of view of the male?

OATES

Absolutely not. I am as sympathetic with any of my male characters as I am with any of my female characters. In many respects I am
closest in temperament to certain of my male characters—Nathan
Vickery of *Son of the Morning*, for instance—and feel an absolute kinship with them. The Kingdom of God *is* within.

INTERVIEWER

Can you tell the sex of a writer from the prose?

OATES

Never.

INTERVIEWER

What male writers have been especially effective, do you think, in
their depiction of women?

OATES

Tolstoy, Lawrence, Shakespeare, Flaubert . . . Very few, really.
But then very few women have been effective in their depiction of
men.

INTERVIEWER

Do you enjoy writing?

OATES

I do enjoy writing, yes. A great deal. And I feel somewhat at a loss,
aimless and foolishly sentimental, and disconnected, when I've finished one work and haven't yet become absorbed in another. All of us
who write, work out of a conviction that we are participating in some
sort of communal activity. Whether my role is writing, or reading and
responding, might not be very important. I take seriously Flaubert's
statement that we must love one another in our art as the mystics love
one another in God. By honoring one another's creation we honor
something that deeply connects us all, and goes beyond us.

Of course, writing is only one activity out of a vast number of activities that constitute our lives. It seems to be the one that some of us have concentrated on, as if we were fated for it. Since I have a great deal of faith in the processes and the wisdom of the unconscious, and have learned from experience to take lightly the judgments of the ego and its inevitable doubts, I never find myself constrained to answer such questions. Life is energy, and energy is creativity. And even when we as individuals pass on, the energy is retained in the work of art, locked in it and awaiting release if only someone will take the time and the care to unlock it.

Issue 74, 1978

Jean Rhys

The Art of Fiction

Jean Rhys was born in Dominica, in the Windward Islands, in 1894, of a Welsh doctor and a native-born Creole. She was sixteen when she was sent to school in England. Her first stories, collected in *The Left Bank*, were published in 1927. Four novels in the twelve years before World War II—*Quartet* (1929); *After Leaving Mr. Mackenzie* (1931); *Voyage in the Dark* (1934); and *Good Morning, Midnight* (1939)—established a fragile literary reputation, which eroded when she dropped out of the publishing world for thirty years only to emerge from her retreat in the west of England when the BBC did a radio adaptation of her novel, *Good Morning, Midnight*. The obscurity had been such that in October, 1956, the *New Statesman* carried an advertisement to find her: "Would Jean Rhys or anyone who knows her whereabouts please get in touch with Sasha Moorsom, Features Department, BBC, in connection with future Third Programme broadcast of *Good Morning, Midnight*." The renaissance of Jean Rhys brought with it the publication of two collections of short stories, *Tigers Are Better Looking* (1968) and *Sleep It Off, Lady* (1976), and her most famous novel, *Wide Sargasso Sea* (1966), an invented biography of Bertha, the mad wife in Charlotte Brontë's *Jane Eyre*.

She has been married three times—first, after World War I, to a Dutch *chansonnier* who wrote songs and sang them in such Paris spots as Le Lapin Agile. He deserted her after ten years of traveling about Europe, mostly to Vienna and Paris, and she divorced him.

if everything is in me. good evil &
so on so must strength be in me
if I know how to get at it.

This is the way?
I think so.
All right but be damned careful
not to leave this books about.

In this place the ropemaker
arms I have a small living room
The feeling is peaceful in the room
nothing is unpleasant except
the black elephants on the
mantelpiece. three big ones two
small. They are not unpleasant
either. They are bearable but very black

There is a table in the middle with
a white cloth on it. a square table.
three chairs stand round it. There
is a deep comfortable armchair.

A manuscript page from *Smile Please*, an unfinished autobiography
by Jean Rhys.

Her second husband, an editor at the publishing firm of Hamish Hamilton, died at the end of the last war. Her third husband, a retired naval officer, died just after the couple moved to the small cottage in Devon where she now lives.

The chief character in almost all her work is a woman who seems to follow in her creator's path step by step: from a West Indian childhood, through the ordeal of life in the provincial theater in pre–World War I England, to an elderly solitude in the English countryside.

Miss Rhys's eyes are sapphire, wide set, and long lashed against a pale English skin; one cannot help thinking that had she stayed in Dominica she would not have that skin, even with the daily hour-and-a-half attention she says she gives to her face and makeup. She was wearing a white silk blouse hidden by an opalescent pink lamé jacket, made to seem somewhat coquettish with ribbons and puffed sleeves.

On the table stood a vase of huge yellow purple-hued cabbage roses, so voluptuous that they looked artificial, as if made of silk for an Edwardian hat.

Outside, the sun sparkled on the giant hedgerows that seclude Jean Rhys's cottage from a quiet Devon village. Here, she has continued at her writer's work, insisting on privacy that secluded her even from her fellow villagers.

—Elizabeth Vreeland, 1979

JEAN RHYS

We moved here because I wanted a place of my own. We bought it—my late husband and I—sight unseen because anything was better than rooms. That's all we'd been in. A room is, after all, a place where you hide from the wolves. That's all any room is. It was difficult here at first. The gales came through the crevices. The mice were everywhere. A frog in the bathroom. Then when I first came here I was accused of being a witch. A neighbor told the whole village that I practiced black magic. I got very cross, but gradually it all died down.

INTERVIEWER

What a shock it must have been when you first arrived from the West Indies.

RHYS

Of course, I hated the cold. England was terribly cold when I first came there. There was no central heating. There were fires, but they were always blocked by people trying to get warm. And I'd never get into the sacred circle. I was always outside, shivering. They had told me when I left Dominica that I would not feel the cold for the first year— that my blood would still be warm from the tropic sun. Quite wrong!

INTERVIEWER

Where did you go to school?

RHYS

It was at Cambridge—the town, not the university. The east wind comes right across from . . . Russia, I suppose. I used to lie in bed and shiver and shiver, wondering why I'd ever dream of wanting to see daffodils and snowflakes. Then the maid would bring me this hot water bottle. It was very sweet of her. Oh, I found England bitterly cold.

INTERVIEWER

And the people?

RHYS

I didn't find them terribly warm. I was so unhappy in England. I was delighted to get away.

INTERVIEWER

Where did you go after Cambridge?

RHYS

I left school early because I wanted to become an actress. While I was studying at the Royal Academy of Dramatic Arts in London, my father died in the West Indies. My mother wrote me that she couldn't afford to keep me at school. But I didn't want to go back to Dominica. I knew I'd miss my father too much. So I joined the chorus of a show on tour around England.

INTERVIEWER

How did your family in Dominica react?

RHYS

There wasn't much they could do about it. Anyway, I believe in fate.

INTERVIEWER

But you could have gone back. You did have the choice.

RHYS

I suppose so. But I wanted to be an actress. I was a very bad actress, but that's what I wanted to be. I do believe that life's all laid out for one. One's choices don't matter much. It is really a matter of being adapted. If you can adapt, you're all right. But it's not always easy if you're born not adapted, a bit of a rebel; then it's difficult to force yourself to adapt. One is born either to go with or to go against.

INTERVIEWER

In your first written, but not your first published, novel, *Voyage in the Dark*, the heroine is also born in the Antilles. She becomes a chorus girl who travels about the dreary towns of the English provinces, is deflowered by a rich Englishman who cares for her, who then abandons her. Did you write it as a form of purgation?

RHYS

I wrote it because it relieved me. I never wrote for money at the start. I wrote the makings of *Voyage in the Dark* long, long ago. I wrote it in several exercise books and then I put it away for years. Someone described the result as "unpublishably sordid but with great sensitiveness and persuasiveness"—so I went on to other things. Then, twenty years later, fate had it that I tackle it again. I hadn't really written a book; it was more or less a jumble of facts. From the notes I'd done ages before I managed to put together *Voyage in the Dark*.

INTERVIEWER

And is it still your favorite?

RHYS

I suppose so. Because it came easiest.

INTERVIEWER

The contrast of the sunny Caribbean landscape with the bleak English one is very moving in *Voyage in the Dark*. Mango trees, hammocks, mauve shadows, purple sea, and the fight not to have a dark patch under your arms while putting on your gloves . . . the business of being a lady. One gets brilliant flashes of what it must have been like.

RHYS

It's all a bit romanticized. Now I'm trying to do it again as it really was. For my memoirs. I hope I've succeeded. It may be a bit dull, perhaps.

INTERVIEWER

But the colors weren't romanticized, and the smells . . .

RHYS

No, it's a very beautiful place, Dominica, and that wasn't romanticized. The mountains are lovely; but it hasn't got any nice beaches, none of those lovely white beaches the tourists love. It's a volcanic island . . . the beaches are black.

INTERVIEWER

What did you do all those years when you weren't writing?

RHYS

When I was excited about life, I didn't want to write at all. I've never written when I was happy. I didn't want to. But I've never had a long period of being happy. Do you think anyone has? I think you can be peaceful for a long time. When I think about it, if I had to choose, I'd rather be happy than write. You see, there's very little invention in my books. What came first with most of them was the wish to get rid of this awful sadness that weighed me down. I found when I was a child that if I could put the hurt into words, it would go. It leaves a sort of melancholy behind and then it goes. I think it was Somerset Maugham who said that if you "write out" a thing . . . it doesn't trouble you so much. You may be left with a vague melancholy, but at least it's not misery—I suppose it's like a Catholic going to confession, or like psychoanalysis.

INTERVIEWER

Did you keep a journal?

RHYS

Not exactly. I wrote things down. Not each day. More in spurts. I would write to forget, to get rid of sad moments. Once they were written down, they were gone.

INTERVIEWER

Is it always a sadness for you to write?

RHYS

No. Writing can also be very exciting. If you're really in the mood to write, you write without apparently wanting to. But it doesn't always happen that way. It's a struggle, and it's very tiring.

INTERVIEWER

What is the story of the publication of *The Left Bank*?

RHYS

It's an odd story. My first husband was a poet, half-French, half-Dutch. He had been on the Disarmament Commission in Vienna after the First World War. There were two Japanese officers in the Allied Commission. But one was supposed to speak French and couldn't, and the other was supposed to speak English and couldn't. So they both got secretaries who were in fact interpreters and translators, and that was the job my husband got, to the one who was supposed to speak English, Mr. Miyaki. Someone in his office became interested in my writing and showed my stories to Ford Madox Ford. Ford cared terribly about writers. If he thought anyone had any good in him at all, he'd go to any lengths to help, pulling every string he could to help. He did that for any amount of people. He really got D. H. Lawrence started, and a lot of the writers who are not so well known.

INTERVIEWER

In his introduction to *The Left Bank*, Ford praised your "singular instinct for form," which he says is "possessed by singularly few English writers and almost no English women writers."

RHYS

The things you remember have no form. When you write about them, you have to give them a beginning, a middle, and an end. To give life shape—that is what a writer does. That is what is so difficult.

INTERVIEWER

Were there others beside Ford who helped you as you started to write?

RHYS

The whole atmosphere of Paris helped, and I learned to read French pretty well. All that no doubt had an influence on me. But Ford helped me more than anybody else: Do this! Don't do that! He insisted on my reading French books and I think they helped me a lot. They had clarity. Ford always said that if you weren't sure of a passage, to translate it into another language. If it looked utterly silly, one got rid of it. English can be so imprecise. Ford published several of my stories in the *Transatlantic Review*, and he helped me with money. He really helped. It was he who found the publisher for *The Left Bank*: After that there was a quarrel and I never saw him again. He went to America to live.

INTERVIEWER

Hemingway takes a lot of swipes at him in *A Moveable Feast*.

RHYS

I think it's a spiteful book. He bullies everybody. Ford wasn't at all the way Hemingway described him.

INTERVIEWER

Then he wasn't pretentious and snobbish and evil-smelling?

RHYS

Not at all. And back then Hemingway wasn't catty. He always seemed to me as if he were enjoying himself terribly. He was a very nice-looking young man. But in that book, he was disparaging about everybody—Fitzgerald, Gertrude Stein, everybody. I didn't like it at all.

INTERVIEWER

An actress recently asked to play Marya in a film version of *Quartet* hesitated because she said she found it dated—dated in that today Marya would have some other option than having to live *à trois* with the Heidlers. She could take a job. . . .

RHYS

In those days, if you were English, or supposed to be English, and you were in Paris and didn't know French well, it was pretty well impossible. I mean what job could you get? One of the things the Heidlers tell Marya when she goes there is that they'll find her a job. "Come stay with us for a little bit. Sooner or later we'll pull a string and find you a job." That was how they convinced her. In England you could get some sort of job, but in Paris it wasn't so easy. You might get a job as a mannequin, or in a shop, but then you wouldn't know the prices, or anything. Of course, it did all happen in the twenties.

INTERVIEWER

It happens today. Three people in a trap.

RHYS

Yes, much the same sort of thing, perhaps, slightly changed. I think that, as usual, people will do what they have to do. That's where fate comes in.

INTERVIEWER

Why did you leave Paris finally and settle back in England?

RHYS

I was told, You must go to London to sell *Quartet*. I didn't want to particularly, but everyone said I must; so in the end I did. I went right to London, then back to Paris for a short time to write *After Leaving Mr. Mackenzie*, and then I came back to England, remarried, and stayed.

INTERVIEWER

In *After Leaving Mr. Mackenzie*, Julia Martin finds herself alone and broke in Paris in such an apathy that she can only lie in bed, allowing her decisions to be made by chance: "If a taxi hoots before I count to three, I'll go to London. If not, I won't."

RHYS

Don't you think that by the time she arrived at that stage, she was rather tired? I mean you can get very tired. And then it is rather a temptation to just lie down and see what happens.

INTERVIEWER

And pull the covers over your head.

RHYS

That's right. I did that as a child. I was so afraid of cockroaches and centipedes and spiders.

INTERVIEWER

They're so large in the Indies.

RHYS

But that was nothing like my fear of *obeah*. That's West Indian black magic. I remember we had this *obeah* woman as a cook once. She was rather a gaudy kind of woman, very tall and thin and always wore a red handkerchief on her wrist. She once told my fortune and a lot of it has come true. My life was peopled with fears. I think that's one of the reasons I don't go back. Maybe my big reason.

INTERVIEWER

But you wrote a wonderful story about going back to your convent school there after twenty-five years.

RHYS

I did go back once. For a very short time. But all my nuns had gone. Everything's very changed. I'm trying to do an autobiography now and I find it very difficult to remember when I was a child in the West Indies.

INTERVIEWER

You wrote that you have such a great memory, that you can shut your eyes and remember conversations . . .

RHYS

That's what I've tried to do, but it's a very long time ago now.

INTERVIEWER

You write in *Quartet* that when you tell lies people think it's a cri de coeur, and then when you tell the truth, nobody believes you.

RHYS

That's always so. I've noticed that. They believe the lies far more than they believe the truth.

INTERVIEWER

Then you really haven't a problem of veracity with your childhood in the book.

RHYS

If I had a problem I doubt that anybody would contradict me. I don't think anybody's alive to contradict me. I try to be more or less truthful, though I suppose the whole thing's a bit romanticized.

INTERVIEWER

You wrote in *Voyage in the Dark* that the fantastic is what you don't do, and the real is what you do.

RHYS

I suppose the fantastic is what you imagine, but as soon as you do a fantastic thing, it's no longer fantastic, it becomes real.

INTERVIEWER

And the difference between romance and reality?

RHYS

Reality is what I remember. You can push onto reality what you feel. Just as I felt that I disliked England so much. It was my feeling that made me dislike it. Now I make a lot of the nice part of the Indies, and I've sort of more or less forgotten the other part, like going to the dentist who only came to the island every now and again. I'm trying to write the beauty of it and how I saw it. And how I did see it as a child. That's what I've been toiling at. It's such a battle. I can't waste much more time on it.

INTERVIEWER

Have you written of your relations with the black people in Dominica?

RHYS

That's very complicated because at the start I hated my nurse. A horrid woman. It was she who told me awful stories of zombies and *sucriants*, the vampires; she frightened me totally. I was a bit wary of the black people. I've tried to write about how I gradually became even a bit envious. They were so strong. They could walk great distances, it seemed to me, without getting tired, and carry those heavy loads on their heads. They went to the dances every night. They wore turbans. They had lovely dresses with a belt to tuck the trains through that were lined with paper and rustled when they moved. Then, my chief worry was that I was expected to get married. I thought, My God, what will I do? At first I doubted that I'd ever get a proposal. Then I knew I was *bound* to marry, otherwise I'd be an old maid which would be perfectly awful. That worry made one very self-conscious. But the black people didn't worry a hoot about that. They had swarms of children and no marriages. I did envy them that.

INTERVIEWER

Did you have young friends who were black?

RHYS

No, it was more divided then. There were a lot of colored girls at the convent I went to. I didn't always like them—but I was kind of used to them.

INTERVIEWER

Was the incident real in *Wide Sargasso Sea* when you go swimming in a pool in the woods with the black girl, Tia?

RHYS

That might have happened. But the girl never stole my dress as we bathed. That was fiction.

INTERVIEWER

Although you are one of five children, one gets the feeling you had a lonely childhood.

RHYS

Yes, I never saw much of them. They left early and came to England. One brother went to India and spent his life there. I didn't see him at all. The other wandered about rather. He went to Canada and Australia and East Africa, then he went back to the West Indies. In Australia he got married, came to London, fell down the stairs, and died. I don't think he was drunk or anything. My other brother said, Just like Orin, he would die in a melodramatic way.

INTERVIEWER

You say your motto is "not harrowing." What does this phrase mean for you?

RHYS

Don't surprise or amaze or make me angry, or make me sorry about something. Lots of words that used to be quite common one doesn't hear any more. It's sad about words that meant quite a lot. I mean a word like *splendid*. Nobody says a thing is *splendid*. You never say a thing is splendid, or a person is splendid. Do you? Splendor's gone. Magnificent is gone.

INTERVIEWER

How do you work now?

RHYS

I can't write anymore. My hand is unsteady, so I have a very nice girl who comes along twice a week, sometimes three times, and I dictate to her. It was difficult at the start.

INTERVIEWER

Do you ever try dictating into a tape recorder?

RHYS

No, because mechanical things always go wrong with me. If they possibly can, they do. If there is a thought or an idea that has been worrying me, I try to write it out, and try very hard to make it clear.

Then when she comes I can dictate it to her. Of course it's by no means the same thing as writing.

INTERVIEWER

Is it an all-consuming occupation when you feel you must write?

RHYS

It seems as if I was fated to write . . . which is horrible. But I can only do one thing. I'm rather useless, but perhaps not as useless as everyone thinks. I tried to be an actress—a chorus girl—and the whole thing ended when I was handed a line to say: "Oh Lottie, don't be epigrammatic." When the cue came, the words just disappeared. That was that. I was interested in beauty—cosmetics—but when I tried to make a face cream, it blew up.

INTERVIEWER

Someone wrote that you have been fighting oblivion since the twenties—do you think this true?

RHYS

I'm not fighting oblivion now. I'm fighting . . . eternity? I feel very isolated. I'm not sure men need women, but I'm sure that women need men. But then loneliness is a part of writing, isn't it? Though week after week, if you never see anyone, it can become rather trying. If there's a knock at the door, I expect some wonderful stranger. I fly to the door. But it's only the postman. I've got myself a bit depressed over this autobiography. When I began it I wrote a lot about the years after I came to England and I was more or less grown up, and of being in France, and lot of that. And then I got this idea that I wanted to write about the West Indies as they were, as I remembered them. And I find it very difficult; also I feel that nobody's going to believe me.

INTERVIEWER

Has anyone seen it?

RHYS

My editor's seen a sort of rough copy of it and she likes it, but it wasn't right. And I haven't got it quite right yet. Another worry is that I can't seem to find a title.

INTERVIEWER

Did you always have a title before you started a book?

RHYS

I've always known it before, but this time I can't. I've got a title, but the publisher's not pleased with it. They want to call it "Smile Please," but I want to call it "And the Walls Came Tumbling Down." That's what I feel is happening. Of course, I don't know. I only know what I read in the papers.

INTERVIEWER

You write in *After Leaving Mr. Mackenzie* that it is always places you recall in your memory, not people. Is that still the case?

RHYS

That was a character in the book who says that. I remember some places very well, but I think I remember people better.

INTERVIEWER

Was Paris your favorite place to be?

RHYS

In the twenties Paris was a very interesting place. Of course, I was delighted to get away from England. I like Paris. I made friends. Whenever I had some money, I'd shoot back to Paris. Paris sort of lifted you up. It's pink, you know, not blue or yellow; there's nothing like it anywhere else.

INTERVIEWER

You went back after you wrote *Good Morning, Midnight*.

RHYS

Oh yes, I went back in 1939, just before the war. The publisher was awfully pleased with the book. He rang me up to tell me how pleased he was, and I was very hopeful. But then war was declared, almost immediately, and they didn't want books. . . . I was forgotten and I gave up writing.

INTERVIEWER

Absolutely?

RHYS

I didn't write for a long time. And then I wrote some short stories. And then there was this thing about doing *Good Morning, Midnight* on the BBC radio. And then I started *Wide Sargasso Sea*.

INTERVIEWER

Where did the idea come from of reconstructing Bertha's life—the *Jane Eyre* heiress who sets fire to the house and jumps from the parapet?

RHYS

When I read *Jane Eyre* as a child, I thought, why should she think Creole women are lunatics and all that? What a shame to make Rochester's first wife, Bertha, the awful madwoman, and I immediately thought I'd write the story as it might really have been. She seemed such a poor ghost. I thought I'd try to write her a life. Charlotte Brontë must have had strong feelings about the West Indies because she brings the West Indies into a lot of her books, like *Villette*. Of course, once upon a time, the West Indies were very rich, and very much more talked about than they are now.

INTERVIEWER

How about films of your books?

RHYS

Films are always going to happen but then they never do. They had an option on *Wide Sargasso Sea*. They even went out to the West Indies to see where they were going to shoot it and even picked the house. Now I'm very skeptical. The director and the scriptwriter went out, that was several years ago . . . They made all sorts of arrangements, but some backer pulled away. They seem to think it would be a very expensive film. I really don't see why.

INTERVIEWER

Whenever you have costumes or houses that burn up, it's expensive, and you have *two* houses that burn up.

RHYS

But extras are very cheap. I suppose they have to take photographers, cameras, people . . . costs rather a lot, but I don't see that it would be too much more expensive than any other.

INTERVIEWER

Have you any desire to go to Paris?

RHYS

I'll never go back now. I went back to the West Indies and I hated it. No, I think "never go back" is a good motto.

INTERVIEWER

There's a title for your book. "Never go back."

RHYS

But that's just what I'm doing. I *am* going back.

INTERVIEWER

What are you reading now?

RHYS

I'm reading a book of Daphne du Maurier. She's a good writer; I like the man who wrote *From Russia with Love* . . . Ian Fleming. He's one who can take you away from everything if you're bored and sad. Some books can really take you away. It's marvelous. Thrillers are my great thing now. I must say Americans dream up such awful horrors. But I'd like to get away myself. I'm always thinking of some place to run away to, like the desert, or Morocco. But I haven't got a car; so I can't drive. It means I'm always stuck here. But you know, one gets into a groove.

INTERVIEWER

But why not go to Morocco this winter?

RHYS

Do the women still wear veils there?

INTERVIEWER

Yes, many still do.

RHYS

They aren't very kind to women in Morocco, or perhaps that is exaggerated. One thinks of it as being exaggerated.

INTERVIEWER

Au fond, I think women really run things there, though it would not seem as if they do.

RHYS

They are just as smart in France. It really doesn't look as if they are running things. But they often have control of the money. Not always, but often.

INTERVIEWER

You once wrote in *The Lotus* that people live much longer than they should, especially women.

RHYS

I'd planned to die at thirty, and then I'd push it on ten years, forty, and then fifty. You always push it on. And then you go on and on and on. It's difficult. Too much trouble. I've thought about death a great deal. One day in the snow I felt so tired. I thought, Damn it, I'll sit down. I can't go on. I'm tired of living here in the snow and ice. So I sat down on the ground. But it was so cold I got up. Oh yes, I used to try to imagine death, but I always come up against a wall.

INTERVIEWER

And the book, that's the reason to go on now, no?

RHYS

But you know I'm beginning to feel that I don't want to do a mental striptease any more. Which would mean tearing up all I've written. I don't mind writing about when I was a child, but I don't quite know why I should go on writing so much about myself. I've had rather a rum life, but I was thinking the other day, would I go through it all again. I think not. I guess I write about myself because that's all I really know.

Issue 76, 1979

Raymond Carver

The Art of Fiction

Raymond Carver lives in a large, two-story, wood-shingled house on a quiet street in Syracuse, New York. The front lawn slopes down to the sidewalk. A new Mercedes sits in the driveway. An older VW, the other household car, gets parked on the street.

The entrance to the house is through a large, screened-in porch. Inside, the furnishings are almost without character. Everything matches—cream-colored couches, a glass coffee table. Tess Gallagher, the writer with whom Raymond Carver lives, collects peacock feathers and sets them in vases throughout the house—the most noticeable decorative attempt. Our suspicions were confirmed; Carver told us that all the furniture was purchased and delivered in one day.

Gallagher has painted a detachable wood NO VISITORS sign, the lettering surrounded by yellow and orange eyelashes, which hangs on the screen door. Sometimes the phone is unplugged and the sign stays up for days at a time.

Carver works in a large room on the top floor. The surface of the long oak desk is clear; his typewriter is set to the side, on an L-shaped wing. There are no knicknacks, charms, or toys of any kind on Carver's desk. He is not a collector or a man prone to mementos and nostalgia. Occasionally, one manila folder lies on the oak desk, containing the story currently in the process of revision. His files are well in order. He can extract a story and all its previous versions at a moment's notice. The walls of the study are painted white like the rest of the house, and, like the rest of the house, they are mostly bare.

Four drafts of the opening page of Raymond Carver's "The Bridle."

Through a high rectangular window above Carver's desk, light filters into the room in slanted beams, like light from high church windows.

Carver is a large man who wears simple clothes—flannel shirts, khakis or jeans. He seems to live and dress as the characters in his stories live and dress. For someone of his size, he has a remarkably low and indistinct voice; we found ourselves bending closer every few minutes to catch his words and asking the irritating "What, what?"

Portions of the interview were conducted through the mail, during 1981–1982. When we met Carver, the NO VISITORS sign was not up and several Syracuse students dropped by to visit during the course of the interview, including Carver's son, a senior. For lunch, Carver made us sandwiches with salmon he had caught off the coast of Washington. Both he and Gallagher are from Washington State and at the time of the interview, they were having a house built in Port Angeles, where they plan to live part of each year. We asked Carver if that house would feel more like a home to him. He replied, "No, wherever I am is fine. This is fine."

—Mona Simpson, Lewis Buzbee, 1983

INTERVIEWER

What was your early life like, and what made you want to write?

RAYMOND CARVER

I grew up in a small town in eastern Washington, a place called Yakima. My dad worked at the sawmill there. He was a saw filer and helped take care of the saws that were used to cut and plane the logs. My mother worked as a retail clerk or a waitress or else stayed at home, but she didn't keep any job for very long. I remember talk concerning her "nerves." In the cabinet under the kitchen sink, she kept a bottle of patent "nerve medicine," and she'd take a couple of tablespoons of this every morning. My dad's nerve medicine was whiskey. Most often he kept a bottle of it under that same sink, or else outside in the woodshed. I remember sneaking a taste of it once and hating it, and wondering how anybody could drink the stuff. Home was a little two-bedroom house. We moved a lot when I was a kid, but it was always into another little two-bedroom house. The first house I can remember living in, near the fairgrounds in Yakima, had an outdoor toilet. This was in the late 1940s. I was eight or ten years old then. I used to wait at the bus stop for my dad to come home from work. Usually he was as regular as clockwork. But every two weeks or so, he wouldn't be on the bus. I'd stick around then and wait for the next bus, but I already knew he wasn't going to be on that one, either. When this happened, it meant he'd gone drinking with friends of his from the sawmill. I still remember the sense of doom and hopelessness that hung over the supper table when my mother and I and my kid brother sat down to eat.

INTERVIEWER

But what made you want to write?

CARVER

The only explanation I can give you is that my dad told me lots of stories about himself when he was a kid, and about his dad and his grandfather. His grandfather had fought in the Civil War. He fought for both sides! He was a turncoat. When the South began losing the war, he crossed over to the North and began fighting for the Union forces. My dad laughed when he told this story. He didn't see anything wrong with it, and I guess I didn't either. Anyway, my dad would tell me stories, anecdotes really, no moral to them, about tramping around in the woods, or else riding the rails and having to look out for railroad bulls. I loved his company and loved to listen to him tell me these stories. Once in a while he'd read something to me from what he was reading. Zane Grey westerns. These were the first real hardback books, outside of grade-school texts, and the Bible, that I'd ever seen. It wouldn't happen very often, but now and again I'd see him lying on the bed of an evening and reading from Zane Grey. It seemed a very private act in a house and family that were not given to privacy. I realized that he had this private side to him, something I didn't understand or know anything about, but something that found expression through this occasional reading. I was interested in that side of him and interested in the act itself. I'd ask him to read me what he was reading, and he'd oblige by just reading from wherever he happened to be in the book. After a while he'd say, "Junior, go do something else now." Well, there were plenty of things to do. In those days, I went fishing in this creek that was not too far from our house. A little later, I started hunting ducks and geese and upland game. That's what excited me in those days, hunting and fishing. That's what made a dent in my emotional life, and that's what I wanted to write about. My reading fare in those days, aside from an occasional historical novel or Mickey Spillane mystery, consisted of *Sports Afield* and *Outdoor Life* and *Field & Stream*. I wrote a longish thing about the fish that got away, or the fish I caught, one or the other, and asked my mother if she would type it up for me. She couldn't type, but she did go rent a typewriter, bless her heart, and between the two of us, we typed it up in some terrible fashion and sent it out. I remember there were two addresses on the masthead of the outdoors magazine; so we sent it to the office closest to us, to Boulder, Colorado, the circulation department. The piece came back, finally, but that was fine. It had gone out in the world, that manuscript—it had been places. Somebody had read it besides my mother, or so I hoped anyway. Then I saw an ad in *Writer's Digest*. It was a photograph of a man, a successful author, obviously, testifying to something called the Palmer Institute of Authorship. That seemed like just the thing for me. There was a monthly payment plan involved. Twenty dollars down, ten or fifteen dollars a month for three years or thirty years, one of those things. There were weekly assignments with personal responses to the assignments. I stayed with it for a few months. Then, maybe I got bored; I stopped doing the work. My folks stopped making the payments. Pretty soon a letter arrived from the Palmer Institute telling me that if I paid them up in full, I could still get the certificate of completion. This seemed more than fair. Somehow I talked my folks into paying the rest of the money, and in due time I got the certificate and hung it up on my bedroom wall. But all through high school it was assumed that I'd graduate and go to work at the sawmill. For a long time I wanted to do the kind of work my dad did. He was going to ask his foreman at the mill to put me on after I graduated. So I worked at the mill for about six months. But I hated the work and knew from the first day I didn't want to do that for the rest of my life. I worked long enough to save the money for a car, buy some clothes, and so I could move out and get married.

INTERVIEWER

Somehow, for whatever reasons, you went to college. Was it your wife who wanted you to go on to college? Did she encourage you in this respect? Did she want to go to college and that made you want to go? How old were you at this point? She must have been pretty young, too.

CARVER

I was eighteen. She was sixteen and pregnant and had just graduated from an Episcopalian private school for girls in Walla Walla, Washington. At school she'd learned the right way to hold a teacup; she'd had religious instruction and gym and such, but she also learned about physics and literature and foreign languages. I was terrifically impressed that she knew Latin. Latin! She tried off and on to go to college during those first years, but it was too hard to do that; it was impossible to do that and raise a family and be broke all the time, too. I mean broke. Her family didn't have any money. She was going to that school on a scholarship. Her mother hated me and still does. My wife was supposed to graduate and go on to the University of Washington to study law on a fellowship. Instead, I made her pregnant, and we got married and began our life together. She was seventeen when the first child was born, eighteen when the second was born. What shall I say at this point? We didn't have any youth. We found ourselves in roles we didn't know how to play. But we did the best we could. Better than that, I want to think. She did finish college finally. She got her B.A. degree at San Jose State twelve or fourteen years after we married.

INTERVIEWER

Were you writing during these early, difficult years?

CARVER

I worked nights and went to school days. We were always working. She was working and trying to raise the kids and manage a household. She worked for the telephone company. The kids were with a babysitter during the day. Finally, I graduated with the B.A. degree from Humboldt State College and we put everything into the car and in one of those carryalls that fits on top of your car, and we went to Iowa City. A teacher named Dick Day at Humboldt State had told me about the Iowa Writers' Workshop. Day had sent along a story of mine and three or four poems to Don Justice, who was responsible for getting me a five-hundred-dollar grant at Iowa.

Five hundred dollars?

That's all they had, they said. It seemed like a lot at the time. But I didn't finish at Iowa. They offered me more money to stay on the second year, but we just couldn't do it. I was working in the library for a dollar or two an hour, and my wife was working as a waitress. It was going to take me another year to get a degree, and we just couldn't stick it out. So we moved back to California. This time it was Sacramento. I found work as a night janitor at Mercy Hospital. I kept the job for three years. It was a pretty good job. I only had to work two or three hours a night, but I was paid for eight hours. There was a certain amount of work that had to get done, but once it was done, that was it—I could go home or do anything I wanted. The first year or two I went home every night and would be in bed at a reasonable hour and be able to get up in the morning and write. The kids would be off at the babysitter's and my wife would have gone to her job—a door-to-door sales job. I'd have all day in front of me. This was fine for a while. Then I began getting off work at night and going drinking instead of going home. By this time it was 1967 or 1968.

When did you first get published?

When I was an undergraduate at Humboldt State in Arcata, California. One day, I had a short story taken at one magazine and a poem taken at another. It was a terrific day! Maybe one of the best days ever. My wife and I drove around town and showed the letters of acceptance to all of our friends. It gave some much needed validation to our lives.

INTERVIEWER

What was the first story you ever published? And the first poem?

CARVER

It was a story called "Pastoral" and it was published in the *Western Humanities Review*. It's a good literary magazine and it's still being published by the University of Utah. They didn't pay me anything for the story, but that didn't matter. The poem was called "The Brass Ring," and it was published by a magazine in Arizona, now defunct, called *Targets*. Charles Bukowski had a poem in the same issue, and I was pleased to be in the same magazine with him. He was a kind of hero to me then.

INTERVIEWER

Is it true—a friend of yours told me this—that you celebrated your first publication by taking the magazine to bed with you?

CARVER

That's partly true. Actually, it was a book, the Best American Short Stories annual. My story "Will You Please Be Quiet, Please?" had just appeared in the collection. That was back in the late sixties, when it was edited every year by Martha Foley and people used to call it that—simply, "The Foley Collection." The story had been published in an obscure little magazine out of Chicago called *December*. The day the anthology came in the mail I took it to bed to read and just to look at, you know, and hold it, but I did more looking and holding than actual reading. I fell asleep and woke up the next morning with the book there in bed beside me, along with my wife.

INTERVIEWER

In an article you did for *The New York Times Book Review* you mentioned a story "too tedious to talk about here"—about why you choose to write short stories over novels. Do you want to go into that story now?

CARVER

The story that was "too tedious to talk about" has to do with a number of things that aren't very pleasant to talk about. I did finally talk about some of these things in the essay "Fires," which was published in *Antaeus*. In it I said that a writer is judged by what he writes, and that's the way it should be. The circumstances surrounding the writing are something else, something extraliterary. Nobody ever asked me to be a writer. But it *was* tough to stay alive and pay bills and put food on the table and at the same time to think of myself as a writer and to *learn* to write. After years of working crap jobs and raising kids and trying to write, I realized I needed to write things I could finish and be done with in a hurry. There was no way I could undertake a novel, a two- or three-year stretch of work on a single project. I needed to write something I could get some kind of a pay-off from immediately, not next year, or three years from now. Hence, poems and stories. I was beginning to see that my life was not—let's say it was not what I wanted it to be. There was always a wagonload of frustration to deal with—wanting to write and not being able to find the time or the place for it. I used to go out and sit in the car and try to write something on a pad on my knee. This was when the kids were in their adolescence. I was in my late twenties or early thirties. We were still in a state of penury, we had one bankruptcy behind us, and years of hard work with nothing to show for it except an old car, a rented house, and new creditors on our backs. It was depressing, and I felt spiritually obliterated. Alcohol became a problem. I more or less gave up, threw in the towel, and took to full-time drinking as a serious pursuit. That's part of what I was talking about when I was talking about things "too tedious to talk about."

INTERVIEWER

Could you talk a little more about the drinking? So many writers, even if they're not alcoholics, drink so much.

CARVER

Probably not a whole lot more than any other group of profession-als. You'd be surprised. Of course there's a mythology that goes along with the drinking, but I was never into that. I was into the drink-ing itself. I suppose I began to drink heavily after I'd realized that the things I'd wanted most in life for myself and my writing, and my wife and children, were simply not going to happen. It's strange. You never start out in life with the intention of becoming a bankrupt or an alcoholic or a cheat and a thief. Or a liar.

INTERVIEWER

And you were all those things?

CARVER

I was. I'm not any longer. Oh, I lie a little from time to time, like everyone else.

INTERVIEWER

How long since you quit drinking?

CARVER

June 2, 1977. If you want the truth, I'm prouder of that, that I've quit drinking, than I am of anything in my life. I'm a recovered alco-holic. I'll always be an alcoholic, but I'm no longer a practicing alco-holic.

INTERVIEWER

How bad did the drinking get?

CARVER

It's very painful to think about some of the things that happened back then. I made a wasteland out of everything I touched. But I might add that toward the end of the drinking there wasn't much left anyway. But specific things? Let's just say, on occasion, the police were involved and emergency rooms and courtrooms.

INTERVIEWER

How did you stop? What made you able to stop?

CARVER

The last year of my drinking, 1977, I was in a recovery center twice, as well as one hospital; and I spent a few days in a place called DeWitt, near San Jose, California. DeWitt used to be, appropriately enough, a hospital for the criminally insane. Toward the end of my drinking career I was completely out of control and in a very grave place. Blackouts, the whole business—points where you can't remember anything you say or do during a certain period of time. You might drive a car, give a reading, teach a class, set a broken leg, go to bed with someone, and not have any memory of it later. You're on some kind of automatic pilot. I have an image of myself sitting in my living room with a glass of whiskey in my hand and my head bandaged from a fall caused by an alcoholic seizure. Crazy! Two weeks later I was back in a recovery center, this time at a place called Duffy's, in Calistoga, California, up in the wine country. I was at Duffy's on two different occasions; in the place called DeWitt, in San Jose; and in a hospital in San Francisco—all in the space of twelve months. I guess that's pretty bad. I was dying from it, plain and simple, and I'm not exaggerating.

INTERVIEWER

What brought you to the point where you could stop drinking for good?

CARVER

It was late May, 1977. I was living by myself in a house in a little town in Northern California, and I'd been sober for about three weeks. I drove to San Francisco, where they were having this publishers' convention. Fred Hills, at that time editor in chief at McGraw-Hill, wanted to take me to lunch and offer me money to write a novel. But a couple of nights before the lunch, one of my friends had a party. Midway through, I picked up a glass of wine and drank it, and that's the last thing I remember. Blackout time. The next morning when the stores opened, I was waiting to buy a bottle. The dinner that night was a disaster; it was terrible, people quarreling and disappearing from the table. And the next morning I had to get up and go have this lunch with Fred Hills. I was so hungover when I woke up I could hardly hold my head up. But I drank a half pint of vodka before I picked up Hills and that helped, for the short run. And then he wanted to drive over to Sausalito for lunch! That took us at least an hour in heavy traffic, and I was drunk and hungover both, you understand. But for some reason he went ahead and offered me this money to write a novel.

INTERVIEWER

Did you ever write the novel?

CARVER

Not yet! Anyway, I managed to get out of San Francisco back up to where I lived. I stayed drunk for a couple more days. And then I woke up, feeling terrible, but I didn't drink anything that morning. Nothing alcoholic, I mean. I felt terrible physically—mentally, too, of course—but I didn't drink anything. I didn't drink for three days, and when the third day had passed, I began to feel some better. Then I just kept not drinking. Gradually I began to put a little distance between myself and the booze. A week. Two weeks. Suddenly it was a month. I'd been sober for a month, and I was slowly starting to get well.

INTERVIEWER

Did AA help?

CARVER

It helped a lot. I went to at least one and sometimes two meetings a day for the first month.

INTERVIEWER

Did you ever feel that alcohol was in any way an inspiration? I'm thinking of your poem "Vodka," published in *Esquire*.

CARVER

My God, no! I hope I've made that clear. Cheever remarked that he could always recognize "an alcoholic line" in a writer's work. I'm not exactly sure what he meant by this but I think I know. When we were teaching in the Iowa Writers' Workshop in the fall semester of 1973, he and I did nothing *but* drink. I mean we met our classes, in a manner of speaking. But the entire time we were there—we were living in this hotel they have on campus, the Iowa House—I don't think either of us ever took the covers off our typewriters. We made trips to a liquor store twice a week in my car.

INTERVIEWER

To stock up?

CARVER

Yes, stock up. But the store didn't open until ten o'clock A.M. Once we planned an early morning run, a ten o'clock run, and we were going to meet in the lobby of the hotel. I came down early to get some cigarettes and John was pacing up and down in the lobby. He was wearing loafers, but he didn't have any socks on. Anyway, we headed out a little early. By the time we got to the liquor store the clerk was just unlocking the front door. On this particular morning, John got out of the car before I could get it properly parked. By the time I got inside the store he was already at the checkout stand with a half gallon of Scotch. He lived on the fourth floor of the hotel and I lived on the second. Our rooms were identical, right down to the same reproduction of the same painting hanging on the wall. But when we drank together, we always drank in his room. He said he was afraid to come down to drink on the second floor. He said there was always a chance of him getting mugged in the hallway! But you know, of course, that fortunately, not too long after Cheever left Iowa City, he went to a treatment center and got sober and stayed sober until he died.

INTERVIEWER

Do you feel the spoken confessions at Alcoholics Anonymous meetings have influenced your writing?

CARVER

There are different kinds of meetings—speaker meetings where just one speaker will get up and talk for fifty minutes or so about what it was like then, and maybe what it's like now. And there are meetings where everyone in the room has a chance to say something. But I can't honestly say I've ever consciously or otherwise patterned any of my stories on things I've heard at the meetings.

INTERVIEWER

Where do your stories come from, then? I'm especially asking about the stories that have something to do with drinking.

CARVER

The fiction I'm most interested in has lines of reference to the real world. None of my stories really happened, of course. But there's always something, some element, something said to me or that I witnessed, that may be the starting place. Here's an example: "That's the last Christmas you'll ever ruin for us!" I was drunk when I heard that, but I remembered it. And later, much later, when I was sober, using only that one line and other things I imagined, imagined so accurately that they could have happened, I made a story—"A Serious Talk." But the fiction I'm most interested in, whether it's Tolstoy's fiction, Chekhov, Barry Hannah, Richard Ford, Hemingway, Isaac Babel, Ann Beattie, or Anne Tyler, strikes me as autobiographical to some extent. At the very least it's referential. Stories long or short don't just come out of thin air. I'm reminded of a conversation involving John Cheever. We were sitting around a table in Iowa City with some people and he happened to remark that after a family fracas at his home one night, he got up the next morning and went into the bathroom to find something his daughter had written in lipstick on the bathroom mirror: "D-e-r-e daddy, don't leave us." Someone at the table spoke up and said, I recognize that from one of your stories. Cheever said, Probably so. Everything I write is autobiographical. Now of course that's not literally true. But everything we write is, in some way, autobiographical. I'm not in the least bothered by "autobiographical" fiction. To the contrary. *On the Road*. Céline. Roth. Lawrence Durrell in *The Alexandria Quartet*. So much of Hemingway in the Nick Adams stories. Updike, too, you bet. Jim McConkey. Clark Blaise is a contemporary writer whose fiction is out-and-out autobiography. Of course, you have to know what you're doing when you turn your life's stories into fiction. You have to be immensely daring, very skilled and imaginative and willing to tell everything on yourself. You're told time and again when you're young to write about what you know, and what do you know better than your own secrets? But unless you're a special kind of writer, and a very talented one, it's dangerous to try and write volume after volume on The Story of My Life. A great danger, or at least a great temptation, for many writers is to become too autobiographical in their approach to their fiction. A little autobiography and a lot of imagination are best.

INTERVIEWER

Are your characters trying to do what matters?

CARVER

I think they are trying. But trying and succeeding are two different matters. In some lives, people always succeed; and I think it's grand when that happens. In other lives, people don't succeed at what they try to do, at the things they want most to do, the large or small things that support the life. These lives are, of course, valid to write about, the lives of the people who don't succeed. Most of my own experience, direct or indirect, has to do with the latter situation. I think most of my characters would like their actions to count for something. But at the same time they've reached the point—as so many people do—that they know it isn't so. It doesn't add up any longer. The things you once thought important or even worth dying for aren't worth a nickel now. It's their lives they've become uncomfortable with, lives they see breaking down. They'd like to set things right, but they can't. And usually they do know it, I think, and after that they just do the best they can.

INTERVIEWER

Could you say something about one of my favorite stories in your most recent collection? Where did the idea for "Why Don't You Dance?" originate?

CARVER

I was visiting some writer friends in Missoula back in the mid-1970s. We were all sitting around drinking and someone told a story about a barmaid named Linda who got drunk with her boyfriend one night and decided to move all of her bedroom furnishings into the backyard. They did it, too, right down to the carpet and the bedroom lamp, the bed, the nightstand, everything. There were about four or five writers in the room, and after the guy finished telling the story, someone said, "Well, who's going to write it?" I don't know who else might have written it, but I wrote it. Not then, but later. About four or five years later, I think. I changed and added things to it, of course. Actually, it was the first story I wrote after I finally stopped drinking.

INTERVIEWER

What are your writing habits like? Are you always working on a story?

CARVER

When I'm writing, I write every day. It's lovely when that's happening. One day dovetailing into the next. Sometimes I don't even know what day of the week it is. The "paddle wheel of days," John Ashbery has called it. When I'm not writing, like now, when I'm tied up with teaching duties as I have been the last while, it's as if I've never written a word or had any desire to write. I fall into bad habits. I stay up too late and sleep in too long. But it's OK. I've learned to be patient and to bide my time. I had to learn that a long time ago. Patience. If I believed in signs, I suppose my sign would be the sign of the turtle. I write in fits and starts. But when I'm writing, I put in a lot of hours at the desk, ten or twelve or fifteen hours at a stretch, day after day. I love that, when that's happening. Much of this work time, understand, is given over to revising and rewriting. There's not much that I like better than to take a story that I've had around the house for a while and work it over again. It's the same with the poems I write. I'm in no hurry to send something off just after I write it, and I sometimes keep it around the house for months doing this or that to it, taking this out and putting that in. It doesn't take that long to do the first draft of the story, that usually happens in one sitting, but it does take a while to do the various versions of the story. I've done as many as twenty or thirty drafts of a story. Never less than ten or twelve drafts. It's instructive, and heartening both, to look at the early drafts of great writers. I'm thinking of the photographs of galleys belonging to Tolstoy, to name one writer who loved to revise. I mean, I don't know if he loved it or not, but he did a great deal of it. He was always revising, right down to the time of page proofs. He went through and rewrote *War and Peace* eight times and was still making corrections in the galleys. Things like this should hearten every writer whose first drafts are dreadful, like mine are.

INTERVIEWER

Describe what happens when you write a story.

CARVER

I write the first draft quickly, as I said. This is most often done in longhand. I simply fill up the pages as rapidly as I can. In some cases, there's a kind of personal shorthand, notes to myself for what I will do later when I come back to it. Some scenes I have to leave unfinished, unwritten in some cases; the scenes that will require meticulous care later. I mean all of it requires meticulous care—but some scenes I save until the second or third draft, because to do them and do them right would take too much time on the first draft. With the first draft it's a question of getting down the outline, the scaffolding of the story. Then on subsequent revisions I'll see to the rest of it. When I've finished the longhand draft I'll type a version of the story and go from there. It always looks different to me, better, of course, after it's typed up. When I'm typing the first draft, I'll begin to rewrite and add and delete a little then. The real work comes later, after I've done three or four drafts of the story. It's the same with the poems, only the poems may go through forty or fifty drafts. Donald Hall told me he sometimes writes a hundred or so drafts of his poems. Can you imagine?

INTERVIEWER

Has your way of working changed?

CARVER

The stories in *What We Talk About* are different to an extent. For one thing, it's a much more self-conscious book in the sense of how intentional every move was, how calculated. I pushed and pulled and worked with those stories before they went into the book to an extent I'd never done with any other stories. When the book was put together and in the hands of my publisher, I didn't write anything at all for six months. And then the first story I wrote was "Cathedral," which I feel is totally different in conception and execution from any stories that have come before. I suppose it reflects a change in my life as much as it does in my way of writing. When I wrote "Cathedral" I experienced this rush and I felt, This is what it's all about, this is the reason we do this. It was different than the stories that had come before. There was an opening up when I wrote the story. I knew I'd gone as far the other way as I could or wanted to go, cutting everything down to the marrow, not just to the bone. Any farther in that direction and I'd be at a dead end—writing stuff and publishing stuff I wouldn't want to read myself, and that's the truth. In a review of the last book, somebody called me a "minimalist" writer. The reviewer meant it as a compliment. But I didn't like it. There's something about "minimalist" that smacks of smallness of vision and execution that I don't like. But all of the stories in the new book, the one called *Cathedral*, were written within an eighteen-month period; and in every one of them I feel this difference.

INTERVIEWER

Do you have any sense of an audience? Updike described his ideal reader as a young boy in a small Midwestern town finding one of his books on a library shelf.

CARVER

It's nice to think of Updike's idealized reader. But except for the early stories, I don't think it's a young boy in a small Midwestern town who's reading Updike. What would this young boy make of *The Centaur* or *Couples* or *Rabbit Redux* or *The Coup*? I think Updike is writing for the audience that John Cheever said he was writing for—"intelligent adult men and women," wherever they live. Any writer worth his salt writes as well and as truly as he can and hopes for as large and perceptive a readership as possible. So you write as well as you can and hope for good readers. But I think you're also writing for other writers to an extent—the dead writers whose work you admire, as well as the living writers you like to read. If they like it, the other writers, there's a good chance other "intelligent adult men and women" may like it, too. But I don't have that boy you mentioned in mind, or anyone else for that matter, when I'm doing the writing itself.

INTERVIEWER

How much of what you write do you finally throw away?

CARVER

Lots. If the first draft of the story is forty pages long, it'll usually be half that by the time I'm finished with it. And it's not just a question of taking out or bringing it down. I take out a lot, but I also add things and then add some more and take out some more. It's something I love to do, putting words in and taking words out.

INTERVIEWER

Has the process of revision changed now that the stories seem to be longer and more generous?

CARVER

Generous, yes, that's a good word for them. Yes, and I'll tell you why. Up at school there's a typist who has one of those space-age typewriters, a word processor, and I can give her a story to type and once she has it typed and I get back the fair copy, I can mark it up to my heart's content and give it back to her; and the next day I can have my story back, all fair copy once more. Then I can mark it up again as much as I want, and the next day I'll have back a fair copy once more. I love it. It may seem like a small thing, really, but it's changed my life, that woman and her word processor.

INTERVIEWER

Did you ever have any time off from not having to earn a living?

CARVER

I had a year once. It was a very important year for me, too. I wrote most of the stories in *Will You Please Be Quiet, Please?* in that year. It was back in 1970 or 1971. I was working for this textbook publishing firm in Palo Alto. It was my first white-collar job, right after the period when I'd been a janitor at the hospital in Sacramento. I'd been working away there quietly as an editor when the company, it was called SRA, decided to do a major reorganization. I planned to quit, I was writing my letter of resignation, but then suddenly—I was fired. It was just wonderful the way it turned out. We invited all of our friends that weekend and had a firing party! For a year I didn't have to work. I drew unemployment and had my severance pay to live on. And that's the period when my wife finished her college degree. That was a turning point, that time. It was a good period.

INTERVIEWER

Are you religious?

CARVER

No, but I have to believe in miracles and the possibility of resurrection. No question about that. Every day that I wake up, I'm glad to wake up. That's why I like to wake up early. In my drinking days I would sleep until noon or whatever and I would usually wake up with the shakes.

INTERVIEWER

Do you regret a lot of things that happened back then when things were so bad?

CARVER

I can't change anything now. I can't afford to regret. That life is simply gone now, and I can't regret its passing. I have to live in the present. The life back then is gone just as surely—it's as remote to me as if it had happened to somebody I read about in a nineteenth-century novel. I don't spend more than five minutes a month in the past. The past really *is* a foreign country, and they do do things differently there. Things happen. I really do feel I've had two different lives.

INTERVIEWER

Can you talk a little about literary influences, or at least name some writers whose work you greatly admire?

CARVER

Ernest Hemingway is one. The early stories. "Big Two-Hearted River," "Cat in the Rain," "The Three-Day Blow," "Soldier's Home," lots more. Chekhov. I suppose he's the writer whose work I most admire. But who doesn't like Chekhov? I'm talking about his stories now, not the plays. His plays move too slowly for me. Tolstoy. Any of his short stories, novellas, and *Anna Karenina*. Not *War and Peace*. Too slow. But *The Death of Ivan Ilyich*, *Master and Man*, "How Much Land Does a Man Need?" Tolstoy is the best there is. Isaac Babel, Flannery O'Connor, Frank O'Connor. James Joyce's *Dubliners*. John Cheever. *Madame Bovary*. Last year I reread that book, along with a new translation of Flaubert's letters written while he was composing— no other word for it—*Madame Bovary*. Conrad. Updike's *Too Far to Go*. And there are wonderful writers I've come across in the last year or two like Tobias Wolff. His book of stories *In the Garden of the North American Martyrs* is just wonderful. Max Schott. Bobbie Ann Mason. Did I mention her? Well, she's good and worth mentioning twice. Harold Pinter. V. S. Pritchett. Years ago I read something in a letter by Chekhov that impressed me. It was a piece of advice to one of his many correspondents, and it went something like this: Friend, you don't have to write about extraordinary people who accomplish extraordinary and memorable deeds. (Understand I was in college at the time and reading plays about princes and dukes and the overthrow of kingdoms. Quests and the like, large undertakings to establish heroes in their rightful places. Novels with larger-than-life heroes.) But reading what Chekhov had to say in that letter, and in other letters of his as well, and reading his stories, made me see things differently than I had before. Not long afterwards I read a play and a number of stories by Maxim Gorky, and he simply reinforced in his work what Chekhov had to say. Richard Ford is another fine writer. He's primarily a novelist, but he's also written stories and essays. He's a friend. I have a lot of friends who are good friends, and some of them are good writers. Some not so good.

INTERVIEWER

What do you do in that case? I mean, how do you handle that—if one of your friends publishes something you don't like?

CARVER

I don't say anything unless the friend asks me, and I hope he doesn't. But if you're asked you have to say it in a way that it doesn't wreck the friendship. You want your friends to do well and write the best they can. But sometimes their work is a disappointment. You want everything to go well for them, but you have this dread that maybe it won't and there's not much you can do.

INTERVIEWER

What do you think of moral fiction? I guess this has to lead into talk about John Gardner and his influence on you. I know you were his student many years ago at Humboldt State College.

CARVER

That's true. I've written about our relationship in the *Antaeus* piece and elaborated on it more in my introduction to a posthumous book of his called *On Becoming a Novelist*. I think *On Moral Fiction* is a wonderfully smart book. I don't agree with all of it, by any means, but generally he's right. Not so much in his assessments of living writers as in the aims, the aspirations of the book. It's a book that wants to affirm life rather than trash it. Gardner's definition of morality is life affirming. And in that regard he believes good fiction is moral fiction. It's a book to argue with, if you like to argue. It's brilliant, in any case. I think he may argue his case even better in *On Becoming a Novelist*. And he doesn't go after other writers as he did in *On Moral Fiction*. We had been out of touch with each other for years when he published *On Moral Fiction*, but his influence, the things he stood for in my life when I was his student, were still so strong that for a long while I didn't want to read the book. I was afraid to find out that what I'd been writing all these years was immoral! You understand that we'd not seen each other for nearly twenty years and had only renewed our friendship after I'd moved to Syracuse and he was down there at Binghamton, seventy miles away. There was a lot of anger directed toward Gardner and the book when it was published. He touched nerves. I happen to think it's a remarkable piece of work.

INTERVIEWER

But after you read the book, what did you think then about your own work? Were you writing "moral" or "immoral" stories?

CARVER

I'm still not sure! But I heard from other people, and then he told me himself, that he liked my work. Especially the new work. That pleases me a great deal. Read *On Becoming a Novelist*.

INTERVIEWER

Do you still write poetry?

CARVER

Some, but not enough. I want to write more. If too long a period of time goes by, six months or so, I get nervous if I haven't written any poems. I find myself wondering if I've stopped being a poet or stopped being able to write poetry. It's usually then that I sit down and try to write some poems. This book of mine that's coming in the spring, *Fires*—that's got all of the poems of mine I want to keep.

INTERVIEWER

How do they influence each other? The writing of fiction and the writing of poetry?

CARVER

They don't any longer. For a long time I was equally interested in the writing of poetry and the writing of fiction. In magazines I always turned to the poems first before I read the stories. Finally, I had to make a choice, and I came down on the side of the fiction. It was the right choice for me. I'm not a "born" poet. I don't know if I'm a "born" anything except a white American male. Maybe I'll become an occasional poet. But I'll settle for that. That's better than not being any kind of poet at all.

INTERVIEWER

How has fame changed you?

CARVER

I feel uncomfortable with that word. You see, I started out with such low expectations in the first place—I mean, how far are you going to get in this life writing short stories? And I didn't have much self-esteem as a result of this drinking thing. So it's a continual amazement to me, this attention that's come along. But I can tell you that after the reception for *What We Talk About*, I felt a confidence that I've never felt before. Every good thing that's happened since has conjoined to make me want to do even more and better work. It's been a good spur. And all this is coming at a time in my life when I have more strength than I've ever had before. Do you know what I'm saying? I feel stronger and more certain of my direction now than ever before. So "fame"—or let's say this newfound attention and interest—has been a good thing. It bolstered my confidence, when my confidence needed bolstering.

INTERVIEWER

Who reads your writing first?

CARVER

Tess Gallagher. As you know, she's a poet and short-story writer herself. I show her everything I write except for letters, and I've even shown
her a few of those. But she has a wonderful eye and a way of feeling herself into what I write. I don't show her anything until I've marked it up
and taken it as far as I can. That's usually the fourth or fifth draft, and then
she reads every subsequent draft thereafter. So far I've dedicated three
books to her and those dedications are not just a token of love and affec-
tion; they also indicate the high esteem in which I hold her and an ac-
knowledgment of the help and inspiration she's given me.

INTERVIEWER

Where does Gordon Lish enter into this? I know he's your editor
at Knopf.

CARVER

Just as he was the editor who began publishing my stories at *Esquire*
back in the early 1970s. But we had a friendship that went back before
that time, back to 1967 or 1968, in Palo Alto. He was working for a
textbook publishing firm right across the street from the firm where I
worked. The one that fired me. He didn't keep any regular office
hours. He did most of his work for the company at home. At least once
a week he'd ask me over to his place for lunch. He wouldn't eat anything himself, he'd just cook something for me and then hover around
the table watching me eat. It made me nervous, as you might imagine.
I'd always wind up leaving something on my plate, and he'd always
wind up eating it. Said it had to do with the way he was brought up.
This is not an isolated example. He still does things like that. He'll take
me to lunch now and won't order anything for himself except a drink
and then he'll eat up whatever I leave in my plate! I saw him do it once
in the Russian Tea Room. There were four of us for dinner, and after
the food came he watched us eat. When he saw we were going to leave
food on our plates, he cleaned it right up. Aside from this craziness,
which is more funny than anything, he's remarkably smart and sensitive to the needs of a manuscript. He's a good editor. Maybe he's a

great editor. All I know for sure is that he's my editor and my friend, and I'm glad on both counts.

INTERVIEWER

Would you consider doing more movie script work?

CARVER

If the subject could be as interesting as this one I just finished with Michael Cimino on the life of Dostoyevsky, yes, of course. Otherwise, no. But Dostoyevsky! You bet I would.

INTERVIEWER

And there was real money involved.

CARVER

Yes.

INTERVIEWER

That accounts for the Mercedes.

CARVER

That's it.

INTERVIEWER

What about *The New Yorker*? Did you ever send your stories to *The New Yorker* when you were first starting out?

CARVER

No, I didn't. I didn't read *The New Yorker*. I sent my stories and poems to the little magazines and once in a while something was accepted, and I was made happy by the acceptance. I had some kind of audience, you see, even though I never met any of my audience.

INTERVIEWER

Do you get letters from people who've read your work?

CARVER

Letters, tapes, sometimes photographs. Somebody just sent me a cassette—songs that had been made out of some of the stories.

INTERVIEWER

Do you write better on the West Coast—out in Washington—or here in the East? I guess I'm asking how important a sense of place is to your work.

CARVER

Once, it was important to see myself as a writer from a particular place. It was important for me to be a writer from the West. But that's not true any longer, for better or worse. I think I've moved around too much, lived in too many places, felt dislocated and displaced, to now have any firmly rooted sense of "place." If I've ever gone about consciously locating a story in a particular place and period, and I guess I have, especially in the first book, I suppose that place would be the Pacific Northwest. I admire the sense of place in such writers as Jim Welch, Wallace Stegner, John Keeble, William Eastlake, and William Kittredge. There are plenty of good writers with this sense of place you're talking about. But the majority of my stories are not set in any specific locale. I mean, they could take place in just about any city or urban area; here in Syracuse, but also Tucson, Sacramento, San Jose, San Francisco, Seattle, or Port Angeles, Washington. In any case, most of my stories are set indoors!

INTERVIEWER

Do you work in a particular place in your house?

CARVER

Yes, upstairs in my study. It's important to me to have my own place. Lots of days go by when we just unplug the telephone and put out our NO VISITORS sign. For many years I worked at the kitchen table, or in a library carrel, or else out in my car. This room of my own is a luxury *and* a necessity now.

INTERVIEWER

Do you still hunt and fish?

CARVER

Not so much anymore. I still fish a little, fish for salmon in the summer, if I'm out in Washington. But I don't hunt, I'm sorry to say. I don't know where to go! I guess I could find someone who'd take me, but I just haven't gotten around to it. But my friend Richard Ford is a hunter. When he was up here in the spring of 1981 to give a reading from his work, he took the proceeds from his reading and bought me a shotgun. Imagine that! And he had it inscribed, *For Raymond from Richard, April 1981.* Richard is a hunter, you see, and I think he was trying to encourage me.

INTERVIEWER

How do you hope your stories will affect people? Do you think your writing will change anybody?

CARVER

I really don't know. I doubt it. Not change in any profound sense. Maybe not any change at all. After all, art is a form of entertainment, yes? For both the maker and the consumer. I mean in a way it's like shooting billiards or playing cards, or bowling—it's just a different, and I would say higher, form of amusement. I'm not saying there isn't spiritual nourishment involved too. There is, of course. Listening to a Beethoven concerto or spending time in front of a van Gogh painting or reading a poem by Blake can be a profound experience on a scale that playing bridge or bowling a 220 game can never be. Art is all the things art is supposed to be. But art is also a superior amusement. Am I wrong in thinking this? I don't know. But I remember in my twenties reading plays by Strindberg, a novel by Max Frisch, Rilke's poetry, listening all night to music by Bartók, watching a TV special on the Sistine Chapel and Michelangelo and feeling in each case that my life *had* to change after these experiences, it couldn't help but be affected by these experiences and *changed*. There was simply no way I would not become a different person. But then I found out soon enough my life was not going to change after all. Not in any way that I could see, perceptible or otherwise. I understood then that art was something I could pursue when I had the time for it, when I could afford to do so, and that's all. Art was a luxury and it wasn't going to change me or my life. I guess I came to the hard realization that art doesn't make anything happen. No. I don't believe for a minute in that absurd Shelleyan nonsense having to do with poets as the "unacknowledged legislators" of this world. What an idea! Isak Dinesen said that she wrote a little every day, without hope and without despair. I like that. The days are gone, if they were ever with us, when a novel or a play or a book of poems could change people's ideas about the world they live in or even about themselves. Maybe writing fiction about particular kinds of people living particular kinds of lives will allow certain areas of life to be understood a little better than they were understood before. But I'm afraid that's it, at least as far as I'm concerned. Perhaps it's different in poetry. Tess has had letters from people who have read her poems and say the poems saved them from jumping off a cliff or drowning themselves, et cetera. But that's something else. Good fiction is partly a bringing of the news from one world to another. That end is good in and of itself, I think. But changing things through fiction, changing somebody's political affiliation or the political system itself, or saving the whales or the redwood trees, no. Not if these are the kinds of changes you mean. And I don't think it should have to do any of these things, either. It doesn't *have* to do anything. It just has to be there for the fierce pleasure we take in doing it, and the different kind of pleasure that's taken in reading something that's durable and made to last, as well as beautiful in and of itself. Something that throws off these sparks—a persistent and steady glow, however dim.

Chinua Achebe

The Art of Fiction

C hinua Achebe was born in Eastern Nigeria in 1930. He went to the local public schools and was among the first students to graduate from the University of Ibadan. After graduation, he worked for the Nigerian Broadcasting Corporation as a radio producer and Director of External Broadcasting, and it was during this period that he began his writing career.

He is the author, coauthor, or editor of some seventeen books, among them five novels: *Things Fall Apart*, 1958; *No Longer at Ease*, 1960; *Arrow of God*, 1964; *A Man of the People*, 1966; and *Anthills of the Savannah*, 1987. He is the editor of several anthologies, including the essay collections *Morning Yet on Creation Day* and *Hopes and Impediments*, and the collection of poetry *Beware Soul Brother*. He is the editor of the magazine *Okike* and founding editor of the Heinemann series on African literature, a list that now has more than three hundred titles. He is often called the father of modern African literature. He is the recipient, at last count, of some twenty-five honorary doctorates from universities throughout the world and is currently the Charles P. Stevenson Jr. Professor of English at Bard College.

This interview took place on two very different occasions. The first meeting was before a live audience at the Unterberg Poetry Center of the 92nd Street Y on a bitterly cold and rainy January evening; the weather made the sidewalks and roads treacherous. We were all the more surprised at the very large and enthusiastic audience. The theater was almost packed. It was Martin Luther King Jr.'s birthday; Achebe give headaches! "

Uproarious laughter.

" Well, on that note we say thank you to Mr Osodi for a most entertaining evening."

13

One of the ~~very~~ many questions which he ~~had to~~ ~~field~~ ~~answered~~ in the course of ~~the~~ his lecture, some briefly and some at ~~great~~ length, ~~covered~~ a rumour that the Central Bank of Kangan was ~~planning~~ completing plans to ~~print~~ float the President's image on the nation's currency. Was it true & if so what did Mr Osodi think about such an eventuality.

Yes I heard of it like everybody else.

" My position is simple. Fortunately I can speak as a private citizen now. All I can say is I hope the rumour is unfounded. Any serious President foolish enough to lay his head on a coin should know ~~if he loses it~~, I mean the head, which was roundly applauded in the auditorium.

This statement I was to reverberate through the country beginning from the very next morning when the National Gazette came out brandishing in the heaviest possible type the following headline: EX-EDITOR ADVOCATES REGICIDE!

A manuscript page from Chinua Achebe's *Anthills of the Savannah*.

paid gracious tribute to him and then answered questions from the interviewer and audience. The interviewer and Achebe sat on a stage with a table and a bouquet of flowers between them. Achebe was at ease and captured the audience with stories of his childhood and youth.

The second session took place on an early fall day at Achebe's house on the beautiful grounds where he lives in upstate New York. He answered the door in his wheelchair and graciously ushered his guest through his large, neat living room to his study—a long, narrow room lined with many books on history, religion, and literature. There is a small, slightly cluttered desk where he writes.

Achebe favors traditional Nigerian clothes and reminds one more of the priest in *Arrow of God* than Okonkwo in *Things Fall Apart*. His appearance is peaceful and his eyes wise. His demeanor is modest, but when he begins to talk about literature and Nigeria, he is transformed. His eyes light up; he is an assured, elegant, and witty storyteller.

The year 1990 marked Achebe's sixtieth birthday. His colleagues at the University of Nigeria at Nsukka, where he is a professor of English and chairman emeritus of the department, sponsored an international conference entitled Eagle on Iroko in his honor. Participants came from around the world to appraise the significance of his work for African and world literature. The conference opened on the day Nelson Mandela was liberated from prison, and the day was declared a national holiday. There was a festive mood during the weeklong activities of scholarly papers, traditional drama, dancing, and banquets. The iroko is the tallest tree in that part of Africa and the eagle soars to its height.

Scarcely a month later, while on his way to the airport in Lagos to resume a teaching post at Dartmouth, Achebe was severely injured in a car accident. He was flown to a London hospital where he underwent surgery and spent many months in painful recuperation. Although confined to a wheelchair, he has made a remarkable recovery in the past three years and, to the surprise of his family and many friends throughout the world, is beginning to look and sound like his old self.

—*Jerome Brooks, 1994*

INTERVIEWER

Would you tell us something about the Achebe family and growing up in an Igbo village, your early education, and whether there was anything there that pointed you that early in the direction of writing?

CHINUA ACHEBE

I think the thing that clearly pointed me there was my interest in stories. Not necessarily *writing* stories, because at that point, writing stories was not really viable. So you didn't think of it. But I knew I loved stories, stories told in our home, first by my mother, then by my elder sister—such as the story of the tortoise—whatever scraps of stories I could gather from conversations, just from hanging around, sitting around when my father had visitors. When I began going to school, I loved the stories I read. They were different, but I loved them, too. My parents were early converts to Christianity in my part of Nigeria. They were not just converts; my father was an evangelist, a religious teacher. He and my mother traveled for thirty-five years to different parts of Igboland, spreading the gospel. I was the fifth of their six children. By the time I was growing up, my father had retired, and had returned with his family to his ancestral village.

When I began going to school and learned to read, I encountered stories of other people and other lands. In one of my essays, I remember the kind of things that fascinated me. Weird things, even, about a wizard who lived in Africa and went to China to find a lamp . . . fascinating to me because they were about things remote, and almost ethereal.

Then I grew older and began to read about adventures in which I didn't know that I was supposed to be on the side of those savages who were encountered by the good white man. I instinctively took sides with the white people. They were fine! They were excellent. They were intelligent. The others were not . . . they were stupid and ugly. That was the way I was introduced to the danger of not having your own stories. There is that great proverb—that until the lions have their own historians, the history of the hunt will always glorify the hunter. That did not come to me until much later. Once I realized that, I had to be a writer. I had to be that historian. It's not one man's job. It's not one person's job. But it is something we have to do, so that the story of the hunt will also reflect the agony, the travail—the bravery, even, of the lions.

INTERVIEWER

You were among the first graduates of the great University of Ibadan. What was it like in the early years of that university, and what did you study there? Has it stuck with you in your writing?

ACHEBE

Ibadan was, in retrospect, a great institution. In a way, it revealed the paradox of the colonial situation, because this university college was founded toward the end of British colonial rule in Nigeria. If they did any good things, Ibadan was one of them. It began as a college of London University, because under the British, you don't rush into doing any of those things like universities just like that. You start off as an appendage of somebody else. You go through a period of tutelage. We were the University College of Ibadan of London. So I took a degree from London University. That was the way it was organized in those days. One of the signs of independence, when it came, was for Ibadan to become a full-fledged university.

I began with science, then English, history, and religion. I found these subjects exciting and very useful. Studying religion was new to me and interesting because it wasn't only Christian theology; we also studied West African religions. My teacher there, Dr. Parrinder, now an emeritus professor of London University, was a pioneer in the area. He had done extensive research in West Africa, in Dahomey. For the first time, I was able to see the systems—including my own—compared and placed side by side, which was really exciting. I also encountered a professor, James Welch, in that department, an extraordinary man, who had been chaplain to King George VI, chaplain to the BBC, and all kinds of high-powered things before he came to us. He was a very eloquent preacher. On one occasion, he said to me, We may not be able to teach you what you need or what you want. We can only teach you what we know. I thought that was wonderful. That was really the best education I had. I didn't learn anything there that I really needed, except this kind of attitude. I have had to go out on my own. The English department was a very good example of what I mean. The people there would have laughed at the idea that any of us would become a writer. That didn't really cross their minds. I remember on one occasion a departmental prize was offered. They put up a notice—write a short story over the long vacation for the departmental prize. I'd never written a short story before, but when I got home, I thought, Well, why not. So I wrote one and submitted it. Months passed; then finally one day there was a notice on the board announcing the result. It said that no prize was awarded because no entry was up to the standard. They named me, said that my story deserved mention. Ibadan in those days was not a dance you danced with snuff in one palm. It was a dance you danced with all your body. So when Ibadan said you deserved mention, that was very high praise.

I went to the lecturer who had organized the prize and said, You said my story wasn't really good enough but it was interesting. Now what was wrong with it? She said, Well, it's the form. It's the wrong form. So I said, Ah, can you tell me about this? She said, Yes, but not now. I'm going to play tennis; we'll talk about it. Remind me later, and I'll tell you. This went on for a whole term. Every day when I saw her, I'd say, Can we talk about form? She'd say, No, not now. We'll talk about it later. Then at the very end she saw me and said, You know, I looked at your story again and actually there's nothing wrong with it. So that was it! That was all I learned from the English department about writing short stories. You really have to go out on your own and do it.

INTERVIEWER

When you finished university, one of the first careers you embarked upon was broadcasting with the Nigerian Broadcasting Corporation.

ACHEBE

I got into it through the intervention of Professor Welch. He had tried to get me a scholarship to Trinity College, Cambridge, and it didn't work out. So the next thing was the broadcasting department, which was newly started in Nigeria, with a lot of BBC people. So that's how I got into it. It wasn't because I was thinking of broadcasting. I really had no idea what I was going to do when I left college. I'm amazed when I think about students today. They know from day one what they are going to be. We didn't. We just coasted. We just knew that things would work out. Fortunately, things *did* work out. There were not too many of us. You couldn't do that today and survive. So I got into broadcasting and then discovered that the section of it where I worked, the spoken word department, the Talks Department, as it's called, was really congenial. It was just the thing I wanted. You edited scripts. People's speeches. Then short stories. I really got into editing and commissioning short stories. Things were happening very fast in our newly independent country, and I was soon promoted out of this excitement into management.

INTERVIEWER

The titles of your first two books—*Things Fall Apart* and *No Longer at Ease*—are from modern Irish and American poets. Other black writers—I'm thinking particularly of Paule Marshall—borrow from Yeats. I wonder if Yeats and Eliot are among your favorite poets.

ACHEBE

They are. Actually, I wouldn't make too much of that. I was showing off more than anything else. As I told you, I took a general degree, with English as part of it, and you had to show some evidence of that. But I liked Yeats! That wild Irishman. I really loved his love of language, his flow. His chaotic ideas seemed to me just the right thing for a poet. Passion! He was always on the right side. He may be wrongheaded, but his heart was always on the right side. He wrote beautiful poetry. It had the same kind of magic about it that I mentioned the wizard had for me. I used to make up lines with anything that came into my head, anything that sounded interesting. So Yeats was that kind of person for me. It was only later I discovered his theory of circles or cycles of civilization. I wasn't thinking of that at all when it came time to find a title. That phrase "things fall apart" seemed to me just right and appropriate.

T. S. Eliot was quite different. I had to study him at Ibadan. He had a kind of priestly erudition—eloquence, but of a different kind. Scholarly to a fault. But I think the poem from which I took the title of *No Longer at Ease*, the one about the three magi, is one of the great poems in the English language. These people who went and then came back to their countries were "no longer at ease". . . . I think that that is great—the use of simple language, even when things talked about are profound, very moving, very poignant. So that's really all there is to it. But you'll notice that after those first two titles I didn't do it anymore.

INTERVIEWER

I once heard your English publisher, Alan Hill, talk about how you sent the manuscript of *Things Fall Apart* to him.

ACHEBE

That was a long story. The first part of it was how the manuscript was nearly lost. In 1957 I was given a scholarship to go to London and study for some months at the BBC. I had a draft of *Things Fall Apart* with me, so I took it along to finish it. When I got to the BBC, one of my friends—there were two of us from Nigeria—said, Why don't you show this to Mr. Phelps? Gilbert Phelps, one of the in-structors of the BBC school, was a novelist. I said, What? No! This went on for some time. Eventually I was pushed to do it and I took the manuscript and handed it to Mr. Phelps. He said, Well . . . all right, the way I would today if anyone brought me a manuscript. He was not really enthusiastic. Why should he be? He took it anyway, very politely. He was the first person, outside of myself, to say, I think this is interesting. In fact, he felt so strongly that one Saturday he was compelled to look for me and tell me. I had traveled out of London; he found out where I was, phoned the hotel, and asked me to call him back. When I was given this message, I was completely floored. I said, Maybe he doesn't like it. But then why would he call me if he doesn't like it? So it must be he *likes* it. Anyway, I was very excited. When I got back to London, he said, This is wonderful. Do you want me to show it to my publishers? I said, Yes, but not yet, because I had decided that the form wasn't right. Attempting to do a saga of three families, I was covering too much ground in this first draft. So I real-ized that I needed to do something drastic, really give it more body.

So I said to Mr. Phelps, OK, I am very grateful but I'd like to take this back to Nigeria and look at it again. Which is what I did.

When I was in England, I had seen advertisements about typing agencies; I had learned that if you really want to make a good impression, you should have your manuscript well typed. So, foolishly, from Nigeria I parceled my manuscript—handwritten, by the way, and the only copy in the whole world—wrapped it up and posted it to this typing agency that advertised in the *Spectator*. They wrote back and said, Thank you for your manuscript. We'll charge thirty-two pounds. That was what they wanted for two copies and which they had to receive before they started. So I sent thirty-two pounds in British postal order to these people and then I heard no more. Weeks passed, and months. I wrote and wrote and wrote. No answer. Not a word. I was getting thinner and thinner and thinner. Finally, I was very lucky. My boss at the broadcasting house was going home to London on leave. A very stubborn Englishwoman. I told her about this. She said, Give me their name and address. When she got to London she went there! She said, What's this nonsense? They must have been shocked, because I think their notion was that a manuscript sent from *Africa*—well, there's really nobody to follow it up. The British don't normally behave like that. It's not done, you see. But something from Africa was treated differently. So when this woman, Mrs. Beattie, turned up in their office and said, What's going on? they were confused. They said, The manuscript was sent but customs returned it. Mrs. Beattie said, Can I see your dispatch book? They had no dispatch book. So she said, Well, send this thing, typed up, back to him in the next week, or otherwise you'll hear about it. So soon after that, I received the typed manuscript of *Things Fall Apart*. One copy, not two. No letter at all to say what happened. My publisher, Alan Hill, rather believed that the thing was simply neglected, left in a corner gathering dust. That's not what happened. These people did not want to return it to me and had no intention of doing so. Anyway, when I got it I sent it back up to Heinemann. They had never seen an African novel. They didn't know what to do with it. Someone told them, Oh, there's a professor of economics at London School of Economics and Political Science who just came back from those places. He might be able to advise you. Fortunately, Don MacRae was a very literate professor, a wonderful man. I got to know him later. He wrote what they said was the shortest report they ever had on any novel—seven words: "The best first novel since the war." So that's how I got launched.

INTERVIEWER

Heinemann was also perplexed as to how many copies should be printed. . . .

ACHEBE

Oh yes. They printed very, very few. It was a risk. Not something they'd ever done before. They had no idea if anybody would want to read it. It went out of print very quickly. It would have stayed that way if Alan Hill hadn't decided that he was going to gamble even more and launch a paperback edition of this book. Other publishers thought it was mad, that this was crazy. But that was how the African Writers Series came into existence. In the end, Alan Hill was made a Commander of the British Empire for bringing into existence a body of literature they said was among the biggest developments in British literature of this century. So it was a very small beginning, but it caught fire.

INTERVIEWER

You have said that you wrote *Things Fall Apart* as a response to Joyce Cary's *Mr. Johnson*.

ACHEBE

I wish I hadn't said that.

INTERVIEWER

You made *Mr. Johnson* famous! But your most trenchant essay on the colonial novel is your subsequent essay on Conrad's *Heart of Darkness*. I wonder what you think is the image of Africa today in the Western mind.

ACHEBE

I think it's changed a bit. But not very much in its essentials. When I think of the standing, the importance, and the erudition of all these people who see nothing about racism in *Heart of Darkness*, I'm convinced that we must really be living in different worlds. Anyway, if you don't like someone's story, you write your own. If you don't like what somebody says, you say what it is you don't like. Some people imagine that what I mean is, Don't read Conrad. Good heavens, no! I *teach* Conrad. I teach *Heart of Darkness*. I have a course on *Heart of Darkness* in which what I'm saying is, Look at the way this man handles Africans. Do you recognize humanity there? People will tell you he was opposed to imperialism. But it's not enough to say, I'm opposed to imperialism. Or, I'm opposed to these people—these poor people—being treated like this. Especially since he goes on straight away to call them "dogs standing on their hind legs." That kind of thing. Animal imagery throughout. He didn't see anything wrong with it. So we must live in different worlds. Until these two worlds come together we will have a lot of trouble.

INTERVIEWER

Have you ever taught creative writing?

ACHEBE

No.

INTERVIEWER

Why not?

ACHEBE

Well, I don't know how it's done. I mean it. I really don't know. The only thing I can say for it is that it provides work for writers. Don't laugh! It's very important. I think it's very important for writers who need something else to do, especially in these precarious times. Many writers can't make a living. So to be able to teach how to write is valuable to them. But I don't really know about its value to the student. I don't mean it's useless. But I wouldn't have wanted anyone to teach me how to write. That's my own taste. I prefer to stumble on it. I prefer to go on trying all kinds of things, not to be told, This is the way it is done. Incidentally, there's a story I like about a very distinguished writer today, who shall remain nameless, who had been taught creative writing in his younger days. The old man who taught him was reflecting about him one day: I remember his work was so good that I said to him, Don't stop writing, never stop writing. I wish I'd never told him that. So I don't know. I teach literature. That's easy for me. Take someone else's work and talk about it.

INTERVIEWER

Has your work been translated into Igbo? Is it important for it to be translated into Igbo?

ACHEBE

No, my work has not been translated. There is a problem with the Igbo language. It suffers from a very serious inheritance, which it received at the beginning of this century from the Anglican mission. They sent out a missionary by the name of Dennis. Archdeacon Dennis. He was a scholar. He had this notion that the Igbo language—which had very many different dialects—should somehow manufacture a uniform dialect that would be used in writing to avoid all these different dialects. Because the missionaries were powerful, what they wanted to do they did. This became the law. An earlier translation of the Bible into one of the dialects—an excellent translation, by the way—was pushed aside and a new dialect was invented by Dennis. The way he did it was to invite six people from six different dialectal areas. They sat round a table and they took a sentence from the Bible: In the beginning, God created . . . or whatever. *In*. What is it in your dialect? And they would take that. *The*. Yours? *Beginning*. Yours? And in this way, around the table, they created what is called Standard Igbo, with which the Bible was translated. The result is incredible. I can speak about it because in my family we read the Bible day and night. I know the Bible very well. But the standard version cannot sing. There's nothing you can do with it to make it sing. It's heavy. It's wooden. It doesn't go anywhere. We've had it now for almost a hundred years so it has established a kind of presence; it has created its own momentum among our own scholars. There are grammarians who now sit over the Igbo language in the way that Dennis did in 1906 and dictate it into Standard Igbo. I think this is a terrible tragedy. I think dialects should be left alone. People should write in whatever dialect they feel they want to write. In the fullness of time, these dialects will sort themselves out. They actually were beginning to do so, because Igbo people have always traveled and met among themselves; they have a way of communicating. But this has not been allowed to happen. Instead, the scholars are all over the place. I don't really have any interest in these translations. If someone said, I want to translate your novel into Igbo, I would say, Go ahead. But when I write in the Igbo language, I write my own dialect. I write some poetry in that dialect. Maybe someday I will, myself, translate *Things Fall Apart* into the Igbo language. Just to show what I mean, though for me, being bilingual, the novel form seems to go with the English language. Poetry and drama seem to go with the Igbo language.

INTERVIEWER

How much do you think writers should engage themselves in public issues?

ACHEBE

I don't lay down the law for anybody else. But I think writers are not only writers, they are also citizens. They are generally adults. My position is that serious and good art has always existed to help, to serve, humanity. Not to indict. I don't see how art can be called art if its purpose is to frustrate humanity. To make humanity uncomfortable, yes. But intrinsically to be against humanity, that I don't take. This is why I find racism impossible, because this is against humanity. Some people think, Well, what he's saying is we must praise his people. For God's sake! Go and read my books. I don't praise my people. I am their greatest critic. Some people think my little pamphlet, *The Trouble with Nigeria*, went too far. I've got into all kinds of trouble for my writing. Art should be on the side of humanity. I think it was Yevtushenko talking about Rimbaud, the Frenchman who went to Ethiopia and came back with all kinds of diseases. Yevtushenko said of him that a poet cannot become a slave trader. When Rimbaud became a slave trader, he stopped writing poetry. Poetry and slave trading cannot be bedfellows. That's where I stand.

INTERVIEWER

Can you say something about the germination of a work? What comes first? A general idea, a specific situation, a plot, a character?

ACHEBE

It's not the same with every book. Generally, I think I can say that the general idea is the first, followed almost immediately by the major characters. We live in a sea of general ideas, so that's not a novel, since there are so many general ideas. But the moment a particular idea is linked to a character, it's like an engine moves it. Then you have a novel underway. This is particularly so with novels that have distinct and overbearing characters like Ezeulu in *Arrow of God*. In novels like *A Man of the People*, or better still, *No Longer at Ease*, with characters who are not commanding personalities, there I think the general idea plays a stronger part at the initial stage. But once you pass that initial state, there's really no difference between the general idea and the character; each has to work.

INTERVIEWER

What is the place of plot? Do you think of a plot as you go along? Does the plot grow out of the character, or out of the idea?

ACHEBE

Once a novel gets going and I know it is viable, I don't then worry about plot or themes. These things will come in almost automatically because the characters are now pulling the story. At some point it seems as if you are not as much in command, in control, of events as you thought you were. There are things the story must have or else look incomplete. And these will almost automatically present themselves. When they don't, you are in trouble and then the novel stops.

INTERVIEWER

Then is writing easy for you? Or do you find it difficult?

ACHEBE

The honest answer is, it's difficult. But the word *difficult* doesn't really express what I mean. It is like wrestling; you are wrestling with ideas and with the story. There is a lot of energy required. At the same time, it is exciting. So it is both difficult and easy. What you must accept is that your life is not going to be the same while you are writing. I have said in the kind of exaggerated manner of writers and prophets that writing, for me, is like receiving a term of imprisonment—you know that's what you're in for, for whatever time it takes. So it is both pleasurable and difficult.

INTERVIEWER

Do you find a particular time or place that you like to write—a time of day or a place in your house or your office?

ACHEBE

I have found that I work best when I am at home in Nigeria. But one learns to work in other places. I am most comfortable in the surroundings, the kind of environment about which I am writing. The time of day doesn't matter, really. I am not an early-morning person; I don't like to get out of bed, and so I don't begin writing at five A.M., though some people, I hear, do. I write once my day has started. And I can work late into the night, also. Generally, I don't attempt to produce a certain number of words a day. The discipline is to work whether you are producing a lot or not, because the day you produce a lot is not necessarily the day you do your best work. So it's trying to do it as regularly as you can without making it—without imposing too rigid a timetable on yourself. That would be my ideal.

INTERVIEWER

Do you write with a pen, a typewriter, or have you been seduced by computers?

ACHEBE

No! No, no—I'm very primitive; I write with a pen. A pen on paper is the ideal way for me. I am not really very comfortable with machines; I never learned to type very well. Whenever I try to do anything on a typewriter, it's like having this machine between me and the words; what comes out is not quite what would come out if I were scribbling. For one thing, I don't like to see mistakes on the typewriter. I like a perfect script. On the typewriter I will sometimes leave a phrase that is not right, not what I want, simply because to change it would be a bit messy. So when I look at all this . . . I am a preindustrial man.

INTERVIEWER

As the author of one of the most famous books in the world, *Things Fall Apart*, does it bother you that your other books are not discussed to the same extent as your first one?

ACHEBE

Well, sometimes, but I don't let it become a problem. You know, they're all in the family; *Things Fall Apart* was the first to arrive and that fact gives it a certain position of prominence, whether in fact other books excel in other particular virtues. *Things Fall Apart* is a kind of fundamental story of my condition that demanded to be heard, to retell the story of my encounter with Europe in a way acceptable to me. The other books do not occupy that same position in my frame of thinking. So I don't resent *Things Fall Apart* getting all the attention it does get. If you ask me, Now, is it your best book? I would say, I don't really know. I wouldn't even want to say. And I'd even go on and say, I don't even think so. But that's all right. I think every book I've done has tried to be different; this is what I set out to do, because I believe in the complexity of the human story and that there's no way you can tell that story in one way and say, This is it. Always there will be someone who can tell it differently depending on where they are standing; the same person telling the story will tell it differently. I think of that masquerade in Igbo festivals that dances in the public arena. The Igbo people say, If you want to see it well, you must not stand in one place. The masquerade is moving through this big arena. Dancing. If you're rooted to a spot, you miss a lot of the grace. So you keep moving, and this is the way I think the world's stories should be told—from many different perspectives.

INTERVIEWER

I wonder if you would comment on any tension you see between aesthetics and being politically engaged as an African writer.

ACHEBE

I don't see any tension for myself. It has always been quite apparent to me that no important story can fail to tell us something of value to us. But at the same time I know that an important message is not a novel. To say that we should all be kind to our neighbors is an important statement; it's not a novel. There is something about important stories that is not just the message, but also the way that message is conveyed, the arrangement of the words, the felicity of the language. So it's really a balance between your commitment, whether it's political or economic or whatever, and your craft as an artist.

INTERVIEWER

Is there a difference between telling a story and writing a story?

ACHEBE

Well, there must be. I remember that when our children were young, we used to read them stories at bedtime. Occasionally I would say to them, I want to *tell* you a story, and the way their eyes would light up was different from the way they would respond to hearing a story read. There's no doubt at all that they preferred the story that was told to the one that was read. We live in a society that is in transition from oral to written. There are oral stories that are still there, not exactly in their full magnificence, but still strong in their differentness from written stories. Each mode has its ways and methods and rules. They can reinforce each other; this is the advantage my generation has—we can bring to the written story something of that energy of the story told by word of mouth. This is really one of the contributions our literature has made to contemporary literature.

INTERVIEWER

Nigerian literature.

ACHEBE

Yes, yes. Bringing into the written literature some of that energy that was always there—the archaic energy of the creation stories.

INTERVIEWER

When you write, what audience do you have in mind? Is it Nigerian? Is it Igbo? Is it American?

ACHEBE

All of those. I have tried to describe my position in terms of circles, standing there in the middle. These circles contain the audiences that get to hear my story. The closest circle is the one closest to my home in Igboland, because the material I am using is their material. But unless I'm writing in the Igbo language, I use a language developed elsewhere, which is English. That affects the way I write. It even affects to some extent the stories I write. So there is, if you like, a kind of paradox there already. But then, if you can, visualize a large number of ever-widening circles, including all, like Yeats's widening gyre. As more and more people are incorporated in this network, they will get different levels of meaning out of the story, depending on what they already know, or what they suspect. These circles go on indefinitely to include, ultimately, the whole world. I have become more aware of this as my books become more widely known. At this particular time, mostly the news I hear is of translations of my books, especially *Things Fall Apart* . . . in Indonesia, in Thailand, Korea, Japan, China, and so on. Fortunately you don't think of all those people when you are writing. At least, I don't. When I'm writing, I really want to satisfy myself. I've got a story that I am working on and struggling with, and I want to tell it the most effective way I can. That's really what I struggle with. And the thought of who may be reading it may be there somewhere in the back of my mind—I'll never say it's not there because I don't know—but it's not really what I'm thinking about. After all, some people will say, Why does he put in all these Nigerian-English words? Some critics say that in frustration. And I feel like saying to them, Go to hell! That's the way the story was given to me. And if you don't want to make this amount of effort, the kind of effort that my people have always made to understand Europe and the rest of the world, if you won't make this little leap, then leave it alone!

INTERVIEWER

Are you ever surprised, when you travel around the world, by what readers make of your writings, or how they bond to them?

ACHEBE

Yes. Yes, yes, yes. I am. People make surprising comments to me. I think particularly of a shy-looking, white American boy who came into my office once—in the seventies, I think—at the University of Massachusetts and said to me, That man, Okonkwo, is my father!

INTERVIEWER

You were surprised!

ACHEBE

Yes! I was surprised. I looked at him and I said, All right! As I've said elsewhere, another person said the same thing: in a public discussion—a debate the two of us had in Florida—James Baldwin said, That man is my father.

INTERVIEWER

Okonkwo?

ACHEBE

Okonkwo.

INTERVIEWER

Did you ever know anybody named Okonkwo? When I was in Nigeria visiting you some years ago, I met a small young man who was a student at the university, who introduced himself to me as Okonkwo. I thought he was an impostor! Is it a real name?

ACHEBE

A very common name. Oh, yes. It's one of the commonest names in Igboland because there are four days in the Igbo week, and each of them is somebody's name. In other words, you are born on Monday or Tuesday or Wednesday or Thursday, if you like, and you will be given the name—"The Son of Monday," or "The Son of Tuesday," or "The Son of Wednesday," or "The Son of Thursday"—if you are Igbo. That's what Okonkwo means: it means a man born on *nkwo* day. The first day of the week. If you are not born on that day, you will be Okeke, Okoye, or Okafo. Not everybody answers to these. Your parents might give you another name, like Achebe; then you prefer to answer that. But you always have a name of the day of the week on which you were born. So Okonkwo is very common.

INTERVIEWER

One of the great women characters you have created, I think, is Beatrice in *Anthills of the Savannah*. Do you identify with her? Do you see any part of yourself in that character? She's sort of a savior, I think.

ACHEBE

Yes, yes, I identify with her. Actually, I identify with all my characters, good and bad. I have to do that in order to make them genuine. I have to understand them even if I don't approve of them. Not completely—it's impossible; complete identification is, in fact, not desirable. There must be areas in which a particular character does not represent you. At times, though, the characters—like Beatrice—do contain, I think, elements of my own self and my systems of beliefs and *hopes* and aspirations. Beatrice is the first *major* woman character in my fiction. Those who do not read me as carefully as they ought have suggested that this is the only woman character I have ever written about and that I probably created her out of pressure from the feminists. Actually, the character of Beatrice has been there in virtually all my fiction, certainly from *No Longer at Ease*, *A Man of the People*, right down to *Anthills of the Savannah*. There is a certain increase in the importance I assign to women in getting us out of the mess that we are in, which is a reflection of the role of women in my traditional culture—that they do not interfere in politics until men really make such a mess that the society is unable to go backward or forward. Then women will move in . . . this is the way the stories have been constructed, and this is what I have tried to say. In one of Sembene Ousmane's films he portrays that same kind of situation where the men struggle, are beaten, and cannot defend their rights against French colonial rule. They surrender their rice harvest, which is an abomination. They dance one last time in the village arena and leave their spears where they danced and go away—this is the final humiliation. The women then emerge, pick up the spears, and begin their own dance. So it's not just in the Igbo culture. It seems to be something that other African peoples also taught us.

INTERVIEWER

You wrote a very passionate piece a year or so ago for *The New York Times* op-ed page about the present status of life in Nigeria. Are you pessimistic or hopeful about Nigeria's return to democracy?

ACHEBE

What is going on is extremely sad. It's appalling. And extremely disappointing to all lovers or friends or citizens of Nigeria. I try as hard as possible not to be pessimistic because I have never thought or believed that creating a Nigerian nation would be easy; I have always known that it was going to be a very tough job. But I never really thought that it would be *this* tough. And what's going on now, which is a subjection of this potentially great country to a clique of military adventurers and a political class that they have completely corrupted— this is really quite appalling. The suffering that they have unleashed on millions of people is quite intolerable. What makes me so angry is that this was quite avoidable. If a political class—including intellectuals, university professors, and people like that, who have read all the books and know how the world works—if they had based their actions on *principle* rather than on opportunity, the military would not have dared to go as far as they are going. But they looked around and saw that they could buy people. Anybody who called himself president would immediately find everyone lining up outside his home or his office to be made minister of this or that. And this is what they have exploited—they have exploited the divisions, the ethnic and religious divisions in the country. These have always been serious, but they were never insurmountable with good leadership. But over the last ten years these military types have been so cynical that they didn't really care what they did as long as they stayed in power. And they watched Nigeria going through the most intolerable situation of suffering and pain. And I just hope, as nothing goes on forever, that we will find a way to stumble out of this anarchy.

INTERVIEWER

Do you miss Nigeria?

ACHEBE

Yes, very much. One reason why I am quite angry with what is happening in Nigeria today is that everything has collapsed. If I decide to go back now, there will be so many problems—where will I find the physical therapy and other things that I now require? Will the doctors, who are leaving in *droves*, coming to America, going to everywhere in the world—Saudi Arabia—how many of them will be there? The universities have almost completely lost their faculties and are hardly ever in session, shut down for one reason or another. So these are some of the reasons why I have not yet been able to get back. So I miss it. And it doesn't have to be that way.

INTERVIEWER

I wanted to ask, how are you coming along? Have you been able to resume writing since your accident?

ACHEBE

I am feeling my way back into writing. The problem is that in this condition you spend a lot of time just getting used to your body again. It does take a lot of energy and time, so that your day does not begin where it used to begin. And the result is that there are very few hours in the day. That's a real problem, and what I have been trying to do is reorganize my day so that I can get in as much writing as possible before the discomfort makes it necessary for me to get up or go out. So, I am beginning. . . .

INTERVIEWER

What advice would you give to someone with literary promise? I would assume that you are constantly being asked by budding novelists to give them advice, to read their manuscripts, and so on.

ACHEBE

I don't get the deluge of manuscripts that I would be getting in Nigeria. But some do manage to find me. This is something I understand, because a budding writer wants to be encouraged. But I believe myself that a good writer doesn't really need to be told anything except to keep at it. Just think of the work you've set yourself to do, and do it as well as you can. Once you have really done all you can, then you can show it to people. But I find this is increasingly not the case with the younger people. They do a first draft and want somebody to finish it off for them with good advice. So I just maneuver myself out of this. I say, Keep at it. I grew up recognizing that there was nobody to give me any advice and that you do your best and if it's not good enough, someday you will come to terms with that. I don't want to be the one to tell somebody, You will not make it, even though I know that the majority of those who come to me with their manuscripts are not really good enough. But you don't ever want to say to a young person, You can't, or, You are no good. Some people might be able to do it, but I don't think I am a policeman for literature. So I tell them, Sweat it out, do your best. Don't publish it yourself—this is one tendency that is becoming more and more common in Nigeria. You go and find someone—a friend—to print your book.

INTERVIEWER

We call that a vanity press here.

ACHEBE

Yes, vanity printing, yes. That really has very severe limitations. I think once you have done all you can to a manuscript, let it find its way in the world.

Issue 133, 1994

Ted Hughes

The Art of Poetry

Ted Hughes lives with his wife, Carol, on a farm in Devonshire. It is a working farm—sheep and cows—and the Hugheses are known to leave a party early to tend to them. "Carol's got to get the sheep in," Hughes will explain.

He came to London for the interview, which took place in the interviewer's dining room. The poet was wearing a tweed jacket, dark trousers, and a tie whose predominantly blue color matched his eyes. His voice is commanding. He is often invited to read his work, the flow of his language enlivening the text. In appearance he is impressive, and yet there is very little aggression or intimidation in his look. Indeed, one admirer has said that her first thought sitting opposite him was that this was what God should look like "when you get there."

Born Edward James Hughes on August 17, 1930, in the small mill town of Mytholmroyd, he is the youngest of the three children of Edith Farrar Hughes and William Henry Hughes. The first seven years of his life were spent in West Yorkshire, on that area's barren, windswept moors. Hughes once said that he could "never escape the impression that the whole region [was] in mourning for the First World War."

He began to write poetry at age seven, after his family moved to Mexborough. It was under the tutelage of his teacher at the town's only grammar school that Hughes began to mature—his work evolving into the rhythmic passionate poetry for which he has become known throughout the world.

When Crow was white he decided the sun was too bright
he decided it glared too white
he decided to attack it defeat it

Crow got his strength ... in full glitter.
He clawed and ... his rage up
He aimed his beak direct at the sun's centre.

He ... his confidence, like a ...
He ... his determination, like a ...
He launched himself to the centre of ... himself
and attacked.
At his battle cry trees grew suddenly old,
Shadows flattened.

But the sun, brightened ... grew ... bigger
and brightened
and Crow returned clawed black (or
unrecognisable)

He opened his mouth but what he said was charred (or
incomprehensible)

"Up there," he managed,
"where white is black, and black is white, I won."

A manuscript page of a poem by Ted Hughes.

Following two years of service in the Royal Air Force, Hughes enrolled at Pembroke College, Cambridge University. He had initially intended to study English literature but found that department's curriculum too limited; archaeology and anthropology proved to be areas of the academic arena more suited to his taste.

Two years after graduating, Hughes and a group of classmates founded the infamous literary magazine *St. Botolph's Review*—known more for its inaugural party than its longevity (it lasted only one issue). It was at that party that Hughes met Sylvia Plath, an American student studying in England. Plath would recall the event in a journal entry: "I met the strongest man in the world, ex-Cambridge, brilliant poet whose work I loved before I met him, a large, bulky, healthy Adam, half French, half Irish, with a voice like the thunder of god—a singer, story-teller, lion, and world wanderer, a vagabond who will never stop." They were wed on June 16, 1956, and remained married for six and a half years, having two children, Frieda and Nicholas. In the fall of 1962 they became estranged over Hughes's alleged infidelities. On February 11, 1963, while residing in a separate apartment, Plath placed towels under the door of the room where her children were napping, laid out a snack for them, turned on the gas jet of her kitchen stove and placed her head in the oven—asphyxiating herself.

A few months after their marriage, Plath had entered a number of her husband's poems in a competition judged by W. H. Auden, among others. Hughes was awarded first prize for his collection *Hawk in the Rain*. It was published in 1957 by Faber & Faber in England and Harper & Row in America. With his next publication, *Lupercal*, in 1960, Hughes became recognized as one of the most significant English poets to emerge since World War II, winning the Somerset Maugham Award in 1960 and the Hawthornden Prize in 1961.

His next notable work was *Wadwo*, a compilation of five short stories, a radio play, and some forty poems. Although it contained many of the violent animal images of Hughes's earlier work, it reflected the poet's growing enchantment with mythology. *Wadwo* led Hughes into an odd fascination with one of the most solitary and ominous images in folklore, the crow. While his aspiration to create an epic tale centering on this bird has not been fulfilled, he did publish *Crow: From the Life and Songs of the Crow* in 1970, sixty-six poems or "songs," as Hughes referred to them. The American version, published by Harper the following year, was well received. *The New York Review of Books* said that *Crow* was "perhaps a more plausible explanation for the present condition of the world than the Christian sequence."

Still deeply interested in mythology and folklore, Hughes created *Orghast*, a play based largely on the Prometheus legend, in 1971, while he was in Iran with members of the International Center for Theater Research. He wrote most of the play's dialogue in an invented language to illustrate the theory that sound alone could express very complex human emotions. Hughes continued on this theme with his next work of poetry entitled *Prometheus on His Crag*, published in 1973 by Rainbow Press.

His next two works of note, *Cave Birds* and *Gaudete*, were predominantly based on the Gravesian concept that mankind has sinned by denying the "White Goddess," the natural, primordial aspect of modern man, while choosing to nurture a conscious, almost sterile intellectual humanism.

Following the publication of his 1983 work *River*, Ted Hughes was named poet laureate of Great Britain. His recent publications, *Flowers and Insects* (1987) and *Wolfwatching* (1991), show a return to his earlier nature-oriented work—possessing a raw force that evokes the physical immediacy of human experience.

Hughes has shown a great range in his work, and aside from his adult verse, he has written children's stories (*Tales of the Early World*), poetry (*Under the North Star*), and plays (*The Coming of the Kings*). Hughes has also edited selections of other writers' work, most notably the late Plath's. The controversy surrounding Hughes's notorious editing and reordering of Plath's poetry and journals, the destruction of at least one volume of the latter, as well as the mysterious disappearance of her putative final novel have mythologized both poets and made it difficult for Hughes to live the anonymous life he has sought in rural Devonshire.

—*Drue Heinz, 1995*

INTERVIEWER

Would you like to talk about your childhood? What shaped your work and contributed to your development as a poet?

TED HUGHES

Well, as far as my writing is concerned, maybe the crucial thing was that I spent my first years in a valley in West Yorkshire in the north of England, which was really a long street of industrial towns—textile mills, textile factories. The little village where I was born had quite a few; the next town fifty. And so on. These towns were surrounded by a very wide landscape of high moorland, in contrast to that industry into which everybody disappeared every day. They just vanished. If you weren't at school you were alone in an empty wilderness.

When I came to consciousness my whole interest was in wild animals. My earliest memories are of the lead animal toys you could buy in those days, wonderfully accurate models. Throughout my childhood I collected these. I had a brother, ten years older, whose passion was shooting. He wanted to be a big game hunter or a game warden in Africa—that was his dream. His compromise in West Yorkshire was to shoot over the hillsides and on the moor edge with a rifle. He would take me along. So my early memories of being three and four are of going off with him, being his retriever. I became completely preoccupied by his world of hunting. He was also a very imaginative fellow; he mythologized his hunting world as North American Indian, Paleolithic. And I lived in his dream. Up to the age of seventeen or eighteen, shooting and fishing and my preoccupation with animals were pretty well my life, apart from books. That makes me sound like more of a loner than I was. Up to twelve or thirteen I also played with my town friends every evening, a little gang, the innocent stuff of those days, kicking about the neighborhood. But weekends I was off on my own. I had a double life.

The writing, the reading came up gradually behind that. From the age of about eight or nine I read just about every comic book available in England. At that time my parents owned a newsagent's shop. I took the comics from the shop, read them, and put them back. That went on until I was twelve or thirteen. Then my mother brought in a sort of children's encyclopedia that included sections of folklore. Little folktales. I remember the shock of reading those stories. I could not believe that such wonderful things existed. The only stories we'd had as younger children were ones our mother had told us—that she made up, mostly. In those early days ours wasn't a house full of books. My father knew quite long passages of "Hiawatha" that he used to recite, something he had from his school days. That had its effect. I remember I wrote a good deal of comic verse for classroom consumption in Hiawatha meter. But throughout your life you have certain literary shocks, and the folktales were my first. From then on I began to collect folklore, folk stories, and mythology. That became my craze.

INTERVIEWER

Can you remember when you first started writing?

HUGHES

I first started writing those comic verses when I was eleven, when I went to grammar school. I realized that certain things I wrote amused my teacher and my classmates. I began to regard myself as a writer, writing as my specialty. But nothing more than that until I was about fourteen, when I discovered Kipling's poems. I was completely bowled over by the rhythm. Their rhythmical, mechanical drive got into me. So suddenly I began to write rhythmical poems, long sagas in Kiplingesque rhythms. I started showing them to my English teacher—at the time a young woman in her early twenties, very keen on poetry. I suppose I was fourteen, fifteen. I was sensitive, of course, to any bit of recognition of anything in my writing. I remember her—probably groping to say something encouraging—pointing to one phrase saying, This is really . . . interesting. Then she said, It's real poetry. It wasn't a phrase; it was a compound epithet concerning the hammer of a punt gun on an imaginary wildfowling hunt. I immediately pricked up my ears. That moment still seems the crucial one. Suddenly I became interested in producing more of that kind of thing. Her words somehow directed me to the main pleasure in my own life, the kind of experience I lived for. So I homed in. Then very quickly—you know how fast these things happen at that age—I began to think, Well, maybe this is what I want to do. And by the time I was sixteen that was all I wanted to do.

I equipped myself in the most obvious way: whatever I liked I tried to learn by heart. I imitated things. And I read a great deal aloud to myself. Reading verse aloud put me on a kind of high. Gradually all this replaced shooting and fishing. When my shooting pal went off to do his national service, I used to sit around in the woods, muttering through my books. I read the whole of *The Faerie Queene* like that. All of Milton. Lots more. It became sort of a hobby-habit. I read a good deal else as well and was constantly trying to write something, of course. That same teacher lent me her Eliot and introduced me to three or four of Hopkins's poems. Then I met Yeats. I was still preoccupied by Kipling when I met Yeats via the third part of his poem "The Wandering of Oisin," which was in the kind of meter I was looking for. Yeats sucked me in through the Irish folklore and myth and the occult business. My dominant passion in poetry up to and through university was Yeats, Yeats under the canopy of Shakespeare and Blake. By the time I got to university, at twenty-one, my sacred canon was fixed: Chaucer, Shakespeare, Marlowe, Blake, Wordsworth, Keats, Coleridge, Hopkins, Yeats, Eliot. I knew no American poetry at all except Eliot. I had a complete Whitman but still didn't know how to read it. The only modern foreign poet I knew was Rilke in Spender's and Leishmann's translation. I was fascinated by Rilke. I had one or two collections with me through my national service. I could see the huge worlds of other possibilities opening in there. But I couldn't see how to get into them. I also had my mother's Bible, a small book with the Psalms, Jeremiah, the Song of Songs, Proverbs, Job, and other bits here and there all set out as free verse. I read whatever contemporary verse I happened to come across, but apart from Dylan Thomas and Auden, I rejected it. It didn't give me any leads somehow, or maybe I simply wasn't ready for it.

INTERVIEWER

Was it difficult to make a living when you started out? How did you do it?

HUGHES

I was ready to do anything, really. Any small job. I went to the United States and taught a little bit, though I didn't want to. I taught first in England in a secondary school, fourteen-year-old boys. I experienced the terrific exhaustion of that profession. I wanted to keep my energy for myself, as if I had the right. I found teaching fascinating but wanted too much to do something else. Then I saw how much money could be made quite quickly by writing children's books. A story—perhaps not true—is that Maxine Kumin wrote fifteen children's stories and made a thousand dollars for each. That seemed to me preferable to attempting a big novel or a problematic play, which would devour great stretches of time with doubtful results in cash. Also, it seemed to me I had a knack of a kind for inventing children's stories. So I did write quite a few. But I didn't have Maxine Kumin's magic. I couldn't sell any of them. I sold them only years later, after my verse had made a reputation for me of a kind. So up to the age of thirty-three, I was living on what one lives on: reviews, BBC work, little radio plays, that sort of thing. Anything for immediate cash. Then, when I was thirty-three, I suddenly received in the post the news that the Abraham Woursell Foundation had given me a lecturer's salary at the University of Vienna for five years. I had no idea how I came to be awarded this. That salary took me from thirty-four years old to thirty-eight, and by that time I was earning my living by my writing. A critical five years. That was when I had the children, and the money saved me from looking for a job outside the house.

INTERVIEWER

Do you have a favorite place to write or can you write anywhere?

HUGHES

Hotel rooms are good. Railway compartments are good. I've had several huts of one sort or another. Ever since I began to write with a purpose I've been looking for the ideal place. I think most writers go through it. I've known several who liked to treat it as a job—writing in some office well away from home, going there regular hours. Sylvia had a friend, a novelist, who used to leave her grand house and go into downtown Boston to a tiny room with a table and chair where she wrote facing a blank wall. Didn't Somerset Maugham also write facing a blank wall? Subtle distraction is the enemy—a big beautiful view, the tide going in and out. Of course, you think it oughtn't to matter, and sometimes it doesn't. Several of my favorite pieces in my book *Crow* I wrote traveling up and down Germany with a woman and small child—I just went on writing wherever we were. Enoch Powell claims that noise and bustle help him to concentrate. Then again, Goethe couldn't write a line if there was another person anywhere in the same house, or so he said at some point. I've tried to test it on myself, and my feeling is that your sense of being concentrated can deceive you. Writing in what seems to be a happy concentrated way, in a room in your own house with books and everything necessary to your life around you, produces something noticeably different, I think, from writing in some empty silent place far away from all that. Because however we concentrate, we remain aware at some level of everything around us. Fast asleep, we keep track of the time to the second. The person conversing at one end of a long table quite unconsciously uses the same unusual words, within a second or two, as the person conversing with somebody else at the other end—though they're amazed to learn they've done it. Also, different kinds of writing need different kinds of concentration. Goethe, picking up a transmission from the other side of his mind, from *beyond* his usual mind, needs different tuning than Enoch Powell when he writes a speech. Brain rhythms would show us what's going on, I expect. But for me successful writing has usually been a case of having found good conditions for real, effortless concentration. When I was living in Boston, in my late twenties, I was so conscious of this that at one point I covered the windows with brown paper to blank out any view and wore earplugs—simply to isolate myself from distraction. That's how I worked for a year. When I came back to England, I think the best place I found in that first year or two was a tiny cubicle at the top of the stairs that was no bigger than a table really. But it was a wonderful place to write. I mean, I can see now, by what I wrote there, that it was a good place. At the time it just seemed like a convenient place.

INTERVIEWER
What tools do you require?

HUGHES
Just a pen.

INTERVIEWER
Just a pen? You write longhand?

HUGHES
I made an interesting discovery about myself when I first worked for a film company. I had to write brief summaries of novels and plays to give the directors some idea of their film potential—a page or so of prose about each book or play and then my comment. That was where I began to write for the first time directly onto a typewriter. I was then about twenty-five. I realized instantly that when I composed directly onto the typewriter my sentences became three times as long, much longer. My subordinate clauses flowered and multiplied and ramified away down the length of the page, all much more eloquently than anything I would have written by hand. Recently I made another similar discovery. For about thirty years I've been on the judging panel of the W. H. Smith children's writing competition. Annually there are about sixty thousand entries. These are cut down to about eight hundred. Among these our panel finds seventy prizewinners. Usually the entries are a page, two pages, three pages. That's been the norm. Just a poem or a bit of prose, a little longer. But in the early 1980s we suddenly began to get seventy- and eighty-page works. These were usually space fiction, always very inventive and always extraordinarily fluent—a definite impression of a command of words and prose, but without exception strangely boring. It was almost impossible to read them through. After two or three years, as these became more numerous, we realized that this was a new thing. So we inquired. It turned out that these were pieces that children had composed on word processors. What's happening is that as the actual tools for getting words onto the page become more flexible and externalized, the writer can get down

almost every thought or every extension of thought. That ought to be an advantage. But in fact, in all these cases, it just extends everything slightly too much. Every sentence is too long. Everything is taken a bit too far, too attenuated. There's always a bit too much there, and it's too thin. Whereas when writing by hand you meet the terrible resistance of what happened your first year at it when you couldn't write at all . . . when you were making attempts, pretending to form letters. These ancient feelings are there, wanting to be expressed. When you sit with your pen, every year of your life is right there, wired into the communication between your brain and your writing hand. There is a natural characteristic resistance that produces a certain kind of result analogous to your actual handwriting. As you force your expression against that built-in resistance, things become automatically more compressed, more summary and, perhaps, psychologically denser. I suppose if you use a word processor and deliberately prune everything back, alert to the tendencies, it should be possible to get the best of both worlds.

Maybe what I'm saying applies only to those who have gone through the long conditioning of writing only with a pen or pencil up through their mid-twenties. For those who start early on a typewriter or, these days, on a computer screen, things must be different. The wiring must be different. In handwriting the brain is mediated by the drawing hand, in typewriting by the fingers hitting the keyboard, in dictation by the idea of a vocal style, in word processing by touching the keyboard and by the screen's feedback. The fact seems to be that each of these methods produces a different syntactic result from the same brain. Maybe the crucial element in handwriting is that the hand is simultaneously drawing. I know I'm very conscious of hidden imagery in handwriting—a subtext of a rudimentary picture language. Perhaps that tends to enforce more cooperation from the other side of the brain. And perhaps that extra load of right-brain suggestions prompts a different succession of words and ideas. Perhaps that's what I am talking about.

INTERVIEWER

So word processing is a new discipline.

HUGHES

It's a new discipline that these particular children haven't learned. And which I think some novelists haven't learned. "Brevity is the soul of wit." It makes the imagination jump. I think I recognize among some modern novels the supersonic hand of the word processor uncurbed. When Henry James started dictating, his sentences became interminable, didn't they? And the physical world, as his brother William complained, suddenly disappeared from them. Henry hadn't realized. He was astonished.

INTERVIEWER

How long does it take to write a poem? Of course it depends on length and hibernation time, but still . . .

HUGHES

Well, in looking back over the whole lot, the best ones took just as long as it took to write them down; the not-so-satisfactory ones I'd tinker with sometimes for two or three years, but certainly for a few days, and I'd continue making changes over months. Some of them I'd still like to change.

INTERVIEWER

Are poems ever truly finished?

HUGHES

My experience with the things that arrive instantaneously is that I can't change them. They are finished. There is one particular poem, an often anthologized piece that just came—"Hawk Roosting." I simply wrote it out just as it appeared in front of me. There is a word in the middle that I'm not sure about. I always have this internal hiccup when I get to it because I had to make the choice between the singular and the plural form and neither of them is right.

INTERVIEWER

Has the answer occurred to you since?

HUGHES

No. I don't know that it could be solved. It's just one of those funny things. So that poem was abandoned insofar as I couldn't solve that problem. But otherwise it's a poem that I could no more think of changing than physically changing myself. Poems get to the point where they are stronger than you are. They come up from some other depth and they find a place on the page. You can never find that depth again, that same kind of authority and voice. I might *feel* I would like to change something about them, but they're still stronger than I am and I cannot.

INTERVIEWER

Do you read or show your work to others while it is in progress?

HUGHES

I try not to. There's a Jewish proverb that Leonard Baskin's always quoting: Never show fools half-work. That "fools" is a bit hard, but I imagine most people who make things know what is meant.

INTERVIEWER

How has criticism of your work affected you or your poetry?

HUGHES

I think it's the shock of every writer's life when their first book is published. The shock of their lives. One has somehow to adjust from being anonymous, a figure in ambush, working from concealment, to being and working in full public view. It had an enormous effect on me. My impression was that I had suddenly walked into a wall of heavy hostile fire. That first year I wrote verses with three magical assonances to the line with the intention of abolishing certain critics! Now I read those reviews and they seem quite good. So it was writer's paranoia. The shock to a person who's never been named in public of being mentioned in newspapers can be absolutely traumatic. To everybody else it looks fairly harmless, even enviable. What I *can* see was that it enormously accelerated my determination to bring my whole operation into my own terms, to make my own form of writing and to abandon a lot of more casual paths that I might have followed. If I'd remained completely unknown, a writer not commented on, I think I might have gone off in all kinds of other directions. One can never be sure, of course.

Wasn't there ever a desire to do something else?

Yes, always. Yes. I've sometimes wondered if it wouldn't be a good idea to write under a few pseudonyms. Keep several quite different lines of writing going. Like Fernando Pessoa, the Portuguese poet who tried four different poetic personalities. They all worked simultaneously. He simply lived with the four. What does Eliot say? "Dance, dance, / Like a dancing bear, / Cry like a parrot, chatter like an ape, / To find expression." It's certainly limiting to confine your writing to one public persona, because the moment you publish your own name you lose freedom. It's like being in a close-knit family. The moment you do anything new, the whole family jumps on it, comments, teases, advises against, does everything to make you self-conscious. There's a unanimous reaction to keep you as you were. You'd suppose any writer worth his salt could be bold and fearless and not give a damn. But in fact very few can. We're at the mercy of the groups that shaped our early days. We're so helplessly social—like cells in an organ. Maybe that's why madness sometimes works—it knocks out the over-sensitive connection. And maybe that's why exile is good. I wonder if the subjective impression of most writers is that whenever they take a new step, some big, unconscious reaction among readers tries to stop them . . . often a big conscious reaction among colleagues. Hardy stopped writing novels by just that. In his late years, while he was up in an apple tree, pruning it, he had a vision of the most magnificent novel—all the characters, many episodes, even some dialogue—the one ultimate novel that he absolutely had to write. What happened? By the time he came down out of the tree the whole vision had fled. And it never reappeared. Even Goethe, back then, made some remark about the impossibility of producing a natural oeuvre of fully ripened works when everything was instantly before the public and its hectic, printed reactions. Of course Goethe himself was a terrible stopper of other young writers. One of the strongest arguments that Shakespeare's plays were written by somebody unsuspected, maybe, was the uniquely *complete* development of that creative mind and its vision.

Also, there's a tendency to lay down laws for yourself about the kind of thing you want to do—an ideal of style, an exemplary probity of some kind, or maybe an ideal of thuggery, a release into disregard for all conventions and so on. Once they become your expected product, these are all traps. One way out of this might be to write a kind of provisional drama where you can explore all sorts of different provisional attitudes and voices. Remember the unresolved opposition of Trigorin and Treplev in Chekhov's *The Seagull?* Chekhov had a huge nostalgia for Treplev's weird vision. Somewhere he described the sort of work he longed to write—full of passionate, howling women, Greek tragedy dimension—and he bemoans the gentle doctor's attentiveness that imbues his actual writing. Now, if he'd been anonymous from the start, might he have explored the other things, too? In poetry, living as a public persona in your writing is maybe even more crippling. Once you've contracted to write only the truth about yourself—as in some respected kinds of modern verse, or as in Shakespeare's sonnets—then you can too easily limit yourself to what you imagine are the truths of the ego that claims your conscious biography. Your own equivalent of what Shakespeare got into his plays is simply foregone. But being experimental isn't enough. The plunge has to be for real. The new thing has to be not you or has to seem so till it turns out to be the new you or the other you.

INTERVIEWER

You say that every writer should have a pseudonym for writing things different than their usual work. Have you ever used one?

HUGHES

Never—except once or twice at university. But I wish I had. I wish I'd established one or two out there. The danger, I suppose, of using pseudonyms is that it interferes with that desirable process—the unification of the personality. Goethe said that even the writing of plays, dividing the imagination up among different fictional personalities, damaged what he valued—the mind's wholeness. I wonder what he meant exactly, since he also described his mode of thinking as imagined conversations with various people. Maybe the pseudonyms, like other personalities conjured up in a dramatic work, can be a preliminary stage of identifying and exploring new parts of yourself. Then the next stage would be to incorporate them in the unifying process. Accept responsibility for them. Maybe that's what Yeats meant by seeking his opposite. The great Sufi master Ibn el-Arabi described the essential method of spiritual advancement as an inner conversation with the personalities that seem to exist beyond what you regard as your own limits . . . getting those personalities to tell you what you did not know, or what you could not easily conceive of within your habitual limits. This is commonplace in some therapies, of course.

INTERVIEWER

What kind of working relationship have you had with editors of both poetry and prose?

HUGHES

On the whole I've been lucky with them. Extremely lucky. I was more than lucky to have T. S. Eliot as my first editor in England. Sylvia had typed up and sent off my manuscript to a 92nd Street Y first poetry book competition—judged by Marianne Moore, Stephen Spender, and Auden. First prize was publication by Harper Brothers. When it won, Sylvia sent Faber the typescript and a letter with that information in which, in American style, she referred to me as Ted. They replied that Faber did not publish first books by American authors. When she told them I was British they took it. That's how I came to be Ted rather than something else.

Eliot's editorial hand on me could not have been lighter. In my second book of verse he suggested one verbal change, but I didn't follow it. I should have. He made some very useful suggestions in a book of verse for children that I wrote. I certainly followed those. My present children's editor at Faber, Janice Thompson, is brilliant in that she definitely gets me to write more things than I otherwise might and makes very acute judgments and suggestions about what I do produce. Editors in the United States—well, I've liked and got on with them all. But at that long distance I've never got to know any so well as I've known the Faber succession. Except for Fran McCullough at Harper. Fran became a close friend while she was editing Sylvia's books and mine. She edited Sylvia's novel *The Bell Jar* and *Letters Home*. Later she edited Sylvia's *Journals*. Some explosive drama in all that. Only the beginning of bigger explosions. I hope we've remained friends in the fallout.

INTERVIEWER

Has it ever become impossible to write?

HUGHES

The nearest I've ever felt to a block was a sort of unfitness in the athletic sense—the need for an all-out, sustained effort of writing simply to get myself into shape before starting on what I imagined would be the real thing. One whole book arrived like that, not a very long book, but one which I felt I needed to galvanize my inertia, break through the huge sloth I was up against. On the spur I invented a little plot: nine birds come to the fallen Adam urging him to get up and be birdlike. I wrote the whole as a bagatelle to sweat myself out of that inertia—and to conjure myself to be a bit more birdlike. Then, suddenly there it was, a sort of book. *Adam and the Sacred Nine*. I'd written a book just trying to get to the point where I might begin to write something that might go into a book. Still, did it break through to the real thing? That's the question, isn't it? A block is when we can't get through to the real thing. Many writers write a great deal, but very few write more than a very little of the real thing. So most writing must be displaced activity. When cockerels confront each other and daren't fight, they busily start pecking imaginary grains off to the side. That's displaced activity. Much of what we do at any level is a bit like that, I fancy. But hard to know which is which. On the other hand, the machinery has to be kept running. The big problem for those who write verse is keeping the machine running without simply exercising evasion of the real confrontation. If

Ulanova, the ballerina, missed one day of practice, she couldn't get back to peak fitness without a week of hard work. Dickens said the same about his writing—if he missed a day he needed a week of hard slog to get back into the flow.

Could I ask about your relationship with other poets? You knew Auden and Eliot.

I met Auden for more than a hello only twice. It was at a poetry festival in 1966. Our conversation was very brief. He said, What do you make of David Jones's *Anathemata*? I replied, A work of genius, a masterpiece. Correct, he said. That was it. The other occasion was after one of the 1966 International Poetry Festival evenings on the South Bank in London when he was fuming against Neruda. I listened to his diatribe. We'd asked Neruda to read for twelve minutes, maybe fifteen. He'd read for over half an hour, longer—apparently from a piece of paper about four inches square. Auden always timed his readings to the minute. Neruda and Auden died almost on the same day; *The New Statesman* gave Neruda the front page and tucked Auden inside. I felt pained by that, though I have no doubt that Neruda is in a different class, a world class, as a poet. I sort of swallowed Auden whole sometime in my early twenties—or tried to. He was so much part of the atmosphere. Some of his work I have always admired a lot. And I admire him—the Goethean side, the dazzle of natural brilliance in all his remarks. But I never felt any real poetic affinity with him. I suppose he is not a poet who taps the sort of things I am trying to tap in myself. Eliot was. I met Eliot only rarely and briefly. Once he and his wife Valerie invited Sylvia and myself to dinner. We were a bit overawed. Fortunately Stephen Spender, who was there, knew how to handle it. What do I recall? Many small humorous remarks. His very slow eating. The size of his hands—very large hands. Once I asked him if the *Landscapes*, those short beautiful little pieces each so different from the others, were selections from a great many similar unpublished things. I thought they might be the sort of poem he whittled away at between the bigger works. No, he said. That's all there were. They just came. It's a mystery. He wins the big races with such ease—but how did he keep in trim? How did he get into form? He seems to me one of the very great poets. One of the very few.

INTERVIEWER

What did you think of Ezra Pound? Did he give you pleasure?

HUGHES

He did, yes. Still does. But as a personality—he doesn't have the power to fascinate as a personality that, for instance, Eliot does; or Yeats, perhaps because his internal evolution, or whatever it was, was so broken, so confused by a militance that took it over from the outside. Perhaps one recoils from what feels like a disintegration. But many pages of the verse seem to me wonderful in all kinds of ways.

INTERVIEWER

You have been associated with Mark Strand and W. S. Merwin. How do you see their work as compared to yours?

HUGHES

I know Merwin's work pretty well. Mark Strand's less well, though I look at it very closely wherever I find it. I've been close to Bill Merwin in the past. I got to know him in the late fifties through Jack Sweeney who was then running the Lamont Poetry Library at Harvard. They had a house in London, and when Sylvia and I got back there in late 1959 they helped us a lot, in practical and other ways. Dido Merwin found us our flat, then half furnished it, then cooked things for Sylvia in the run-up to our daughter being born. That was the high point of my friendship with Bill. He was an important writer for me at that time. It was a crucial moment in his poetry—very big transformations were going on in there; it was coming out of its chrysalis. And I suppose because we were so close, living only a couple of hundred yards apart, his inner changes were part of the osmotic flow of feelings between us. Very important for me. That's when I began to get out of my second collection of poems and into

my third—which became the book entitled *Wodwo*. He helped me out
of my chrysalis, too. Partway out. And he was pretty important for
Sylvia a little later when the *Ariel* poems began to arrive in early 1962.
One of the hidden supply lines behind *Ariel* was the set of Neruda
translations that Bill did for the BBC at that time. I still have her copy.
It wasn't just Neruda that helped her. It was the way she saw how Bill
used Neruda. That wasn't her only supply line, but it was one. I think
Bill's traveled further on his road than any contemporary U.S. or
British writer I can think of. Amazing resources and skills.

INTERVIEWER

What do you think of the label "confessional poetry" and the tendency for more and more poets to work in that mode?

HUGHES

Goethe called his work one big confession, didn't he? Looking at his
work in the broadest sense, you could say the same of Shakespeare:
a total self-examination and self-accusation, a total confession—very
naked, I think, when you look into it. Maybe it's the same with any writing that has real poetic life. Maybe all poetry, insofar as it moves us and
connects with us, is a revealing of something that the writer doesn't actually want to say but desperately needs to communicate, to be delivered of. Perhaps it's the need to keep it hidden that makes it
poetic—makes it poetry. The writer daren't actually put it into words,
so it leaks out obliquely, smuggled through analogies. We think we're
writing something to amuse, but we're actually saying something we
desperately need to share. The real mystery is this strange need. Why
can't we just hide it and shut up? Why do we have to blab? Why do
human beings need to confess? Maybe if you don't have that secret
confession, you don't have a poem—don't even have a story. Don't
have a writer. If most poetry doesn't seem to be in any sense confessional, it's because the strategy of concealment, of obliquity, can be so
compulsive that it's almost entirely successful. The smuggling analogy
is loaded with interesting cargo that seems to be there for its own
sake—subject matter of general interest—but at the bottom of *Paradise
Lost* and *Samson Agonistes*, for instance, Milton tells us what nearly got

him executed. The novelty of some of Robert Lowell's most affecting pieces in *Life Studies*, some of Anne Sexton's poems, and some of Sylvia's was the way they tried to throw off that luggage, the deliberate way they stripped off the veiling analogies. Sylvia went furthest in the sense that her secret was most dangerous to her. She desperately needed to reveal it. You can't overestimate her compulsion to write like that. She had to write those things—even against her most vital interests. She died before she knew what *The Bell Jar* and the *Ariel* poems were going to do to her life, but she had to get them out. She had to tell everybody . . . like those Native American groups who periodically told everything that was wrong and painful in their lives in the presence of the whole tribe. It was no good doing it in secret; it had to be done in front of everybody else. Maybe that's why poets go to such lengths to get their poems published. It's no good whispering them to a priest or a confessional. And it's not for fame, because they go on doing it after they've learned what fame amounts to. No, until the revelation's actually published, the poet feels no release. In all that, Sylvia was an extreme case, I think.

INTERVIEWER

Could you talk a bit more about Sylvia?

HUGHES

Sylvia and I met because she was curious about my group of friends at university and I was curious about her. I was working in London but I used to go back up to Cambridge at weekends. Half a dozen or so of us made a poetic gang. Our main cooperative activity was drinking in the Anchor and our main common interest, apart from fellow feeling and mutual attraction, was Irish, Scottish, and Welsh traditional songs—folk songs and broadsheet ballads. We sang a lot. Recorded folk songs were rare in those days. Our poetic interests were more mutually understood than talked about. But we did print a broadsheet of literary comment. In one issue, one of our group, our Welshman, Dan Huws, demolished a poem that Sylvia had published, "Caryatids." He later became a close friend of hers, wrote a beautiful elegy when she died. That attack attracted her attention. Also, she had met one of our group, Lucas Myers, an American, who was an especially close friend of mine. Luke was very dark and skinny. He could be incredibly wild. Just what you hoped for from Tennessee. His poems were startling to us—Hart Crane, Wallace Stevens vocabulary, zany. He interested Sylvia. In her journals she records the occasional dream in which Luke appears unmistakably. When we published a magazine full of our own poems, the only issue of *St. Botolph's*, and launched it at a big dance party, Sylvia came to see what the rest of us looked like. Up to that point I'd never set eyes on her. I'd heard plenty about her from an English girlfriend who shared supervisions with her. There she suddenly was, raving Luke's verses at Luke and my verses at me.

Once I got to know her and read her poems, I saw straight off that she was a genius of some kind. Quite suddenly we were completely committed to each other and to each other's writing. The year before, I had started writing again after the years of the devastation of university. I'd just written what have become some of my more anthologized pieces—"The Thought Fox," the Jaguar poems, "Wind." I see now that when we met, my writing, like hers, left its old path and started to circle and search. To me, of course, she was not only herself—she was America and American literature in person. I don't know what I was to her. Apart from the more monumental classics—Tolstoy, Dostoyevsky, and so on—my background reading was utterly different from hers. But our minds soon became two parts of one operation. We dreamed a lot of shared or complementary dreams. Our telepathy was intrusive. I don't know whether our verse exchanged much, if we influenced one another that way—not in the early days. Maybe others see that differently. Our methods were not the same. Hers was to collect a heap of vivid objects and good words and make a pattern; the pattern would be projected from somewhere deep inside, from her very distinctly evolved myth. It appears distinctly evolved to a reader now—despite having been totally unconscious to her then. My method was to find a thread end and draw the rest out of a hidden tangle. Her method was more painterly, mine more narrative, perhaps. Throughout our time together we looked at each other's verses at every stage—up to the *Ariel* poems of October 1962, which was when we separated.

INTERVIEWER

Do you know how Sylvia used her journals? Were they diaries or notebooks for her poetry and fiction?

HUGHES

Well, I think Janet Malcolm in *The New Yorker* made a fair point about the journals: a lot of what's in them is practice . . . shaping up for some possible novel, little chapters for novels. She was constantly sketching something that happened and working it into something she thought might fit into a novel. She thought of her journals as working notes for some ultimate novel although, in fact, I don't think any of it ever went into *The Bell Jar*. She changed certain things to make them *work*, to make some kind of symbolic statement of a feeling. She wasn't writing an account of this or that event; she was trying to get to some other kind of ancient, i.e., childhood, material. Some of her short stories take the technique a stage further. Wanting to express that ancient feeling.

INTERVIEWER

What happened to Plath's last novel that was never published?

HUGHES

Well, what I was aware of was a fragment of a novel, about seventy pages. Her mother said she saw a whole novel, but I never knew about it. What I was aware of was sixty, seventy pages that disappeared. And to tell you the truth, I always assumed her mother took them all on one of her visits.

INTERVIEWER

Would you talk about burning Plath's journals?

HUGHES

What I actually destroyed was one journal that covered maybe two or three months, the last months. And it was just sad. I just didn't want her children to see it, no. Particularly her last days.

INTERVIEWER

What about *Ariel*? Did you reorder the poems there?

HUGHES

Well, nobody in the United States wanted to publish the collection as she left it. The one publisher over there who was interested wanted to cut it to twenty poems. The fear seemed to be that the whole lot might provoke some sort of backlash—some revulsion. And at the time, you know, few magazine editors would publish the *Ariel* poems; few liked them. The qualities weren't so obvious in those days. So right from the start there was a question over just how the book was to be presented. I wanted the book that would display the whole range and variety. I remember writing to the man who suggested cutting it to twenty—a longish intemperate letter, as I recall—and saying I felt that was simply impossible. I was torn between cutting some things out and putting some more things in. I was keen to get some of the last poems in. But the real problem was, as I've said, that the U.S. publishers I approached did not want Sylvia's collection as it stood. Faber in England were happy to publish the book in any form. Finally it was a compromise—I cut some things out and I put others in. As a result I have been mightily accused of disordering her intentions and even suppressing part of her work. But those charges have evolved twenty, thirty years after the event. They are based on simple ignorance of how it all happened. Within six years of that first publication all her late poems were published in collections—all that she'd put in her own *Ariel* and those she'd kept out. It was her growing fame, of course, that made it possible to publish them. And years ago, for anybody who was curious, I published the contents and order of her own typescript—so if anybody wants to see what her *Ariel* was it's quite easy. On the other hand, how final was her order? She was forever shuffling the poems in her typescripts—looking for different connections, better sequences. She knew there were always new possibilities, all fluid.

INTERVIEWER

Could you say a bit more about how your own poems originate and how you begin writing?

HUGHES

Well, I have a sort of notion. Just the tail end of an idea, usually just the thread of an idea. If I can feel behind that a sort of waiting momentum, a sense of some charge there to tap, then I just plunge in. What usually happens then—inevitably I would say—is that I go off in some wholly different direction. The thread end of an idea burns away and I'm pulled in—on the momentum of whatever was there waiting. Then that feeling opens up other energies, all the possibilities in my head, I suppose. That's the pleasure—never quite knowing what's there, being surprised. Once I get onto something I usually finish it. In a way it goes on finishing itself while I attend to its needs. It might be days, months. Later, often enough, I see exactly what it needs to be and I finish it in moments, usually by getting rid of things.

INTERVIEWER

What do birds mean for you? The figures of the hawk and the crow—so astonishing. Are you tired to death of explaining them?

HUGHES

I don't know how to explain them. There are certain things that are just impressive, aren't there? One stone can be impressive and the stones around it aren't. It's the same with animals. Some, for some reason, are strangely impressive. They just get into you in a strange way. Certain birds obviously have this extra quality that fascinates your attention. Obviously hawks have always done that for me, as a great many others have—not only impressive in themselves but also in that they've accumulated an enormous literature making them even more impressive. And crows, too. Crows are the central bird in many mythologies. The crow is at every extreme, lives on every piece of land on earth, the most intelligent bird.

INTERVIEWER

Your poem "The Thought Fox" is thought to be your ars poetica. Do you agree with that?

HUGHES

There is a sense in which every poem that comes off is a description or a dramatization of its own creation. Within the poem, I sometimes think, is all the evidence you need for explaining how the poem came to be and why it is as it is. Then again, every poem that works is like a meta-phor of the whole mind writing, the solution of all the oppositions and imbalances going on at that time. When the mind finds the balance of all those things and projects it, that's a poem. It's a kind of hologram of the mental condition at that moment, which then immediately changes and moves on to some other sort of balance and rearrangement. What counts is that it be a symbol of that momentary wholeness. That's how I see it.

INTERVIEWER

Why do you choose to speak through animals so often?

HUGHES

I suppose because they were there at the beginning. Like parents. Since I spent my first seventeen or eighteen years constantly thinking about them more or less, they became a language—a symbolic language which is also the language of my whole life. It was not something I be-gan to learn about at university or something that happened to me when I was thirty, but part of the machinery of my mind from the be-ginning. They are a way of connecting all my deepest feelings to-gether. So when I look for or get hold of a feeling of that kind, it tends to bring up the image of an animal or animals simply because that's the deepest, earliest language that my imagination learned. Or one of the deepest, earliest languages. People were there, too.

INTERVIEWER

What would you say is the function of poetry as opposed to the function of prose?

HUGHES

In the seventies I got to know one or two healers. The one I knew best believed that since everybody has access to the energies of the autoimmune system, some individuals develop a surplus. His own history was one of needing more than most—forty years of ankylosing spondylitis. In the end, when he was past sixty, a medium told him that no one could heal him, but that he could heal himself if he would start to heal others. So he started healing and within six months was virtually cured. Watching and listening to him, the idea occurred to me that art was perhaps this—the psychological component of the autoimmune system. It works on the artist as a healing. But it works on others, too, as a medicine. Hence our great, insatiable thirst for it. However it comes out—whether a design in a carpet, a painting on a wall, the shaping of a doorway—we recognize that medicinal element because of the instant healing effect, and we call it art. It consoles and heals something in us. That's why that aspect of things is so important, and why what we want to preserve in civilizations and societies is their art—because it's a living medicine that we can still use. It still works. We feel it working. Prose, narratives, et cetera, can carry this healing. Poetry does it more intensely. Music, maybe, most intensely of all.

INTERVIEWER

On another matter entirely, do you think the literary communities in England and America differ from each other?

HUGHES

Yes, profoundly. The world and the whole grounding of experience for American writers is so utterly different from that of English writers. The hinterlands of American writing are so much more varied and the scope of their hinterlands is so infinitely vast. Many more natural and social worlds are available to American writers. For every generation of Americans there's more material that is utterly new and strange. I think the problem for American writers is to keep up with their material, whereas the problem for English writers is to find new material—material that isn't already in some real sense secondhand, used up, dog-eared, predigested. You see this in a very simple way in the contrast between the American and English writing about field sports—shooting and fishing. The range, richness, variety, quantity, quality of the American sports writing is stupefying. There are some fine writers on these subjects in the UK, but one has the impression that they are simply updating, modernizing material that was used up generations ago, and a very limited range of material it is.

What do you think of writing workshops and M.F.A. programs?

Sometimes they work wonders. When the Arvon Writing Foundation—what would be called a creative writing college in the United States—was started here in England in 1969, I was asked to join the founders. I had taught creative writing classes at the University of Massachusetts and it had been rather a wonderful experience. I learned an awful lot from the students themselves. I saw how those classes worked, how the students educated each other in writing skills, how one talented student can somehow transform the talents of a whole class. But on the whole I felt that the idea was impractical for England. I thought I knew too well the bigoted antagonism that most of our older writers felt about transatlantic ideas of creative writing. I'd heard it expressed too often. So I thought the idea could not work here simply because the writers would not cooperate. But the founders of Arvon, two poets, went ahead and invited me to give a reading of my verses to the first course. The students were a group of fourteen-year-olds from a local school. Within that one week they had produced work that astonished me. Within five days, in fact. They were in an incredible state of creative excitement. Here in England the idea worked in a way that I had never seen in the United States. So Arvon developed. Younger writers, and most of the older writers as it turned out, tutored the courses with an almost natural skill and very often with amazing results. The experience persuaded me that a creative writing course of Arvon's kind has more impact here, perhaps because the English personality and character tend to be comparatively fixed and set, rigid, so that any change comes with a bang. You get revelations of talent in people who had never dreamed they could write a word. Amazing conversions.

INTERVIEWER

Would you like to have had such a program available to you when you started out?

HUGHES

I've often wondered. I'm not sure if I would have gone. What I wanted to do was work it all out in my own terms and at my own pace. I didn't want to be influenced, or at least I wanted to choose my influences for myself. Between the age when I began to write seriously and the time I left the university at the age of twenty-four, I read very little in poetry, novels, and drama apart from the great authors—the authors I considered to be great. Within that literature I was a hundred-great-books reader. My first real encounter with the possibilities of contemporary poetry came only in 1954 or 1955 when a Penguin anthology of American poetry came out. I'd become aware of some names of course—Frost, Wallace Stevens, even Theodore Roethke, Hart Crane. That anthology came out just as I was ready to look further. So I completely bypassed contemporary English poetry, apart from Auden and Dylan Thomas, and came fresh to the American. Everything in that book seemed exciting to me—exciting and familiar. Wilbur, Bill Merwin, Elizabeth Bishop, Lowell. But most of all John Crowe Ransom. For two or three years Ransom became a craze of mine, and he still was when I met Sylvia. I managed to enthuse her to the point that he seriously affected her style for a period. But many things in that anthology hit me, pieces like Karl Shapiro's "Auto Wreck." When I met Sylvia I also met her library, and the whole wave hit me. I began to devour everything American. But my point is that up to then my exciting new discoveries in poetry had been things like the first act of *Two Noble Kinsmen* (not usually included in Shakespeare's complete works), or Lady Gregory's translation of the Arran song: "It was late last night the dog was speaking of you." What I felt I wanted to do didn't seem to exist. I was conscious mainly of a kind of musical energy. My notion was to make real and solid what would contain it—something to do with the way I read poems to myself.

INTERVIEWER

And you eventually burst out of that.

HUGHES

The earliest piece of mine that I kept was a lyric titled "Song" that came to me as such things should in your nineteenth year—literally a voice in the air at about three o'clock A.M. when I was on night duty just after I'd started national service. Between that and the next piece that I saved, the poem I titled "The Thought Fox," lay six years of total confusion. Six years! That's when I read myself to bits, as Nietzsche said students do. Also, I ran smack into the first part of the English lit tripos at Cambridge. I got out of that and into anthropology none too soon. I was writing all the time, but in confusion. I mopped up everything that was going on inside me with Beethoven's music. Throughout that time, he was my therapy. After university I lived in London, did various jobs, but I was removed from friends and from constant Beethoven, and for the first time in years I thought about nothing but the poem I was trying to write. Then one night up came "The Thought Fox" and, soon after, the other pieces I mentioned. But I had less a sense of bursting out, I think, more a sense of tuning in to my own transmission. Tuning out the influences, the static and interference. I didn't get there by explosives. My whole understanding of it was that I could get it only by concentration.

INTERVIEWER

In the late twentieth century is there a tradition of British poetry that is different from other English-speaking nations?

HUGHES

Well, when I began to write I certainly felt there to be. The tradition had its gods, the great sacred national figures of the past. Some of them not so great. But they policed the behavior of young poets and they policed the tastes of readers—most of all the tastes of readers. Yes, in the 1950s it was still a strong orthodoxy. Eliot and Pound had challenged it, but they hadn't fractured it. I'm not even sure if they modified it much. Mainly you were aware that this tradition was distinctly not-continental and distinctly not-American. It had hypersensitive detectors for any trace of contamination from those two sources. In general, I suppose, it was defensive. We were made very aware of it in the early fifties by Robert Graves. He gave a series of lectures at Cambridge that purged the tradition of its heretics—bad Wordsworth and so on—and of its alien stowaways Eliot and Pound. Graves had a strange kind of authority through the late fifties—the man of tradition, the learned champion of the British tradition. I fancied he had an effect even on Auden, who certainly admired him a lot. But then came the sixties. In the UK the shock of the sixties is usually tied to the Beatles. But as far as poetry was concerned their influence was marginal, I think. The poetry shock that hit the UK in the sixties started before the Beatles. Sylvia responded to the first ripples of it. In a sense, *Ariel* is a response to those first signs, and she never heard the Beatles. What happened were two big simultaneous events in the world of poetry—the first was the sudden waking up of the world from the ice age of the war. Countries that had been separated by blockades or crushed under the Communist ice suddenly seemed to wake up. In poetry they rushed to embrace one another, first on that amazing boom of translation, then in the International Poetry Festivals that got going mid-decade. Maybe the Pasternak explosion in the late fifties was the beginning. But in general, Bill Merwin had translated a huge amount of various authors. We had Robert Bly's first volumes of his *Sixties* magazine. We collected the first translations of Zbigniew Herbert and Holub—unearthed by Alvarez in, I think, 1962. I'm not sure when the Penguin translations began, but their first Lorca edition had appeared in 1960. The boom began early and then simply grew right through the decade.

The other momentous event came from the United States—the shockwave not so much of pop music but of the lifestyle of the Beat poets, with Allen Ginsberg as high priest. That shockwave, which swept America at the end of the fifties, hit England in the beginning of the sixties. The Beatles were its English amplifiers in one sense, but the actual thing at the time was the lifestyle. You saw all your friends transformed in a slow flash. And with the lifestyle came the poetry, the transcendentalism, the Beat publications. Those two big waves—one of international poetry and the other, the California revolution, blend into one. What was really very strange was the way the fans of the new pop music and folk music craze all took to buying poetry—especially translated modern poetry. Penguin stepped up their output of new titles; every publisher seemed to be commissioning new translations of foreign poets. Those fans bought huge numbers of the books. They were packed in at the first of the Art Council's big International Poetry Festivals in 1966, which I helped organize. Our program was based on an issue of Daniel Weissbort's new magazine, *Modern Poetry in Translation*, which I think was the first such magazine in Britain. It was an amazing occasion. Almost every big figure I invited accepted and came. And by chance, on the day of the festival, London happened to be full of poets from all over the place. We invited quite a few and they joined in. Any young poet in the UK aware of that must have been hit pretty hard. The variety of different poetries that were not only suddenly available, but in high fashion, was staggering.

The mad atmosphere of those early International Festivals only lasted a year or two. Probably that one in 1966 and the earlier, more spontaneous one in 1965 were the great ones. But the rest of it reeled on into the early seventies until finally the translation boom began to flag. Still, the best of the books haven't gone away. And that awakening of all the countries to one another's poetry hasn't gone to sleep. Poets like Holub have become almost honorary British poets. In many ways, none of that has closed down. Has it modified British tradition? Well, it must have modified it one way: at least all young British poets now know that the British tradition is not the only one among the traditions of the globe. Everything is now completely open, every approach, with infinite possibilities. Obviously the British tradition still exists as a staple of certain historically hard-earned qualities if anybody is still there who knows how to inherit them. Raleigh's qualities haven't become irrelevant. When I read Primo Levi's verse I'm reminded of Raleigh. But for young British poets it's no longer the only tradition, no longer a tradition closed in on itself and defensive.

INTERVIEWER

You've just come back from Macedonia—a poetry festival that was obviously very important. What was the understanding of British poetry there?

HUGHES

I had a curious experience on the airplane coming back. I boarded in Skopje and noticed this young woman on the opposite side of the aisle, oh, about thirty-five. I saw her look at me and I thought because the whole festival in Struga had been so publicized and televised throughout Macedonia—that maybe she felt she had seen me, maybe even recognized me since they gave me the Laurel Wreath of Gold this year and there'd been a certain amount of camera concentration. But neither of us said anything. Then there she was again on the next leg of the flight in the seat in front of me, and she asked if I was who I was. She had seen me on TV. Finally she said, I was very surprised that they gave the prize to British poetry. Naturally I asked her why. And she replied, Well, I thought British poetry was dead. It turned out she was a doctor in Dubai. I had with me this rather magnificent Macedonian-made volume of my poems translated into Macedonian. So I handed her the book and said, Here's an opportunity to examine the patient. When she returned it to me half an hour later she was very gracious. Ten minutes after that I saw she was reading the latest *Times Literary Supplement*!

INTERVIEWER

It's like the British poet is dead every few years, isn't it?

HUGHES

What struck me was that it came out so pat. A sort of obvious truism, as if everybody over the continental landmass simply knew it. And in the *TLS* she had her finger on the pulse.

INTERVIEWER

Is poetry as vital to people now as it was thirty years ago? Aren't sales of poetry going up?

HUGHES

Well, it's a fact—not much observed maybe, except by the judges of children's writing competitions—that the teaching of how to write poetry is now producing extraordinary results. Mainly at the lower ages. This might not be so new in the United States, but in the UK it's a phenomenon of the last fifteen years, especially of the last ten. The twenty-five-year influence of the Arvon Foundation can't be ignored. You only have to ask around among young published poets and look at the prizewinners of the various competitions. And Arvon has spawned a host of other places doing a similar job. All this must be helping sales in the UK. It's a new kind of reading and writing public that simply didn't exist in Britain before the early seventies. And it's definitely not confined to the universities.

But I expect the real reasons must be deeper. Poetry sales are supposed to rise during a war, aren't they, when people are forced to become aware of what really matters. You could invent an explanation, I'm sure. Maybe something to do with the way we all live on two levels—a top level where we scramble to respond moment by moment to the bombardment of impressions, demands, opportunities. And a bottom level where our last-ditch human values live—the long-term feelings like instinct, the bedrock facts of our character. Usually, we can live happily on the top level and forget the bottom level. But, all it takes to dump the population on the top level to the lowest pits of the bottom level, with all their values and all their ideas totally changed, is a war. I would suggest that poetry is one of the voices of the bottom level.

The poetry translation boom of the sixties was inseparable, I think, from the Vietnam War. That war felt like the Cold War finally bursting into flames—the beginning of war with the combined Communist regimes. And the translated modern poetry boom was inseparable from that catastrophe. It pervaded everything. Two societies, the United States and the UK, that were notably stuck on the top level were trying to divine the bottom-level reality being lived out in Southeast Asia. But in general everyone under the Communist regimes was on the bottom level. You remember all those attempts to actualize it, to live it secondhand? To be part of it somehow?

Pasternak was the first big voice to be heard from under the Russian ice. But then came Yevtushenko and Voznesensky on their reading tours through the West. Their popularity, their glamour, was amazing. I remember C. P. Snow introducing Yevtushenko onstage at the South Bank by characterizing him as "what we really mean by a celebrity." Behind that, Mandelshtam, Akhmatova, Mayakovsky, and the rest were suddenly the greatest names; translations began to pour out. There was a huge thirst. And I remember the big shock—another of the big literary shocks in my life—of discovering the poetry of Russia's victims in Herbert, Holub, Popa, and so on, and along with that the poetry of Amichai, Celan . . . So you could say the great craving of the United States and the UK on the top level to anticipate and experience that reality on the bottom level did take in one way the form of a craze for translated poetry, an almost undiscriminating appetite for any news whatsoever through that hotline. The market for those books was colossal.

Now what's going on in the Balkans is making that bottom level resonate again, as well as the African famines, the thirty-odd horrible little wars crackling away, and behind all that a new sense of impending global disaster, an obscure mix of environmental and political breakdowns, runaway populations, and the economic threat of the Far East. Anyway, a sense of big trouble coming, with all the evidence of the first phases jamming the TV screens. Here in the UK we're still only an audience on the top level watching the calamities taking place on the bottom level. But we're a twenty-four-hour-a-day top-level audience, supersaturated with impressions of life on the bottom level. The war in former Yugoslavia has raised the curtain on it all. So given that model of the two levels, the appetite for poetry should be rising again, a little. Or slowly.

INTERVIEWER

Finally, what does this progression mean in terms of form? What are your thoughts on free as opposed to formal verse?

HUGHES

In the way you've put the question "formal" suggests regular metrics, regular stanzas, and, usually, rhyme. But it also suggests some absolute form that doesn't have those more evident features; it suggests any form governed by a strong, inflexible inner law that the writer finds himself having to obey, that he can't just play around with as he can play around with, say, the wording of a letter. That kind of deeper, hidden form, though it doesn't show regular metrical or stanzaic patterning or end rhyme, can't in any way be called "free." Take any passage of "The Waste Land," or maybe a better example is Eliot's poem "Marina." Every word in those poems is as formally fixed, as locked into flexible inner laws, as words can be. The music of those words, the musical inevitability of the pitch, the pacing, the combination of inflections—all that is in some way absolute, unalterable, the ultimate perfect containment of unusually powerful poetic forces. You could say the same of many other examples: Smart's "Jubilate Agno," any passages in Shakespeare's blank verse, Shakespeare's prose. To my mind, the best of the kind of verse usually called free always aspires towards that kind of formal inevitability—a fixed, unalterable, musical, and yet hidden dramatic shape. One difference between this kind of verse and regular, metrical, rhymed stanzas is the problem it sets the reader at first reading. Regular formal features give the reader immediate bearings, the A-B-C directions for reading or performing the piece being nursery simple; the poem has a familiar, friendly look from that very first encounter. But when these are missing—no regular meter, no stanza shape, no obvious rhyme—the reader has to grope, searching for that less obvious, deeper set of musical dramatic laws. That takes time, more than one or two readings. And it takes poetic imagination—or some talent for rhythmical, expressive speech. But if those laws are actually there, as they are in the Eliot, the Smart, and the Shakespeare, sooner or later they assert their inevitability in the reader's mind, and the reader begins to recognize the presence of some absolute, inner form. Of course if those laws aren't there, they can never assert themselves. The piece never gets a grip on the reader. It might be interesting and even exciting to read at first encounter, but then it will slowly fall to bits. The reader will begin to recognize the absence of any law that makes it go one way rather than another . . . the absence of any deeper pattern of hidden forces. So the thing ceases to be read.

In the long run, the same fate—to be rejected and forgotten—overtakes most formally shaped verse, too, no matter how strict its meter or how accurate and dexterous its rhymes. Good metrical rhymed verse, if it's to grip the imagination and stay readable, has to have, as well as those external formal features, the same dynamo of hidden musical dramatic laws as the apparently free verse.

Having said that, I think you are then left with the pro and contra arguments for using or not using those features of regular meter, stanza, rhyme. The main argument, to my mind, for *not* using them is to gain access to the huge variety of musical patterns that they shut out. Imagine if Shakespeare had stuck to sonnets and long-rhymed poems and had never got onto the explorations of his blank verse and those wonderful musical flights of dialogue or onto his prose. Imagine what might have come out of the eighteenth century in England if the regime of the couplet hadn't been so absolute. How could Whitman ever have happened if he'd stuck to his crabby rhymes? That seems to me a strong argument. But the main argument for using meter, rhyme, stanza also seems strong. It's not just that rhymes and the requirement of meter actually stimulate invention—which they obviously do, at certain levels—but it's the strange satisfaction of making that square treasure chest and packing it. Or making that locket with its jewel or its portrait. Or making that periscope box of precisely arranged lenses. There's mystery to it, I'm quite sure. Maybe a mathematical satisfaction. Take the ballad stanza, which is basically just an old English couplet. The best of those quatrains have a kind of primal force, not just musical finality but an inner force, a weight of paid-for experience that most people can recognize. Yet when you break the meter, lose or disarray the rhymes, everything's gone. Then there's Primo Levi's remark. He found that in the death camps, where it became very important to dig poems out of the memory, the poems of regular meter and rhyme proved more loyal, and I'm not sure he didn't say that they were more consoling. You don't forget his remark.

Jan Morris

The Art of the Essay

Jan Morris was born James Humphrey Morris on October 2, 1926, in Somerset, England. As she recalled in her memoir, *Conundrum*, "I was three or four when I realized that I had been born into the wrong body, and should really be a girl." First intimations. But he would live as a man for the next thirty-six years, mentioning his sexual confusion only to his wife Elizabeth, whom he married at twenty-two in Cairo, where he was working for the local Arab News Agency.

Morris left boarding school at the age of seventeen and served for the next five years in the 9th Queen's Lancers, one of Britain's best cavalry regiments. He then moved to Cairo, but soon returned to Britain, attending Oxford for two years before reentering journalism as a reporter for the *Times*, which assigned him, because no one else was available, to cover the Hillary and Tensing expedition to Mount Everest. At twenty-six, having never before climbed a mountain, he scaled three-quarters (twenty-two thousand feet) of Everest to report the first conquest of the mountain. It was a world scoop, and won him international renown. He went on to a distinguished career as a foreign correspondent, for both the *Times* and the *Guardian*.

In 1956, he was awarded a Commonwealth Fellowship, which allowed him to travel through America for a year and resulted in his first book: *As I Saw the U.S.A.* A similar book was published to great acclaim in 1960, *The World of Venice*, the product of a year's sabbatical in that city with his family. Morris ended his career as a full-time

PREFACE| (ch. head) — 16 pt. Plate Caps #d

These letters from Hav, originally contributed to the magazine <u>New Gotham</u>, were written during the months leading up to the events, in the late summer of 1985, which put an end to the character of the city. They thus constitute the only substantial civic portrait ever published, at least in modern times. Countless visitors, of course, left passing descriptions. They marvelled at the Iron Dog and the House of the Chinese Master, they pontificated about New Hav, they caught something of the atmosphere in memoirs, in novels, in poetry

...the green-grey shape that seamen swear is Hav,
Beyond the racing tumble of its foam.

Nobody, however, wrote a proper book about the place. It was almost as though a conspiracy protected the peninsula from too frank or thorough a description.

I count myself lucky in having seen it for the first time late in a travelling life, for it was itself a little compendium of the world's experience, historically, aesthetically, even perhaps spiritually. It reminded me constantly of places elsewhere, but remained to the end absolutely, often paradoxically and occasionally absurdly itself.

A manuscript page from *Last Letter from Hav* by Jan Morris.

journalist in 1961, in part because of a newspaper policy that prevented him from expanding his journalistic assignments into books. He went on to publish numerous books, including *The Road to Huddersfield: A Journey to Five Continents* (1963), *The Presence of Spain* (1965), and the Pax Britannica trilogy.

In 1964, there was another change, personal rather than professional: Morris started taking hormone pills to begin his transformation into a female. The process was completed in 1972, when he traveled to Casablanca for the definitive operation. Her first book as Jan Morris, *Conundrum*, chronicles the passing from male to female. But when asked to discuss the sex change further, she demurs, preferring to let that account speak for itself and referring to the whole matter simply as "the conundrum thing." Since then she has published thirteen books, including *Travels* (1976), *Manhattan '45* (1987), *Hong Kong* (1988), and two novels, *Last Letter from Hav* (1985) and *Fisher's Face* (1995).

Divorce necessarily followed the sex change (it is required by British law), although Morris still lives with his former wife, currently in a house in North Wales called Trefan Morys. Morris describes the house in her book *Pleasures of a Tangled Life* (1989): "I love it above all inanimate objects, and above a good many animate ones, too. . . . It consists in essence simply of two living rooms, each about forty feet long. Both are full of books, and there is a little suite of functional chambers on two floors at one end, linked by a spiral staircase." They have four children.

At seventy-one, she looks remarkably youthful, perhaps a result of the hormone pills. And she still travels, this summer to Hong Kong to cover the transfer of power from Britain to China. The interview was begun in 1989 under the auspices of the 92nd Street Y, at Hunter College in New York City, and continued through telephone calls and letters.

—Leo Lerman, 1997

INTERVIEWER

You resist being called a travel writer.

JAN MORRIS

Yes. At least I resist the idea that travel writing has got to be factual. I believe in its imaginative qualities and its potential as art and literature. I must say that my campaign, which I've been waging for ages now, has borne some fruit because intelligent bookshops nowadays do have a stack called something like travel *literature*. But what word does one use?

INTERVIEWER

Writing about place?

MORRIS

Yes, that's what I do. Although I think of myself more as a belletrist, an old-fashioned word. Essayist would do; people understand that more or less. But the thing is, my subject has been mostly concerned with place. It needn't be. I believe my best books to be far more historical than topographical. But like most writers, I think far too much about myself anyway, and in my heart of hearts don't think I am worth talking about in this way.

INTERVIEWER

Basically, what you are then is a historian.

MORRIS

Well, my best books have been histories. That's all.

INTERVIEWER

So let's start with your Pax Britannica trilogy. Did you have Gibbon's *Decline and Fall of the Roman Empire* in mind when you began?

MORRIS

No, not at all. When I began the trilogy I didn't know I was going to write it. I ought to tell you how I got into writing it. I'm old enough to remember the empire when it still was the empire. I was brought up in a world whose map was painted very largely red, and I went out into the world when I was young in a spirit of imperial arrogance. I felt, like most British people my age, that I was born to a birthright of supremacy; out I went to exert that supremacy. But gradually in the course of my later adolescence and youth my views about this changed.

INTERVIEWER

Did they change at a particular moment?

MORRIS

Yes. I was living in what was then Palestine, and I had occasion to call upon the district commissioner of Gaza. He was an Englishman. It was a British mandate in those days, and he was the British official in charge of that part of Palestine. I knocked on his door and out he came. Something about this guy's hat made me think twice about him. It was kind of a bohemian hat. Rather a floppy, slightly rakish or raffish hat; a very, very civilian hat—a sort of fawn color, but because it was bleached by imperial suns and made limp by tropical rainstorms all of the empire was in that hat. He seemed to be rather a nice man. I admired him. He had none of my foolish, cocky arrogance at all. He was a gentleman in the old sense of the word. And through him, and through meeting some of his colleagues, I began to see that my imperial cockiness was nonsense and that the empire, in its last years at least, wasn't a bit arrogant, it wasn't a bit cocky. People like that were simply trying to withdraw from an immense historical process and hand it over honorably to its successors. Because of this, my view of the empire changed.

I went on and wrote a book about an imperial adventure, which was a crossing of southeast Arabia, with the Sultan of Oman, but under the auspices of the Raj, really. One of the reviewers of the book said, Why does this author fiddle around along the edges, along the perimeters of this imperial subject? Why not get down to the heart of it? For once a writer did take notice of what a reviewer suggested: because of what he said, I decided I'd write a large, celebratory volume at the center of the imperial story, 1897, which was the time of the queen's Diamond Jubilee and the climax of the whole imperial affair. I wrote that book, and I loved doing it. Then I thought, Well, I'll add one on each side of it and make a triptych. I'll have a volume showing how Queen Victoria came to the throne and the empire splurged into this great moment of climax. Then we'll have the climactic piece. Finally, we'll have an elegiac threnody, letting the thing die down until the end, which I took to be the death of Winston Churchill. Nothing at all to do with Gibbon.

INTERVIEWER

In what's now the Queen Victoria volume you demonstrated something you do frequently. You began with the particular, with Emily Eden, and then spread out over the British Empire. The reader sort of grows up with Queen Victoria. In the preface of the first volume you state that you are "chiefly attracted by the aesthetic of empire." Did this dictate a different approach?

MORRIS

Yes, it did. Because I did not set out to exhibit a moral stance about the empire. I treated it as an immense exhibition. By and large, I accepted the moral views of those who were doing it at the time. Things that would seem wicked to us now didn't always seem wicked to people in the Victorian age. I accepted that. Since this is an escapist point of view, really, I decided that I would not in any way make it an analysis of empire but rather an evocation. The looks and smells and sensations of it. What I later tried to imagine was this: Supposing in the last years of the Roman Empire one young centurion, old enough to remember the imperial impulses and the imperial splendor but recognizing that it was passing, sat down and wrote a large book about his sensations at that moment. Wouldn't that be interesting? Said I, But somebody *could* do it about this still greater empire, the British Empire. Who is that? I asked myself. Me!

INTERVIEWER

As the empire began its decline, more frightening than the loss of territory, you say, was the possibility that the British might have lost the will to rule. In what ways was the empire's decline an expression of British character at the time?

MORRIS

In several ways it was. In the more honorable way, I think it was in
the way that I was trying to express my responses to the district commissioner of Gaza. There were a great many very decent men who
were devoting their lives to the empire. Perhaps, when they began
their careers, they did it in a paternalistic way, which is in itself a form
of arrogance; by the time I got into it, very few of them were arrogant.
They were only anxious to hand it over honorably and at a reasonable
speed. I think they did it very well on the whole. Compared with the
record of the French leaving their empire, the British did it in a successful, kindly way. But at the same time, of course, the British had
been absolutely shattered by two world wars. The first one left the
empire physically larger than ever before. The second one was an obvious death knell for it. The British came out of the Second World
War an extremely tired and disillusioned nation, exemplified by the
fact that they immediately gave the boot to their great hero, Winston
Churchill. All they were interested in then was getting back to their island and trying to make it a more decent place to live. In that respect,
the will to empire had most certainly gone. And the sense of enter-
prise and of adventure and of push and of just a touch of arrogance
too—of swagger, at least—that had been essential to the extension of
the empire. All that had been kicked out of the British. Perhaps a very
good thing too.

INTERVIEWER

There was such a show of panache, such a show of grandeur, such
pageantry.

MORRIS

You mean the ending of it or the running of it?

INTERVIEWER

The running of it.

MORRIS

The ending of it, too, was done with a certain panache, a lot of grand pullings down of flags and trumpet calls and royalty going out to kiss prime ministers lately released from jail.

INTERVIEWER

You begin the trilogy as James Morris. The second volume was written during the ten years of sexual ambiguity when you were taking female hormones but had not yet changed your gender. And the third was written as Jan Morris. To what extent is the character of the trilogy seasoned by this change?

MORRIS

I truly don't think at all, really. I've reread the books myself with this in mind. I don't think there is a great deal of difference. It was a purely intellectual or aesthetic, artistic approach to a fairly remote subject. It wasn't anything, I don't think, that could be affected much by my own personal affairs . . . less than other things I've written.

INTERVIEWER

The very heart of this question is: do you feel your sensibilities at all changed?

MORRIS

That is a different question. The trilogy: I started it and finished it in the same frame of mind. But I suppose it is true that most of my work has been a protracted potter, looking at the world and allowing the world to look at me. And I suppose there can be no doubt that both the world's view of me and my view of the world have changed. Of course they have. The point of the book *Pleasures of a Tangled Life* is to try to present, or even to present to myself what kind of sensibility has resulted from this experience. I'm sick to death of talking about the experience itself, as you can imagine, after twenty years. But I've come to recognize that what I am is the result of the experience itself. The tangle that was there is something that has gone subliminally through all my work. The one book I think isn't affected is the Pax Britannica trilogy.

INTERVIEWER

At the end of the trilogy you say that you've come to view empire less in historical than in redemptory terms. What do you mean?

MORRIS

I was thinking of Teilhard de Chardin's concept of "infurling," in which he thought that history, by a process of turning in upon itself, was very gradually bringing humanity and nature into a unity. When I was in Canada I came across an old newspaper article about a lecture on imperialism given in about 1902. Nearly all imperialist talk of that time was about the majesty of the British economic power or the strength of the navy. But this one wasn't at all; this lecturer viewed empire as an agent of love. He thought that among all these mixed emotions there was a common thread of love—of people being fond of each other and trying to do the best for each other. And I've come to think that the good is simply more resilient than the bad. If you have a great historical process like the British Empire, the bad is dross; it is thrown away. The good is what stays on. There was some good in imperialism. It did enable people to get to know each other better than they had before. It allowed people to break away from shackling old traditions and heritages. It introduced the world to fresh ideas and new opportunities. These are the contributions that matter for the redemption and the unity of us all. Although I am at heart against empires, I do think that the British did leave behind them a great number of friends.

INTERVIEWER

At the end of the trilogy you ask, "Is that the truth? Is that how it was? It is my truth. Its emotions are mine. Its scenes are heightened or diminished by my vision. If it is not invariably true in the fact, it is certainly true in the imagination." In what way is this statement true of any history?

MORRIS

Oh, I think it can be untrue of some histories. . . . There are people who write history as a deliberate distortion because they want to deliver a message or shove over a creed. Mine wasn't false in that sense. I tried to present both sides of the story. I didn't try to distort anything to fit another purpose.

INTERVIEWER

I was thinking of that extra inch or half-inch that Lytton Strachey added onto the archbishop. Such is the temptation when one is writing history—to add that extra inch.

MORRIS

Of course, there is one small distortion in my kind of history in that it aims to entertain. So it does in effect ignore little matters like economics. But I have a story, too. In *Pleasures*, I have a piece about first enjoying food and drink. Until I was in my mid-twenties, I didn't take much interest in them. But when I lunched in Australia at the famous cartoonist George Molnar's house on the lawn overlooking Sydney Harbor, the meal was something quite simple but delicious: pâté, crusty rolls, a bottle of wine, an apple, this sort of thing. There was something about the way this man presented and served the food. He crunched the bread in sort of a lascivious way. He spread the pâté kind of unguently. He almost slurped the wine. I thought it was so marvelous. When I came to describe it, I could see it all again so clearly: the dancing sea, the clear Australian sky, the green lawn; above us were the wings of the Sydney opera house, like a benediction over this experience. It was only when I finished the chapter that I remembered that the Sydney opera house hadn't been built yet!

INTERVIEWER

I would like to ask you about *The World of Venice*. Judging from the book and from the entire trilogy, you seem supremely interested in declines and falls. Are you trying to tell us about the decline and fall of the whole world, of reality in our time? And if so, is there any new beginning?

I certainly don't think that I'm trying to describe the decline and fall of the world. Rather, it seems more vigorous as every year goes by. Perhaps it is because I am aware of the excitement of the present age—the explosive beauty of the new technologies that are overcoming us, the vivacity of the world—that I am attracted to decline, to the melancholy spectacle of things that get old and die. But another reason I tend to write about decline is because I don't believe in pretending it doesn't exist. I believe in age; I believe in recognizing age. I'm sure that I shall always love Venice, but in a way I do wish it wasn't being touched up. I think it's trying to deny its age, pretending that it isn't antiquated and decrepit, which it is, really. One part of me is very attracted to that decline, and another part of me is fascinated by the fact that Venice denies that decline so adamantly. Such a scenario is not part of my view of the world in the 1990s. Rather, I take the opposite stance. I see the world today as in a very vigorous, virile, and interesting state.

You first published *The World of Venice* in 1960 as James Morris. In the preface to the 1974 reprinted edition, you, as Jan Morris, see the book as a period piece: "Venice seen through a particular pair of eyes at a particular moment," which "cannot be modernized with a few deft strokes of a felt-tip pen." Would Jan have written a different book than James?

It's extremely hard to say. As a reprint it was no longer a contemporary portrait of the city because a lot had changed in the meantime. I resigned myself to the fact that the Venice I had described was my Venice, really. As to whether Jan Morris would write the book differently . . . I used to think that as Jan I tend to concentrate more on the smaller things, the details, rather than on the grand sweep of things.

But as I've got older, I've come to think that the grand sweep and the details are exactly the same; the macrocosm and the microcosm are identical.

INTERVIEWER

You speak of the book on Venice as "a highly subjective, romantic, impressionistic picture, less of a city than of an experience." Is that true of any city you portray? Is it more true in some cases than in others?

MORRIS

It's true of them all, certainly. I'm not the sort of writer who tries to tell other people what they are going to get out of the city. I don't consider my books travel books. I don't like travel books, as I said before. I don't believe in them as a genre of literature. Every city I describe is really only a description of me looking at the city or responding to it. Of course, some cities have a more brilliant image. In this case the city overtakes me so that I find I am not, after all, describing what I feel about the city but describing something very, very powerful about the city itself. For example, Beijing: I went to that city in my usual frame of mind, in which I follow two precepts. The first I draw from E. M. Forster's advice that in order to see the city of Alexandria best one ought to wander around aimlessly. The other I take from the Psalms; you might remember the line "grin like a dog and run about the city."

INTERVIEWER

And scare the hell out of the populace!

MORRIS

Yes. Well, I went into Beijing wandering aimlessly and grinning like a dog and running about in the usual way, but it didn't work! Beijing was too big for me. Its size imposed upon what I wrote about the city.

INTERVIEWER

In the introduction to your collection of writings about cities you say that you've accomplished at last what you set out to do.

MORRIS

I drew an imaginary, figurative line between two cities, Budapest and Bucharest. All cities above that line qualify as what seem to me "great cities," and all below that line could be very interesting but not in the same class. So I resolved that before I died I would visit and write about all the cities above the Bucharest line. I could do some below if I wanted to, but I would try to do all the ones above. In the end I did. Beijing was the last one.

INTERVIEWER

Is there any place you haven't written about that you would like to?

MORRIS

I think I'm tired of writing about places qua places—if I ever did that. But I've never been into Tibet proper (only on the frontier) and I would like to go there, also Vladivostok—both places where the situation would be as interesting to write about as the locality.

INTERVIEWER

Is there any place you have been unable to capture?

MORRIS

I always think London has defeated me; probably heaps of other places, too—who am I to judge?

INTERVIEWER

You say that by 1980 you had fallen out of love with Venice. What happened?

MORRIS

I fall in and out of love with Venice very frequently as a matter of fact. I've known Venice since the end of the Second World War. For most of that time Venice has been trying to find a role for itself, to be a creative, living city, or to be a kind of museum city that we all go and look at. At one time it was intended to be a dormitory town for the big industrial complex around the lagoon and Mestre. That fell through because of pollution, so Venice was out on a limb again. The attempt to bring it into the modern world had failed. Then one day I saw that the golden horses of Saint Mark's were no longer on the facade of the basilica. They'd taken the statues down and put them inside. Outside they'd placed some dummies . . . good replicas, but without the sheen and the scratches, the age and the magic of the old ones. I thought, This is the moment when Venice has decided. It won't be a great diplomatic, mercantile, or political city, nor will it be a great seaport of the East. Instead it will be a museum that we can all visit. Maybe that's the right thing for it, anyway. Age has crept up on it. It can't do it anymore. Perhaps that's the answer. For a time I went along with that, but in the last five or ten years mass tourism has taken such a turn, especially in Europe and particularly in Venice. It seems to me that the poor old place is too swamped with tourism to survive as even a viable museum unless it takes really drastic steps to keep people out.

INTERVIEWER

Still, there are strange, haunted squares in Venice that one can find, away from tourists.

MORRIS

There are haunted squares where one can sit in Indianapolis!

INTERVIEWER

Those dummy horses are very significant to me too, but to me they meant something slightly different. They seemed to be symbols of the decline and fall of reality in my time.

MORRIS

If it is true about the decline and fall of reality, then its chief agency is tourism. Tourism encourages unreality. It's easier in the tourist context to be unreal than real. It's the easiest thing in the world to buy a funny old Welsh hat and pop it on and sit outside selling rock in some bogus tavern. It's much easier than being real, contemporary.

Tourism encourages and abets this sham-ness wherever it touches. I detest it.

INTERVIEWER

For those who don't know what *rock* is, it's a very sweet candy.

MORRIS

And it can have the name of the place written all the way through it. However much you chew it, it still says *Wales*. Wales, Wales, Wales.

INTERVIEWER

In your book *Conundrum* you answer almost every conceivable question about your decision to change your gender and the process involved. Your life seems made up of journeys, both in terms of travel and of personal exploration. To what extent was travel a relief or escape from feeling trapped in a man's body?

MORRIS

You mean just ordinary travel, don't you, not travel in a metaphysical sense?

INTERVIEWER

We can come to metaphysical travel later.

MORRIS

Well, I used to think it hadn't anything to do with escape because I've always enjoyed traveling; it's one of my great pleasures. My original travels were not quite voluntary. I went abroad with the British army, and there wasn't much sense of escape in that. But later I did begin to believe that maybe there was some sort of allegorical meaning to my traveling. I thought that the restlessness I was possessed by was, perhaps, some yearning, not so much for the sake of escape as for the sake of quest: a quest for unity, a search for wholeness. I certainly didn't think of it that way in the beginning, but I've come to think it might be so.

INTERVIEWER

From what I know of you, both personally and through your writing, I think it must be so.

MORRIS

I've become obsessed with the idea of reconciliation, particularly reconciliation with nature but with people, too, of course. I think that travel has been a kind of search for that, a pursuit for unity and even an attempt to contribute to a sense of unity.

INTERVIEWER

Your description of climbing Mount Everest is such an extraordinary symbolic venture.

MORRIS

Well, it's nice to have it thought of as symbolism, but I really don't think of it that way. It was just an assignment, and I did it.

INTERVIEWER

So you have nothing to say about metaphysical travel then?

MORRIS

No, because it seems to me such an inner, indeed inmost matter that, old pro as I am, I can't put it into words.

INTERVIEWER

Is there a book you've written as Jan that James would not have written?

MORRIS

Pleasures of a Tangled Life. The whole point of this book of essays is to try to present the sensibility that has been created or has evolved out of "the conundrum experience," as we say in our evasive, euphemistic way. People who come to interview me at home often ask, Do you mind if we talk about the conundrum thing? The book tries to present, to readers as well as myself, what kind of a sensibility has resulted from this sort of thing. I think the conundrum aspect runs subliminally through the whole book. I recognize that the pleasures, nearly all of them, are ones that I enjoy in a particular way because of "the conundrum thing."

INTERVIEWER

Let's talk about *Sydney*. How do you prepare yourself for a particular book?

MORRIS

First of all I decide why I want to write the book. The reason I wanted to write *Sydney* gets me back to the good old empire once again. It seems to me that when the tide of empire withdrew it left behind on the sands of the world a whole lot of objects, some of them unpleasant, some of them dull, but one of them particularly glittering. Not the nicest object, rather a sharp, hard object, but a brilliant one. And that seemed to me the city of Sydney, New South Wales, a city that is not only a remnant of that old empire but also, in a way, the New City. It is creating new people in the same way that America created new people in the 1780s. So I decided that would be a good book to do. I wanted to conclude my commitment, my obsession with the empire. And I thought Sydney was a good place to end with. Somebody reviewing *Sydney* said that most of the books I'd written were cousins to empire in some way; they're related.

INTERVIEWER

At what point during the progress of the book do you feel that you've captured your subject, that the place is yours?

MORRIS

It varies. I usually write the first draft in a sort of stream-of-consciousness way, without thinking very hard about it. I let it all go through. Then when I go back to the second draft, very often I find that what I've already got is much better than what I've planned. Sometimes the unconscious bit is very much better than the conscious bit. I'm a weak person, and so I do, in fact, always replace the unconscious with the conscious bit, but I'm often wrong in doing so. Sometimes I go back and see that the early draft is better and more natural. Incidentally, talking of stream of consciousness, after forty years of trying I've finished Joyce's *Ulysses*. I must say I still think life is too short for *Finnegans Wake*.

INTERVIEWER

Do you feel you got to the *bottom* of Sydney in this book?

MORRIS

No, I don't think so. I got to the bottom, as I say, of my own feelings about it. Sydney is not a city that at first sight is going to incite one's sensibilities. It wants to be frank, macho, fun, you know. But the more I felt the city, the more I thought about the city, the more I realized that sort of *wistful* quality in it, which perhaps is behind all such macho places, really.

INTERVIEWER

A wistful quality?

MORRIS

Yes. It's a kind of yearning. Often what I feel about the Australians themselves is that they resist it a bit because they don't feel they ought to feel these sort of feelings. But they probably do, really, I think. It has something to do with the landscape. D. H. Lawrence got it all those years ago.

INTERVIEWER

But when you have a city, such as Sydney, that's a little bit elusive in terms of its wistful quality, how does that reveal itself to you? Is the realization an active process on your part, or is it something that just flowers as you spend time there?

MORRIS

I think that it is purely passive. All I do, really, is to go to the place and just think about nothing else whatever except that place. I have to say in the case of Sydney that if its transcendental quality hadn't emerged, the book might have been a little bit boring. I didn't know it was going to show itself. I felt it more and more the longer I stayed there.

INTERVIEWER

So it wasn't an immediate transcendence?

MORRIS

No. A lot of people see *Sydney* as if it were a "road to Damascus" experience. It wasn't.

INTERVIEWER

You use anecdotes and stories in certain places to punctuate the narrative. Do you consciously use the techniques of fiction to move a narrative along?

MORRIS

I do believe in the techniques of fiction, so I'm very gratified you should ask this. I really don't see that there's much difference between writing a book of this kind and writing a novel. The situations that arise are the sort of situations you'd often make up—the background you would devise for a novel, the characters you would produce for a novel. And you have an added attraction, of course: the fact that the overwhelming character of the whole book is the city itself, which is an advantage you have over the novelist. Paul Theroux said to me once that he liked writing travel books because they gave him a plot; he didn't have to think one up. It works the other way around, too. I edited the travel writings of Virginia Woolf. *To the Lighthouse* is in many ways a travel book: the descriptions of the journey across the bay, the views that she provides, are exactly what she would do if she were writing a work of literary travel.

INTERVIEWER

What aspect did the sensibility and change of sensibility based on "the conundrum experience," which you discussed in *Pleasures of a Tangled Life*, play in writing *Sydney*?

MORRIS

Well, of course, *Pleasures of a Tangled Life* was a very much more varied book. It dealt specifically with personal aspects of life, personal views: what happened to me at home, how I feel about different aspects of life and of living and of art and of religion . . . So, naturally, that presents a sensibility far more directly, doesn't it, more immediately, than a book like *Sydney*. On the other hand, I think if you compare with a compassionate eye, a sympathetic eye, a book like *Sydney* with a book like *Oxford*, which I wrote in 1965, I think you would think, if you were intelligent enough, that there was a different person writing. You might not think the style had changed enormously, but I think you'd find the mind behind it or the feeling behind it, the sensibility behind it, had changed. Yes, I think I would think that about *Sydney*. It's a gentler book, of course.

INTERVIEWER

When you're researching a book, do you travel alone?

MORRIS

I generally travel alone, but sometimes with my partner, with whom I've lived for forty years. But dearly though I love her, if I'm going to be working I find I'm better on my own. Love is rather inhibiting in my view. We are always thinking about what each other wants to do. Whereas, to be writing about a place you've got to be utterly selfish. You've only got to think about the place that you're writing. Your antenna must be out all the time picking up vibrations and details. If you've got somebody with you, especially somebody you're fond of, it doesn't work so well. So, although I never have the heart to tell her this, I would really rather not have her come along.

INTERVIEWER

If you're going to be any kind of writer you've got to be utterly selfish.

MORRIS

And lonely, I suppose.

INTERVIEWER
How long do you stay in a place?

MORRIS

That depends entirely on the nature of the thing that I'm writing. If I'm commissioned by a magazine to write an essay, what I do is go to the place for a week and think about nothing but that place. And then, the last few days, in a kind of frenzy of ecstasy or despair, I write three drafts of the essay, one draft each day. I write continuously—it doesn't matter how many hours—until the thing is done. I love the feeling of wrapping the whole thing up, popping it off in the post, and going somewhere else. It is very satisfying. I do think that the impact of it, the suddenness and abruptness of it, makes it go better.

The best book about a place I've ever written is the one about Spain. I hardly knew Spain, but I was commissioned to go there for six months to write a book about it. So I bought a Volkswagen camper-bus, and off I set to this country that I knew nothing about. The impact was tremendous; I thought about nothing but Spain for the entire six months. When it was finished I remember watching an airplane going overhead and thinking, There goes my lovely manuscript, on its way to New York. That book, because it was done in a mood of high ecstasy and excitement, was the best of the lot.

INTERVIEWER

How does your mood affect your impression of a place? What you write about it?

MORRIS

I am nothing if not a professional, and I long ago learned to aim off for mood, weather, or chance encounters: but of course if I spent a week somewhere with a permanent headache, in perpetual drizzle, encountering only grumpy citizens, I can see that my essay might not be as exuberant as it might be.

INTERVIEWER

You mentioned being lonely. . . .

MORRIS

Yes. Well, I'm not lonely when I travel, but like every writer, I'm a bit lonely when I have to sit down and write the thing, because you can only do that by yourself. I do it rather laboriously, three times over. It's a long process. During that time I'm pretty reclusive and shuttered. But traveling, no, less so than it used to be, really, because, you know, I've been doing it an awfully long time. Wherever I go now I know people. So there's no need for me to be lonely if I don't want to be lonely. The lonely part of it is the technicality of being a writer, which is naturally a lonely one anyway. You can't talk to people while you're writing. You can't work while the television is on.

INTERVIEWER

You could have music.

MORRIS

Lately I bought a little electronic keyboard so that every now and then I break off and play something.

INTERVIEWER

What do you play?

MORRIS

Sometimes if I've got the score, I play the solo part of concertos. I'm very good on the Mendelssohn violin concertos.

INTERVIEWER

How important are languages? How many languages do you speak and to what extent is that critical in investigating a place?

MORRIS

Well, it has been crucial in a way in my choice of subjects. Because so much of my time has been spent with the British Empire and its cousinships, English was the lingua franca so that was no problem. But because I am a poor linguist I've done very few—no books, really, except *Venice*—about cities where the foreign language is essential. I speak sort of pidgin French and Italian. I learned some Arabic years ago, but that wouldn't, for example, qualify me to write a book about Moscow or Berlin, would it? And unlike some of my colleagues, I'm not sure I've got the dedication to learn an entirely new language in order to write a book about that country. Colin Thubron, for example, to write a book about traveling through China actually sat down and learned Mandarin.

INTERVIEWER

So what did you do, say, when you were investigating Venice? Did you use translators?

MORRIS

Well, I'm not too bad in Italian. Do you know that story? Hemingway said what an easy language Italian was, and his Italian friend said, In that case, Mr. Hemingway, why not undertake the use of grammar? When I went to Spain, commissioned to do a short, sixty-thousand-word book, I bought a recorded language course. And the book's been in print ever since.

INTERVIEWER

Has technology, notably the advent of the word processor, changed your technique or style in any way?

MORRIS

I do use a word processor, but it hasn't changed my writing in any way whatever. The belief that style and mental capacity depend upon the instrument one uses is a superstition. I will write with anything at any time. I've used them all—the fountain pen, manual typewriter, electric typewriter—and none have made the slightest difference. But with a word processor I won't type the first few drafts on disk because there is the temptation simply to fiddle with the text, to juggle with it. The word processor is useful to me only for the final draft of the thing. I do think that the word processor for a writer's last draft is a wonderful thing because you can go on and on polishing the thing.

INTERVIEWER

Do you feel that having been a man at one time in your life gives you more courage to make excursions on your own?

MORRIS

Yes. There's a hangover from the confidence I had as a man. When I started, the feminist movement hadn't really happened, so, of course, there was more of a gulf between a male and female traveler. Now things are very, very different. Many women are unnecessarily timid about travel. I don't believe it is so different for a woman or a man nowadays. Of course, there are actual physical dangers of a different kind. But the general run of hazard is exactly the same for men as for women, and the treatment that a woman gets when traveling is, by and large, better. People are less frightened of you. They tend to trust you more. The relationship between women, between one woman and another, is a much closer one than the relationship between men. Wherever a woman travels in the world she's got a few million friends waiting to help her.

INTERVIEWER

You say that you read about and study a place you've never been to before going there to write about it. Do you find that the place turns out to be largely what you expect it to be or exactly what you did not expect it to be?

MORRIS

It's a long time since I've had to write about a place I didn't know. Nowadays, I generally write about places I know about already. But I think some of the great travel books have not prepared me for the place I'm going to. One of them is one of my favorite books, Doughty's *Arabia Deserta*; it's a marvelous book and a great work of art, but the image it presents of the desert and its life isn't the image I felt. I'm not grumbling at all. He wasn't trying to tell me what *I* was going to see in the desert. He was just telling me what the desert was like to him. But that's one book that doesn't seem to match up to my own conceptions of the desert. Sterne, for example, too. I can't say that France seems very much like *A Sentimental Journey* to me. There are some other people too, like Kingslake, who wrote deliberately in an entertaining mode, consciously painting an arresting picture of life. It isn't much like it when you get there.

INTERVIEWER

Back to the dissolution of empires. We've watched the waning and extinction of another great empire, the Soviet Union.

MORRIS

The tragedy of the Soviet Union was that it marked the decline of an ideological empire. The British Empire really had no ideology, except one that had evolved by a kind of rule of thumb, changing as it went along. There was a general rule of fair play about it. But the moral purpose behind the Soviet Empire seems to have been a different thing altogether. I've always been very attracted to the idea of communism. If I'd been alive in those days I probably would have been a communist. The tragedy of it was, it seems to me, that it was so soon perverted. The revolution was betrayed. It sank into the horrors of Stalinism, sliding slowly into the awful mires of inefficiency, disillusion, unhappiness and despair that we see now. The failure of it seems to be that although it set out ideologically to provide welfare for a people, it utterly lacked the idea of giving its people happiness. If political ideology doesn't take into account the human desire for happiness, it seems to me bound to fail. Perhaps this is why your system is so successful, because it actually does talk about the pursuit of happiness, doesn't it? That's a different matter altogether.

INTERVIEWER

I once met someone who had visited London and had refused to go back so as not to obliterate the memory she had of it twenty-eight years earlier. Have you ever felt that way about any place?

MORRIS

Yes, I think I have. I've often had doubts about going back, but I find that often they are ill-founded. Chicago is one of them. I first went to Chicago in 1953, and I've been commissioned several times since then to go back. Each time I thought, This is a mistake. It's not going to be what you thought it was; you'll be disappointed. But it wasn't so. Recently I wrote a very long essay about it, and it came off just as well as it had in previous times. Although in principle I agree with your friend, in practice it doesn't seem to be true.

INTERVIEWER

Why do you think Chicago works so well for you? Has it changed?

MORRIS

Yes, of course, it has changed enormously since I first went there, but it's not the change that excites me; it's the sameness—the fact that it still feels like most of us foreigners really want America to feel. There's a touch of an immensely urbane, sophisticated Norman Rockwell to Chicago that we innocents like.

INTERVIEWER

You've called Chicago the perfect city. Is that still true?

MORRIS

I don't think I said perfect. What I do mean is that, among twentieth-century cities, Chicago comes nearest to the ideal of a perfect city . . . an aesthetically perfect city. The shape of it seems to me fine and logical, and the buildings are magnificent. It is the most underrated of all the metropolises of the world in my opinion. I don't think many people say, I must go and look at that Chicago! Dickens did, though. As he drove in by train the conductor came through and said, Mr. Dickens, you're entering the boss city of the universe.

INTERVIEWER

You've written thirty-two books to date, by our count eighteen as James, fourteen as Jan. You've accomplished everything you set out to do?

MORRIS

By no means. There's one particular thing I've failed to do. This experience of mine that every now and then crops up . . . I think I've failed to use it artistically in the way I might have used it. A sex change is a very extraordinary thing for someone to have gone through and particularly extraordinary for a writer, I think. But although, as I say and you recognize, the effects of it appear kind of subliminally through everything I've written, I don't believe I've created a work of art around it.

I think *Fisher's Face* was, as some percipient critics saw, a kind of artistic product of this predicament—it is my favorite among my books—but I still haven't devised any more explicit way of using it. Perhaps I've left it too late?

Issue 143, 1997

Martin Amis

The Art of Fiction

Martin Amis was born on August 25, 1949, in Oxford, England, where his father, the Booker Prize–winning author Sir Kingsley Amis, was a doctoral student. He grew up in the various university towns in which his father taught literature: Swansea, Princeton, and Cambridge. His parents divorced when he was twelve.

At eighteen, a role in the film *A High Wind in Jamaica* took him to the West Indies. He returned to England in 1968 and, after taking "crammers" (courses designed to prepare one for university), he enrolled in Exeter College, Oxford. He graduated with first-class honors in English. In his early twenties, he wrote book reviews for the London *Observer* and soon thereafter worked as an editorial assistant for *The Times Literary Supplement*. His first novel, *The Rachel Papers*, was published in 1973 and received critical acclaim, winning the Somerset Maugham Award (a prize his father had also been awarded). While at the *TLS*, he published his second novel, *Dead Babies* (1975), which Auberon Waugh referred to as "nothing less than brilliant."

From 1977 to 1980 he served as literary editor of *The New Statesman*, a socialist weekly, and wrote two more novels, *Success* (1978) and *Other People* (1981). In 1984, his best-selling *Money* appeared, followed by a collection of journalism, *The Moronic Inferno* (1986), and a collection of short stories, *Einstein's Monsters* (1987), which focused on the nuclear threat and contained a polemical element previously unseen in his fiction.

the death explanation : a world view

It places us in a strange position. What was I for?
The death loophole. You got rid of it and something
much worse stares at you in the mirror. Ending.

Dying, as a career move : it might
help the book.

I hope you will tone it
down for my sake. It
is my intention to write
a family novel

(a desperate
charlatan

Sam to Ni : I never think about my readers.
It's all too precise. I can leave things out.
I can edit reality, at least.

Then you don't get it, do you.
The death of god — but he isn't dying, is he.
He has a vampire life. God always stood in for d. The
d of god is just what d always wanted. The d of g
just leaves you with d.
And then?
'The death of love. It is happening, as the night
follows the day. What do you make of me?'

I climbed to my feet saying, 'You're a bad dream,
baby. I keep thinking I'm going wake up' — and I
snapped my fingers weakly — 'and you'll disappear.'

She came toward me and held my head gently and
gave me the FP.
'Your yeah,' I said.
'There's a new one. You'd borrow my it. Shall I tell you
now what it's called, or afterwards?'
'Afterwards.'
Well?'
'It's called ... No. What did you think?'
'It's a baby,' I said.
'It's called The Kiss of Death.'
'The title needs some work
You'll need to work on that title. I can't.'
She felt with her hand, I just
'You you can. You can. Don't think about love. Think
about the same thing.'

A manuscript page from *London Fields* by Martin Amis.

dying like
m. age. 8
m. age like
dying
I felt I was dying
(ma)

London Fields (1990) again confronted nuclear holocaust and the death of the planet. One critic described the novel as "ferociously impressive." Amis subsequently published another collection of journalism, *Visiting Mrs. Nabokov*, and a novel, *Time's Arrow* (1992).

Soon thereafter, at the time of his divorce, Amis found himself the focus of a literary feud. When he left his longtime agent, Pat Kavanagh, the wife of his friend and fellow author Julian Barnes, to sign with Andrew Wylie, A. S. Byatt accused him of selling out to pay for his divorce and extensive dental work. His response to the scandal: "Envy never comes to the ball dressed as envy; it comes dressed as high moral standards or distaste for materialism."

Since then, he has written two novels: *The Information* (1995) and *Night Train*, a best-selling detective thriller set in an unnamed city in the United States.

The following interview is the result of several meetings, the first of which took place in the summer of 1990, on a former turkey ranch near Wellfleet, Massachusetts, where he was vacationing. Dressed in tennis gear, tan and relaxed, Amis drank coffee and throughout the afternoon rolled his own cigarettes with a frequency reminiscent of John Self (in *Money*), who explains to the reader, "Unless I specifically inform you otherwise, I'm always smoking another cigarette." Amis now lives in northwest London.

—*Francesca Riviere, 1998*

INTERVIEWER

When you are writing a novel, how do you start out? Is it with character or with theme? Or does something else come to you first?

MARTIN AMIS

The common conception of how novels get written seems to me to be an exact description of writer's block. In the common view, the writer is at this stage so desperate that he's sitting around with a list of characters, a list of themes, and a framework for his plot, and ostensibly trying to mesh the three elements. In fact, it's never like that.

What happens is what Nabokov described as a throb. A throb or a glimmer, an act of recognition on the writer's part. At this stage the writer thinks, Here is something I can write a novel about. In the absence of that recognition I don't know what one would do. It may be that nothing about this idea—or glimmer, or throb—appeals to you other than the fact that it's your destiny, that it's your next book. You may even be secretly appalled or awed or turned off by the idea, but it goes beyond that. You're just reassured that there is another novel for you to write. The idea can be incredibly thin—a situation, a character in a certain place at a certain time. With *Money*, for example, I had an idea of a big fat guy in New York, trying to make a film. That was all. Sometimes a novel can come pretty consecutively and it's rather like a journey in that you get going and the plot, such as it is, unfolds and you follow your nose. You have to decide between identical-seeming dirt roads, both of which look completely hopeless, but you nevertheless have to choose which one to follow.

INTERVIEWER

Do you worry, as you go along, that what you've already written isn't up to par?

AMIS

You try to think about where you are going, not where you came from, though what sometimes happens is that you get stuck, and it's really not what you're about to do that's stumping you, it's something you've already done that isn't right. You have to go back and fix that. My father described a process in which, as it were, he had to take himself gently but firmly by the hand and say, Now all right, calm down. What is it that's worrying you? The dialogue will go: Well, it's the first page, actually. What is it about the first page? He might say, The first sentence. And he realized that it was only a little thing that was holding him up. Actually, my father, I think, sat down and wrote what he considered to be the final version straightaway, because he said there's no point in putting down a sentence if you're not going to stand by it.

INTERVIEWER

So that assumed he knew where he was going.

AMIS

He knew a lot more than I do about where he was going. That may come with experience in the craft. I tend to be more headlong.

INTERVIEWER

How important is plot to you?

AMIS

Plots really matter only in thrillers. In mainstream writing the plot is—what is it? A hook. The reader is going to wonder how things turn out. In this respect, *Money* was a much more difficult book to write than *London Fields* because it is essentially a plotless novel. It is what I would call a *voice* novel. If the voice doesn't work you're screwed. *Money* was only one voice, whereas *London Fields* was four voices. The eggs weren't in one basket. They were in four baskets. I was fairly confident that the hook, this idea of a woman arranging her own murder, pricked the curiosity. So although nothing much happens in five hundred pages, people are still going to want to know how it ends. It's a *tease* novel, in that respect.

INTERVIEWER

Did you read or hear somewhere that certain people were predisposed to being murdered?

AMIS

Yes. I can't even remember when the idea or the scratch on the mind occurred. It wasn't even a book I read; it was a book review I read or heard about, or a conversation I listened to in a pub or a tube train. Anyway, all I needed was one sentence, which was the sentence you just outlined. And at that point I was thinking in terms of a very short novel, about the murderer and the murderee and their eventual conjunction. Then the introduction of a third character,

Guy, the foil, opened the novel out into a broader kind of society, and then the narrator had his own demands for space to be met. And finally, time and place took over, i.e., London, a modern city at the end of the century, at the end of the millennium. That brought together all kinds of interests and preoccupations. Again, it must be stressed that you don't have your themes tacked up on the wall like a target, or like a dartboard. When people ask, What did you mean to say with this novel? The answer to the question is, of course, The *novel*, all four hundred and seventy pages of it. Not any catchphrase that you could print on a badge or a T-shirt. It's a human failing to reduce things either to a slogan or a personality, but I seem to have laid myself open to this—the personality getting in the way of the novel.

INTERVIEWER

How do you mean that?

AMIS

Judging by everything from reviews to letters I receive, I find that people take my writing rather personally. It's interesting when you're doing signing sessions with other writers and you look at the queues at each table and you can see definite human types gathering there.

INTERVIEWER

Which type is in your queue?

AMIS

Well, I did one with Roald Dahl and quite predictable human divisions were observable. For him, a lot of children, a lot of parents of children. With Julian Barnes, his queue seemed to be peopled by rather comfortable, professional types. My queue is always full of, you know, wild-eyed sleazebags and people who stare at me very intensely, as if I have some particular message for them. As if I must know that they've been reading me, that this dyad or symbiosis of reader and writer has been so intense that I must somehow know about it.

INTERVIEWER

When did you know you wanted to write, or when did you consider yourself a writer?

AMIS

I might as well do my dad here.

INTERVIEWER

Sure.

AMIS

I'm not at all reluctant to talk about my father, since it's become clearer to me that it is more or less a unique case. First of all, it doesn't seem that literary ability is very strongly inherited. As far as I know, my father and I are the only father-and-son team who both have a body of work, or, as my father would put it, who are both "some good." And you know, Auberon Waugh and David Updike may have come up with a novel or two here and there, but not two chunks of work, either in succession or synchronously, as we have. I want to make it clear that it's been nothing but a help to me. Maybe it was more difficult for him, funnily enough; it took me a long time to realize that. I don't know how I'd feel if one of my little boys started to write, but I do know that I feel generally resentful of younger writers.

INTERVIEWER

You do?

AMIS

You're not thrilled to see some blazing talent coming up on your flank. Dislike and resentment of younger writers is something fairly universal among writers, and it may be more annoying, you know, when it's your own son. Also, it seems to me quite natural that I should admire my father's work and that he should have been suspicious and only half-engaged about my work. My father said to me that when a writer of twenty-five puts pen to paper he's saying to the writer of fifty that it's no longer like that, it's like *this*. The older writer, at some point, is going to lose touch with what the contemporary moment feels like, although some writers do amazing jobs of keeping able to do them, Saul Bellow being a good example. When my father started writing, he was saying to older writers—for instance, Somerset Maugham—it's not like that, it's like this. Of course, there was a reaction. One of the paperback editions of *Lucky Jim* has a quote from Somerset Maugham, which says something like today's universities are filling up with the new generation that has emerged since the war; Mr. Amis's observations are so sharp, his ear so acute, that he has caught their manners and mores exactly. That's where the quote ends on the book cover, but the original piece goes on—they are scum, they have no respect for values, for culture, et cetera. So a bit of "they are scum" is inevitable in the assessment of the younger writer.

Anyway, to get back to what it was like to start. All people rather like the idea of being a writer or painter at the age of thirteen or fourteen, but only the ones who succeed at it are ever asked when they first got the idea. I have said that I was aware at that age that my father was a writer, but I wasn't sure what kind of books he wrote. For all I knew they could have been westerns or bodice rippers.

INTERVIEWER

You didn't read him?

AMIS

I didn't, no. I was too young really, and I wasn't reading anyone.

INTERVIEWER

Did you ever discuss writing with him when you began?

AMIS

Not really. He was brilliantly indolent: he never gave me any encouragement at all. I later realized how valuable and necessary that was. I know one or two writers who've encouraged their children to write and it's a completely hollow promise because, to return to the more or less unique situation of my father and me, literary talent isn't inherited. When a writer-father says to a writer-son—and all sons, all people are writers for a little while—you can be me, you can be a writer, you can have my life, it's a complicated offer. It's certain to fall flat. So, perhaps out of natural indolence rather than prescience, he never did encourage me at all, and I never appealed for encouragement. What makes you a writer? You develop an extra sense that partly excludes you from experience. When writers experience things, they're not really experiencing them anything like a hundred percent. They're always holding back and wondering what the significance of it is, or wondering how they'd do it on the page. Always this disinterestedness . . . as if it really isn't to do with you, a certain cold impartiality. That faculty, I think, was pretty fully developed in me quite early on. One day, when I was still living at home, my father came into my room and I placed my hands protectively over the piece of paper in my typewriter. I didn't want him to see it. He said, later, that was his first suspicion. But then I did announce that I was writing a novel; I left home, and a year later the novel was done. I left the proofs of it on his desk and went off on holiday. When I came back, *he'd* gone on holiday. But he left a brief, charming note saying he thought it was enjoyable and fun and all that. I think that was the last novel of mine he read all the way through.

INTERVIEWER

That was *The Rachel Papers*?

AMIS

The Rachel Papers, yes. I think he slaved his way to the end of my third novel, *Success*, of which he said, The beginning and the end worked, but the middle didn't. As for the subsequent books, he read about twenty pages and then gave up. It took a bit of getting used to, this, because you felt it as a son *and* as a fellow writer. There was no sore feeling at all, partly because I was inured, but also because I saw that it was impossible for him to tell white lies as writers tend to do to their friends. I would much rather revise upward my opinion of a friend's book than endanger a friendship. But he was not like that; in that way he was much tougher than me.

INTERVIEWER

Did you feel you were carrying the mantle of your father's legacy or competing with that? Was there any intimidation at the beginning, or did you just want to write and that was it?

AMIS

I suppose it was nice to know that however bad your first novel was, it probably would have been published out of mercenary curiosity. It was like having a lot of ballast; it was reassuring. The more eminent my father became, the more secure it made me feel. People were very generous to me to begin with, out of a mistaken feeling that it must have been hard for me. The only entry on the deficit side came later, after people who had been generous to me for a while probably expected me to write a couple of novels and then shut up, as writers' sons usually do. There's a feeling that it's a bit bloody much that I've gone on and on and here I still am. "Why were we so nice to him in the beginning?" Interestingly, only recently did I realize that it was much harder for my father than for me. Not *very* hard; I think he was quite pleased, most of the time, that I'm a writer. But much more annoying for him. I was never annoyed. It's natural to admire your elders and to despise your youngsters. That's the way of the world. There was a brief period when my father would snipe at me in print and use me as an example of the incomprehensibility and uninterestingness of modern prose. Thanks for the plug, Dad. But that was just amusing, that was just in character for him. And I sniped back.

INTERVIEWER

I read that when he came across your name as a character in *Money*, he flung the book across the room.

AMIS

I'm almost certain that it was the introduction of a minor character called Martin Amis that caused my father to send the book windmilling through the air. Because I had broken the contract between writer and reader, which says no messing about, no fooling with the reality level.

I once cornered him and asked him which prose writers he *did* admire—as usual, at dinner, he'd been dismissing great swathes of literature, one after the other. He was once asked to contribute an article in a series called Sacred Cows. My father said, What about my doing American literature? They said, Well, all right. My father said, How many words? They said, Eight hundred. My father said, Oh, I don't think I'll need as much space as *that*. When challenged, he said he did like one book by Evelyn Waugh, some books by Anthony Powell, and after about another thirty seconds he was reduced to Dick Francis. He didn't like Jane Austen, didn't like Dickens, didn't like Fielding, didn't like Lawrence, didn't like Joyce, didn't like any Americans. And was ill-equipped to judge any of the Russians, the French, the South Americans, et cetera. So I began to feel a bit better about him not liking my stuff either.

INTERVIEWER

In good company.

AMIS

Exactly.

INTERVIEWER

Is there someone whose work you read that was pivotal or a turning point?

AMIS

The first literature I read was Jane Austen.

INTERVIEWER

Was it influential?

AMIS

I would say that the writers I like and trust have at the base of their prose something called the English sentence. An awful lot of modern writing seems to me to be a depressed use of language. Once, I called it "vow-of-poverty prose." No, give me the king in his countinghouse.

Give me Updike. Anthony Burgess said there are two kinds of writers, A-writers and B-writers. A-writers are storytellers, B-writers are users of language. And I tend to be grouped in the Bs. Under Nabokov's prose, under Burgess's prose, under my father's prose—his early rather than his later prose—the English sentence is like a poetic meter. It's a basic rhythm from which the writer is free to glance off in unexpected directions. But the sentence is still there. To be crude, it would be like saying that I don't trust an abstract painter unless I know that he can do hands.

INTERVIEWER

Their experimentations are based on a structure or knowledge . . .

AMIS

They're based on the ability to write a good English sentence. Much modern prose is praised for its terseness, its scrupulous avoidance of curlicue, et cetera. But I don't feel the deeper rhythm there. I don't think these writers are being terse out of choice. I think they are being terse because it's the only way they can write.

INTERVIEWER

Out of limitation.

AMIS

Out of limitation. So if the prose isn't there, then you're reduced to what are merely secondary interests, like story, plot, characterization, psychological insight, and form. I get less and less interested in form, although I have the English writer's addiction to it. Form seems to me like decor in a restaurant. Form is easy. You can make shapely novels, everything working like a well-made watch. You can do all these little balancing acts and color schemes—like an American campus novel, meaning a novel written on campus, rather than about campus. A creative-writing novel. What is important is to write freely and passionately and with all the resources that the language provides. I'm not interested in limiting the language to the capabilities—or the accepted, obvious capabilities—of my narrators. I'm not interested in writing a realistically *stupid* novel. Some of my characters have been semiliterate, but I fix it one way or the other so that I can write absolutely flat out in their voice. Nabokov said something like, I think like a genius, I write like a distinguished man of letters, I talk like an idiot. The first and third propositions are true of everyone. As many writers have shown, supposedly ordinary, inarticulate, uneducated people have mystical and poetical thoughts that just don't quite make it into expression. What could be a better job for a novelist than to do it for them? They say that everyone has a novel in them but it doesn't often get written. If you write that novel *for* them at the highest pitch of your powers, you don't end up with a realistically stupid novel, one that begins, you know, I get up in de morning.

INTERVIEWER

What would be something really difficult for you to write?

AMIS

I did have the idea of writing—I may yet, when it falls together—a short story narrated by a two year old. But even then I think I would try to fix it so that I could write flat out. I rather like these impositions of difficulty. In *Other People*, I used the localized third person, where everything is seen through the heroine's point of view. She's not only a woman, she's also suffering from an amnesia so total that she doesn't know what a chair is, or a sink, or a spoon. In *Money*, I had a semiliterate alcoholic. In *Time's Arrow*, I have a kind of super-innocent narrator living in a world where time runs backwards. You're always looking for a way to see the world as if you've never seen it before. As if you'd never really got used to living here on this planet. Have you heard of the Martian school of poets?

INTERVIEWER

No, I haven't.

AMIS

It all goes back to a poem written by Craig Raine called "A Martian Sends a Postcard Home." The poem consists of little riddles about what the Martian sees of life on Earth. Such as, at night they hide in pairs and watch films about each other with their eyelids shut. Only the young are allowed to suffer openly. Adults go to a punishment room, with water but nothing to eat. They sit and suffer the noises in silence and everyone's pain has a different smell.

INTERVIEWER

Yikes!

AMIS

It's a marvelous poem. As with most schools, the Martian label means everything and nothing, since I think all writers are Martians. They come and say, You haven't been seeing this place right; it's not like *that*, it's like *this*. Seeing the world anew, as if it were new, is as old as writing. It's what all painters are trying to do, to see what's there, to see it in a way that renews it. It becomes more and more urgent as the planet gets worn flat and forest after forest is slain to print the paper for people's impressions to be scrawled down on. It becomes harder and harder to be original, to see things with an innocent eye. Innocence is much tied up with it. As the planet gets progressively less innocent, you need a more innocent eye to see it.

INTERVIEWER

How would you respond to this quote from Paul Valéry? He says, "Hide your god, men must hide their true gods with great care."

AMIS

Writers very seldom talk about their gods in the sense Valéry meant, because it's mysterious even to them. They don't know what makes them write; they don't know in any psychoanalytical sense what makes them write. They don't know why, when they come up against a difficulty and then go for a walk, they can come back and the difficulty is solved. They don't know why they plant minor characters early on in a novel who turn up with a specific function later on. When things are going well, you do have the sense that what you're writing is being fed to you in some way. Auden compared writing a poem to cleaning an old piece of slate until the letters appear. The only way you could reveal your god is perhaps under hypnosis. It's sacred and it's secret, even to the writer.

INTERVIEWER

Can you talk about the influence of other writers or poets? I know one of them is Saul Bellow.

AMIS

I would say they are more *inspirers* than influences. When I am stuck with a sentence that isn't fully born, it isn't yet there, I sometimes think, How would Dickens go at this sentence, how would Bellow or Nabokov go at this sentence? What you hope to emerge with is how *you* would go at that sentence, but you get a little shove in the back by thinking about writers you admire. I was once winding up a telephone conversation with Saul Bellow and he said, Well you go back to work now, and I said, All right, and he said, Give 'em hell. And it's Dickens saying, Give 'em hell. Give the reader hell. Stretch the reader.

INTERVIEWER

What do you mean by stretching the reader? Making things difficult for them?

AMIS

Yes, I think you throw all modesty and caution aside and say that the reader is you. Inevitably, you are writing the sort of stuff that you would like to read, that would give you the most pleasure to read. Looking back on your work, if it's more than ten years old or five years old, it's usually pretty painful.

INTERVIEWER

You've moved on.

AMIS

You've moved on. But even when you read the page with the half-averted eyes, you'll see something and you'll think, That paragraph is still alive. In the same kind of way you might think about a younger self of yours that whatever you were up to, you had vigor.

INTERVIEWER

Would you say there's a certain continuity in a writer's body of work, which may zig or zag, but actually follows a sequence over the long term.

AMIS

I think that novels are about the author's voice, and this perhaps is why I haven't got much time for the novel that dutifully apes the voice of the bricklayer or even the etymologist or whatever it might be. What gives the voice its own timbre and its own resonance is what interests me, and that is always there, right from the start. It has to do with what is inimitable about the writer. This tends to get confused with what is parodiable about a writer.

INTERVIEWER

The writer's voice is his style?

AMIS

It's all he's got. It's not the flashy twist, the abrupt climax, or the seamless sequence of events that characterizes a writer and makes him unique. It's a tone, it's a way of looking at things. It's a rhythm, it's what in poetry is called a sprung rhythm. Instead of having a stress every other beat, it has stress after stress after stress. One's a little worried about having one's logo on every sentence. What's that phrase about a painting consisting entirely of signatures? That obviously is something to be avoided, but it would never inhibit me. I never think, Let's write a piece of prose that is unmistakably mine. Really, it's an internal process, a tuning-fork process. You say the sentence or you write the sentence again and again until the tuning fork is still, until it satisfies you.

INTERVIEWER

Do you say the sentence aloud when you're writing?

AMIS

No, entirely in the mind. Oh, you might have a few stabs at it and then when you read it through, something jars, something . . . the rhythm doesn't feel right, one word is suspect, and you may then recast the sentence entirely, until it's got no elbows left, if you know what I mean, until it looks completely comfortable. What each writer will find comfortable will vary with each writer. Until it suits you, and then you needn't do anything more to it.

INTERVIEWER

Will you go straight through a whole first draft, beginning, middle, and end?

AMIS

On the first draft. Then sequence comes into it, and you transfer from what I think of as the more painterly hand-eye medium of longhand. If I showed you a notebook of mine, it would have lots of squiggles and transpositions and lots of light crossings-out so that you can see what the original was. You move from that into the typewritten, which immediately looks more convincing and more immovable. By the way, it's all nonsense about how wonderful computers are because you can shift things around. Nothing compares with the fluidity of longhand. You shift things around without shifting them around—in that you merely indicate a possibility while your original thought is still there. The trouble with a computer is that what you come out with has no memory, no provenance, no history—the little cursor, or whatever it's called, that wobbles around the middle of the screen falsely gives you the impression that you're thinking. Even when you're not.

INTERVIEWER

Do you get someone to type the final version?

AMIS

No, no. When I finish a novel, I do think that whether or not I should get a prize for writing the book, I should certainly get a prize for typing it. The Booker Prize is for typing. Even going from second draft to final draft, hardly a page survives without being totally rewritten. You know that the very act of retyping will involve you in thirty or forty little improvements per page. If you don't retype, you are denying that page those improvements.

INTERVIEWER

There's more momentum in the typing stage.

AMIS

Absolutely. It begins to look like a book rather than a collection of doodles.

INTERVIEWER

What's a good day of writing? How many hours, how many pages?

AMIS

Everyone assumes I'm a systematic and nose-to-the-grindstone kind of person. But to me it seems like a part-time job, really, in that writing from eleven to one continuously is a very good day's work. Then you can read and play tennis or snooker. Two hours. I think most writers would be very happy with two hours of concentrated work. Toward the end of a book, as you get more confident, and also decidedly more hysterical about getting this thing away from you, then you can do six or seven hours. But that means you are working on hysterical energy.

I want to clean my desk again (not that it ever is clean); I want this five years' worth of preoccupation off my desk. Because I started writing when I was relatively young, every novel I've written contains everything I know, so that by the time I'm finished I'm completely out of gas. I'm a moron when I finish a novel. It's all in *there* and there's nothing left in *here*.

INTERVIEWER

You said that after *London Fields* you felt a supervoid.

AMIS

I felt like a clinical moron. My IQ was about sixty-five. For weeks I shambled about, unable to do my own shoelaces. Also faintly happy and proud.

INTERVIEWER

In your work, do you feel more strongly affected by visual stimuli or aural stimuli or something else?

AMIS

Through the ear, probably. My mind, like everyone else's mind, is full of jabbering voices. Any phrase that sticks in my mind, I tend to think is resonant and I will use it. Visual stimuli are not so naturally processed by me. For visual description I sort of have to roll my sleeves up.

INTERVIEWER

You write a fair amount of journalism.

AMIS

Journalism, particularly book reviewing, brings with it another magnitude of difficulty. Fiction writing is basically what I want to do when I get up in the morning. If I haven't done any all day, then I feel dissatisfied. If I wake up knowing that I have some journalism to write, then it's with a heavy tread that I go to the bathroom—without relish, for many and obvious reasons. You're no longer in complete control.

INTERVIEWER

Do you think it's a good training ground?

AMIS

I think you have a duty to contribute, to go on contributing to what Gore Vidal calls "book chat." For certain self-interested reasons, you want to keep standards up so that when your next book comes out, it's more likely that people will get the hang of it. I have no admiration for writers who think at a certain point they can wash their hands of book chat. You should be part of the ongoing debate.

INTERVIEWER

How much of your fiction comes from fact?

AMIS

Tom Wolfe wrote that piece—in *Harper's*, was it?—where he said that writers are neglecting the real world; that it's all out there and it's interesting and novelists should be writing about it. He suggested a ratio of seventy percent research, thirty percent inspiration. But the trouble is that the real world probably isn't going to fit into the novel. In a sense, it's better to do the research in your mind. You need detail, you need pegs, but you don't want too much truth, you don't want too much fact. I would reverse the ratio—thirty percent research, seventy percent inspiration. Perhaps even thirty percent research is too much. You want a few glimmers from the real world but then you need to run it through your psyche, to reimagine it. Don't transcribe, reimagine. Mere fact has no chance of being formally perfect. It will get in the way, it will be all elbows. This reminds me of something I once said about the nonfiction novel—*In Cold Blood*, *The Executioner's Song*, and so on. There is a great deal of artistry in that form. The first couple of hundred pages in *The Executioner's Song*, where Mailer is reimagining the locale and the characters, are wonderfully artistic. But the trouble with the nonfiction fiction is that the facts are there. The murder is there. That's what you're given. And that makes the nonfiction fiction artistically very limited. The larger act of transformation can't take place because you're stymied by the truth.

INTERVIEWER

Can we talk about how your characters develop?

AMIS

I'm very fond of quoting these two remarks. E. M. Forster said he used to line up his characters, as it were, at the starting line of the novel, and say to them, Right. No larks. Nabokov used to say that his characters cringed as he walked past with his switch, and that he'd seen whole avenues of imagined trees lose their leaves in terror as he approached. I don't think I'm really like that. I think character is destiny within the novel as well as outside the novel . . . that characters you invent will contribute vitally to the kind of novel you're going to write. I feel that if they are alive in your mind, they're going to have ideas of their own and take you places you wouldn't perhaps have gone. In *London Fields*, certainly, the dynamic character in my mind was the girl. Rather as the narrator, Sam, keeps appealing to her to spice up a scene or to give it a bit of form, she was doing that for *me*. She was vigorous enough, and shifty enough, for me to appeal to her to help me out. Fix it, get me to the next stage. I think I rather resist the idea of characters being pawns in a formal game. I'm almost daring them to strike out in a way that might surprise me.

INTERVIEWER

So you give them license.

AMIS

A bit of license, yes. But *I'm* the boss. I'm the boss but they're on the team. They're "my people," in the sense that a politician might have his people—his in-depth backup. I'm always willing to hear their ideas, although of course I retain the right of absolute veto; I slap them down but I want to hear what they've got to say.

INTERVIEWER

How will the characters present themselves?

AMIS

I think they have to have a physical hook, a physical plinth of some kind, and they will have a human model. But you don't want to know the model too well. Better to base a character on someone you've known for ten minutes than someone you've known for ten years, because you want them to be plastic, to be malleable.

It seems the source of a lot of what you are talking about is intuition.

Well, you become a grizzled old pro, too, in that the craft side of it gets easier and more natural. You know more what you're about, you know more what you don't have to say. You get your characters around town more economically, you get them in and out of places without so much fuss. You learn more about modulation. After a scene dominated by dialogue, you don't want much dialogue in the next scene. It becomes kind of rule of thumb. So that if you are going to break that rule, then you have to have a good reason for it. But, otherwise, you trust entirely to instinct. It's all you've got. Writer's block, disintegration of the writer, that's all to do with failing confidence.

How often do you write?

Every weekday. I have an office where I work. I leave the house and I'm absent for the average working day. I drive my powerful Audi three quarters of a mile across London to my flat. And there, unless I've got something else I have to do, I will sit down and write fiction for as long as I can. As I said earlier, it never feels remotely like a full day's work, although it can be. A lot of the time seems to be spent making coffee or trolling around, or throwing darts, or playing pinball, or picking your nose, trimming your fingernails, or staring at the ceiling.

You know that foreign correspondent's ruse; in the days when you had your profession on the passport, you put writer; and then when you were in some trouble spot, in order to conceal your identity you simply changed the *r* in *writer* to an *a* and became a *waiter*. I always thought there was a great truth there. Writing is waiting, for me certainly. It wouldn't bother me a bit if I didn't write one word in the morning. I'd just think, you know, not yet. The job seems to be one of making yourself receptive to whatever's on the rise that day. I was quite surprised to read how much dread Father felt as he approached the typewriter in the morning.

INTERVIEWER

Yes, he really sidled up to it.

AMIS

I seldom have that kind of squeamishness. Any smoker will sympathize when I say that after your first cup of coffee you have a sobbing, pleading feeling in the lungs as they cry out for their first cigarette of the day, and my desire to write is rather like that. It's rather physical.

INTERVIEWER

The physical activity balances the mental purpose.

AMIS

All under the general heading of a game.

INTERVIEWER

Do you have any superstitions about writing?

AMIS

It's amazing—I do sometimes feel tempted by computers until I realize what an amazing pleasure a new Biro is.

INTERVIEWER

A new Biro?

AMIS

A Biro, you know—a ballpoint. The pleasure you get from a new Biro that works. So you have the childish pleasure of paper and pen.

INTERVIEWER

New supplies.

AMIS

New supplies. Superstitions . . . I think someone must have told me at some point that I write a lot better if I'm smoking. I'm sure if I stopped smoking, I would start writing sentences like, It was bitterly cold. Or, It was bakingly hot.

INTERVIEWER

Do you need complete isolation to write or is it more portable than that?

AMIS

I can write in the midst of—not very conveniently—but I can make progress in the midst of the usual family clamor. But it has to be said, perhaps with some regret, that the first thing that distinguishes a writer is that he is most alive when alone, most fully alive when alone. A tolerance for solitude isn't anywhere near the full description of what really goes on. The most interesting things happen to you when you are alone.

INTERVIEWER

You make yourself laugh or cry . . . ?

AMIS

Yes . . . crazy scientist's laughter comes from the study—the laughter scientists use to signify life created out of a grimy test tube.

INTERVIEWER

Out of a Biro.

AMIS

Yes. A good deal of that. When I worked on my first book at home, my bedroom was above my father's study, and I would often hear, not crazy scientist's laughter, but the sort of laughter where the shoulders are shaking, coming from below. And I continue that tradition. I do find that not only the comic scenes make you laugh but anything that works well. Really, laughter is the successful serendipity of the whole business.

How important is the ego, self-confidence?

Novelists have two ways of talking about themselves. One in which they do a very good job of pretending to be reasonably modest individuals with fairly realistic opinions of their own powers and not atrociously ungenerous in their assessments of their contemporaries. The second train of thought is that of the inner egomaniac; your immediate contemporaries are just blind worms in a ditch, slithering pointlessly around, getting nowhere. You bestride the whole generation with your formidability. The only thing your contemporaries are doing—even the most eminent of them—is devaluing literary eminence. Basically they're just stinking up the place. You open the book pages and you can't understand why it isn't all about you. Or, indeed, why the whole *paper* isn't all about you. I think without this kind of feeling you couldn't operate at all. The ego has to be roughly this size. I'm not sure it's true, but I was told by a poet friend that even William Golding can come into a literary party at six-thirty and do a good imitation of a self-effacing man of letters, but at nine o'clock the whole room may be brought to silence by his cry of *I'm a genius!* Just give him a bullhorn. They may have their little smiles and demurrals and seem twinkly and manageable characters but really . . . Is there anything you'd like to add? Yes. *I'm a genius!* End of interview.

There's also the flip side, of course—terrific vulnerability, crying jags, the seeking of the fetal position after a bad review and all that kind of stuff. One of the perks of being a writer–son of a writer is that I don't think I've had much of that myself—a *huge* self-love. Or maybe I see it clearly because writing has never seemed to me to be an unusual way of making a living or spending your time. Whereas, friends of mine, Julian Barnes, the son of schoolteachers, Ian McEwan, the son of a military man, they must be drunk with power when they sit down at their typewriters, and think I earn a living because what I think has

universal interest, or semiuniversal interest, anyway, enough interest
to pay the rent. It must be gratifying in extraordinary ways. It would
take a lot of getting over, it seems to me. I've never had that intoxicat-
ing pleasure, but perhaps I haven't suffered either. It just seemed to
me a very natural way of proceeding with my life, and I haven't felt
singled out at all. To me, it's all about perceptions, perceptions about
life or human nature or the way something looks or the way something sounds. Two or three of them on a page in a notebook, that's
what it's really all about. Getting enough of them to enliven every
page of a novel, like light. I mean, to call them *felicities* is wrong. You
have to have a clumsier formulation, something like droplets of origi-
nality, things that are essentially your own, and are you. If I die tomorrow, well, at least my children, who are approaching as we speak,
at least they will have a very good idea of what I was like, of what my
mind was like, because they will be able to read my books. So maybe
there is an immortalizing principle at work even if it's just for your
children. Even if they've forgotten you physically, they could never
say that they didn't know what their father was like.

Issue 146, 1998

Salman Rushdie

The Art of Fiction

S alman Rushdie was born in Bombay in 1947, on the eve of India's independence. He was educated there and in England, where he spent the first decades of his writing life. These days Rushdie lives primarily in New York, where this interview was conducted in several sessions over the past year. By coincidence, the second conversation took place on Valentine's Day 2005, the sixteenth anniversary of the Ayatollah Khomeini's fatwa against Rushdie, which proclaimed him an apostate for writing *The Satanic Verses* and sentenced him to death under Islamic law. In 1998, Iran's president, Mohammed Khatami, denounced the fatwa, and Rushdie now insists that the danger has passed. But Islamic hard-liners regard fatwas as irrevocable and Rushdie's home address remains unlisted.

For a man who occasioned such furor, who has been lauded and blamed, threatened and feted, burnt in effigy and upheld as an icon of free expression, Rushdie is surprisingly easygoing and candid— neither a hunted victim nor a scourge. Clean shaven, dressed in jeans and a sweater, he actually looks like a younger version of the condemned man who stared out at his accusers in Richard Avedon's famous 1995 portrait. "My family can't stand that picture," he said, laughing. Then, asked where the photograph is stored, he grinned and replied, "On the wall."

When he is working, Rushdie said, "it is rather unusual of me to come out in the daytime." But late last year he handed in the manuscript for *Shalimar the Clown*, his ninth novel, and he has not yet each other, so that when the letter from Shalimar the clown arrived it seemed anachronistic, like a punch thrown long after the final bell.

Everything I am your mother makes me, the letter began. *Every blow I suffer your father deals.* There followed more along these lines, and then ended with the sentence that Shalimar the clown had carried within him all his life. *Your father deserves to die, and your mother is a whore.* She showed the letter to Yuvraj. 'Too bad he hasn't improved his English in San Quentin,' he said, trying to dismiss the ugly words, to rob them of their power. 'He puts the past into the present tense.'

*

Night in the A/C was a little quieter than the day. There was a certain amount of screaming but after the 1 a.m. inspection it quietened down. Three in the morning was almost peaceful. Shalimar the clown lay on his steel cot and tried to conjure up the sound of the running of the Muskadoon, tried to taste the gushtaba and roghan josh and firni of Pandit Pyarelal Kaul, tried to remember his father. *I wish I was still held in the palm of your hand.* His brothers came into the cell to say hello. They were out of focus, like amateur photographs, and they soon disappeared again. The Muskadoon died away and the taste of the dishes of the wazwaan turned back into the usual bitter blood-flecked shit taste he'd grown used to over the years. Then there was a loud hissing noise and the cell door sprang open. He moved quickly on to his feet and crouched slightly, ready for whatever was coming. Nobody entered but there was a noise of running feet. Men in prison fatigues were running in the corridors. *It's a jailbreak,* he realized. There was no gunfire yet but it would start soon. He stood staring at the open

A manuscript page from *Shalimar the Clown* by Salman Rushdie.

started a new project. Although he claimed he'd exhausted his resources finishing the book, he seemed to gain energy as he talked
about his past, his writing, his politics. In conversation, Rushdie per-
forms the same mental acrobatics that one finds in his fiction—
snaking digressions that can touch down on several continents and
historical eras before returning to the original point.

The fatwa ensured that the name Salman Rushdie is better known
around the world than that of any other living novelist. But his reputation as a writer has hardly been eclipsed by the political assaults. In
1993, he was awarded the "Booker of Bookers"—a medal honoring
his novel *Midnight's Children* as the best book to win the Man Booker
Prize since it was established twenty-five years earlier—and he is currently the president of the PEN-American Center. In addition to his
novels, he is the author of five volumes of nonfiction, and a short-
story collection. On Valentine's Day, as he arranged himself in a
padded chair, a light snow fell, and the incinerator stack of a building
a few blocks east blew a column of black smoke into the sky. Rushdie
drank from a glass of water and talked about finding his wife the right
gift before settling into questions.

—*Jack Livings, 2005*

INTERVIEWER

When you're writing, do you think at all about who will be reading you?

SALMAN RUSHDIE

I don't really know. When I was young, I used to say, No, I'm just
the servant of the work.

INTERVIEWER

That's noble.

RUSHDIE

Excessively noble. I've gotten more interested in clarity as a virtue,
less interested in the virtues of difficulty. And I suppose that means I

do have a clearer sense of how people read, which is, I suppose, partly created by my knowledge of how people have read what I have written so far. I don't like books that play to the gallery, but I've become more concerned with telling a story as clearly and engagingly as I can. Then again, that's what I thought at the beginning, when I wrote *Midnight's Children*. I thought it odd that storytelling and literature seemed to have come to a parting of the ways. It seemed unnecessary for the separation to have taken place. A story doesn't have to be simple, it doesn't have to be one-dimensional but, especially if it's multidimensional, you need to find the clearest, most engaging way of telling it.

One of the things that has become, to me, more evidently my subject is the way in which the stories of anywhere are also the stories of everywhere else. To an extent, I already knew that because Bombay, where I grew up, was a city in which the West was totally mixed up with the East. The accidents of my life have given me the ability to make stories in which different parts of the world are brought together, sometimes harmoniously, sometimes in conflict, and sometimes both—usually both. The difficulty in these stories is that if you write about everywhere you can end up writing about nowhere. It's a problem that the writer writing about a single place does not have to face. Those writers face other problems, but the thing that a Faulkner or a Welty has—a patch of the earth that they know so profoundly and belong to so totally that they can excavate it all their lives and not exhaust it—I admire that, but it's not what I do.

INTERVIEWER

How would you describe what you do?

RUSHDIE

My life has given me this other subject: worlds in collision. How do you make people see that everyone's story is now a part of everyone else's story? It's one thing to say it, but how can you make a reader feel that is their lived experience? The last three novels have been attempts to find answers to those questions: *The Ground Beneath Her Feet* and *Fury* and the new one, *Shalimar the Clown*, which begins and ends in L.A., but the middle of it is in Kashmir, and some is in Nazi-occupied Strasbourg, and some in 1960s England. In *Shalimar*, the character Max Ophuls is a resistance hero during World War II. The resistance, which we think of as heroic, was what we would now call an insurgency in a time of occupation. Now we live in a time when there are other insurgencies that we don't call heroic—that we call terrorist. I didn't want to make moral judgments. I wanted to say, That happened then, this is happening now, this story includes both those things, just look how they sit together. I don't think it's for the novelist to say, It means this.

INTERVIEWER

Do you have to restrain yourself from saying, It means this?

RUSHDIE

No. I'm against that in a novel. If I'm writing an op-ed piece, it's different. But I believe that you damage the novel by instructing the reader. The character of Shalimar, for example, is a vicious murderer. You're terrified of him, but at certain points—like the scene where he flies off the wall in San Quentin—you're rooting for him. I wanted that to happen, I wanted people to see as he sees, to feel as he feels, rather than to assume they know what kind of man he is. Of all my books this was the book that was most completely written by its characters. Quite a lot of the original conception of the book had to be jettisoned because the characters wanted to go another way.

INTERVIEWER

What do you mean?

RUSHDIE

Moment by moment in the writing, things would happen that I hadn't foreseen. Something strange happened with this book. I felt completely possessed by these people, to the extent that I found myself crying over my own characters. There's a moment in the book where Boonyi's father, the pandit Pyarelal, dies in his fruit orchard. I couldn't bear it. I found myself sitting at my desk weeping. I thought,

What am I doing? This is somebody I've made up. Then there was a moment when I was writing about the destruction of the Kashmiri village. I absolutely couldn't bear the idea of writing it. I would sit at my desk and think, I can't write these sentences. Many writers who have had to deal with the subject of atrocity can't face it head-on. I've never felt that I couldn't bear the idea of telling a story—that it's so awful, I don't want to tell it, can something else happen? And then you think, Oh, nothing else *can* happen, *that's* what happens.

INTERVIEWER

Kashmir is family territory for you.

RUSHDIE

My family's from Kashmir originally, and until now I've never really taken it on. The beginning of *Midnight's Children* is in Kashmir, and *Haroun and the Sea of Stories* is a fairy tale of Kashmir, but in my fiction I've never really addressed Kashmir itself. The year of the real explosion in Kashmir, 1989, was also the year in which there was an explosion in my life. So I got distracted, and . . . By the way, today is the anniversary of the fatwa. Valentine's Day is not my favorite day of the year, which really annoys my wife. Anyway, *Shalimar* was a kind of attempt to write a Kashmiri *Paradise Lost*. Only *Paradise Lost* is about the fall of man—paradise is still there, it's just that we get kicked out of it. *Shalimar* is about the smashing of paradise. It's as if Adam went back with bombs and blew the place up.

I've never seen anywhere in the world as beautiful as Kashmir. It has something to do with the fact that the valley is very small and the mountains are very big, so you have this miniature countryside surrounded by the Himalayas, and it's just spectacular. And it's true, the people are very beautiful, too. Kashmir is quite prosperous. The soil is very rich, so the crops are plentiful. It's lush, not like much of India, in which there's great scarcity. But of course all that's gone now, and there is great hardship.

The main industry of Kashmir was tourism. Not foreign tourism, Indian tourism. If you look at Indian movies, every time they wanted an exotic locale, they would have a dance number in Kashmir. Kashmir was India's fairyland. Indians went there because in a hot country you go to a cold place. People would be entranced by the sight of snow. You'd see people at the airport where there's dirty, slushy snow piled up by the sides of the roads, standing there as if they'd found a diamond mine. It had that feeling of an enchanted space. That's all gone now, and even if there's a peace treaty tomorrow it's not coming back, because the thing that was smashed, which is what I tried to write about, is the tolerant, mingled culture of Kashmir. After the way the Hindus were driven out, and the way the Muslims have been radicalized and tormented, you can't put it back together again. I wanted to say: It's not just a story about mountain people five or six thousand miles away. It's our story, too.

INTERVIEWER

We're all implicated in it?

RUSHDIE

I wanted to make sure in this book that the story was personal, not political. I wanted people to read it and form intimate, novelistic attachments to the characters and if I did it right it won't feel didactic, and you'll care about everybody. I wanted to write a book with no minor characters.

INTERVIEWER

Were you keenly aware of Kashmiri politics when you were growing up?

RUSHDIE

When I was probably no older than twelve we went on a family trip to Kashmir. There were beautiful hikes you could take with little ponies up into the high mountains, onto the glaciers. We all went— my sisters, my parents, and I—and there were villages where you could spend the night at a government rest house, very simple places. When we got to our rest house my mother discovered that the pony that should have been carrying all the food didn't have the food on board. She had three fractious children with her, so she sent the pony guy off to the village to see what could be had, and he came back and said, There's no food, there's nothing to be had. They don't have anything. And she said, What do you mean? There can't be nothing. There must be some eggs—what do you mean *nothing*? He said, No, there's nothing. And so she said, Well, we can't have dinner, nobody's going to eat.

About an hour later we saw this procession of a half-dozen people coming up from the village, bringing food. The village headman came up to us and said, I want to apologize to you, because when we told the guy there wasn't any food we thought you were a Hindu family. But, he said, when we heard it was a Muslim family we had to bring food. We won't accept any payment, and we apologize for having been so discourteous.

I thought, Wow. This is in Kashmir, which is supposed to have this tradition of tolerance. I would go all the time, and the moment they heard the name Salman, which is a Muslim name, they would talk to me in a way that if I were called, you know, Raghubir, they might not. So I would have long conversations about their lives and their resentments. But when I went back to Delhi or Bombay and relayed this information there was a desire even amongst the Indian intelligentsia not to acknowledge how deep those resentments had become. People would say, You shouldn't talk this way because you're sounding communalist. Me, the Muslim communalist!

INTERVIEWER

Could you possibly write an apolitical book?

RUSHDIE

Yes, I have great interest in it, and I keep being annoyed that I haven't. I think the space between private life and public life has disappeared in our time. There used to be much more distance there. It's like Jane Austen forgetting to mention the Napoleonic wars. The function of the British army in the novels of Jane Austen is to look cute at parties. It's not because she's ducking something, it's that she can fully and profoundly explain the lives of her characters without a reference to the public sphere. That's no longer possible, and it's not just because there's a TV in the corner of every room. It's because the events of the world have great bearing on our daily lives. Do we have a job or not? How much is our money worth? This is all determined by things outside of our control. It challenges Heraclitus's idea that character is destiny. Sometimes your character is not your destiny. Sometimes a plane flying into a building is your destiny. The larger world gets into the story not because I want to write about politics, but because I want to write about people.

INTERVIEWER

But in American writing there seems to be a rift of sorts—politics over there, fiction over here—because what an American novelist writes is not going to influence policy in Washington.

RUSHDIE

Yes, but who cares about that?

INTERVIEWER

Do you think that in India, for instance, fiction is politically relevant?

RUSHDIE

No. If only it was. But what does happen is that well-known writers are still considered—in a way that American writers are not—to be a part of the conversation. Their opinions are sought out. This happens in England, too. It happens in Europe. In America it was true not so long ago. It was true in the generation of Mailer, Sontag, Arthur Miller—

INTERVIEWER

What happened?

RUSHDIE

I don't know. At the height of the British Empire very few English novels were written that dealt with British power. It's extraordinary that at the moment in which England was the global superpower the subject of British power appeared not to interest most writers. Maybe there's an echo of that now, when America is the global superpower. Outside this country, America means power. That's not true in the United States itself. There are still writers here who take on politics—Don DeLillo, Robert Stone, Joan Didion, and so on. But I think many American writers are relatively uninterested in the way America is perceived abroad. As a result there's relatively little written about the power of America.

INTERVIEWER

Alongside your interest in politics and power, there's a lot of fantastic invention in your work. In fact, you've said that *The Wizard of Oz* made a writer of you.

RUSHDIE

After I saw the film, I went home and wrote a short story called "Over the Rainbow." I was probably nine or ten. The story was about a boy walking down a sidewalk in Bombay and seeing the beginning of the rainbow, instead of the end—this shimmering thing arcing away from him. It had steps cut in it—usefully—rainbow-colored steps all the way up. He goes up over the rainbow and has fairy-tale adventures. He meets a talking Pianola at one point. The story has not survived. Probably just as well.

INTERVIEWER

I thought your father had it.

RUSHDIE

He said he had it, but when we looked through his papers after he died, we never found it. So either he was bullshitting or he lost it. He died in '87, so it was a long time ago, and certainly nothing's going to come to light now. There are no trunks in the attic. I think it's gone, along with a much later thing, the first full-length piece of writing that I did. When I was eighteen, and I'd just left school—Rugby, in England—I had a gap of about five months before I was due to go to Cambridge. In that period I wrote a typescript called "Terminal Report" about my last term or two at school, thinly fictionalized. I went to Cambridge and forgot about it, and then about twenty years later my mother said that they'd found this manuscript. It was like a message from my eighteen-year-old self. But I didn't much like that self, who was very politically conservative, and in other ways a fairly standard product of an English boarding-school education. The exception was the material about racism, which was incredibly sophisticated. That eighteen-year-old boy knew everything I know now, except he knew it more sharply because it had just happened to him. Still, I had such a negative reaction to that text that when my mother asked if I wanted it, I told her to keep it. And then she lost it. When she died, we didn't find it.

INTERVIEWER

An act of kindness?

RUSHDIE

Maybe. It was absolutely terrible. But I regret its loss because it was like a diary. If I ever wanted to write about that period it would have given me raw material I couldn't otherwise get. Now I feel really stupid to have left it at home.

INTERVIEWER

You had a bad time at Rugby?

RUSHDIE

I wasn't beaten up, but I was very lonely and there were few people that I thought of as friends. A lot of that had to do with prejudice. Not from the staff—I was extremely well taught. I remember two or three teachers who were inspirational teachers of the kind that you see in Robin Williams movies. There was a sweet, elderly gentleman called Mr. J. B. Hope-Simpson, who apart from being a good history teacher was also the person who introduced me to *The Lord of the Rings* when I was fifteen. I completely fell in love with it, somewhat to the harm of my studies. I still remember it in uncanny detail. I really responded to the language project, all the imaginary languages. I got quite good at Elvish at one point.

INTERVIEWER

Did you have anyone to speak Elvish with?

RUSHDIE

There were one or two other *Lord of the Rings* nerds.

INTERVIEWER

What else were you reading?

RUSHDIE

Before I came to England, my favorite authors were P. G. Wodehouse and Agatha Christie. I used to devour both. My grandparents lived in Aligarh, not far from New Delhi, where my grandfather was involved with the Tibbiya College at Aligarh Muslim University. He was a Western-trained doctor, trained in Europe, but he became very interested in Indian traditional medicine. He would take me on the back of his bike to the university library and turn me loose. I remember it as a place with giant stacks disappearing into the dark, with those rolling ladders that you could climb, and I would come down out of the gloom with these big heaps of P. G. Wodehouse and Agatha Christie, which my grandfather would solemnly check out for me. I'd take them back and read them in a week and come back for more. Wodehouse was very popular in India, and I think still is.

INTERVIEWER

Why is that?

RUSHDIE

Funny is funny. Wodehouse has something in common with the Indian sense of humor. It may just be the silliness.

INTERVIEWER

So between the age of ten and the time you left for Rugby, when you were thirteen and a half, were you writing stories?

RUSHDIE

I don't have any memory of much besides that "Over the Rainbow" thing, but I was good at English. I remember a particular class in which we were asked to write a limerick about anything. If we managed one, we should write two. And during the course of this class, when everyone else had been fighting to get down one or two that didn't even scan properly, I wrote maybe thirty-seven. The teacher accused me of having cheated. The sense of injustice still lingers. How could I cheat? I didn't just happen to have a copy of Edward Lear with me, nor had I spent the last five years memorizing limericks in anticipation of this possible task. I felt I should be praised, and instead I was accused.

INTERVIEWER

Bombay has many languages. What is your mother tongue?

RUSHDIE

Urdu. Urdu is literally my mother's tongue. It's my father's tongue, too. But in northern India one also spoke Hindi. Actually, what we spoke was neither of them, or rather more like both. I mean, what people in northern India actually speak is not a real language. It's a colloquial mixture of Hindi and Urdu called Hindustani. It isn't written. It's the language of Bollywood movies. And some mixture of Hindustani and English is what we spoke at home. When I went to England for school, when I was thirteen and a half, I would have been more or less exactly bilingual—equally good in both languages. And I'm still very colloquially comfortable in Hindi and Urdu, but I wouldn't consider writing in them.

INTERVIEWER

Were you a good student?

RUSHDIE

I wasn't as smart as I thought I was. In general that was a good school, Cathedral School in Bombay. When I came to England I didn't feel behind, but if you look at the school reports, I'm not doing that well. Before Rugby my father, like many Indian fathers, would assign me extra work. I remember having to do essays and things at home and resenting them colossally. He'd make me do précis of Shakespeare. It is not unusual in an Indian household that children, especially eldest and only sons, should be driven that way. At Rugby, partly because of the social unhappiness, I plunged into work. It wasn't so much creative writing, though; I was more attracted in those days to history. I won prizes for long theses and essays. I don't know why it was, given my love of reading, that it never occurred to me, either at school or at university, to study literature. It didn't really seem like work to read novels. Actually, my father didn't think history was work, either. He wanted me to do something sensible at Cambridge—economics.

INTERVIEWER

You resisted him?

RUSHDIE

My life was saved by the director of studies, Dr. John Broadbent. I went to see him and said, Look, my father says that history is not useful and that I should switch to economics, otherwise he won't pay the fees. Broadbent said, Leave it to me. And he wrote my father a ferocious letter: Dear Mr. Rushdie, your son has told us this. Unfortunately we do not believe that he has the qualifications to study economics at Cambridge, therefore, if you insist on making him give up the study of history, I will have to ask you to remove him from the university to make room for somebody who is properly qualified. That was a very strange moment, because I'd left the subcontinent for Cambridge in the middle of a war—India and Pakistan, September '65. I couldn't get through on the phone because all of the lines had been taken over by the military. Letters were all being censored and took weeks to arrive, and I was hearing about bombings and air raids. But after Broadbent's letter my father never said a word about economics again. When I graduated and told him I wanted to write novels he was shocked. A cry burst out of him: What will I tell my friends? What he really meant was that all his friends' less intelligent sons were pulling down big bucks in serious jobs and what—I was going to be a penniless novelist? It would be a loss of face for him because he thought of writing as, at best, a hobby. Fortunately, he lived long enough to see that it might not have been such a dumb choice.

INTERVIEWER

Did he say so?

RUSHDIE

He somehow couldn't praise the books; he was curiously strangled emotionally. I was the only son, and as a result we had a difficult relationship. He died in '87, so *Midnight's Children* and *Shame* had come out, but *The Satanic Verses* had not, and he never said a kind word to me about my writing until a week or two before he died. But he'd read my books a hundred times. He probably knew them better than I did. Actually, he was annoyed about *Midnight's Children* because he felt that the father character was a satire of him. In my young, pissed-off way I responded that I'd left all the nasty stuff out. My father had studied literature at Cambridge so I expected him to have a sophisticated response to the book, but the person who did was my mother. I'd thought that if anybody was going to be worried that the family in the book is an echo of my family, it would be her. But she understood it at once as fiction. My father took a while to, as he put it, forgive me. Of course, I got more annoyed about being forgiven than I had about him being pissed off.

INTERVIEWER

But, as you say, he didn't live to read *The Satanic Verses*.

RUSHDIE

I'm absolutely certain that my father would have been five hundred percent on my side. He was a scholar of Islam, very knowledgeable about the life of the Prophet and the origins of early Islam, and indeed the way in which the Koran was revealed, and so on, but completely lacking in religious belief. We would go to the mosque once a year. Even when he was dying there was not a single moment when he took refuge in religion or called out to God, nothing. He never was under any illusion that death was anything other than an ending. It was very impressive. So the fact that I decided to study the origins of Islam at university is not an accident. It's partly to do with having that kind of example at home. And he'd have seen that what I was doing in that book was a nonreligious person's investigation into the nature of revelation, using Islam's example because it's what I knew most about.

INTERVIEWER

Where did you go after Cambridge?

RUSHDIE

First, I tried to be an actor. I had done all this undergraduate acting and I thought I might like to go on doing it, especially while I was trying to be a writer. I didn't find it at all easy to begin. I was living in an attic room in a house I was sharing with four friends in London, just futzing around. I didn't know what I was doing. I was pretending to write. There was a kind of panic inside me, which made me quite a nervous person at that time. I had some college friends who were in London, involved in fringe theater groups. There were a lot of interesting writers working there—David Hare, Howard Brenton, Trevor Griffiths—and some very good actors, too. I learned from working with good actors that I wasn't as good as they were. A good actor will make you look better on stage, but you know that they're doing it, not you.

Partly because of that, and partly because I just had no money at all, I decided after a while that I needed to do something else. One of my theatrical friends with whom I'd been at Cambridge, a writer called Dusty Hughes, got a job at the J. Walter Thompson advertising agency in London. Suddenly he had this office overlooking Berkeley Square and he was doing photo shoots for shampoo with supermodels. And he had money. He had a car. And he said, You should do this, Salman, it's really easy. He arranged for me to have a copy test in the J. Walter Thompson agency, which I failed.

The question I remember is: Imagine that you meet a Martian who speaks English but doesn't know what bread is—you have a hundred words to explain to him how to make a piece of toast. In Satyajit Ray's film *Company Limited*, one million people apply for the same job. The protagonist is one of the million, and the interviewers, not knowing how to choose between a million people, start asking increasingly lunatic questions. The question that finally destroys his chances of getting the job is: What is the weight of the moon? The Martian question was a question like that.

Eventually I got a position at a much smaller agency called Sharp McManus, on Albemarle Street. That was my first job, and I really had no idea how to approach it. I was given a project for a cheap cigar made by Player's. It was a Christmas offer; they were going to have a little box of Christmas crackers—you know, those classic British party favors—and inside each cracker there'd be a little tube with a cigar in it. I was told to write something for this, and I blanked. Eventually I went to see the creative director, Oliver Knox—who later in his life wrote three or four novels himself—and said, I don't know what to do. And he immediately said, Oh—six cracking ideas from Player's to help Christmas go off with a bang. That was my education in advertising.

INTERVIEWER

Were you writing fiction at the same time?

RUSHDIE

I was beginning. I was very unsuccessful. I hadn't really found a direction as a writer. I was writing stuff that I didn't show anyone, bits that eventually came together into a first novel-length thing that everybody hated. This was before *Grimus*, my first published novel. I tried to write the book in a Joycean stream of consciousness when really it needed to be written in straight, thrillerish language. It was called *The Book of the Peer*. A peer in Urdu is a saint or holy man. It was a story about an unnamed Eastern country in which a popular holy man is backed by a rich man and a general who decide that they're going to put him in power in order to pull his strings; and when they do, they discover that he's actually much more powerful than they are. It was, in a way, prescient about what happened afterwards with Khomeini, about the ways in which Islamic radicalism rose as a result of people thinking they could use it as a facade. Unfortunately, the book is almost unbearable to read because of the way it's written. Really, nobody—even people who were well disposed towards me—wanted anything to do with it. I put it away and went on working in advertising.

INTERVIEWER

All novelists seem to have at least one in the drawer that's just garbage.

RUSHDIE

I have three. Until I started writing *Midnight's Children*, which would probably have been about late '75, early '76, there was this period of flailing about. It was more than a technical problem. Until you know who you are you can't write. Because my life had been jumbled up between India and England and Pakistan, I really didn't have a good handle on myself. As a result the writing *was* garbage—sometimes clever garbage, but garbage nonetheless. I think that also goes for *Grimus*. To me, it doesn't feel like my writing. Or only fitfully. It makes me want to hide behind the furniture. But there we are. It's in print, I've never withdrawn it. If you make the mistake of publishing something you have to leave it out there. It's steadily found a readership, and there are even people who've said good things about it, much to my mystification.

But one of the novels that I abandoned—"The Antagonist," a dreadful sub-Pynchon piece set in London—contained the germ of what became *Midnight's Children*, a marginal character called Saleem Sinai who was born at the moment of Indian independence. That's the only thing that survived. I threw away a year's work and kept that germ.

After the critical beating *Grimus* took, I completely rethought everything. I thought, OK, I have to write about something that I care about much more. I was very scared all the time. See, I thought my career as a writer had gone nowhere at all. Meanwhile, many people in that very gifted generation I was a part of had found their ways as writers at a much younger age. It was as if they were zooming past me.

Martin Amis, Ian McEwan, Julian Barnes, William Boyd, Kazuo Ishig-
uro, Timothy Mo, Angela Carter, Bruce Chatwin—to name only a few.
It was an extraordinary moment in English literature, and I was the
one left in the starting gate, not knowing which way to run. That didn't
make it any easier.

INTERVIEWER

What was it about Saleem Sinai that released you?

RUSHDIE

I'd always wanted to write something that would come out of my
experience as a child in Bombay. I'd been away from India for a while
and began to fear that the connection was eroding. Childhood—that
was the impetus long before I knew what the story was and how big
it would become. But if you're going to have the child born at the
same time as the country, so that they're twins in a way, you have to
tell the story of both twins. So it forced me to take on history. One of
the reasons it took five years to write is that I didn't know how to
write it. One early version opened with the line, "Most of what matters in our lives takes place in our absence." I meant that children
don't come naked into the world, they come burdened with the accumulated history of their family and their world. But it was too Tol-
stoyan. I thought, If there's one thing this book is not, it's *Anna
Karenina*. The sentence is still there in the book somewhere, but I
buried it.

The third-person narration wasn't working, so I decided to try a
first-person narrative, and there was a day when I sat down and I
wrote more or less exactly what is now the first page of *Midnight's
Children*. It just arrived, this voice of Saleem's: quite savvy, full of all
kinds of arcana, funny but sort of ridiculous. I was electrified by what
was coming out of my typewriter. It was one of those moments when
you believe that the writing comes through you rather than from you.
I saw how to drag in everything from the ancient traditions of India to
the oral narrative form to, above all, the noise and the music of the Indian city. That first paragraph showed me the book. I held onto
Saleem's coattails and let him run. As the book developed, as Saleem

grew up, there were moments where I felt frustrated by him. As he got older, he became more and more passive. I kept trying to force him to be more active, to take charge of events—and it just didn't work. Afterwards, people assumed the book was autobiographical, but to me Saleem always felt very unlike me, because I had a kind of wrestling match with him, which I lost.

INTERVIEWER

Have you written another book where the voice just arrives like that?

RUSHDIE

Each book has to teach you how to write it, but there's often an important moment of discovery. The only thing that's comparable was when I was writing *Haroun and the Sea of Stories*, in which the big problem was tone of voice, how to walk the line that would allow both children and grown-ups to get pleasure out of it. There was a particular day when, after some false starts, I wrote what is now the beginning of the book. And again I thought, Oh, I see, you do it like this: "There was once, in the country of Alifbay . . ." I had to find that once-upon-a-time formula. Because the thing about the fable is that the words used are very simple but the story is not. You see this in Indian fables like the Panchatantra stories, in Aesop, and even in modern fables, like Calvino's books. You say something like, Once upon a time there was a cat who wore boots as high as his knees and used a sword. Words of one syllable, but the thing created is very strange.

Joseph Heller said that once in a while he would find a sentence that contained a hundred more sentences. That happened to him when he started *Catch-22*, the moment he wrote the sentence about Yossarian falling in love with the chaplain. That sentence told him where the rest of the novel was going. That happened to me when I wrote the beginning of *Midnight's Children* and *Haroun*. I had that lightbulb moment. But when I wrote *The Satanic Verses* I had hundreds of pages before I wrote the scene that is now the beginning of the novel, these people falling out of the sky. When I wrote that scene I thought, What's this doing here? This doesn't belong here.

INTERVIEWER

And there was your beginning.

RUSHDIE

It's a funny thing, that scene. When the book came out, a lot of people really hated it. That's when the joke started about there being a page fifteen club of Rushdie readers—you know, people who couldn't get beyond page fifteen. I myself thought it a good opening and I still do. You almost always discover that the book you're writing is not quite the book you set out to write. When you discover that, you solve the problem of the book. When I was writing *Fury* the title changed every day, and I was uncertain for a long time what the book was about. Was it about dolls, or New York, or violence, or divorce? Every day I'd wake up and I'd see it a slightly different way. Not until I figured out the title did I understand the central idea behind the book. Same thing happened with *Midnight's Children*. I didn't know what it was called at first. When I started writing it, I just put "Sinai" on the cover. Then there was a moment when I thought, If I don't know what the title is, I don't know what the book's about. I stopped writing prose and started writing titles. After several days of fooling around I ended up with two: "Children of Midnight" and "Midnight's Children." I typed them out manically, one after the other, over and over again. And then, after about a day of typing, I suddenly thought, "Children of Midnight," that's a really boring title, and "Midnight's Children," that's a really good title. And it showed me the center of the novel. It's about those children. With *The Satanic Verses* I didn't know if it was one book or three. It took me quite a while to be brave enough to decide it was a single work. Even though it would have to be a novel of discontinuities, I decided that was the book I wanted to write. I must have been feeling very confident. I'd had these two very successful books, and that put a lot of fuel in my tank, and I thought I could do anything.

INTERVIEWER

With fame, and with the fatwa, there has come to be almost a cult of Rushdie. Does that ever follow you back to the desk?

RUSHDIE

No. Writers are really good at creating that quiet space. When I'm in my room with the door shut, nothing signifies except what I'm trying to wrestle with. Writing's too hard, it just requires so much of you, and most of the time you feel dumb. I always think you start at the stupid end of the book, and if you're lucky you finish at the smart end. When you start out, you feel inadequate to the task. You don't even understand the task. It's so difficult, you don't have time to worry about being famous. That just seems like shit that happens outside.

What's harder to deal with is hostility from the press. It was a strange feeling to be characterized by some in the British press as an unlikable person. I'm not quite sure what I did to deserve it. I understand that in a literary life there are cycles when it's your turn to be praised and your turn to be hammered. It was clear that when *Fury* came out it was my turn to be hammered. I felt that a lot of the critical response was not about the book at all—it was about me. It was bizarre that so many of the reviews of *Fury* were headed with a picture of me with my then-girlfriend, now my wife. I thought, What's that got to do with it? Do you put John Updike's wife next to him at the top of a review? Or Saul Bellow's wife?

INTERVIEWER

In *Fury*, Solanka is born in Bombay, educated at Cambridge, and lives in Manhattan. Maybe that's why reviewers assumed it was about your own life in New York.

RUSHDIE

Yes, I was saying I'm over here now. It felt scary to write so close to the present in time, and to my own experience, but both were deliberate choices. I wanted to write about arrival. I didn't want to pretend that I was Don DeLillo or Philip Roth or anyone who'd grown up in these streets. I wanted to write about the New York of people who come here and make new lives, about the ease with which stories from all over the world can become New York stories. Just by virtue of showing up, your story becomes one of the many stories of the city. London's not like that. Yes, there's an immigrant culture in London that enriches it and adds to it, but London has a dominant narrative. There is no comparable dominant narrative in New York; just the collected narratives of everyone who shows up. That's one of the reasons why I am attracted to it.

As for Solanka, he's a grumpy bastard. I put the world's grumpiness about America into Solanka, and then surrounded him with a kind of carnival. Whereas I love being in New York, I'm as interested in the carnival as in the grumpiness. And even Solanka—you know he may be someone who bitches a lot about America, but it's to America that he's come to save himself. I thought it was silly the way the book was read as being about me. It's not my diary. You can start close to your life, but that's a starting place. The question is, what's the journey? The journey is the work of art. Where do you finish up?

INTERVIEWER

You've lived in—and between—very different parts of the world. Where would you say you're from?

RUSHDIE

I've always had more affinity to places than nations. I suppose if you were asking me formally, I would still think of myself as a British citizen of Indian origin. But I think of myself as a New Yorker and as a Londoner. I probably think of those as being more exact definitions than the passport or the place of birth.

INTERVIEWER

Will you ever write a memoir?

RUSHDIE

Until the whole fatwa thing happened it never occurred to me that my life was interesting enough. I'd just write my novels and hopefully those would be interesting, but who cares about the writer's life? Then this very unusual thing happened to me, and I found myself keeping an occasional journal just to remind myself what was happening. When things went back to normal, it occurred to me that a memoir would be a way of being done with it. Nobody would ever ask me about it again. But then I realized I'd have to spend a year researching it, at least a year writing it, and at least a year talking about it. So I'd be sentencing myself to three or four more years of the thing I'd just got out of. I didn't think I could bear that.

INTERVIEWER

Did the fatwa shake your confidence as a writer?

RUSHDIE

It made me wobble a lot. Then, it made me take a very deep breath, and in a way rededicate myself to the art, to think, Well, to hell with that. But at first what I felt was: That book took me more than five years to write. That's five years of my life giving my absolute best effort to make a thing as good as I can possibly make it. I do believe that writers, in the act of writing, are altruistic. They're not thinking about money and fame. They're just thinking about being the best writer they can be, making the page as good as it can be, making a sentence the best sentence you can write, the person interesting, and the theme developed. Getting it right is what you're thinking about. The writing is so difficult and makes such demands of you that the response—sales and so on— doesn't signify. So I spent five years like this, and what I got for it was worldwide vilification and my life being threatened. It wasn't even so much to do with the physical danger as with the intellectual contempt, the denigration of the seriousness of the work, the idea that I was a worthless individual who had done a worthless thing, and that, unfortunately, there were a certain number of Western fellow travelers who agreed. Then you think, What the fuck am I doing it for? It's not worth it. Just to spend five years of your life being as serious as you can be, and then to be accused of being frivolous and self-seeking, opportunistic: He did it on purpose. Of course I did it on purpose! How do you spend five years of your life doing something accidentally?

INTERVIEWER

When people said you did it on purpose they meant you set out to provoke, that you asked for it. Were you conscious, while writing the book, that your secular take on Islam might be provocative?

RUSHDIE

I knew my work did not appeal to the likes of radical mullahs.

INTERVIEWER

Still, it's a big leap from that to a fatwa.

RUSHDIE

Well, that was, of course, something that nobody could have fore-seen. Nobody. It had never happened before. It never occurred to me. And you know, I found out some time afterwards that there had been an unauthorized translation into Farsi of my previous novel, *Shame*, done by the Iranians, who had then given it a major prize as the best translated novel that year. This meant that when *The Satanic Verses* was published, even Iranian booksellers thought that I was probably cool, because the mullahs had given my previous book a stamp of approval. So it surprised people in Iran as much as else-where.

INTERVIEWER

But this idea that you should have seen it coming was heavily sub-scribed to at the time.

RUSHDIE

After the book was finished there were one or two early readers, in-cluding Edward Said, who noticed that I'd taken these guys on and asked whether I was concerned about it. And in those innocent days, I said no. I mean, why would they bother? It's a five hundred and fifty page literary novel in English. The idea that it would even float across their field of vision seemed improbable, and I truthfully didn't care.

Why shouldn't literature provoke? It always has. And this idea that somehow the person under attack is responsible for the attack is a shifting of the blame—which seemed easy to do in 1989. Recently, in England, in the aftermath of the Al Qaeda bombings, there's been a lot of journalistic comment saying it all began with *The Satanic Verses*, and there's total sympathy now for what was happening to me

then. Nobody these days is saying it was my fault and I did it on purpose, because people understand the nature of radical Islam better.

INTERVIEWER

So, what—we're all Salman Rushdie now?

RUSHDIE

Yeah. Phrases like that are used all the time now in the English
press, whereas in 1989 there was a widespread tabloid belief that I
was this troublemaker who had to be saved from his own kind by a
government he'd opposed—the Thatcher government. And then
when I decided to make a life for myself in New York, that proved my
ingratitude. As if, in order to be grateful, I had to live in London for
the rest of my life.

INTERVIEWER

But you were saying that in 1989, at the outset, the fatwa made you
question whether literature was actually worth the effort.

RUSHDIE

It made me think, for a period of many months, that maybe I
didn't want to be a writer anymore. It wasn't to do with the fact that
it's dangerous. It was that I felt disgusted with what had happened to
me, and at a loss to know how to continue if that was how my work
was going to be treated. I thought, you know, I could be a bus conductor. Anything is better than this. I've often said—and it's true—
that I think the thing that saved me as a writer was having promised
my son a book. His life was substantially derailed, too. Not just mine.
There are all kinds of things I couldn't do with him, and things that
were very difficult to do, so this was a promise I knew I had to keep. It
made me go back to being a writer. When I discovered the voice for
Haroun and the Sea of Stories, I felt happy again. It was the first time
I'd felt happy since February of 1989. It gave me back my sense of
why I liked to do my job. Then I thought, I can't go on, I'll go on.

I actually remember reading the Beckett trilogy at that time. *The
Unnamable* is almost as difficult as *Finnegans Wake*, but that stoicism,

that great last line, is valuable. I found myself reading Enlightenment writers—Voltaire—and realizing that I was not the only writer who'd had a hard time. It may seem ridiculously romantic, but I was actually strengthened by the history of literature. Ovid in exile, Dostoyevsky in front of the firing squad, Genet in jail—and look what they did: the *Metamorphoses*, *Crime and Punishment*, everything that Genet wrote is prison literature. I thought, Well, if they can do it, I can have a go at doing it. It became easier for me to know where I stood in the world, and that was good. It just got rid of some confusions.

But I still never know how people are going to respond to a book. I just have no idea. I thought *The Satanic Verses* was my least political novel. Maybe that's beginning to be true now. After all this fuss, at last that book is beginning to have a literary life—particularly in the academy. It's being read not just in comparative religion courses or in Middle Eastern politics courses. I get letters that don't even mention the Islamic stuff. I get letters from people responding to the comedy in the novel, which is one of the things nobody ever talked about— how could it be funny when the thing that happened to it was so unfunny?—and I think: Finally! In a way, it makes it worth having fought the battle, that this book has managed somehow to survive, and can now finally be a book instead of being a hot potato, a sloganized scandal. It is, at last, a novel.

INTERVIEWER

In both *The Satanic Verses* and *Midnight's Children*, as well as some essays, there's a notion that you've ascribed to yourself and your characters alike: the god-shaped hole. Does that phrase still speak to you?

RUSHDIE

There is in human beings a need for something that is not material, a thing that gets called spiritual. We all have a need for the idea that there is something beyond our physical being in the world. We need exaltation. If you don't believe in God you still have the need to feel exalted from time to time and consoled, and you still need an explanation. And you need the other thing that religion gives you, which is community, the sense of something shared, a common language, a common metaphor structure, a way of explaining yourself to people. A shorthand. Religion provides all of that to people who can have it. Now, if you can't have religion, then those are big absences that you have to find somewhere else. That's the hole. The two big questions of religion are where do we come from and how shall we live. I'm interested as a fiction writer in the fictions we have made up as a race to explain our origins, but I'm not interested in them as explanations. I don't go to priests for the answers to these questions. When we do, look what happens. Khomeini happens. The Taliban happens. The Inquisition happens.

INTERVIEWER

So where do you go?

RUSHDIE

Almost anywhere else. The question of how shall we live is a never-answered question. It's a constant argument. In a free society we argue about how we shall live, and that's how we live. The argument is the answer, and I want to be in that argument. It's democracy: the least bad system available. The explanatory power of religion is the easiest thing to do without. The rest of it—the consolation, the exaltation, the community—that's harder. The place I've gone in my life to fulfill that is literature, and not just literature, but movies, music, painting, the arts in general. And then there is love. The love of your wife, the love of your children, the love of your parents, the love of your friends. I invest a lot in the idea of friendship. Always have. Particularly because my life has been torn away from its place of origin and flung around the world. My family relationships were not broken, but they were strained in many ways. Friends are the family you build. I live very passionately among the people I choose to live with. It gives me my sense of community and of being more than just a machine.

I grew up in a country where almost everybody has deep religious beliefs—including the urban intelligentsia—and where people don't just think of religion as something abstract, but believe that making offerings to the gods has a direct impact on their happiness and their progress in the world. It's a country where hundreds of millions of people believe that the gods are directly intervening in their daily lives, so their relationship with the gods is a daily matter, pragmatic. That's my world; I have to take it seriously. Also, it's important to enter the heads of people who think in ways that are not your own, and to let that way of thinking determine the outcome of their stories.

INTERVIEWER

Can you talk about your procedure when you sit down at the desk?

RUSHDIE

If you read the press you might get the impression that all I ever do is go to parties. Actually, what I do for hours, every day of my life, is sit in a room by myself. When I stop for the day I always try to have some notion of where I want to pick up. If I've done that, then it's a little easier to start because I know the first sentence or phrase. At least I know where in my head to go and look for it. Early on, it's very slow and there are a lot of false starts. I'll write a paragraph, and then the next day I'll think, Nah, I don't like that at all, or, I don't know where it belongs, but it doesn't belong here. Quite often it will take me months to get underway. When I was younger, I would write with a lot more ease than I do now, but what I wrote would require a great deal more rewriting. Now I write much more slowly and I revise a lot as I go. I find that when I've got a bit done, it seems to require less revision than it used to. So it's changed. I'm just looking for something that gives me a little rush, and if I can get that, get a few hundred words down, then that's got me through the day.

INTERVIEWER

Do you get up in the morning and start writing first thing?

RUSHDIE

Yes, absolutely. I don't have any strange, occult practices. I just get up, go downstairs, and write. I've learned that I need to give it the first energy of the day, so before I read the newspaper, before I open the mail, before I phone anyone, often before I have a shower, I sit in my pajamas at the desk. I do not let myself get up until I've done something that I think qualifies as working. If I go out to dinner with friends, when I come home I go back to the desk before going to bed and read through what I did that day. When I wake up in the morning, the first thing I do is to read through what I did the day before. No matter how well you think you've done on a given day, there will always be something that is underimagined, some little thing that you need to add or subtract—and I must say, thank God for laptops, because it makes it a lot easier. This process of critically rereading what I did the day before is a way of getting back inside the skin of the book. But sometimes I know exactly what I want to do and I sit down and start on it. So there's no rule.

INTERVIEWER

Is there anything in particular that you read to help you along when you're working?

RUSHDIE

I read poetry. When you're writing a novel, it's so easy to have odd bits of laziness slip in. Poetry is a way of reminding myself to pay attention to language. I've been reading a lot of Czeslaw Milosz recently. And then, from over the other side of the fence, I've been reading Bob Dylan's *Chronicles*, which is wonderful. It's so well written, with moments of really sloppy writing mixed in, misused words—you know, *evidentially* instead of *evidently*. *Incredulously* instead of *incredibly*. Clearly the publisher—somebody—thought it's all part of his Bobness.

INTERVIEWER

Evidentially.

RUSHDIE

I like the Randall Jarrell line: "A novel is a prose narrative of some length that has something wrong with it." I think that's true. If you're going to write a hundred, a hundred and fifty thousand, two hundred thousand words, perfection is a fantasy. If you're Shakespeare and you're writing sixteen lines, you can create a perfect thing. I suspect though that if Shakespeare had written a novel, there would be imperfections. There are imperfections in his plays—there are boring bits, if one's allowed to say this. If you're reading for the love of reading, you look for what it gives you, not for what it doesn't give you. If there's enough there, a misstep is easy to forgive. That also happens in literary criticism. There are critics who approach work on the basis of what they can get from it, and others who approach in terms of what they can find wrong with it. Frankly, you can find something wrong with any book you pick up, I don't care how great it is is. There's a wonderful riff in Julian Barnes's *Flaubert's Parrot*, in the chapter called "Emma Bovary's Eyes," when he points out that her eyes change color four or five times in the book.

INTERVIEWER

In *Shalimar the Clown*, why did you name your main character Max Ophuls? After the film director?

RUSHDIE

I just liked the name. The interesting thing about the Franco-German border near Strasbourg is the way in which history has continually moved it, so that the city has been German sometimes, and French sometimes, and I wanted Max to have a name that is both French and German, because I wanted the history of Strasbourg to be in the name.

INTERVIEWER

But why not make up a name?

RUSHDIE

I don't know. Names stick. I just kept thinking of him like that, and in the end I forgot about the film director.

INTERVIEWER

Can you read fiction while you're working on a novel?

RUSHDIE

Not much. At least, not much contemporary fiction. I read less contemporary fiction than I used to and more of the classics. It seems they've hung around for a reason. When I wrote *Fury*, for instance, I read Balzac, in particular *Eugénie Grandet*. If you look at the opening of *Eugénie Grandet*, it uses a technique like a slow cinematic zoom. It starts with a very wide focus—here is this town, these are its buildings, this is its economic situation—and gradually it focuses in on this neighborhood, and inside the neighborhood on this rather grand house, and inside this house a room, and inside this room, a woman sitting on a chair. By the time you find out her name, she's already imprisoned in her class and her social situation and her community and her city. By the time her own story begins to unfold, you realize it's going to smash into all these things. She is like a bird in this cage. I thought, That's good. That's such a clear way of doing it.

INTERVIEWER

Do you go to the movies a lot?

RUSHDIE

A lot, yes. Much of my thinking about writing was shaped by a youth spent watching the extraordinary outburst of world cinema in the sixties and seventies. I think I learned as much from Buñuel and Bergman and Godard and Fellini as I learned from books. It's hard now to explain what it feels like when the week's new movie is Fellini's *8½*, when the week after that it's the new Godard movie, and the week after that it's the new Bergman, then it's the new Satyajit Ray movie, then Kurosawa. Those filmmakers were consciously building oeuvres that had a coherence, and in which themes were explored until they were exhausted. There was a serious artistic project going on. Now, whether it's films or books, we've become a much lazier culture. Filmmakers get bought out just like that. You make one interesting film and off you go into moneyland. The idea of building a body of work that has intellectual and artistic coherence is gone. Nobody's interested.

INTERVIEWER

What did you learn from watching these movies?

RUSHDIE

Some technical things—for instance, from the New Wave's freedom of technique, a freeing up the language. The classic form of film montage is long shot, medium shot, close-up, medium shot, long shot, medium shot, close-up, medium shot, long shot—like a kind of dance. In two steps, out two steps, in two steps, out two steps. It can be unbelievably tedious. If you look at the films of the fifties being cut like that, it's sort of like editing by numbers. So Godard's heavy use of the jump cut made you jump. To go from the wide scene—bang—into the face of Belmondo or Anna Karina. One of the reasons why, in the films of Godard, a character will sometimes address the camera directly—

INTERVIEWER

—is because they didn't have the money to film the full scene.

RUSHDIE

That's right. But I liked that idea, the breaking of the frame, the fact that many of these films were funny and serious at the same time. In *Alphaville*, which is a very dark film, there's this wonderful scene where Lemmy Caution, the down-at-the-heels private eye, arrives at the flophouse where he discovers that all the superheroes are dead. "Et Batman?" "Il est mort." "Superman?" "Mort." "Flash Gordon?" "Mort." It's hilarious. And I love Buñuel's use of surrealism, which doesn't stop the films from feeling real. In *The Discreet Charm of the Bourgeoisie*, people sit around a table on toilet seats but go quietly to a little room in order to eat. And I like both Bergmans—the mystical Bergman of *The Seventh Seal* and the close-up, psychological Bergman. And Kurosawa taking us into a completely closed culture, the world of the samurai. I don't think like the samurai thought, yet you've gotta love Toshiro Mifune scratching himself—you're immediately on his side. It's one of the things you want a work of art to do, to take you into a world you haven't been in, and to make it part of your world. That great period of filmmaking has a lot to teach novelists. I always thought I got my education in the cinema.

INTERVIEWER

Were you consciously taking this in and applying it?

RUSHDIE

No, I just loved going to the movies. I was having a better time in the movies than in the library. Nowadays I find that people who like my books tend to say that they're very visual, while people who don't like my books tend to say that they're too visual. If you're a writer, people like you for exactly the things that other people dislike you for. Your strengths are your weaknesses. Sometimes the same sentences are held up as examples of how badly I write and how well I write. People who like my writing say they like the female characters. The people who don't like my books say, Well, of course, he can't write about women.

INTERVIEWER

You were talking about how your generation of British writers was loaded with talent. What is it like for you here in New York?

RUSHDIE

In America there is a younger generation with real ambition. But there was a moment when American literature got a little unadventurous. Raymond Carver was a very ambitious writer, and his books are incredibly original because they push the boundaries of how to say things, how to suggest things, but I think that a lot of the school of Carver became an excuse for saying banal things in banal ways. As if that was all you had to do—have two people sitting down across the table with a bottle of whiskey talking to each other in clichés. Now I think there are, once again, attempts to do startling things. Some of them work and some of them don't. But I like to see that spirit again. Oddly, in England in the seventies and eighties, we resisted being called a generation. Most of us didn't know each other. We didn't see that we had a project. It wasn't like the surrealists, who had a manifesto. We didn't discuss our writing with each other. I was having enough trouble finding my way; I didn't want ten other opinions. I thought I had to find my own way.

INTERVIEWER

Do you write letters?

RUSHDIE

I'm notorious for being a bad letter writer. It's my wife's biggest complaint about me. Would I please write her some letters. What's the point of being married to a writer if you don't have any love letters? So, I have to do it. But, no, I have no great literary correspondence. I have some things, though. In 1984, the first time I went to Australia, I began to read Patrick White. I traveled a little bit with Bruce Chatwin on some of the trips that led to *The Songlines*, and I was struck, moved, by the Australian desert. Then I read White's book, *Voss*, and was really taken with it. It was one of the few times in my life that I wrote a fan letter. White wrote back, saying, Dear Mr. Rushdie, *Voss* is a novel I have come to hate. He said, I could send you some of my books that I still have some feeling for, but one does not wish to burden people with books they do not wish to read. And I thought, Fuck you, too. You know, I've written this really warm letter and I get back this crabby old thing. When I went to Australia again, I never made any attempt to contact him. Then he died, and his biographer, David Marr, wrote to me. White threw everything away, but in the top drawer of his desk there was this very small bunch of letters, most of which were from his bank manager, and three or four non-business letters, of which mine was one. And I thought, How stupid can you be? I'd completely misunderstood his letter. I'd read his self-deprecation as grumpiness.

INTERVIEWER

How do you decide when to ship a novel off?

RUSHDIE

Embarrassment is a good test. When you feel you wouldn't be embarrassed by people reading what's on the page, then you can let people read it. But with *Shalimar* I did something I've never done before: I showed it to a few people—my agent, my wife, and my friend, the writer Pauline Melville. I also showed it to my editors, Dan Franklin at Cape and Dan Menaker here at Random House. I showed them the first hundred and fifty pages, then I showed it to them again at about three hundred and fifty, four hundred pages. I don't know why I did that. I just thought, I never do this, so I'm going to do it. I'm getting to the point where I think, I don't have to do things just because I've always done them. I liked that I was able to show people along the way and have their enthusiasm. Whether that means I needed more reassurance, or whether it means I was more confident, I really don't know. I think it's somehow both at once.

INTERVIEWER

What hand have editors had in your work?

RUSHDIE

What I remember best are two really valuable pieces of editing work that Liz Calder did with *Midnight's Children*. One was at the end of what is now Part Two and the beginning of Part Three when there's a time jump of about six years from the end of the Indo-Pakistan War of 1965 to the moment of the Bangladesh war in 1971. What I had originally done was jump further forward—to the end of the Bangladesh war—then jump back to the beginning, and then go forward again. So there'd been seven years forward, one year back, and then forward again, and that scrambling of the timeline was the one moment in the book where Liz said her attention was broken. That was very valuable. There's still the six-year jump, but I went back and restored chronological sequence, and it cleared up those forty or fifty pages enormously.

The other thing was that there used to be a second audience figure in the novel. In the book as you know it, Saleem tells his story to Padma, the pickle woman. In the earlier version he was also writing the story down and sending it to a woman journalist who remained offstage. So the oral narration was to the woman in the pickle factory, and then the written version was being sent to this other figure. Liz and one or two other early readers all agreed that this was the one completely redundant element of the book. They said, You've got a good character sitting in the room with him, with whom he actually has a relationship, and you don't need this abstract second figure of a journalist that he wants to send his writing to. I initially thought they were wrong, and then was persuaded to have a go at removing that character. The character fell out of the book so easily—I remember it took about two days—that it made me see very clearly that a character who could be removed so simply was not properly integrated into the story. They really saved me from a bad mistake. Now if I look at that removed material, it's kind of awful.

The one other book in which I think there was really constructive editing was my Nicaragua book, *The Jaguar Smile*. It was reportage. I came back from Nicaragua in 1986, and wrote it in a few months. It's still quite a short book, but the original version was a bit shorter. Because of the speed, Sonny Mehta—who was, at that time, the editor of Picador in England—said he had some concerns about the text, and he actually more or less line edited the book. In almost every case he asked for more information. It was never that he was taking things out, always that he wanted more. He said, You're assuming too much knowledge—I need to know who these people are, what this moment was, background, et cetera. He just made me flesh out the book much more, and that was valuable.

INTERVIEWER

Besides *The Jaguar Smile*, you've written *Imaginary Homelands*, *Step Across This Line*, and other nonfiction. Is there another nonfiction book in the works?

RUSHDIE

Not yet. At this moment I feel—how shall I put it?—I feel that my life has become rather dramatically nonfictional. In a way there's too much factual material surrounding me, and I feel the need to get out from underneath that rubble of fact and get back to the business of imaginative writing. I feel full of stories, and until I feel I've shaken off the dust and really restored—well, not restored, but explored—the stories I have to tell, which are invented stories, I don't really want to go back to fact. I want to do less and less of it.

One of the things that writing *Shalimar the Clown* taught me was that it doesn't matter how much research you do. I did a lot more research for that book than I've ever done for a novel, but I learned that research will only get you so far. In the end, to make the thing work, there has to be a serious imaginative leap. You have to be able to get inside the skin of people, and feel them and understand their thought processes and learn what they want to do with the story. So even writing this heavily researched book strengthened my belief that what I really am interested in is that imaginative leap. At the moment I've been doing this *New York Times* syndicated column once a month, and I have a contract for this year, but I have a strong feeling that I might leave it at that for a while—because I'd rather be writing short stories. So I'm having a very strong fiction impulse right now.

INTERVIEWER

Is that a fact?

RUSHDIE

Exactly—I could be lying. Never trust a writer when he talks about the future of his writing.

INTERVIEWER

OK, so what will your next book be?

RUSHDIE

The next book I think I'm going to write is a novel that imagines an early connection between Italy of the Renaissance and the early Moghul empire. Originally I had planned to call it "The Enchantress of Florence." Meanwhile, my little boy—my second son—is agitating for a children's book. He loves *Haroun and the Sea of Stories*, but he knows it was written for his brother. If I've got a really long period of serious research to do, it might be nice to write a children's book while I'm doing that. Maybe I can do a little reading and for a few hours a day write a fairy tale.

Then there's "Parallelville," a futuristic, science-fiction-slash-film-noir idea, sort of *Blade Runner* meets *Touch of Evil*. I'm also considering writing a book that I've tentatively titled "Careless Masters." I imagine it as a big, English novel that starts off as a story about boarding school and then takes those characters into adulthood, making it a state-of-England novel. The most extended thing I've ever written about England is *The Satanic Verses*, which no one thinks of as a novel about England, but is actually, in large part, a novel about London. It's about the life of immigrants in Thatcherite London.

INTERVIEWER

Do you get edgy if you don't write every day?

RUSHDIE

I feel much better when I know where I'm going. On the other hand, some of my most creative moments are the moments between books, when I don't know where I'm going, and my head freewheels. Things come to me unexpectedly, and can become a character or a paragraph or just a perception, all of which can turn into stories, or a novel. I work just as hard when I'm not writing a book as when I am. I sit there and let things happen, mostly I throw away the next day what I wrote the day before. But pure creativity is just seeing what shows up. Once something has shown up, then it's more focused, and it's more enjoyable. But this in-between time is when unexpected things happen. Things happen that I previously thought were outside my ability to imagine. They become imaginable. And they come inside. That's where I am right now.

Issue 174, 2005

Norman Mailer

The Art of Fiction

I saw Norman Mailer over the course of two days in April, at his home on Cape Cod. The sun was out long enough to let me see the Provincetown transvestites making their way down Commercial Street in a caravan of fake curls, but then a storm came and it was time to retire to the downstairs sitting room of Mailer's house by the ocean. We sat on two chairs by a large window, and as we spoke a strange northern light crept through the rain and through the glass to make a becoming halo around the eighty-four-year-old author's head. Mailer's wife of twenty-six years, Norris Church, was in New York for the weekend, but her presence could be felt in her paintings around us.

Mailer was last interviewed for this magazine in 1964, the year he published his seventh book. This year he published his forty-second, *The Castle in the Forest*, and dedicated it to his ten grandchildren, as well as various godchildren and a grandniece. Mailer is thinner than he used to be, and he walks with two canes. He is an old prince of duality, so it comes as no surprise to learn that he also has two hearing aids, which allowed him to get most of my questions the first time. We went for supper together the night before the interview began, to Michael Shay's, a nearby restaurant that specializes in oysters. Mailer knows the waiters by their first names and he knows the menu even better. He usually takes his oyster shells home because he likes cleaning them, looking at them, and sometimes drawing on them. "Look here," he said, lifting one. "An oyster shell quite often looks like the face of a Greek god."

Only a few went down at first but before

~~But that hardly mattered.~~ Before long the crowds pushing up from the far

was compressing

rear ~~were crowding~~ the hundred thousand in the middle and that hundred

was

thousand ~~were~~ jamming into ~~the~~ tens of thousands lined up before the *standing*

long in

booths. In every area, on every patch of ground ~~one~~ man *a* ~~crawling on hands~~ *OK*

over him

~~had~~ to do no more than ~~fall or~~ stumble and another would fall. A third would trip, a

Women would

fourth would be knocked over by ~~the~~ bodies pressing behind. ~~In five~~ *scream. Women and children were knocked down,*

down

~~In the next five~~ minutes there were five hundred people ~~on the ground or~~ driven into one of

even as

the sand pits or unable to hold back against ~~the~~ forces pushing behind ~~or~~

others were pushed

~~they were driven into a well.~~ *over the lip of a well, and out—* Bodies piled upon bodies. ~~Cries arose.~~ I had never

roaring

heard such a sound of woe before—it came out of thousands of throats *in*

in rage or screaming in terror at their own agony. The first

~~those ten or fifteen minutes. The mayhem became interchangeable with~~

sounds of physical agony commenced,

~~the carnage.~~ I had an experience I *had* never encountered before. It is an accolade

and

~~that~~ one can offer to ~~very~~ few events. Humans ~~were~~ transmogrified into a

were hurled

storm at sea. ~~They~~ moved forward in waves. Slighter people ~~thrust forward—~~

13

A manuscript page from The Castle in the Forest *by Norman Mailer.*

There was something Zeus-like about Mailer himself as he pondered my questions, yet at times he was as earthy as Studs Lonigan. His blue eyes shone when he told me how often a man needs to pee at his age. "At George Plimpton's memorial service," he said, "in Saint John the Divine, I suddenly had to go and I knew I wouldn't make it down the aisle. So I went into a corridor at the side and there I met Philip Roth. Sometimes I have to go into a telephone kiosk to pee, Phil, I said. You just can't wait at my age. I know, said Roth—it's the same with me. Well, I said, you always were precocious."

Now and then during our interview, Mailer would stop and have a drink. He's not much of a boozer these days, and when he does drink it tends to be in surprising combinations. At one point I made him a red wine and orange juice; at another point it was rum and grapefruit. His intelligence never flickers, and I soon felt that Mailer would be a good person to be stuck with in the army. He is loyal to the spirit of argument and attentive to his opponent's appetites. For instance, after several hours of us locking into one another like two convicts in a Russian novel, Mailer suggested we go lie down, and we were soon asleep on our respective beds with the wind howling outside from Melville's old shipping lanes.

At times, as the interview progressed, it felt as if the beams of the house were twisting in time to Mailer's thoughts. He uses his hands like a filmmaker or a boxing coach, forever framing the idea of movement. But with the storm coming down he was most like Captain Ahab, strung out on this spit of land that beckons to the North Atlantic, struggling still with the big fish. It was pleasant to watch him pitch and roll with the unknowable. After that first meal at Michael Shay's, I helped him into his car and told him I would walk into town. It was a New England evening, and the long straight road to the commercial district was dark and quiet. Mailer's house was very close, and I got there first and stopped across the road. He soon arrived in his car and got himself onto the sidewalk very gingerly, the sticks working hard. I stood watching him for a minute until he disappeared through the gate. As I walked away I noticed a plaque on a house further down stating that John Dos Passos lived there eighty years ago, just as Norman Kingsley Mailer was learning to read. I was happy to see these houses so close, the lights burning bright in the darkness.

—*Andrew O'Hagan, 2007*

INTERVIEWER

Dwight MacDonald once called Provincetown "Eighth Street by the Sea." How long have you been coming here?

NORMAN MAILER

I first came when I was about nineteen. I was having a romance with a girl whom I later married, Beatrice Silverman, my first wife. We decided we wanted to go somewhere for a weekend and she'd heard of this lovely town on the tip of Cape Cod. It must have been 1942 or '43 and I absolutely fell in love with the place. There was a great fear of the Nazis landing suddenly on the back shore—we have more than forty miles of open seacoast here. So there were no lights in the town. Walking on the streets at night it felt like one was back in the American colonial past. All through the war, I kept writing to my wife that the first thing we'd do when I got back—if and when—is we'd go to Provincetown.

INTERVIEWER

And you started to write *The Naked and the Dead* hereabouts?

MAILER

I got out of the army in May of '46 and we came up here in June. I started the book in June, maybe by the beginning of July. I began writing in a rented beach hut in Truro. I usually need a couple of weeks to warm up on a book.

INTERVIEWER

You had notes?

MAILER

I always make a huge number of notes before I start. I tend to read a lot on collateral matters and think about it and brood. Now it takes me a half year to get into a novel. I think it took me a few weeks with *The Naked and the Dead*, because I was young and so full of it and full of the war. I didn't really have to do any research—it was all in the brain. I wrote almost two hundred pages while I was here that summer.

INTERVIEWER

And you knew it was good?

MAILER

In one mood I thought it was terrific, and then in another I'd think, Oh, you don't know how to write. I wasn't a stylist in those days—I knew enough about good writing to know that. Last night at supper you and I spoke about Theodore Dreiser. We agreed more or less, didn't we, that style was not his forte and yet he had something better than style? Dreiser was one of the people I read at that time, and I would rally my literary troops whenever they were showing signs of bad morale by saying to myself, Well, Dreiser doesn't have much of a style.

There's such a thing as having too much style. I think the only one who ever got away with it is Proust. He really had a perfect mating of material and style. Usually if you have a great style your material will be more constrained. That applies to Henry James and it applies to Hemingway. The reverse of that tendency would be Zola, whose style is reasonably decent, nothing remarkable, but the material is terrific.

I think in my own work I've gone through the poles of style. It is at its best in *An American Dream* and virtually nonexistent in *The Executioner's Song*, because the material is prodigious. In *An American Dream* it was all my own imagining. I was cooking the dish.

INTERVIEWER

It may be argued, in your case, that a great subject has a tendency to unlock a secrecy in your style, something that was not obvious before.

MAILER

I'm smiling because you give it such a nice edge. My motives at the time of *The Executioner's Song* were not all that honorable. I'd been running into a lot of criticism of my baroque style, and it was getting to me. My whole thing became, you know—you asses out there, you think a baroque style is easy? It's not easy. It's something you really have to arrive at. It takes years of work. You guys keep talking about the virtues of simplicity—I'll show you. There's absolutely nothing to simplicity, and I'm going to prove it with this book, because I probably have the perfect material for showing that I can write a simple book. So I proceeded to do it. My pride in that book is that the best piece of writing is Gary Gilmore's letter about two-thirds in. I quoted it verbatim. No writing by me up to this point could be superior to that letter, because that letter makes him come to life, and suddenly you see this man was a man of substance, despite all. He might have been a punk, as he was called, he might have killed two people in hideous fashion, but by God, he had a mind and he had a sense of personal literary style, which was in that letter.

One of my basic notions for a long, long time is that there is this mysterious mountain out there called reality. We novelists are always trying to climb it. We are mountaineers, and the question is, Which face do you attack? Different faces call for different approaches, and some demand a knotty and convoluted interior style. Others demand great simplicity. The point is that style is an attack on the nature of reality.

So I wrote the Gilmore book simply. Maybe it led me to think I could take a crack at Hemingway, but the fact of the matter is, when it comes to writing simply, I am not Hemingway's equal. My great admiration for Hemingway is not necessarily for the man, the character. I think if we had met it could have been a small disaster for me. But he showed us, as no one else ever has, what the potential strength of the English sentence could be.

INTERVIEWER

Let's linger on Hemingway for a second. Is it possible he showed a generation how to get emotion into a sentence without mentioning emotion?

MAILER

Yes, and he did it more than anyone ever had before or after. But he's a trap. If you're not careful you end up writing like him. It's very dangerous to write like Hemingway, but on the other hand it's almost like a rite of passage. I almost wouldn't trust a young novelist—I won't speak for the women here, but for a male novelist—who doesn't imitate Hemingway in his youth.

INTERVIEWER

Do you remember where you were when you heard Hemingway had killed himself?

MAILER

I remember it very well. I was with Jeanne Campbell in Mexico and it was before we got married. I was truly aghast. A certain part of me has never really gotten over it. In a way, it was a huge warning. What he was saying is, Listen all you novelists out there. Get it straight: when you're a novelist you're entering on an extremely dangerous psychological journey, and it can blow up in your face.

INTERVIEWER

Did it compromise your sense of his courage?

MAILER

I hated to think that his death might do that. I came up with a thesis: Hemingway had learned early in life that the closer he came to daring death the healthier it was for him. He saw that as the great medicine, to dare to engage in a nearness to death. And so I had this notion that night after night when he was alone, after he said goodnight to Mary, Hemingway would go to his bedroom and he'd put his thumb on the shotgun trigger and put the barrel in his mouth and squeeze down on the trigger a little bit, and—trembling, shaking—he'd try to see how close he could come without having the thing go off. On the final night he went too far. That to me made more sense than him just deciding to blow it all to bits. However, it's nothing but a theory. The fact of the matter is that Hemingway committed suicide.

INTERVIEWER

Might it be said, in any event, that writing is a sort of self-annihilation?

MAILER

It uses you profoundly. There's simply less of you after you finish a book, which is why writers can be so absolutely enraged at cruel criticisms that they feel are unfair. We feel we have killed ourselves once writing the book, and now they are seeking to kill us again for too little. Gary Gilmore once remarked, "Padre, there's nothing fair." And I've used that over and over again. Yet if you're writing a good novel then you're being an explorer—you're getting into something where you don't know the end, where the end is not given. There's a mixture of dread and excitement that keeps you going. To my mind, it's not worth writing a novel unless you're tackling something where your chances of success are open. You can fail. You're gambling with your psychic reserves. It's as if you were the general of an army of one, and this general can really drive that army into a cul-de-sac.

INTERVIEWER

Let's talk about age, growing old, and let's be precise. How does the matter of growing old affect your vanity as a writer? There is perhaps nothing more damaging to one's vanity than the idea that the best years are behind one.

MAILER

Well, I think if you get old and you're not full of objectivity you're in trouble. The thing that makes old age powerful is objectivity. If you say to yourself, My karma is more balanced now that I have fewer things than I've ever had in my life, that can give you sustenance. You end up with a keen sense of what you still have as a writer, and also of what you don't have any longer. As you grow older, there's no reason why you can't be wiser as a novelist than you ever were before. You should know more about human nature every year of your life. Do you write about it quite as well or as brilliantly as you once did? No, not quite. You're down a peg or two there.

INTERVIEWER

Why?

MAILER

I think it's a simple matter of brain damage and nothing else. The brain deteriorates. Why can't an old car do certain things a new car can do? You have to take that for granted. You wouldn't beat on an old car and say, You betrayed me! The good thing is you know every noise in that old car.

INTERVIEWER

It was suggested to me that a certain senior American novelist went to see another senior American novelist at the twilight of the latter's life and said to him, Enough now, no more writing.

MAILER

He said to him don't write anymore?

INTERVIEWER

Yes. It's one of those stories you hear in New York. If it happened, one might think of it as an act of love. One great and elegant swordsman disarming another.

MAILER

No, I can't believe it. I'll tell you if anyone ever came to me with that, I'd say, kidding is kidding, but get your ass off my pillow.

INTERVIEWER

Do you think America is a good place in which to practice the arts?

MAILER

When I was young it was marvelous for a writer. It's the reason we have so many good writers in America—most of our literature had not yet been written. English novelists had all the major eighteenth- and nineteenth-century geniuses to deal with and go beyond. What did we have to go beyond? A few great writers, Melville and Hawthorne. The list is very short. For us, the field was wide open. Now we're beleaguered. The movies were bad enough, though American novelists always felt a certain superiority to what was happening in Hollywood. You weren't learning more about human nature from films, you were just being entertained—at some cost to your ability to learn a little more about why we're here, which I think is one of the remaining huge questions.

Now people grow up with television, which has an element within it that is absolutely inimical to serious reading, and that is the commercial. Any time you're interested in a narrative, you know it's going to be interrupted every seven to ten minutes, which will shatter any concentration. Kids watch television and lose all interest in sustained narrative. As a novelist, I really feel I'm one of the elders of a dying craft. It once was an art, and now it's down to being a craft, and that craft is going to go. The answer to your question is this: America is no longer a good place to be a novelist, and once it was a wonderful place.

INTERVIEWER

Was there a time when the country looked to novelists for the truth?

MAILER

The important writers in my day, back in the early forties, were much more important to me than movie stars. Movie stars were oddities, curiosities. Actors could be dynamic, they could be attractive, but that wasn't important, not in the scheme of things. Novelists were. I can't speak for how people feel when they enter the priesthood, but that was the way I felt as a novelist—vocational. Nothing was more important to me.

The country seems to have been so hungry for great novelists—for a great American novel. Did that feed your sense of vocation?

MAILER

Most certainly. I think a number of us used to dream fifty and sixty years ago of doing just that—writing the great American novel. I will say, that dream dies hard.

INTERVIEWER

There's a story Shelley Winters told about you. The way I heard it, she came to you around 1950 and asked you to help her understand Dreiser's novel *An American Tragedy*. She badly wanted to be cast as the factory girl in George Stevens's screen adaptation. It eventually came out as *A Place in the Sun*, with Montgomery Clift. A sweet story, that.

MAILER

And absolutely true.

INTERVIEWER

I love the idea of a girl coming to a novelist wanting to be educated.

MAILER

Well, we'd known each other. Shelley called me up one day. She was hysterical. She said, I have to go see George Stevens tomorrow. In those days she was viewed as a ditzy blonde who was not much of an actress. She was terribly serious about acting but she played silly blondes in silly movies, and she wanted something better.

She said, I've got to read this book *An American Tragedy*, and it's seven hundred pages, I can't read it by tomorrow, and so forth. So I said, All right, I'll come over and see you. And of course I had my own little agenda tucked into the middle of it. Hey, I'll be alone with this blonde movie actress and maybe good things will come of it. So I get there and she's got a bad case of hives, and she's got a bandanna wrapped around her head, and her chin is swollen, and she looks like hell, and she's in an old kimono, totally unsexy, and she looks ready to go in for a strong case of the weeps.

In those days I wasn't always very effective, but that day I was. I said, Now look, first of all it's a seven-hundred-page book, but your part of it is only in the middle, and I showed her about two hundred and fifty pages in the middle. Read as much as you can tonight, and don't panic. The key thing is that you can play this role, and what you want to remember is, she's a working-class girl you're playing, and she's a girl who's completely without artifice. She is what she is. And that's the core of Roberta Alden. It's what gets her into the love affair with Clyde, and it's what makes her lose it.

So I go home afterward. I might as well have been in the desert for all the sex there was going to be that day. And I speak to my wife, in the righteous tones of a husband who's been out trying to galli-vant and has failed. And then, of course, twenty-four hours later Shelley calls me up and says, Norman, I got the role. She says, I was talking to him and I said, Mr. Stevens, the way I look at it is Roberta Alden is a girl completely without artifice. And he said, Hey, you know, you're not the dummy I thought you were. So she got the role. Once she'd been working on it for a few weeks, she called again and said, Norman, I need some new dialogue. I need some new lines. I've used that statement about artifice a few times now and he's get-ting tired of it.

INTERVIEWER

Much of the interviewer's art is concerned with the question of motive. What made you write this? What caused you to marry her? How did you come to be involved in that particular action? Why did you do it? And it strikes me that your new novel, *The Castle in the Forest*, is likewise shrouded in the question of motive, the overarching one being what made young Adolph Hitler into a personification of evil? The family incest? The example of the bees? The severity of his father's beatings?

MAILER

None of that. None of the above.

INTERVIEWER

Hold on. You mean it doesn't matter? But to what extent was the question of motive your motive for writing the book?

MAILER

Oh, my motive is separate from whatever motives I gave Hitler. I hate it when writers give psychological explanations that pretend to answer questions and don't.

INTERVIEWER

Nevertheless you chose to put these things in the book.

MAILER

Well, they are contributing factors. But my notion of the book from the beginning was to have a devil narrating it. There's a long riff in the novel about how the average intelligent intellectual today finds it hard enough to believe in God, let alone the devil. And my feeling is that there's no better explanation for Hitler than that he was inspired by the devil, as Jesus Christ was inspired by God. If people will believe that Jesus Christ is the son of God then I don't see why you can't see that Hitler is the offspring of the devil. It's the simplest explanation. There's no other.

INTERVIEWER

Do you stand with Milton and with *Paradise Lost* in the understanding that the devil sometimes has the best lines?

MAILER

Oh yeah, more than the best lines. I really do believe that there's a close-knit war between God and the devil that goes on in all our affairs. People hate the thought today, because we live in a technological time where human beings are sick and tired of the heritage of the Middle Ages, a time when we all crawled on our bellies and prayed to God and sobbed and said, Oh, God, please pay attention to me. Oh, God, please save me. Oh, Devil, stay away. Well, we've had the

Enlightenment since then. We've had Voltaire. We've had several centuries in which to forge our vanity as human beings, and now we are a third force. There's God at one end, the devil at the other, and there we are occupying this huge center. And half of us alive don't believe in God or the devil.

INTERVIEWER

Do you believe in God?

MAILER

Oh, of course I do. But I don't mean I believe in God as a lawgiver, as the Jehovah. I think that was a power grab by priests way back then, a power grab implicit in the notion that if you can get people afraid of a powerful force who will punish them if they don't do the right thing, then the agents of that force wield huge power. And so there's no such thing as a priesthood that doesn't believe in God as all-powerful and all-punishing. But I don't believe in that at all. I believe in God as the creator. My notion of God is that God created us, and that like all creators God is not in command of the situation. God is the best that he or she can do under very difficult circumstances.

INTERVIEWER

So is this an existential God?

MAILER

Absolutely. Doesn't know how it's going to turn out, doesn't know whether he or she is going to succeed or fail. Has a war with the devil. This God is a local god, if you will. And there are local gods all over the universe. All with different notions of existence. And some of them are at war with each other and some of them are so far apart they don't have to worry about it. But if we're going to go with rank speculations, absolutely errant speculations, illegal speculations, I'd say that the devil was probably sent here as a counterforce to God. In other words, there were higher forces in the universe that didn't like this upstart God who had a vision of humanity.

INTERVIEWER

A large number of Americans today hold the notion that God and the devil are at work in their daily lives.

MAILER

I think they are. Not in a controlling sense—I don't believe that the devil seizes you and you're gone forever. But can you say that you've never had a fuck where you didn't feel evil for a little while?

INTERVIEWER

A little angelic, maybe.

MAILER

No. A little evil. And I think that's the answer.

INTERVIEWER

In *The Castle in the Forest*, I wonder if you aren't mystifying the process by suggesting that Hitler could only be as he was because the devil was present at the moment of his conception. That would be my argument with the book: a novelist can't ignore the capacity of human beings to create terror in the confines of their own minds, in the structure of their own lives.

MAILER

You can argue that. Hitler is, however, one of a kind: there's no explanation for him. Stalin was a monster of a comprehensible sort. We can read Stalin's biography, we can study the Bolshevik movement, we can study the conditions in Russia, we can study the hideous aftermath of the Russian Revolution. We can add Stalin up bit by bit, piece by piece, and understand him in human terms. He may have been one of the most evil human beings that ever lived, but he was a human being. You don't need to bring in the devil to explain Stalin. But Hitler is different. Hitler is not a strong man the way Stalin was. He's almost weak. He is inexplicable, unless you buy the idea that he was the devil's choice for reasons that go very deep into German nature.

And I would go further than that. I'm now anticipating the next book that I'm going to write. Who knows if I'll be around long enough to write it, but if I can, Hitler will emerge as the devil's choice. By the end of *The Castle*, he's one of tens of hundreds of candidates that the devil has seeded all over humanity as possible monsters. The devil, like God, gives a command for many things, but history is not wholly predictable. God and the devil are warring with one another. Humans are warring against them and among themselves. And the devil does not try to create one Hitler the way God created one Jesus. He's a pragmatist, so he creates hundreds and thousands of potential Hitlers, and this is the one that came through. Why? Because of the extraordinary conditions in Germany, which were not present when Hitler was conceived, and that's what the next book will get into. How this crappy kid ends up being this powerhouse.

INTERVIEWER

We're living in a world increasingly defined by people who believe that the other party is the force of evil.

MAILER

Yeah.

INTERVIEWER

We live with these terms. The Axis of Evil. The Great Satan. The Evil Empire.

MAILER

The brunt of my effort is to make certain that all the bread is buttered equally. Is there evil in America? Yes. Is there evil in Islam? Yes. Is one side more evil than the other? Who knows. We're both immensely evil, we're both immensely good. It's part of our religious beliefs that we are mixtures, profound mixtures. Atheists say they are perfectly happy not believing in God. But they can't be happy philosophically, because they have no answer to the question of how we got here. It's very hard to describe the complexities of human nature having emerged ex nihilo. If you have God as a creator doing the best that he or she can do there's a perfect explanation for why we're here. We're God's creation, and God has great respect for us, the way a father, a good father, has respect for children because the father wants the children to be more interesting than himself. And ditto for the mother. And in that sense we are, you might say, the avant-garde for God. The notion of heaven as Club Med or hell as an overheated boiler room makes no sense to me.

INTERVIEWER

You believe in reincarnation. So what are you coming back as, Norman?

MAILER

Well, I'm waiting, right? I'm in the waiting room. And finally my name is called. I go in and there's a monitoring angel who says, Mr. Mailer, we're very glad to meet you. We've been looking forward to your arrival. Let me tell you the good news, absolutely good news, is you've been passed for reincarnation. I say, Oh thank you, yes, I really didn't want to go into eternal peace. And the monitoring angel says, Well, between us, it isn't really necessarily eternal peace. It can be a little hectic. But nonetheless, the fact of the matter is that you've been passed for reincarnation. Let me see, before I look and see what we've got you down for, we always ask people, What would you like to be in your next life? And I say, Well, I think I'd like to be a black athlete. I don't care where you put me, I'll take my chances, but yes, that's what I want to be, a black athlete. And the monitoring angel says, Listen, Mailer, we're so oversubscribed in that department. Everybody wants to be a black athlete in their next life. I don't know now . . . I can't begin to . . . let me see what we've got you booked for. So he opens the big book, looks, and says, Well, we've got you down for a cockroach. But here's the good news: you'll be the fastest cockroach on the block.

INTERVIEWER

Not bad.

MAILER

Reincarnation is the best evidence of God's sense of wit and judgment. God, I repeat, is not a lawgiver. He is a creator, and creators have judgment.

INTERVIEWER

Was it Gary Gilmore's belief in reincarnation that initially attracted you to him?

MAILER

Oh yeah. But the thought has been with me for years. In 1954, when I was a very proud atheist, very proud, very sure of myself, very sure that God had to be dispensed with, I went out to visit James Jones in Illinois. He started talking about reincarnation. Now, Jones was one of the most practical novelists I've ever met, real Midwestern. He was absolutely solid in his sense of the real and the given and how you dealt with it. His pleasure in life was how you dealt precisely with the difficulties of reality. He was a great believer in the real, and yet he believed in reincarnation. I said to him, I'm sure you don't believe in that stuff, do you? He said, Hell yes I do! It's the only thing that makes sense. So I had to live with that remark for the next ten years before it finally moved over to my head.

INTERVIEWER

Do you have violent dreams?

MAILER

No, I don't. I put those dreams into the work.

INTERVIEWER

A capacity for violence clings to your concerns as a writer, and it clings equally to your reputation.

MAILER

The reputation is worse. The legend is much fatter than I am.

INTERVIEWER

Let's pause over the reputation. There are two recent movies that bring it up. One is *Infamous*, Douglas McGrath's movie about Truman Capote. There's a scene where Capote is having dinner with some of those rich girls he loved. One of them asks him if it isn't frightening to go into the cell with the Clutter murderers, and Capote says, "To be frank, I'm much more concerned for my safety around Norman Mailer."

MAILER

If you've been in five—say, five—fights in your life, the public sees it as fifty fights or one hundred and fifty.

INTERVIEWER

And in the other movie, *Factory Girl*, about Edie Sedgwick, there's a scene in which Andy Warhol is sitting in a confessional box and he's saying to the priest, "I have this friend and Norman Mailer walked up and punched him in the stomach, and all I could think was, Will Norman Mailer ever punch me?"

MAILER

People are always at a loss when they meet me.

INTERVIEWER

Are you sick of it?

MAILER

Oh, I'm beyond being sick of it, you know. You have to shrug.

INTERVIEWER

Yet your work has always been taken up with violence.

MAILER

The interest in violence is legitimate. I always thought it was one of the frontiers left to us as novelists. The great novelists of the nineteenth century dealt with love, they dealt with disappointment and love, they dealt with honesty, they dealt to some degree with corruption, they dealt with the forces of society as general abstract forces that could bend a person's will. Then came the twentieth century. Hemingway was fascinated with violence because his body was torn apart in the war. Violence was central to him. When I read Hemingway I was fascinated with the way he treated violence, but never satisfied.

INTERVIEWER

Was part of it your knowledge that man was living under the threat of mass violence?

MAILER

But that was the irony. That individual violence was taboo and yet we lived very seriously with notions of mass violence. There were perfectly serious people in both the Soviet Union and America in those years who spent their days and nights dreaming about how they could absolutely destroy the other country. I mean, they asked themselves how much damage would we have to suffer to destroy the Soviet Union totally. Those are the kind of calculations that were being made all the time.

INTERVIEWER

Let's keep to the line here. We come into this period when your generation of American novelists really begins to have a nuanced understanding of how violence exists both in our imaginations and in our societies. Please take that up.

MAILER

I was always alert to the animosity that the literary world felt when having to deal with violence. This was during a period when it wasn't at all certain we'd make it to the end of the century. We lived with that— we still live with such uncertainty. At the same time, individual violence is considered very unpleasant and not to be talked about, and for me violent moments are always existential moments. They are crucial. One looks at them and says, Maybe I can do something terrific with this.

INTERVIEWER

So you look at a figure such as Lee Harvey Oswald, a man whose name will always cling to a single devastating act of violence—and what do you see?

MAILER

Well, first of all, I have to decide whether he did it or not. When I started *Oswald's Tale* I felt that if I ever got over to Russia I was going find out an awful lot. I believed there was a conspiracy. And the better I got to know Oswald the more I came to believe that if he was a member of a conspiracy he was only there as some great extension, he wasn't the sort of person who'd be a useful member to the conspiracy, because he was a loner. He was much too proud. He wanted to do it all himself. I could be wrong about all this. When I say I think Oswald killed John F. Kennedy, I come to that conclusion in the way of an intelligence officer, which means I'm seventy-five percent certain he killed Kennedy. Certainly if someone came up with incontrovertible evidence that he was part of a conspiracy, I'd have to say I was wrong. But I believe he did it, for a very simple reason, which is he wanted to be famous. He wanted to be immortal. It stands out about him. Because of his experience in the Soviet Union and in America, he crossed from mass violence to individual violence, and he may indeed have felt that he was afforded a special role in existence.

INTERVIEWER

Do you still stand by your essay "The White Negro"?

MAILER

I stand by it in that I'm sure there are any number of people—particularly young men—who lead their lives according to the quality of their orgasm. In other words they find a chick who gives them a greater orgasm than another chick and that's what they follow, that's their idea of love. And who's to say they're wrong? The orgasm is a very deep expression of ourselves. A lot of black people resent that I ascribed the search for the orgasm more to black people than to white. My feeling was that since many other avenues of achievement were cut off to them, it made perfect sense.

INTERVIEWER

I want to talk to you about how a novelist transfigures factual material. Lawrence Schiller brought you interviews for the Gary Gilmore story and for the book about Lee Harvey Oswald. So can you begin to say what happens to turn facts into art?

MAILER

To make it novelistic? All right. With Gilmore, Larry came in with a third of the interviews, or half of the interviews—something massive like that. And then I did a great many, and my assistant Judith McNally did all the lawyers, because she was very good at that. And so we ended up with about three hundred interviews, and maybe half of them I participated in. From there, it was a little like reducing maple sap to syrup—you boil the stuff all day long until you get down to an essence. Then came the next step, which was to transmute that into a fictional form.

I realized at this point that there exists a funny reciprocal relation between fact and fiction. I had this feeling that I can't really justify or explain, that the closer this book stayed to the given statements the more fictional it would be. When you have a collection of bare facts, the trouble is that most of the facts are not—what's the word I'm looking for—refined. They are warped. They're scabby. They're distorted. Very often they're false facts. And there's a tendency when you don't have to live with these facts to lump them all together, and so the story very often ends, despite good and serious efforts, with a betrayal of the reality.

INTERVIEWER

This is excellent. Break it down.

MAILER

OK. I would go so far as to say that any history that gets built entirely upon fact is going to be full of error and will be misleading. It's the human mind that is able to synthesize what the reality might have been. Now, that reality doesn't have to be the one that took place, it has to be a reality that people can live with in their narrow minds, as the likelihood of how something could take place. And that's the key difference. If you read a book and say, Yes, this is how it could have taken place, your mind has been enriched. The feeling I had with *The Executioner's Song* was that these facts, if very closely examined and reexamined and reduced and refined, would begin to create a manifest of the given that I would call fictional. Fictional because it breathed, and there's the difference. If you put facts together in such a way that they truly breathe for the reader, then you're writing fiction. Fiction is not tales or legends, or saying stuff that's not true as opposed to stuff that is true. Something can be true and still be fiction.

INTERVIEWER

You've never been entirely happy with this. When you wrote *The Armies of the Night* did you feel it was a novel?

MAILER

Yeah, well, I didn't do much of a job with the "history as a novel, the novel as history" label. To this day I'm not sure what I was doing when I did that. I think that *The Armies of the Night* is not a fiction. That book was as real as I could make it. It is an autobiographical narrative, and that's not the same thing as fiction.

INTERVIEWER

Does it bother you that your two Pulitzer Prizes were for works based on factual situations?

MAILER

Some say with bland certitude, Of course Mailer is a good nonfiction writer—he's not much of a novelist. That irritates me, yes. Because the person saying that is just not familiar with my work. No one could read *Harlot's Ghost* and say it's nonfiction, you know. No one could read *Ancient Evenings*, for God's sake, and say that's nonfiction. They're not familiar with those works, that's all. They've made up their minds on the basis of the stuff they have read, which tends to be the nonfictional work.

I accept that I have been living with the problems of nonfiction over the years, and that I have often been happy writing nonfiction because it's easier than writing novels. You don't have to worry about the story.

INTERVIEWER

That won't do, Norman. No way.

MAILER

No, let me go on. When you're writing fiction you can lose your novel on a given morning. You can have your protagonist take up a serious act that appeals to you at the moment, and then you have to follow up on that act, and you have to deal with the consequences of that act. And two months later, six months later, horror of horrors, two years later, you wake up and say, I took the wrong turn that day. That happens in the writing of novels, and it's enough to frighten you to death.

INTERVIEWER

OK. But you're not going to suggest that you wrote nonfiction because it was easier?

MAILER

No—not quite. I wrote nonfiction because the jobs were offered to me. For instance, with *Marilyn*, Scott Meredith, who was my agent at the time, called me to say he's got some pretty terrific money for twenty-five thousand words on Marilyn Monroe. And he named the figure.

INTERVIEWER

What was it?

MAILER

For the sake of the record, it was fifty thousand dollars. In those days that was enormous. And Scott said to me, Look, Norman. It's very good. But don't write too much. I proceeded to get so taken with

Marilyn that I ended up writing ninety-five thousand words. Fifty thousand ended up being a modest payment for the book instead of a coup. The point is, it was such an agreeable book to write. I didn't have to do any thinking. I didn't have to create this incredible blonde star who had such an incredible life—the material was all there. And on top of that, writing the book taught me a great deal about facts and false facts. See, I was dealing with a group of liars. Everybody in Hollywood exaggerates and distorts and trims and manipulates stories, and so it was almost like being an intelligence agent. You had to decide what might be true and what might not.

INTERVIEWER

There's a part of you that enjoys the notion of being an intelligence agent?

MAILER

Does it just! I once did a story on Warren Beatty for *Vanity Fair*. I really liked him, and I think he liked me. I also wanted him to run for president. This was in 1991, and he demurred. And then later Arianna Huffington wrote that he should run for president. So I called Warren up and I said, Will you settle for vice president? And he answered, All right, all right, what do you want? Head of intelligence, I told him. You've got it, he said. How we laughed. Ah, if only Warren Beatty had been president.

INTERVIEWER

Flaubert felt that one could find the model for Emma Bovary very close to the author. How much of you is there in the grand persons that you've taken as your subjects, and would it ever be possible for you to say, Adolf Hitler, *c'est moi*?

MAILER

While I was doing the story on Warren, I went to see *Bugsy*, which hadn't been released yet. And the violence in *Bugsy* was truly apparent. Now Warren Beatty is obviously physically able, he's a bit of an athlete, but you don't think of him as violent. And so it was a shock to see how marvelous and convincing a portrait of violence he managed to give. And I said to him, Aren't you a little bit concerned that your friends won't be comfortable around you now? And he said, Oh, no, most of my friends are actors and they understand it. You don't really need to have more than five percent of a character in yourself to be able to play him. Then he grinned and said, Of course if you've got seventy-five percent it's a lot easier. I'd say with Adolph Hitler, five percent was all I needed.

INTERVIEWER

You've gone quite far with five percent.

MAILER

You bring whatever powers you have to high focus. It's why very few people ever become successful novelists and are able to remain successful novelists. They have the talent, but it's also about bringing the powers to focus. It involves stuff that isn't agreeable. For instance, being a novelist means you have to be ready to live a monastic life. When you're really working on a novel there can be ten days in a row when you're just out there working and offering nothing to your mate and nothing to anyone else. You don't want to be bothered, you don't want to answer the phone, you don't want even to talk a great deal to your kids—you want to be left alone while you're working. And that is hard. And of course every morning you have to go in there and face that blank page and start up again. So this business of bringing your powers to focus is not routine. You have to believe you're going to engage in spiritual discomfort in order to get to the place where you can think. Not just to think as yourself, but to do so as the person who's fashioning the novel.

INTERVIEWER

Has there been an instance of seventy-five percent with you, where you felt that you really knew an extraordinary amount about the subject? I mean natively knew a lot about the subject, as opposed to knowing their dates and the names of their wives. I'm thinking of Picasso.

MAILER

That was easier. But no, never seventy-five percent. Always less than half. I mean, these are extraordinary people. You mentioned Lee Harvey Oswald, Gary Gilmore, Marilyn Monroe, Hitler. What's the common denominator in all of them? They're all essentially people without roots—people who've gone through identity crises.

INTERVIEWER

Muhammad Ali?

MAILER

Oh, I think he's had to reforge his identity every few years.

INTERVIEWER

Why?

MAILER

Ali embraces not only the fighter but the ring, and the audience. He has a sense of absolute awareness. So for him every time his status shifted, and it shifted dramatically several times, he was a somewhat different person. So he had identity crises. Or modulations, identity shifts.

INTERVIEWER

Jesus Christ?

MAILER

If you think you're the son of God, you got a lot of identity crisis.

INTERVIEWER

You have been drawn to icons and to the travails of the celebrated ego, but not so much to the minutiae of family life or the American suburbs. Saul Bellow put everything that ever happened to him into his novels. You've been married six times but have not used your private life in that way.

MAILER

Never, and for a reason—which is, I believe that the fundamental experiences of your life form crystals in your imagination, and that you can take your imagination and beam it through from different angles. It hits the crystal, you beam it through this way, you beam it through on another angle, and you end up with different stories, different aperçus, different novels. It's exactly what actors do. I've never written directly about a wife at the time I was married to her. I don't think that I've ever written about a wife. I think I write about aspects of wives, aspects of children, because I don't believe in using one's experience directly. I think if you do, you cut off other possibilities.

INTERVIEWER

Now, it would be impossible to talk to you about the art of fiction without talking about politics. You once called yourself a left conservative.

MAILER

I still do. I am a left conservative.

INTERVIEWER

But let us talk about neoconservatism. It has become such a thing in America. I'm interested in your relationship with people like Norman Podhoretz, people who went on a journey that took them very far from the place where they started.

MAILER

Well, I can understand it. And in fact, I feel partly responsible for Podhoretz. He and I were close friends at one point. He wrote a book called *Making It*, and the book got trashed terribly. He was unpopular on the left. I never quite understood why he was so unpopular. But they trashed his book like you wouldn't believe. It was truly ugly. And I hadn't read it yet—or I'd read the first half of it, which was pretty good. And I witnessed this trashing and said to him, I'm going to write a review. So I read all of the book. And the book betrays itself.

The second half is god-awful. In the first half, his thesis is that the dirty little secret among the left, among artists and intellectuals, is that they really want to make it, and they want to make it big. And they conceal that from themselves and from others. But this is really the motivating factor that is never talked about. You can talk about sex but you can't talk about ambition and desire for success. So he does all that. And then he starts to give portraits of all the people on the left who have made it—pious, sweet little portraits, with people who we know goddamn well are not that at all. And I was horrified at the way he could betray his own book. There was a failure in nerve there—in other words, if you want to be strong theoretically, you better be strong in detail as well. That's what makes a good general. Strong at both ends. And he wasn't.

So I ended up mocking his book, too. And I was pretty cruel. Looking back on it, I was probably too cruel. He went into a depression and stayed there for about a year . . . just didn't do much. Worked on his magazine and listened to music and hardly saw anyone. And by the end of that time, he'd moved over to the right. Podhoretz is nothing if not active and enterprising. So the moment he moved over to the right, it wasn't enough to be on the right, he had to be far to the right. And so I feel that I'm responsible, to whatever degree, for helping to have shoved him over there. Which is too bad, because he now is paying for his sins on the right by having supported the war in Iraq and he has to live with it—has to live with all the idiocies of the neoconservatives.

INTERVIEWER

Politics was a consuming passion for you—on the level of action, for a time, as much as on the level of writing. Did you have the political effect you desired?

MAILER

You spend your life, if you're a politically minded writer, attacking what you hate politically. And it probably has no more than a very small effect. But the inner call is there to do it. At one point I actually went into politics and tried twice to run for mayor of New York and thought I'd make a difference. What I discovered is I might just as well have tried out for a soccer team, when I don't know anything about soccer.

INTERVIEWER

The 1969 campaign for mayor marked the end of your political career.

MAILER

I realized a number of things afterward. One of them was I didn't have enough stamina. I mean, I aged in the three or four months of the campaign, and I was tired all the time. We got very little press. And it really felt, a lot of the time, as if we were just beating our fists against the wall. What I said after it was all over is that a freshman can't be elected president of the fraternity. And right after I made that remark, along came Jimmy Carter. He broke the rule, but he wasn't a very successful president.

INTERVIEWER

So it must interest you to imagine how Václav Havel managed to be a writer and be president, too?

MAILER

I don't know much about his career. We met once and had an unhappy meeting because I'd been in Havana and I talked about meeting Castro, what an interesting man he was, which is undeniably true, but Havel just clammed up. Obviously I was not someone with whom he wished to have anything to do, so my feeling was, Hey, you tell me to get lost? I tell you to get lost! He brought out the old Brooklyn in me.

INTERVIEWER

But at some level you must have understood?

MAILER

I understood, but I also thought it was narrow-minded. Yes, he'd spent his life fighting the communists, and he hated them, but you've got to be able to make distinctions. There is such a thing as a relatively good communist, and if there's one on earth, it was Fidel Castro. I mean, there's a huge difference—the average communist that oppressed Havel was a bureaucrat who had kept his nose clean and in the trough and was an oppressor because he was a mediocrity. And there was Castro, who was hated by every American president for a very simple reason, which is that he had become head of a nation by daring to win. And how had they become president? By shaking hands with people they despised for decades. And Havel should have been able to see that difference.

INTERVIEWER

Flannery O'Connor once asked the question, "Who speaks for America today?" The answer she gave was the advertising agencies. Can you imagine a time again when the answer to that question will be the American novelist?

MAILER

No, not now. I'm gloomy. I wish I could be more positive about it. But the marketeers have taken over the country. There's been a profound shift in the American ethic. We used to be a country that prided itself on the fine products we made. Not necessarily the greatest or most beautiful or most finely machined products, but we made a very good level of product that made economic sense. Now the country's pride is marketing.

INTERVIEWER

F. Scott Fitzgerald knew that America was addicted to illusion. But is it now more true to say that America fully believes its own lies?

MAILER

When it comes to foreign affairs, we've been living lies ever since World War II. Now, maybe for the first five or ten years after World War II, Russia was an ideological threat because it did have great appeal to certain poor countries, no question. And then after that they hit their bad years. They've never been a huge threat to us. Yet for forty-plus years while the Cold War was on, we kept Americans believing we were engaged in a struggle of ideology that had to be won. So there was an awful lot of bullshit slowly rolling down, like lava, over the American mind.

Most of the country believes in Jesus Christ. And they believe that compassion is the greatest virtue. But we only believe this on Sundays. And the other six days of the week, we're an immensely competitive nation. We scramble like hell to make more money than our neighbor. Culture's a word that most Americans don't react to quickly. A European knows exactly what you mean by culture. They've got it there in their architecture. They've got it there in the curve of a street, and we have thoroughfares that go in a straight line because that's the fastest way to get to market. So there's a great guilt in American life, and this guilt is that we're not good Christians. The Karl Rove concoction—stupidity plus patriotism—comes into play here. The basic propaganda machine of the parties, particularly the Republicans, is to enforce the notion that we are a noble, good country that wants only good for the rest of the world, and that we're God's blessing and that God wants us to succeed, that we're God's project. And under this exists, always, an ongoing sense of shame, an ongoing sense of guilt, the feeling that we're not as good as we pretend to be.

INTERVIEWER

Younger American novelists have voiced concern over the neglect of high culture and the rise of Oprah's Book Club. But it seems to me novelists are doing fine, actually; it's the critical culture that's in trouble. You grew up as a writer in conditions of, shall we say, mutual recognition with a generation of literary critics—people who had political feeling and were respectful of high culture. I'm thinking of Irving Howe and Alfred Kazin, Lionel Trilling, of course, and Edmund Wilson. Answer me two things: Did the existence of that critical audience affect your sense of the culture you were writing into? And two, has the disappearance of that critical culture taken away from the good of the novel?

MAILER

The answer to both questions is yes, absolutely. Those critics were my judgmental peers. It was more exciting to me to meet people like Trilling and Howe than to meet most movie stars. Edmund Wilson was the nearest thing to Jehovah. You wanted their respect, and you feared their disapproval. At the same time, as you grew and developed, you didn't feel totally inferior to them. There came that time—that happy, blessed time—when you could say, Well, I might know more about this subject than Irving Howe. That was a nice moment. We don't have it anymore. Those critics have all passed away. There's no one to replace them that I can see.

INTERVIEWER

You were friends with the Trillings. Did you feel such people helped you to define your style as a writer?

MAILER

Lionel was very remote, and he never really engaged with a book of mine as such. But it was nice to be in his presence. He was a very intelligent man. And there was that book he wrote, *The Liberal Imagination*—you could argue with it. You could live with it. You could think about it. And he was a fine man to spend an evening with because his intelligence was so good. Diana was enthusiastic, emotional, open, passionate, furious, absolutely took sides on everything, intolerant, full of fun—the exact opposite of Lionel. I suppose I was really closer to Diana. We were almost like cousins. We fought all the time and loved each other. And of course there was Lillian Hellman: they were impossible friends, the Trillings and the Hellmans, because Lillian was sort of sympathetic to the Party, and they were very much anticommunist. And yet they never brought that up between them until the end, when they parted company.

INTERVIEWER

"Marriage is a workable institution," says the narrator in the new book, "especially for dreadful people." That made me laugh.

MAILER

Well, the devil was speaking. That's not me.

INTERVIEWER

As you prefer. But I still wonder if your marriages have made you a better novelist.

MAILER

Let's transpose the question. Did Picasso's marriages—we'd better say relationships—make him a better painter or a worse one? It's an interesting point of argument.

INTERVIEWER

They certainly afforded him variety.

MAILER

Every wife is a culture, and you enter deep into another culture, one that's not your own, and you learn an awful lot from it. And given the fact that marriage is not always a comfortable institution, you chafe in that culture. For example, suppose you spend ten years of your life in France. And you finally decide to leave. You wouldn't for the rest of your life say, I hate France. You'd say, France has an awful lot to offer. I have my differences with it, but I'm happy I spent ten years in France. Women don't like arguments like that because they consider them denigrating. Oh, here's this man who took my youth and enjoyed me to the hilt and then took off. That's not the way it is. Men are aged quite as much by marriage as women. There's no question in my mind that within each marriage Picasso was a different type of painter. And I think you could probably say—I don't compare myself to Picasso, who had a much mightier effect on the world than I'll ever have—that my writing shifted with each wife. Each relationship had a profound effect on the work. One has different loyalties, different interests, different understandings. One has a different sense of good and evil.

INTERVIEWER

Good and evil?

MAILER

Our understanding of good and evil begins with our parents. Down the road it is altered by one's relationships with one's children.

INTERVIEWER

If one is so minded—or so inclined—is it a good idea for a novelist to have children?

MAILER

I don't prescribe for novelists. I mean, if Henry James followed my prescription, where would he have been?

INTERVIEWER

James himself was full of prescriptions.

MAILER

He made a fetish of point of view. That was as close as he came to an all-out religion.

INTERVIEWER

His most famous essay has the same title as this interview series, "The Art of Fiction." In it he lays down the rules of good writing. "Be generous and delicate and pursue the prize." "Don't think too much about optimism and pessimism; try and catch the color of life itself." He had quite specific notions of what the job demanded.

MAILER

I would never have wanted to live his life. Too much went to too little. Not necessarily in the work, but in the day-to-day living. The matter of what to wear for a given evening. The concern over whether the level of conversation at his end will be high enough or not. All that sort of stuff. No, one must be free of that.

INTERVIEWER

Yet there is the question of friendship. American novelists have often been at least partly directed by their friendships—Fitzgerald and Hemingway, or Sherwood Anderson and Theodore Dreiser.

MAILER

Fitzgerald and Hemingway's friendship was hardly untroubled.

INTERVIEWER

No, but the friendship nevertheless defined something essential for each of them.

MAILER

All right, well, I can give you James Jones and myself, too.

INTERVIEWER

And William Styron?

MAILER

I was rough on William Styron at one point. He was a very talented man. You have to understand something. There was Jones and Styron and myself, and we were all immensely competitive. What's not understood sufficiently about novelists is how competitive we all are. We're as competitive as star athletes. Particularly the ones who break through into public renown. And we don't say, Oh, what do you all have to be so envious of each other for? Isn't it enough that we're all talented? Why can't we just enjoy each other? It doesn't work that way. We're competitive. You can't say to athletes, What are you all competitive for? Isn't it marvelous that you can catch a football with great ease and run quickly? Why do you have to be in competition with the other men? Anyone who talks like that is the silliest sort of liberal.

At the same time we had a lot of respect for each other. I remember I received a copy of *From Here to Eternity*, which I think I'd asked for, and Jones had inscribed it: "To Norman—my most feared friend; my dearest rival." That's the nature of friendship among writers.

Gore Vidal—who has never been at a loss to see the negative side of human nature—pointed out that, "Whenever a friend succeeds, a little something in me dies." That's an exaggeration of this notion of competition. But in time we may try to get to the point where, although something of you does die, some other part of you is encouraged. You say, Well, if he's doing it, I can do it.

INTERVIEWER

But Styron?

MAILER

It was his style. He was a wonderful stylist. Probably the best of us. He was no intellectual, but he had a fine ability to create mood. And I think it was very important to him to be a great writer. So important that when he began to run into trouble as a novelist, I think that's what brought on his depression more than anything else.

INTERVIEWER

What explains your falling out?

MAILER

I don't want to get into it. At a certain point, I wrote him a very ugly letter to tell him to stop trashing my wife. The letter was written without sufficient knowledge to have justified the strong wording.

INTERVIEWER

And your friendship ended with James Jones?

MAILER

What happened with Jim is, we'd been very friendly and then he got married to Gloria. And I was married at the time to Adele, and I think Gloria, who was socially very ambitious, saw Adele as a sea anchor on her social ambitions. So she decided to end it. She turned to Jim and said, Adele insulted me, and Adele was very upset. She said, I didn't insult her. I don't know what's going on. And so I always assumed, Oh, he just made a tough, hard-boiled decision. Gloria was a tough lady. So Jim and I stopped talking to each other for years, and we never became friends again, which was a great loss, but there it was. And then Gloria and I, oddly enough, after Jim was gone, became slight friends again. It was really only one night, enjoying dancing together at some party in New York. I wouldn't have believed it was possible five years earlier.

INTERVIEWER

Much of this provides a little updating of a famous essay you wrote. It was called "Evaluations: Quick and Expensive Comments on the Talent in the Room." It upset a lot of people at the time, but which of that group of writers you wrote about turned out to be the most surprising in the end?

MAILER

With their talents?

INTERVIEWER

Yes.

MAILER

Updike and Roth. Because I dismissed them, you remember. And I was dead wrong. Given the perversity of novelists, I'll even take a little credit. I think I got them angered enough to say, He's going to rue those words!

INTERVIEWER

And does it surprise you, all this posthumous life of Truman Capote?

MAILER

He was an extraordinary person. Extraordinary. Not extraordinary in the depth of his intelligence, but extraordinary in his daring. I once made a comment that he was one of the bravest men in New York. And you've no idea what it meant to walk around the way he did when he was young. I remember he was living in Brooklyn, and there was a set designer—I think it was Oliver Smith—who had a house about two blocks from where I lived in Brooklyn Heights. Truman lived in the basement there, so we'd run into each other on the street once in a while. One time, when we did, we started walking, and I said, Let's have a drink, and we went into the nearest bar. It happened to be an old Irishmen's bar. It was one hundred yards long, or so it seemed, and they all had one foot up on the rail, these tough working-class Irishmen, and probably some Scots, all drinking there.

And we walk in, and there's Truman with the blond hair that he still wore in bangs and he had his little gabardine raincoat. He didn't have his arms in his sleeves, he had it tucked around his shoulders like a cape. And he walked in, and I walked in behind him and suddenly realized, Oh my God. And we went to the back of the place and sat down and talked for a while, nobody bothered us, but you know it was one of those things where you just didn't relax for a moment. I figured there could well be trouble before we got out of there. It occurred to me then that Truman lived with that every minute of every day of his life—he insisted on being himself. And he was ready to take on what might happen. I was most impressed by that.

INTERVIEWER

And what is the lasting enemy? Vanity?

MAILER

It can take you down. Look at poor Truman. His attitude became, If I'm not recognized in my own time then something absolutely awful is taking place in society. And that vanity is something that we all have to approach and walk around with great care. It can destroy a good part of us if we get into it. You know, you really have to be able to exhale, just exhale, and say, Why don't we just leave it to history?

Issue 181, 2007

Contributors

Chinua Achebe was born in 1930 in Ogidi, Nigeria. He learned to speak English at the age of eight, and at thirteen he was one of a small group of students chosen to study at the select Government College in Umuahia, Eastern Nigeria. In 1948 he enrolled in University College, Ibadan, where he studied English and began contributing stories and essays to the *University Herald*. His first novel, *Things Fall Apart*, was published in 1958 and has since been translated into some fifty languages. He is the author of numerous story, poetry, and essay collections, as well as four other novels: *No Longer at Ease* (1960), *Arrow of God* (1964), *A Man of the People* (1966), and *Anthills of the Savannah* (1987). Achebe has been awarded the Nigerian National Merit Award (the country's highest prize for academic work), a UNESCO Fellowship for Creative Artists, and the Man Booker International Prize, and he is an honorary member of the American Academy of Arts and Letters. **Jerome Brooks** (1932–2007) was a professor emeritus in the English Department at the City College of New York. He held a Ph.D. in English and Theology from the University of Chicago, and his many honors included a Fulbright Fellowship (1976) and an NEH grant (1979).

Martin Amis was born in 1949 in Oxford, England, the son of novelist Kingsley Amis. During his youth, Amis lived in England, South Wales, the United States, Spain, and the West Indies. He studied English at Exeter College, Oxford, graduating in 1971. At twenty-four he published his first novel, *The Rachel Papers* (1973), which won the Somerset Maugham Award. His early writing earned him a reputation as a satirist, and during the eighties he cemented his place among the most important and influential voices in contemporary British fiction with the publication of *Money* (1984) and *London Fields* (1989). He also worked as an editor and critic;

during the seventies and eighties he held editorial positions at various periodicals, including the *London Observer*, the *Times Literary Supplement*, and *The New Statesman*. His 1991 novel, *Time's Arrow*, was shortlisted for the Man Booker Prize. Amis is currently a professor of creative writing at Manchester University. He published a new collection of nonfiction, *The Second Plane*, in 2008, and his twelfth novel, *The Pregnant Widow*, is forthcoming from Random House. **Francesca Riviere**'s writing has appeared in the *Los Angeles Times*, *Premiere*, and *Smoke*.

Raymond Carver (1938–1988) was born in Clatskanie, Oregon. At the age of twenty, he moved to California and enrolled in a writing course with John Gardner, who helped him develop his sparse style, often characterized as minimalism or dirty realism. Carver spent a postgraduate year at the Iowa Writer's Workshop. In 1971 *Esquire* published the first of a number of his stories. His first collection, *Will You Please Be Quiet, Please?* (1976), was a critical success and was followed by *Furious Seasons and Other Stories* (1977). Carver's next two collections, *What We Talk About When We Talk About Love* (1981) and *Cathedral* (1983), secured his place as a master of the short-story genre. During the eighties he published three books of poetry— *Where Water Comes Together with Other Water* (1985), *Ultramarine* (1986), and *A New Path to the Waterfall* (1989), which appeared posthumously. His final collection of short fiction was *Where I'm Calling From: New and Selected Stories* (1988). **Lewis Buzbee** is the author of *Fliegelman's Desire, After the Gold Rush*, *The Yellow-Lighted Bookshop*, and *Steinbeck's Ghost*. He lives in San Francisco with his wife and daughter. **Mona Simpson**, a former senior editor of *The Paris Review*, is the author of four novels: *Anywhere But Here* (1987), *The Lost Father* (1992), *A Regular Guy* (1996), and *Off Keck Road* (2000), which was nominated for the PEN/Faulkner Award.

John Cheever (1912–1982) was born in Quincy, Massachusetts, but spent most of his life in New York City and its Westchester County suburbs, the setting for much of his fiction. When he was just eighteen, *The New Republic* published his fictionalized account of being dismissed from high school—he never attended college. Instead, he began to publish a steady string of stories in literary magazines, and in *The New Yorker*, where he continued to publish throughout his career. His first collection, *The Way Some People Live*, appeared in 1943, followed by *The Enormous Radio and Other Stories* a decade later. His first novel, *The Wapshot Chronicle* (1957), won the National Book Award the same year that he was elected to the National Institute of Arts and Letters. In the ensuing decades he published three more novels, including *The Wapshot Scandal* (1964; a sequel to the *The Wapshot Chronicle*) and *Falconer* (1977). *The Stories of John Cheever* (1978), a selection of his best work, won the National Book Critics Circle Award and the Pulitzer Prize. In 1982, two months before his death, he was awarded the National Medal for Literature. **Annette Grant** is an editor and writer.

Isak Dinesen (1885–1962) was the pseudonym of Karen Dinesen, who was born in a rural area near Copenhagen, Denmark. In 1914 Dinesen married Swedish nobleman Bror Blixen and the two moved to East Africa to start up a pioneer coffee farm. Following their divorce in 1925, Dinesen began work on a series of short stories that were later published in her critically acclaimed collection *Seven Gothic Tales* (1934). Dinesen's time in Africa inspired her best-known work, the novel *Out of Africa* (1937), which was made into a film in 1985 starring Robert Redford and Meryl Streep. In spite of failing health, Dinesen continued to write for much of the forties and fifties, producing a sequel to *Out of Africa* and several more volumes of short stories. When Ernest Hemingway accepted the Nobel Prize in Literature in 1954, he spoke of three other writers who he thought should have received the award before him, including "that beautiful writer, Isak Dinesen." A number of her works, including *Daguerreotypes and Other Essays* (1979) and *Letters from Africa: 1914–1931* (1981), have been collected and published posthumously. **Eugene Walter** (1921–1998), a former *Paris Review* associate editor, was a screenwriter, author, translator, actor, and gourmet chef. His many books include *Monkey Poems* (1953), the novel *The Untidy Pilgrim* (1954), and the bestselling *American Cooking: Southern Style*, part of Time-Life's Foods of the World series.

Ralph Ellison (1914–1994) was born in Oklahoma City, Oklahoma. In his youth Ellison wanted to be a musician, and he earned a scholarship to study music at the Tuskegee Institute in Alabama. In 1936 Ellison moved to New York, where he was introduced to Langston Hughes and Richard Wright; Wright and Ellison developed a friendship that set Ellison on the path to his literary career. Ellison joined the Federal Writers' Project and throughout the forties he wrote short stories, reviews, and essays for various periodicals. In 1952 he published *Invisible Man*, which won the 1953 National Book Award. He was also an accomplished essayist; his nonfiction is collected in *Shadow and Act* (1964) and *Going to the Territory* (1986). In the late fifties Ellison began working in earnest on his second novel. Although several excerpts of it were published, the complete work did not appear during Ellison's lifetime. In 1999 Ellison's literary executor published an edited selection of the manuscript under the title *Juneteenth*. The complete manuscript, *Three Days Before the Shooting*, is forthcoming from Modern Library. **Alfred Chester** (1928–1971) was a fiction writer and literary critic. He published short stories in *The New Yorker* and

Esquire, and his novels include *Jamie Is My Heart's Desire* (1956) and *The Exquisite Corpse* (1967). His nonfiction appeared in *The New York Review of Books*, *Partisan Review*, and *Commentary*, among other publications. **Vilma Howard**'s fiction and poetry appeared in *The Paris Review* in the 1950s, and her poems were anthologized by Langston Hughes in his collection *New Negro Poets: U.S.A.* in 1964.

Ted Hughes (1930–1998) was born in Mytholmroyd, England. He served two years in the Royal Air Force before enrolling in Pembroke College, Cambridge, where he studied English literature, archaeology, and anthropology. In 1956 he met the American poet Sylvia Plath, and the two married four months later. Encouraged by Plath, he entered and won a publishing contest with his poetry collection *Hawk in the Rain* in 1957. His second collection of poetry, *Lupercal*, appeared in 1960. After Plath's death in 1963 he began writing children's fiction, including *The Iron Man: A Story in Five Nights* (1968), which was later adapted as a motion picture. Hughes also translated numerous works, including Aeschylus's *Oresteia* and Euripides' *Alcestis*. His many awards include a Guggenheim Fellowship, the Queen's Gold Medal for Poetry, the Somerset Maugham Award, and the Hawthornden Prize. In 1977 he was awarded the Order of the British Empire, and in 1984 served as England's poet laureate. **Drue Heinz** was for many years the publisher of *The Paris Review*.

Norman Mailer (1923–2007) was born in Long Branch, New Jersey. He majored in engineering at Harvard, where he also studied creative writing. Shortly after graduating in 1943, Mailer was drafted into the army. His first novel, *The Naked and the Dead* (1948), which drew on his wartime experience, was nominated for a Pulitzer Prize and stayed on the *New York Times* bestseller list for over a year, making Mailer a literary celebrity at twenty-five. For decades he was a prolific writer of novels, poetry, biography, screenplays, essays, and political journalism, publishing in numerous periodicals including *Esquire*, *Dissent*, *Partisan Review*, and the *Village Voice*, which he cofounded in 1955. He was a key figure in the New Journalism movement, which brought novelistic writing devices to nonfiction narratives, a technique he helped make famous through works such as *Of a Fire on the Moon* (1971), *The Prisoner of Sex* (1971), *Marilyn: A Biography* (1973), and *The Fight* (1975). Mailer won the National Book Award and a Pulitzer Prize in nonfiction for *Armies of the Night* (1968), his third-person account of his involvement in the antiwar movement, and in 1980 he won a second Pulitzer for *The Executioner's Song*. In 2005 the National Book Foundation awarded Mailer the Medal for Distinguished Contribution to American Letters. **Andrew O'Hagan** is a novelist and essayist who lives in London. His latest novel, *Be Near Me* (2007), won the Los Angeles Times Book Award for Fiction, and he has recently published *The Atlantic Ocean*, a book of pieces about Britain and America. He writes regularly for the *London Review of Books* and *The New York Review of Books*.

Jan Morris was born James Humphrey Morris in Clevedon, England, in 1926. He served in the army from 1944 to 1947 before attending Christ Church College at Oxford. In 1953 Morris was assigned to cover the Everest expedition for *The Times*. He accompanied the expedition team to twenty-two thousand feet and was the first to report on Edmund Hillary's successful trip to the summit. He published his first book, *Coast to Coast*, in 1956, followed by *Sultan in Oman* (1957), *The Market of Seleukia* (1957), *South African Winter* (1958), and *Coronation Everest* (1958). Morris's books not only chronicle his travels but explore the political and social situations of the places he visits. In 1960 Morris won a George Polk Memorial Award and the Heinemann Award from the Royal Society of Literature for *Venice*, his first full-length travel work to achieve major commercial success. In 1972 Morris underwent a sex change operation; she published an autobiographical account of the experience, *Conundrum* (1974), under her new name, Jan Morris. Morris has also published children's literature and essay collections. In 1985 she published her first novel, *Last Letters from Hav*, which was nominated for the Man Booker Prize. **Leo Lerman** (1914–1994) was a longtime writer and editor at *Vogue* and *Vanity Fair*, among other publications. His journals, *The Grand Surprise: The Journals of Leo Lerman*, were published in 2007.

Joyce Carol Oates was born in 1938 in Lockport, New York. She was educated in a one-room schoolhouse and was the first member of her family to attend college, earning a B.A. from Syracuse and a master's in English from the University of Wisconsin. She began a Ph.D. program at Rice University but gave up her studies to focus on writing when one of her short stories was listed on the honor roll of Best American Short Stories in 1963. With the publication of her first story collection, *By the North Gate* (1963), Oates began a prolific literary career. She has published more than one hundred books, including novels, story and essay collections, plays, and poetry. Her fourth novel, *them* (1969), earned her a National Book Award; *Black Water* (1992) and *What I Lived For* (1994) were finalists for the Pulitzer Prize; her short fiction has appeared more than twenty times in the O. Henry Prize Stories anthologies; and in 1970 she became the first recipient of an O. Henry special award for continuing achievement. She is currently the Roger S. Berlind Distinguished Professor of Humanities at Princeton University. **Robert Phillips** is the author of thirty books of poetry, fiction, and nonfiction. His interview with Philip Larkin appears in *The Paris Review Interviews, II*. He is Moores Professor of English at the University of Houston.

Harold Pinter was born in 1930 in Hackney, England. He is the author of more than thirty plays and two dozen screenplays, and in 2005 he was awarded the Nobel Prize in Literature. Pinter studied acting at the Royal Academy of Dramatic Art, spending a decade as an actor before beginning to write plays in 1957. His first professionally staged play, *The Birthday Party* (1958), closed within a week, but two years later *The Caretaker* became an international success. His major works include *The Homecoming* (1965), which won a Tony Award and the New York Drama Critics' Circle Award; *No Man's Land* (1975); *Betrayal* (1978); and *Ashes to Ashes* (1996). He also wrote several critically acclaimed screen adaptations, including *The French Lieutenant's Woman* (1981) and *The Handmaid's Tale* (1990). **Larry Bensky**, a former Paris editor of *The Paris Review*, is a longtime print and radio journalist. He won a George Polk Award in 1987 for his coverage of Iran-Contra for Pacifica Radio, and is currently at work on an audiovisual project about Marcel Proust.

Jean Rhys (1890–1979) was born Ella Gwendoline Rees Williams in Roseau, Dominica. At the age of seventeen, Rhys left Dominica to study in England, where she worked as an artist's model and a member of a traveling musical chorus, among other odd jobs. During the twenties Rhys began publishing short stories at the urging of Ford Madox Ford, the novelist and publisher who became Rhys's mentor. She published her first story collection, *The Left Bank and Other Stories*, in 1927 and went on to publish four novels: *Quartet* (1929), *After Leaving Mr. Mackenzie* (1931), *Voyage in the Dark* (1934), and *Good Morning, Midnight* (1939). After the war, Rhys published three volumes of short stories and a final novel, *Wide Sargasso Sea* (1966), which reimagines the story of Bertha Rochester, the madwoman locked in the attic in Charlotte Bronte's *Jane Eyre* (1847). The novel won the W. H. Smith Literary Award in 1967, and resulted in a renewed interest in Rhys's work. **Elizabeth Vreeland** (1928–1985) was an arts commentator for National Public Radio. Her poems were published in *The New York Review of Books*, *The New York Times*, and *The Paris Review*.

Salman Rushdie was born in Bombay, India, in 1947. He attended secondary school and university in the United Kingdom, studying history and acting at Cambridge. He published his first novel, *Grimus*, in 1975; it was followed by *Midnight's Children* (1981), which won the Booker Prize and catapulted him to international literary fame, and another critically acclaimed novel, *Shame* (1983). After *The Satanic Verses* appeared in 1988, a fatwa issued by Ayatollah Khomeini of Iran calling for Rushdie's murder forced the writer underground for nine years. He nevertheless continued to publish fiction and essays, writing a children's novel, *Haroun and the Sea of Stories* (1990), and a short-story collection, *East, West* (1994). His subsequent novels include *The Ground Beneath Her Feet* (1999), *Fury* (2001), and *Shalimar the Clown* (2005). He was knighted by the Queen of England in 2007. His latest novel is *The Enchantress of Florence* (2008). **Jack Livings**, an advisory editor of *The Paris Review*, is at work on a book of short stories, several of which have appeared in *The Paris Review*, *A Public Space*, *StoryQuarterly*, *Tin House*, and Best American Short Stories.

Georges Simenon (1903–1989) was born in Liège, Belgium. As a child, he attended the Collège Saint-Louis and Collège Saint-Servais, but he was forced to withdraw at age fifteen to help support his family. In 1919 he began work as a reporter at the *Gazette de Liège*, and in 1921 he published his first work, *Au Pont des Arches*, under a pseudonym. Simenon wrote under various pen names until the late twenties, and in 1931 published *Pietr-le-Letton*, the first of many detective novels to feature Commissioner Maigret, his best-known character. Though widely known for his Maigret novels, Simenon also wrote a number of more pointedly literary works, including *Strangers in the House* (1940) and *Red Lights* (1953). A prolific master of the noir genre, Simenon published more than four hundred works, and was a member of the Académie Royale Belge de Langue et Littérature Françaises and the American Academy of Arts and Letters. **Carvel Collins** (1913–1990) was a professor who taught at MIT and Notre Dame. His books include *The American Sporting Gallery* (1949) and *Sam Ward in the Gold Rush* (1949). He was an authority on William Faulkner and edited several collections of Faulkner's short fiction as well as two of his novels, *Mayday* and *The Unvanquished*.

Evelyn Waugh (1903–1966) was born in West Hampstead, a suburb of London, to a family of writers, but it was not until 1927, after graduating from Oxford University with brief forays into art and carpentry, that Waugh devoted himself to writing. From the publication of his first novel, *Decline and Fall*, in 1928, Waugh remained prolific until his death, writing novels, travel journals, short stories, biographies, articles, and critical essays, sometimes publishing two books a year. He wrote the novels *Vile Bodies* (1930), *A Handful of Dust* (1934), and *Scoop* (1938) before joining the Royal Marines shortly after World War II broke out. After leaving service in 1943, he wrote what would become his most popular and enduring novel, *Brideshead Revisited* (1945). He revisited the war in a trilogy of highly regarded novels, *Men at Arms* (1952), *Officers and Gentlemen* (1955), and *Unconditional Surrender* (1961; published in the United States as *The End of the Battle*). These were compiled into one volume, *Sword of Honour*, in 1965. He died the following year on Easter Sunday. **Julian Jebb** (1934–1984) was a journalist and television producer in the arts department of BBC television, where he made interview-based documentaries with Christopher Isherwood, Patricia Highsmith, and Anthony Powell, as well as longer documentaries on Virginia Woolf and the Mitford sisters, among other subjects.

William Carlos Williams (1883–1963) was born in Rutherford, New Jersey, where he lived and practiced medicine for most of his life. As a young man he traveled and studied in Europe before returning to the United States to attend medical school at the University of Pennsylvania. As an undergraduate he befriended Ezra Pound and Hilda Doolittle (H.D.), who encouraged his interest in poetry. His first collection, *Poems*, appeared in 1909, and the next year he opened his medical practice. His subsequent collections include *The Tempers* (1913), *Al Que Quiere!* (1917), *Kora in Hell* (1920), *Sour Grapes* (1921), and *Spring and All* (1923), which is considered a landmark of modernist poetry. *Paterson*, an epic, unfinished poem in five parts, dominated the latter part of Williams's writing career. In 1951 and 1952 he suffered a series of strokes that forced him to retire from medicine. Williams remained relatively unknown until late in life, when a new generation of poets including Allen Ginsberg, Denise Levertov, and Robert Creeley named him as a major influence and brought widespread recognition to his work. **Stanley Koehler**, a poet and professor emeritus of English at the University of Massachusetts, Amherst, is the author of *Countries of the Mind: The Poetry of William Carlos Williams* (1998).

Acknowledgments

This book would not have been possible without the care and devotion of *The Paris Review*'s editorial staff: Matt Weiland, Radhika Jones, Nathaniel Rich, Christopher Cox, Meghan O'Rourke, Charles Simic, and Sarah Stein, and a superb group of interns, Richard Beck, Christopher Carroll, Ian Ingram, Ian MacDougall, Daniel Poppick, Rachel Riederer, and Amory Wiggin.

Special thanks also to the generations of *Paris Review* editors who presided over the genesis of the interviews in this volume during the past half century.

Special thanks to Frances Coady, David Rogers, David Logsdon, James Meader, and Tanya Farrell at Picador, and Jamie Byng and Anya Serota at Canongate.

Special thanks to the Wylie Agency.

Ralph Ellison manuscript page reprinted by permission of the Estate of Ralph Ellison. Interview reprinted by permission of the Estate of Alfred Chester and *The Paris Review*.
Georges Simenon interview reprinted by permission of *The Paris Review*.
Isak Dinesen manuscript page reprinted by permission of the Estate of Karen Blixen. Interview reprinted by permission of the Estate of Eugene Walter and *The Paris Review*.
Evelyn Waugh manuscript page reprinted by permission of the Estate of Evelyn Waugh. Interview reprinted by permission of *The Paris Review*.

William Carlos Williams manuscript page reprinted by permission of the Estate of William Carlos Williams. Interview reprinted by permission of Stanley Koehler and *The Paris Review*.

Interview reprinted by permission of Larry Bensky and *The Paris Review*.

John Cheever manuscript page reprinted by permission of The Wylie Agency. Interview reprinted by permission of Annette Grant and *The Paris Review*.

Joyce Carol Oates manuscript page reprinted by permission of Joyce Carol Oates. Interview reprinted by permission of Robert Phillips and *The Paris Review*.

Jean Rhys manuscript page reprinted by permission of the Estate of Jean Rhys. Interview reprinted by permission of Nicholas Vreeland and *The Paris Review*.

Raymond Carver manuscript page reprinted by permission of Tess Gallagher and the Wylie Agency. Interview reprinted by permission of Mona Simpson and Lewis Buzbee and *The Paris Review*.

Chinua Achebe manuscript page reprinted by permission of Chinua Achebe. Interview reprinted by permission of Paul O'Neil and *The Paris Review*.

Ted Hughes manuscript page reprinted by permission of Carol Hughes. Interview reprinted by permission of Drue Heinz and *The Paris Review*.

Jan Morris manuscript page reprinted by permission of Jan Morris. Interview reprinted by permission of Joel Kaye and *The Paris Review*.

Martin Amis manuscript page reprinted by permission of Martin Amis and The Wylie Agency. Interview reprinted by permission of *The Paris Review*.

Salman Rushdie manuscript page reprinted by permission of Salman Rushdie. Interview reprinted by permission of Jack Livings and *The Paris Review*.

Norman Mailer manuscript page reprinted by permission of the Estate of Norman Mailer. Interview reprinted by permission of Andrew O'Hagan and *The Paris Review*.